Contesting Europe

Exploring Euroscepticism in
Online Media Coverage

P. de Wilde, A. Michailidou and H.-J. Trenz

with the collaboration of A. Crespy, O. Fimin,
M. Heller, T. Kohut, B. Kriza and N. Styczyńska

© P. de Wilde, A. Michailidou and H.-J. Trenz 2013

First published by the ECPR Press in 2013

The ECPR Press is the publishing imprint of the European Consortium for Political Research (ECPR), a scholarly association, which supports and encourages the training, research and cross-national cooperation of political scientists in institutions throughout Europe and beyond.

ECPR Press
University of Essex
Wivenhoe Park
Colchester
CO4 3SQ
UK

All rights reserved. No part of this book may be reprinted or reproduced or utilised in any form or by any electronic, mechanical, or other means, now known or hereafter invented, including photocopying and recording, or in any information storage or retrieval system, without permission in writing from the publishers.

Typeset by ECPR Press.

Printed and bound by Lightning Source.

British Library Cataloguing in Publication Data.

A catalogue record for this book is available from the British Library.

Paperback ISBN: 978-1-907301-51-3

www.ecpr.eu/ecprpress

ECPR – Monographs
Series Editors:
Dario Castiglione (University of Exeter)
Peter Kennealy (European University Institute)
Alexandra Segerberg (Stockholm University)
Peter Triantafillou (Roskilde University)

Other books available in this series
Agents or Bosses? (ISBN: 9781907301261) Ozge Kemahlioglu

Causes of War: The Struggle for Recognition (ISBN: 9781907301018) Thomas Lindemann

Citizenship: The History of an Idea (ISBN: 9780954796655) Paul Magnette

Coercing, Constraining and Signalling: Explaining UN and EU Sanctions After the Cold War (ISBN: 9781907301209) Francesco Giumelli

Constraints On Party Policy Change (ISBN: 9781907301490) Thomas M. Meyer

Deliberation Behind Closed Doors: Transparency and Lobbying in the European Union (ISBN: 9780955248849) Daniel Naurin

Democratic Institutions and Authoritarian Rule in Southeast Europe (ISBN: 9781907301438) Danijela Dolenec

European Integration and its Limits: Intergovernmental Conflicts and their Domestic Origins (ISBN: 9780955820373) Daniel Finke

Gender and Vote in Britain: Beyond the Gender Gap? (ISBN: 9780954796693) Rosie Campbell

Globalisation: An Overview (ISBN: 9780955248825) Danilo Zolo

Joining Political Organisations: Institutions, Mobilisation and Participation in Western Democracies (ISBN: 9780955248894) Laura Morales

Organising the European Parliament: Committees' Role and Legislative Influence (ISBN: 9781907301391) Nikoleta Yordanova

Paying for Democracy: Political Finance and State Funding for Parties (ISBN: 9780954796631) Kevin Casas-Zamora

Policy Making In Multilevel Systems: Federalism, Decentralisation, and Performance in the OECD Countries (ISBN: 9781907301339) Jan Biela, Annika Hennl and Andre Kaiser

Political Conflict and Political Preferences: Communicative Interaction Between Facts, Norms and Interests (ISBN: 9780955820304) Claudia Landwehr

Political Parties and Interest Groups in Norway (ISBN: 9780955820366) Elin Haugsgjerd Allern

Regulation in Practice: The de facto Independence of Regulatory Agencies (ISBN: 9781907301285) Martino Maggetti

Representing Women?: Female Legislators in West European Parliaments (ISBN: 9780954796648) Mercedes Mateo Diaz

The Personalisation of Politics: A Study of Parliamentary Democracies
(ISBN: 9781907301032) Lauri Karvonen

The Politics of Income Taxation: A Comparative Analysis
(ISBN: 9780954796686) Steffen Ganghof

The Return of the State of War: A Theoretical Analysis of Operation Iraqi Freedom (ISBN: 9780955248856) Dario Battistella

Urban Foreign Policy and Domestic Dilemmas: Insights from Swiss and EU City-regions (ISBN: 9781907301070) Nico van der Heiden

Why Aren't They There? The Political Representation of Women, Ethnic Groups and Issue Positions In Legislature (ISBN: 9780955820397) Didier Ruedin

Widen the Market, Narrow the Competition: Banker Interests and the Making of a European Capital Market (ISBN: 9781907301087) Daniel Mügge

Please visit www.ecpr.eu/ecprpress for information about new publications.

Contents

List of Figures and Tables   vii

List of Abbreviations   xi

Contributors   xiii

Acknowledgements   xvi

Preface   xvii

Chapter One: Political Contestation and European Integration:
   A Public Sphere Approach   1

Chapter Two: A Comparative Mixed-Methods Approach of Online
   EU Polity Contestation   21

Chapter Three: Contesting Europe: Towards Convergence?   37

Chapter Four: The Mainstreaming of Euroscepticism in Austria:
   EP Campaigning Between Media Populism and Far Right Extremism   61

Chapter Five: EU Polity Contestation in France and French-Speaking Belgium:
   The Bounded Impact of a Referendum
   Amandine Crespy and Olga Fimin   79

Chapter Six: Contending European Integration in Germany:
   From Permissive Consensus to Moderate Euroscepticism   101

Chapter Seven: Reflecting a Morose Political Climate:
   EU Polity Contestation in Hungary
   Maria Heller, Tamás Kohut and Borbála Kriza   119

Chapter Eight: The Netherlands:
   Reliving the 2005 Referendum on the Constitutional Treaty?   137

Chapter Nine: The European Other:
   The EU as External Threat in the Polish Online Debate
   Natasza Styczyńska   155

Chapter Ten: The UK: A Case of Extraordinary Euroscepticism   173

Chapter Eleven: The Limited Convergence in EU Polity Contestation:
   Implications for Democracy   195

Appendices   205

Bibliography   225

Index   259

List of Figures and Tables

Figures

Figure 2.1: Total number of articles covering the 2009 EP elections in each country, period: 18 May–10 June 2009	29
Figure 3.1: Intensity of EU polity debate by country	42
Figure 3.2: Online media users' evaluations of the principle of European integration (values indicate the number of positive and negative evaluations by category)	44
Figure 3.3: Online media users' evaluations of the current institutional set-up of the EU (values indicate the number of positive and negative evaluations by country)	47
Figure 3.4: Online media users' evaluations of the level, scope and inclusiveness of the current institutional set-up of the EU	48
Figure 3.5: Online media users' evaluations of the future of European integration project (values indicate the number of positive and negative evaluations by country)	49
Figure 3.6: Online media users' evaluations of the level, scope and inclusiveness of the future of European integration project	50
Figure 4.1: Distribution of EU polity evaluations across countries: Austrian contributions per actor	69
Figure 4.2: Evaluations of the EU polity in Austria	72
Figure 4.3: Explaining opinions – How EU polity evaluations were justified in Austria and in all countries	74
Figure 5.1: Distribution of EU evaluations across countries: French contributions per actor	87
Figure 5.2: Distribution of EU evaluations across countries: Belgian contributions per actor	88
Figure 5.3: Evaluations of the current EU polity set-up in France and French-speaking Belgium	90
Figure 5.4: Evaluations on the future project of integration in France and French-speaking Belgium	94
Figure 5.5: Explaining opinions: How EU polity evaluations were justified in France and Belgium	97

Figure 6.1: Distribution of EU polity evaluations across countries: German contributions per actor — 110

Figure 6.2: Explaining opinions: how EU polity evaluations were justified in Germany — 113

Figure 7.1: Distribution of EU evaluations across countries: Hungarian contributions per actor — 129

Figure 7.2: Explaining opinions: how EU polity evaluations were justified in Hungary — 133

Figure 8.1: Mapping EU polity evaluations in Dutch online debates — 144

Figure 8.2 EU polity evaluations across countries: Dutch contributions per actor category — 145

Figure 8.3: Explaining opinions: how EU polity evaluations were justified in the Netherlands — 151

Figure 9.1: Distribution of EU evaluations across countries: Polish contributions per actor — 168

Figure 9.2: Explaining opinions: how EU polity evaluations were justified in Poland — 169

Figure 10.1: Mapping EU polity evaluations in British online debates — 190

Figure 10.2 EU polity evaluations across countries: UK contributions per actor category — 190

Figure 10.3: Explaining opinions: how EU polity evaluations were justified in the UK — 191

Tables

Table 1.1: Typology of EU polity evaluations	13
Table 3.1: Online media users' evaluations of the level, scope and inclusiveness of the current institutional set-up of the EU by country	46
Table 3.2: Online media users' evaluations of the level, scope and inclusiveness of the future of European integration project by country	51
Table 3.3: Critical matrix of EU polity contestation: frequencies of specified and under-specified evaluations	53
Table 3.4: Critical matrix of EU contestation: EU polity evaluations by party actors and citizens	55
Table 3.5: Justifications of EU polity worth by actor type	55
Table 3.6: Polity contestation and justifications	57
Table 6.1: Debating the EU online: Topics of the German articles	107
Table 7.1: Debating the EU online: Topics of Hungarian articles	126
Table 8.1: Debating the EU online: Topics of the Dutch articles	143
Table 10.1: Debating the EU online: Topics of the UK articles	185
Table A.1: Typology of EU polity contestation	219
Table A.2: Possible EU polity contestation combinations, categories applied and frequencies	221

List of Abbreviations

ARP	Anti-Revolutionaire Partij
BBC	British Broadcasting Corporation
BZÖ	Bündnis Zukunft Österreich
CDA	Christelijk Democratisch Appèl
CHU	Christelijk-Historische Unie
CNPT	Chasse, pêche, nature et traditions
CPN	Communistische Partij Nederland
D66	Democraten 66
ECR	European Conservatives and Reformists
ECSC	European Coal and Steel Community
ECT	European Constitutional Treaty
EEC	European Economic Community
EFD	Europe of Freedom and Democracy
EMU	Economic and Monetary Union
EP	European Parliament
EPP	European People's Party
EPP-ED	European People's Party/European Democrats
EU	European Union
FGTB	Fédération Générale du Travail de Belgique
FPÖ	Freiheitliche Partei Österreichs
GPV	Gereformeerd Politiek Verbond
IND/DEM	Independence/Democracy
KVP	Katholieke Volkspartij
LCR	Ligue Communiste Révolutionnaire
LDD	Lijst Dedecker
LO	Lutte ouvrière
LPR	Liga Polskich Rodzin
MEP	Member of the European Parliament
MP	Member of Parliament
NOS	Nederlandse Omroep Stichting
NPA	Nouveau Parti Anti-Capitaliste
N-VA	Vlaams Belang and the Nieuw-Vlaamse Alliantie
ÖVP	Österreichische Volkspartei

PC	Parti Communiste
PG	Parti de Gauche
PS	Parti Socialiste
PTB	Parti des Travailleurs Belges
PvdA	Partij van de Arbeid
PVV	Partij voor de Vrijheid
RPF	Reformatorisch Politieke Federatie
RSS	Rich Site Summary or RDF Site Summary (also dubbed Really Simple Syndication)
SGP	Staatkundig-Gereformeerde Partij
SP	Socialistische Partij
SPÖ	Sozialdemokratische Partei Österreichs
SS	Schutzstaffel
UEN	Union for Europe of the Nations
UK	United Kingdom
UMP	L'Union Pour un Mouvement Populaire
VVD	Volkspartij voor Vrijheid en Democratie

Contributors

AMANDINE CRESPY is Assistant Professor at the Université Libre de Bruxelles (ULB) (CEVIPOL/Institute for European Studies – IEE). She holds a PhD from the ULB and was a visiting fellow at the Freie Universität Berlin, Science Po in Paris and Harvard University. Her research mainly deals with the political conflicts related to the economic and social dimension of EU integration. Her research interests include Euroscepticism and resistances to EU integration, services' liberalisation and regulation (especially public services), the Eurocrisis, the role of conflict in deliberation and democracy. She has authored a number of articles in international journals including *Journal of Common Market Studies*, *Journal of European Public Policy* and *Political Studies* as well as a monograph entitled *Qui a peur de Bolkestein? Conflit, résistances et démocratie dans l'Union européenne* (Economica 2012).

PIETER DE WILDE is Senior Researcher at the Department of Global Governance, Social Science Research Center Berlin (WZB). He holds a PhD in political science from the University of Oslo where he conducted research on the politicisation of European integration at ARENA, Center for European Studies. Currently, he is working on the WZB project The Political Sociology of Cosmopolitanism and Communitarianism. His main research interests include European integration, the functioning and legitimacy of the European Union, globalisation and political conflict. His work has been published in the *Journal of Common Market Studies*, *Journal of European Public Policy*, *West European Politics*, *Journal of European Integration*, *Comparative European Politics* and the *European Journal of Social Theory*.

OLGA-ELENA FIMIN holds a Masters degree in European Affairs from the Institute for European Studies, Free University of Brussels, Belgium, where she has successfully defended her thesis on "The role of MEPs as a link between national parties and the European federations of parties. A case-study of the Romanian MEPs". Her academic interests relate to subjects like political parties in Europe, processes and theories of European integration and the protection and promotion of human rights. Pursuing this direction, she has recently graduated from a joint Masters program in human rights law (Académie Universitaire Louvain, Belgium) and is currently working in the Directorate-General Development and Cooperation – EuropeAid, European Commission.

MARIA HELLER, director of the Institute of Sociology, Eötvös Loránd University, Budapest, is a sociologist with a background in linguistics. Her research interests include media and communication, theories of the public sphere, discourse analysis and new ICTs. She has published in several languages on the structure of the public sphere; discourse analyses of public debates (national identity, demography, NATO and EU enlargement, globalisation, Eurosceptic discourses); value analysis of mass culture, commodity aesthetics; symbolic politics and the European public sphere; the structure of the public sphere in state-socialism; new perspectives on 21st-century communications; discursive strategies in advertising and the sociology of games. She is a member of several Hungarian and international scholarly associations, has participated in various international research programmes, and was a "Freedom of Speech" professor at Bergen University (Norway).

TAMÁS KOHUT is a sociologist, currently a doctoral fellow at the Zentrum für Antisemitismusforschung at the Technische Universität, Berlin. His main research interests include the social and political history of anti-Semitism, the First World War, everyday life and the state socialist era of Hungary. His work has been published in the Hungarian social historical journal *Korall*.

BORBÁLA KRIZA is a researcher in political sociology. She obtained her M.A. in Sociology and Minority Studies at Eötvös Loránd University and also studied at the Nationalism Studies Department of Central European University. Currently she is a doctoral fellow at the Center for European Studies at Sciences Po, Paris. In 2008 she was a junior fellow at the Collegium Budapest and also a Marshall Memorial Fellow of the German Marshall Fund of the US. Kriza's research focuses on the topics of democracy and far-right politics, gender equality, media, ethnicity, xenophobia, anti-Semitism, national identity and collective memory in Central and Eastern Europe and the Balkans. She has contributed to projects initiated by, among others, Eötvös Loránd University, the EU Agency for Fundamental Rights, Central European University, the Hungarian Academy of Sciences, the Central Office for Statistics in Hungary and the US Holocaust Memorial Museum. Her work has been widely published in Hungarian and English. Her documentary film "Rocking the Nation" on the Hungarian far-right subculture has been screened in many international film festivals around Europe.

ASIMINA MICHAILIDOU is senior researcher at the ARENA Centre for European Studies, University of Oslo, Norway. She holds a PhD in political communication from Loughborough University, UK. Previous and current projects of hers cover the EU's public communication strategies; online media, mobilisation and crises; online journalism and European elections; Euroscepticism; social media and their impact on political discourse; globalisation and political activism; and theoretical perspectives on the concept of the public sphere. Among her main publications are: *The European Union online* (2012, Akademiker) and articles in the *Journal of European Public Policy*, *Journalism Practice*, *European Journal of Communication Research* and the *Journal of Contemporary European Research*.

NATASZA STYCZYŃSKA is a doctoral fellow at the Institute of European Studies, Jagiellonian University, Krakow, where she conducts research on Europeanisation and Polish party politics. She holds MA degrees in Political Sciences (Pedagogical University of Krakow) and European Studies (Jagiellonian University, Krakow). In 2009-2011 she was a researcher in the RECON (Reconstituting Democracy in Europe) Integrated Project supported by the European Commission's Sixth Framework Programme. Her academic interests include transformation processes in Central and Eastern Europe, party politics and Euroscepticism in the CEE region, as well as Austro-Hungarian heritage in Central and Southern Europe.

HANS-JÖRG TRENZ is Professor in European Studies at University of Copenhagen where he coordinates CEMES, The Centre for Modern European Studies at the Faculty of Humanities, and adjunct Professor at ARENA, Centre for European Studies of University of Oslo. He attained his habilitation at Humboldt University Berlin and a PhD in social and political sciences at the European University Institute in Florence. His main research interests are in the areas of media, communication and public sphere, civil society, European civilization and identity, migration and ethnic minorities, cultural and political sociology, social and political theory, democracy and constitutionalism in the European Union. His main publications include: (2012) *The Politicization of Europe*, London: Routledge (together with Paul Statham), (2010) *The New Politics of European Civil Society*, London: Routledge (together with Ulrike Liebert) and (2005) *Europa in den Medien. Das europäische Integrationsprojekt im Spiegel nationaler Öffentlichkeit,* Frankfurt a.M./New York: Campus.

Acknowledgements

The scholarly exchange that laid the grounds for this volume took place in May 2010, during a two-day workshop on 'Euroscepticism and the Future of European Democracy' in Krakow. We would like to thank the organisers, Zdzisław Mach and Magdalena Góra, as well as the authors and commentators of the various papers: Paul Statham, Nick Jankowski, Dora Husz, Kathrin Packham, Grzegorz Pożarlik, Ann Zimmermann, Florence Haegel, Francois Foret, Petra Guasti, Zdenka Mansfeldová, Barbara Jablonska, and Carlos Cunha. Their input and feedback has been fundamental in shaping this book. Special thanks go to all our coders who meticulously gathered online data and applied our methodology of content analysis to their respective country of expertise: Olga Fimin, Tamás Kohut, Natasza Styczyńska, Jan Klepatz and Katri Vallaste.

A number of colleagues and friends have kindly offered their feedback and support at critical and opportune occasions. Draft versions of the introductory and comparative chapters were presented at ARENA, Oslo, the UACES conference in Bruges, the ESA European Political Sociology Midterm Conference in Lille, the TKI Colloquium of the Wissenschaftszentrum Berlin in Berlin, the DVPW Sektionstagung Internationale Beziehungen in München and the ECPR General Conference in Reykjavik. Our thanks go to all the participants for their constructive feedback. We would particularly like to thank all our colleagues at ARENA, and also Michael Zürn, Martin Binder, Autumn Lockwood-Payton, Matthias Ecker-Ehrhardt, Liesbet Hooghe, Gary Marks and Jürgen Neyer for their inspiring and often enlightening remarks. Many thanks go to Chris Lord for his insightful comments on the UK chapter. The book's final shape is the result of the excellent editorial support of Kadri Miard and Sindre Hervig at ARENA.

The efforts of all those who have been involved in this book would not have been possible without the financial support granted by the European Commission's 6th Framework Programme, which we gratefully acknowledge. We would also like to thank all RECON partners, and in particular the research directors Erik Oddvar Eriksen and John Erik Fossum for their invaluable support and friendship.

The process of transforming our rich data into a concise and coherent manuscript has been rewarding but also challenging. We are indebted to Dario Castiglione, ECPR Press Series Editor, for his continuous support during the publication process.

Pieter de Wilde, Asimina Michailidou and Hans-Jörg Trenz
Berlin, Oslo and Copenhagen, June 2013

Preface

This book on public expressions of Euroscepticism during the 2009 European Parliamentary election campaigns is the result of a collaborative research effort from members of the 'Public Sphere and Democracy' work package within the FP6-funded RECON 'Reconstituting Democracy in Europe' project, coordinated by Ulrike Liebert and Hans-Jörg Trenz. With existing scholarly attention predominantly focused on party politics and public opinion, the question of how Euroscepticism is advanced in public and media discourse remains relatively unchartered. So, the Euroscepticism project set out to accomplish two ambitious tasks: a) to map the formation of public opinion on European integration through the systematic mapping of both positive and negative public statements concerning the EU polity. This goes beyond standard approaches, which have analysed Eurosceptic discourse in isolation from pro-integration discourse; and b) to trace patterns of convergence and divergence of EU polity contestation across national and transnational public spheres. By combining in-depth qualitative discussions in country case studies with overarching quantitative content analysis, we have aimed to capture both nation-state specific and EU-wide trends.

Our focus on the role of online news media as a platform of political contestation and campaigning in the context of EP elections, has further enabled us to assess the performance of both professional and citizens' journalism in the process of making Eurosceptic discourse salient in the public sphere. The result is that we have collected a wealth of data which sheds light not only on the nature of Eurosceptic discourse across several countries but also on the process of public opinion formation in the online European public sphere(s).

'Contesting Europe' is written as a research monograph. As such, it brings together the comparative findings and country cases from the 'Euroscepticism' research project. The three main authors have collectively drafted most of the chapters of this volume but also substantially relied on the collaboration of an international team of researchers, who not only delivered the raw material in the form of media-content data but also contributed to the interpretation of several of the country cases. The partner universities were ARENA, Centre for European Studies, Oslo; Jagiellonian University, Krakov; Eötvös Loránd University, Budapest; Université Libre, Bruxelles; and Academy of Science of the Czech Republic, Prague. Out of the twelve EU countries that were monitored by the Euroscepticism survey, eight were chosen for the in-depth country chapters included in this volume. The country chapters on Belgium, France, Poland and Hungary were delivered by the respective partners and their authorship is acknowledged. The country chapters of Germany and Austria were drafted by Hans-Jörg, the country chapter on the UK by Asimina, and the country chapter on the Netherlands by Pieter.

Since the first initial discussions that started the Euroscepticism project, public contestation about the EU has entered mainstream public discourse in virtually all EU Member States. The role of online news media in shaping public opinion has also been strengthened, with many of the countries that were 'lagging behind' in online news media use for political debating back in 2009, now catching up rapidly. These changes emphasise, for us, the importance of understanding the interplay between Eurosceptic discourse and online news media, but also remind us that research on the internet is very easily and rapidly outdated by new developments. It is therefore important to emphasise that the core of our research represents the state of affairs in June 2009. As far as possible we have added new information on new developments in the country chapters. We have also aimed to add a longer-term perspective to our analysis of time-specific facts and findings. We hope that in this way, our book provides a benchmark and point of departure for future research on the communicative aspects of Euroscepticism, as well as insights that have a longer lifespan that the average online debate or article.

Chapter One | Political Contestation and European Integration: A Public Sphere Approach

What this book is about

Since the early 1950s, European nation states have increasingly pooled sovereignty in a process generally referred to as European integration. Especially since the mid-1980s, the European Union (EU), as formally constituted by the Treaty of Maastricht (1992) and consolidated in subsequent Treaty reforms, made substantial steps from market integration to political integration and entered into a more or less continuous, and still unsettled, process of constitutionalisation (Abromeit 2001; Rittberger and Schimmelfennig 2006). Although there is no agreement on what kind of political entity the EU is, it has developed beyond the status of an international organisation and is now so complex and encompassing that it may be referred to as some kind of 'polity' (Mair 2007) or 'political system' (Hix 2005). Whether this polity should exist, what it should look like, how many competencies it should have and to what extent one wants to be a part of it, are questions of constant debate and controversy. In other words, the polity of the European Union is an issue of political contestation throughout Europe.

The new salience of identity politics, the renationalisation of the European political agenda and the populist backlash we have been witnessing in European politics since the beginning of the Eurozone crisis underline this 'unfinished' and fundamentally contested character of the EU. The contemporary European Union is increasingly subject to regular critique of its policy choices and actors but also to more principled forms of opposition, which question its institutional and constitutional architecture and rationale of existence.

Current developments prominently feature varieties of objections to ongoing European integration that reflect attitudes of 'Euroscepticism' (Leconte 2010). These expressions of Euroscepticism not only respond to the integration process itself (De Wilde and Zürn 2012), they also interact with pro-European arguments supporting and legitimising this integration process (De Wilde and Trenz 2012). How do the various expressions of opposition to European integration manifest themselves in contemporary Europe? How to discern the boundaries between critical discourse and Eurosceptic discourse or between EU legitimation discourse and counter-discourse? Is there an intrinsic link between further integration and Eurosceptic responses in the form of fundamentally contesting the legitimacy of the EU and its achievements?

This volume aims at conceptualising and empirically mapping the political conflicts that shape the public perceptions of the EU. Specifically, it investigates the extent to which there is convergence on Eurosceptic discourse in terms of intensity, substance and justification across Member States, different discussion forums and between citizens and elites. To do this, we adopt a public sphere approach which allows us to study the dynamic formation of public perceptions through discourse. We thus locate 'Euroscepticism' primarily in the public and media debates, which proliferate in response to current challenges to European integration and democracy.

After the era of permissive consensus, the legitimacy of the EU is now contested within and across the Member States, mobilising governments, political parties, civil society and a growing segment of the population.

In line with the existing literature on Euroscepticism (Crespy & Verschueren 2009; Fuchs *et al.* 2009a; Leconte 2010; Szczerbiak & Taggart 2008a, 2008b), we focus in the following on this particular type of contesting the legitimacy of the EU as a political system. More specifically, we introduce the term 'EU polity contestation' to emphasise two core elements of 'Euroscepticism'. First, 'EU polity contestation' captures the public character of 'Euroscepticism', which becomes salient through public and media debates and is not simply measured in latent patterns of citizen dispositions, partisan positions or ideologies. Secondly, 'EU polity contestation' qualifies Euroscepticism as a particular form of contestation of the EU that goes beyond regular competition among politicians or conflicts about specific policies or decision-making processes. It refers to all kinds of debates which raise the 'polity question': i.e. questions of what type of political entity the EU is or should be, on what principles of legitimation it should be based and how its level and scope of authority should be confined. By taking a public sphere perspective, we place at centre stage the ways the legitimacy of the EU is challenged and defended in mediated public debates. Publicly debating the legitimacy of the EU is constitutive of how it is perceived and dealt with in the institutional arena (Koopmans & Statham 2010). Our aim is to supplement existing approaches within EU studies which focus primarily on intra-institutional dynamics of conflicts, the strategic games of national governments or the positioning of political parties (e.g. Marks & Steenbergen 2004; Moravcsik 1998).

The rising politicisation of European integration has arguably contributed to the restructuring of political conflict which now takes place at the level of mass politics (Kriesi *et al.* 2008). Understanding the nature and dynamics of public contestation and responding supportive arguments about European integration helps us to analyse how Europe is made visible, interesting and worthwhile to its citizens. Unlike most of the existing literature, we thus argue that the politicisation of European integration needs to be measured in ongoing public debates and the media and not purely in strategic party interaction or the 'silent' attitudes of the people involved. The politicisation of European integration, which is widely accepted to affect the legitimacy of the EU and the scope and future prospects of integration, is staged in and for the mass media (De Wilde 2011). By taking into account this public character of political conflicts over European integration, we can systematically reconstruct how politicisation shapes public perceptions of the legitimacy of the EU in terms of competing principles of what constitutes a legitimate political order, about the level and scope of political authority and about the future trajectory of integration (Morgan 2005; De Wilde and Trenz 2012).

Today's public sphere is to a large extent constituted by the mass media (Bennett & Entman 2001). They are vital to the analysis of political contestation for at least three related reasons: First, from a normative perspective, mass media are ascribed the role of 'translators' of the political process into such formats that make it accessible to the people. In the EU case, it is of particular relevance whether the media provide a shared knowledge over European affairs and select the same issues across the national media spheres. For many scholars simultaneously unfolding public debates over EU matters are regarded as a key prerequisite for the emergence of a European public sphere – or at least as an indication that national public spheres are becoming 'Europeanized' (Eder & Kantner 2000). Secondly, mass media are central for political contestation because they supply flows of information that link relevant actors and institutions, including activated citizens. For the EU project, it is of significant bearing whether political actors, parties and citizens are linked across national borders and political levels. Some form of 'social transnationalism' (Mau & Mewes 2012; Risse 2010) or 'transnational discursive exchange' (Wessler *et al.* 2008) is therefore considered as a further indicator for the emergence of a European public sphere. Finally, mass media are relevant because they construct public opinion and facilitate collective will formation. This concerns whether interpretations of and concerns with the EU's legitimacy are shared across the political space. The degree of convergence of patterns of EU polity contestation would indicate the emergence of a European public sphere that also facilitates collective will formation of Europeans who can, in principle, agree on what kind of entity the EU is and what should be the future trajectory of integration (Eriksen 2005; Habermas 2003). In contrast, the degree of divergence of patterns of political contestation would indicate a more fundamental controversy about the issues of concern and their possible solutions across and within Member States.

Given the fragmentation of the communicative spaces in the EU, it is generally accepted that political contestation over European integration is still mainly made salient, filtered and framed within national media systems. Our approach shares the premise that the Europeanisation of public debates is carried by national mass media, but also takes into consideration the possibility of media transformation. In particular, we want to test out the scope of contestation on the internet. Through operationalising our public sphere approach and making it applicable for empirical research, the volume presents a comparative analysis of interactive news websites during campaigns for the 2009 European Parliament (EP) elections, where, arguably, the dynamic elements of EU polity contestation can best be observed because citizens are presented with the possibility to directly and publicly respond to news articles and each other's comments.

Mapping the field of EU polity contestation

The political contestation of Europe has come to scholarly attention in the wake of the fading 'permissive consensus' that has followed the enhanced integration process since the early 1990s (Marks & Steenbergen 2004). In particular, extensive efforts have been made to map and explain citizens' attitudes towards the EU and European integration (Eichenberg & Dalton 2007; Gabel 1998b; Hooghe & Marks 2007; Niedermayer 1995) as well as the positions taken up by political parties (Gaffney 1996; Marks et al. 2002; Ray 1999). Further research has investigated the extent to which Europe features as an issue in the media (De Vreese 2001, 2007b; Koopmans & Statham 2010; Peters et al. 2003; Trenz 2004) and the extent to which social movements and civil society organisations mobilise and organise around the EU (Imig & Tarrow 2001; Marks & McAdam 1999; Wessels 2004).

In theoretical terms, the emphasis of this body of literature is placed on actors' strategies and institutional dynamics of contestation. From an agency perspective, scholars have emphasised the strategic choice of political parties to exploit negative opinion of the population and to mobilise a Eurosceptic agenda. From an institutional perspective, the interplay between politicisation and enhanced integration has been emphasised. Political contestation responds to new political competences and authority of the EU that impact on people's lives. At the same time, institutional reform and the drive for democratisation of the existing institutional structures and procedures of decision making creates new opportunities for participation and voice (Bartolini 2005; Kohler-Koch & Rittberger 2007).

Moving beyond the state of the art in this field, this volume adds to the mapping of political conflict over European integration in three original ways. First, we provide an analysis of mass-mediated discourse and citizens' mobilisation as a central element of political contestation that informs both citizens' attitudes and party positions. We emphasise the power of discourse to set boundaries to political agents regarding what is considered acceptable and desirable. Subsequently, we trace the formation of public opinion on European integration through the systematic mapping of both positive and negative public statements concerning the EU polity. This goes beyond standard approaches, which have analysed Eurosceptic discourse in isolation from pro-integration discourse (Fuchs et al. 2009; Leconte 2010). We then conduct a comparative survey of EU polity contestation in the 2009 EP electoral context mapping patterns of convergence and divergence in twelve Member States and transnational websites. By combining in-depth qualitative discussions in country case studies with overarching quantitative content analysis, we aim to capture both nation-state specific and EU-wide trends.

Of course, this is not the first time that mass-mediated public debates on issues related to European integration are examined in a comparative framework (see, for example, De Vreese 2001; Koopmans & Statham 2010; Trenz 2004). However, the existing body of literature provides us mainly with information on the coverage of EU issues in traditional mass media such as newspapers and television, with little, if any, data on the dynamics of political contestation unfolding within this coverage (for a notable exception, see Koopmans & Statham 2010). By making online news media the focus of our study, we are able to map not only the dynamics of EU politicisation in news media reporting but also the spontaneous reactions these provoke from members of the EU constituency. A further shortcoming of this literature is that information and debates filtered by national media are seen mainly as an intervening variable that amplifies or inhibits elite or partisan-driven politicisation and thus accounts for exceptional cases of voters' mobilisation, such as a referendum (Hooghe & Marks 2009: 14). What is missing is a more systematic analysis of media discourse, which does not focus on mass-mediated public debates of exceptional political events but rather accounts for the regular patterns of 'mediatization' (Meyer 2009) and its potential effects on the course of European integration.

With regard to attitudinal research, we reject the assumption that enhanced political conflicts over European integration always correspond to changing attitudes of citizens. Existing surveys often approach public opinion in terms of support of and identification with European integration, EU actors and institutions or specific EU competences and policies (Eichenberg & Dalton 1993, 2007; Hooghe 2007; Hooghe & Marks 2007; Niedermayer 1995). Especially in Eurobarometer and European election surveys, attitudes of European citizens are treated as pre-dispositions, which are incorporated within particular groups, using the common standards to classify people along national lines or using relatively invariable indicators like education and social class (Gabel & Anderson 2004; McLaren 2005; Petithomme 2008). Attitudinal research on European integration has thus aimed to trace general patterns of group polarisation and especially to identify those groups within the larger population, which represent Eurosceptic attitudes (Fuchs and Klingemann 2011).

Against this tendency to attribute Eurosceptic or pro-European attitudes to particular individuals or groups, we argue that political attitudes are not always fixed, predisposed or deeply socialised but can also be activated in particular situations and arise through communicative exchange with others.[1] The validity of this approach is supported by observed fluctuating patterns in public opinion on the EU. Spikes in public opinion to either supportive or critical pole are frequently found to correlate with the media attention cycle (Norris 2000). In reputedly Eurosceptic countries like the United Kingdom (UK) and Austria, public discourse is also driven by strong expressions of media populism against the EU (Mazzoleni 2003). To account for this impact of mass media on public opinion formation, we need to turn to the mass-mediated spaces where attitudes are given expression and are made visible to a wider audience

While research has mainly paid attention to party positions, only little attention

---

1. Even a questionnaire can be seen as a special form of dialogue between the respondent and the researcher (with both having an audience in mind that is seen as being addressed by the data generated).

has been paid to how these are portrayed in the media (Kriesi 2007; Statham & Koopmans 2009). This omission is problematic especially given the reported gap between political elites and citizens regarding European integration. The referendums on treaty change have demonstrated wide differences between political elites and citizens (Hobolt 2009; Hughes *et al.* 2008; Wessels 1995). For instance, in the case of the Netherlands, close to 85 per cent of the Dutch parliamentarians supported the Constitutional Treaty and advocated a yes-vote in the 2005 national referendum, yet only 39 per cent of Dutch citizens voted yes (Aarts & Van der Kolk 2005). Rather than focusing on party manifestos or expert judgments, we identify the mass media as the principal arena where party positioning on the EU is amplified and framed for the broader audience (Koopmans & Statham 2010; Kriesi *et al.* 2008). We are here able to capture the direct confrontation between partisan elite arguments and those of citizens.

This volume, in contrast to previous research on 'Euroscepticism' maps political conflicts over the EU in terms of both promoting and contesting the legitimacy of the EU. Of particular interest to the scientific community so far has been a wide variety of negative attitudes, party positions and behaviour, generally referred to as 'Euroscepticism' (Fuchs *et al.* 2009; Haesly 2001; Harmsen & Spiering 2004; Hooghe 2007; Leconte 2010; Szczerbiak & Taggart 2008a, 2008b; Taylor 2008). The focus on this 'negative side' is warranted, given its increased prominence recently and its possible implications for the EU and European integration as a political project. Furthermore, in response to the integration process, it is negative evaluations of the EU that polity that primarily drive public discourse. However, by focusing predominantly on negative opinions and party positions towards European integration, the interaction between positive and negative arguments in the formation of public opinion has been overlooked. Our approach of public debates as direct exchange of positive and negative evaluations of the EU polity allows us to focus precisely on this aspect of public opinion formation.

Our aim is to make a contribution to the analysis of political contestation over Europe by conceptually fleshing out and empirically mapping the role of public and media debates using a sophisticated methodology of quantitative content analysis. Conceptually, we develop a comprehensive typology of EU polity contestation and its relation to pro-European discourse and arguments. 'Euroscepticism' is used in this context as an umbrella term that comprises varieties of EU resistances and opposition in terms of principle, polity and project. Through the conceptualisation of multiple dimensions, targets and justifications that EU polity contestation can encompass, our typology provides a rich picture of different types of evaluations made in practice, beyond such qualifications as 'soft' and 'hard' Euroscepticism (Szczerbiak & Taggart 2008c), or scaling attitudes on a single dimensional space from pro-European to anti-European (Hix *et al.* 2006; Hooghe & Marks 2007). Methodologically, we study evaluations of the EU polity as expressed on frequently visited political news websites during the 2009 European Parliament elections. Rather than classifying political party positions based on expert surveys (Ray 1999) or manifesto data (Klingemann *et al.* 2006) or analysing citizens' attitudes with survey data (Eichenberg & Dalton 2007; Hooghe & Marks 2007; Reif &

Inglehart 1991), this approach targets evaluations made on interactive websites where citizens respond of their own accord to highly visible news stories which include EU evaluations made by prominent political actors. Our methodology thus captures the discursive dynamics of public opinion formation.

Ultimately, this volume intends to map the degree of convergence or divergence in the patterns of political conflicts over European integration across Member States. Although the targets of contestation – the institutions, competencies and composition of the EU polity – are largely the same in all EU Member States, there remain considerable differences in how and to what extent the EU is contested across Europe. Students of Euroscepticism have consistently reported strong differences between relatively Eurosceptic Member States such as Austria, Sweden and the United Kingdom and relatively pro-European Member States such as Belgium, Germany and the Netherlands. Although important issues of European integration such as the powers of the European Commission, EU foreign policy or Turkish EU Membership are debated in many Member States, they are neither contested to the same degree nor supported by the same justifications. The meaning and value of the EU polity are invariably interpreted within the diverging contexts of national politics. As a result, across the EU we find different patterns in public opinion (Kritzinger 2003), different party politics (Szczerbiak & Taggart 2008a) and different national narratives (Díez Medrano 2003) towards European integration.

A key empirical research question to which the data presented in this volume sheds new light is therefore whether we find the same degree of divergence in opinions expressed in the media spheres of Europe. We ask whether and to what extent the EU is contested by the same types of actors, raising similar issues and expressing similar concerns across EU Member States or dispositions regarding the legitimacy of the EU that diverge and fragment the European political space. This focus on convergence and divergence concerns 1) The content of contentious debates about European integration across Member States; 2) The intensity of EU polity contestation in media debates through an analysis of news coverage of EP election campaigns; and 3) The interactive dynamics of contentious debates about European integration, seeking to establish whether there is convergence in the way different actors – especially political elites and citizens – contest the EU polity.

The extent to which there are commonalities and differences in EU polity contestation across and within EU Member States is particularly important in light of the available options for institutional reform and democratisation of the EU. On the one hand, strongly divergent patterns of contestation generating Member State-specific polity preferences may result in irreconcilable national demands on the EU presenting a centrifugal force that endangers its continued existence (Chryssochoou 1994; Gabel 1998a). On the other hand, convergence in contestation throughout the EU may provide the building blocks of EU-wide collective will-formation concerning the nature of the EU polity and end goals of European integration. In other words, such commonalities in public debates may present the beginnings of a European public sphere with the potential of increasing the democratic legitimacy of the EU (Fossum & Schlesinger 2007; Risse 2010).

Given the importance of convergence and divergence in EU polity contestation for the democratic legitimacy of the EU, it makes sense to study contestation in relation to an EU electoral context since this represents an important mechanism for collective will-formation involving the general electorate. EP elections focus public attention and facilitate collective will formation by means of public argumentation and discussion. For this purpose, political parties prepare electoral platforms and manifestos, which define the agenda for campaigning and aim to bind the candidates that stand for election. The forging of a European collective will presupposes, however, certain social and institutional prerequisites presently unavailable or only insufficiently developed in the EU (Eder & Trenz 2006). Most importantly, collective will formation relies on the mass media which serve a unified attentive mass public. In complex societies such as the EU, the public sphere is increasingly diversified with functional or territorial sub-publics being served by different media (Gitlin 1998). Democracy is only made possible to the extent that the diversification of the public sphere is conducive to the expression of a pluralism of opinions that remain mutually understandable and that fragmentation is prevented (Benhabib 1996). In the transnational electoral setting of EP elections, which operates through nationally diversified public spheres (Van der Brug & Van der Eijk 2007), it is therefore crucial to measure convergence and divergence in the patterns of political contestation and degrees of interaction between national sub-publics. This can serve as an indicator of the viability of democracy in the EU transnational context and the stability of the European political order.

Our interest in convergence and divergence in EU polity contestation within the context of EP elections draws our attention to the fact that these elections are often considered 'second order' (Reif & Schmitt 1980; Van der Brug & Van der Eijk 2007). That is, the campaigns for European Parliament elections are often conducted by national politicians based on national rather than European political issues. As a result, the campaigns and issues diverge substantially from country to country (Van der Brug & Van der Eijk 2007). To the extent that EP elections are second-order elections, we may find very little EU polity contestation going on combined with a substantial focus of the debates on domestic political issues, rather than EU policies or politicians. We would label such campaign debates to be *domestic debates*. A lack of EU polity contestation, however, does not automatically mean elections are second order. If the campaigns focus on policy questions regarding the issue fields in which the EU and the EP have regulatory powers or on candidates for the European Parliament or European Commission, we label these *substantial debates*. These debates are on the substance of EU policies in which the EP has a direct say as co-legislator. This may, for example, involve questions of more or less market regulation at EU level along the lines of left-right party politics resembling domestic politics. According to our definition provided above, neither domestic nor substantial debates would feature EU polity contestation prominently. If the campaigns feature extensive debates on the institutional design of the EU, the process of European integration, division of powers between Brussels and the Member States, enlargement and other constitutional issues, we will label these *existential debates*. In such a case of prominent EU polity contestation, the topical context in which this takes place – either domestic or European – does not change the classification of these debates as existential. Varieties of existential debates are dominated by the criticism of what the EU is and should be as polity, or to what extent a particular Member State should be involved in the EU, which we defined as EU polity contestation earlier. The intensity with which EU polity contestation takes place, therefore, will bring media coverage of the EP election campaigns closer to the existential ideal type. The question of convergence and divergence is thus understood to include both the nature as well as the intensity of EU polity contestation across Member States.

In the country chapters, we are able to deliver an informed account of national discourses about European integration based on systematic state-of-the-art review and qualitative media content analysis. Instead of introducing national public discourse as a diffuse variable that shapes European integration over time (Harmsen 2008; Larsen 1999), we employ a sophisticated and transparent online media sampling and coding methodology where the units of analysis are clearly operationalised contributions to debates on the EU polity rather than a holistic black box of 'national discourse'. This allows us to aggregate to the Member-State level, capturing nation state specifics, while at the same time facilitating the analysis of public opinion formation and party positioning as unfolding within the national public spheres of the Member States in more detail.

Towards a conceptual framework of EU Polity Contestation

As has been argued by Peter Mair, it is precisely the unsettled nature of the EU as a political entity and its permanent constitutionalisation that opens up the possibility of a form of polity contestation that in many of Europe's established nation states would be considered as exceptional and, in some cases, even illegal (Mair 2007; 4). In laying down the responsiveness of EU polity contestation, we argue in the next step that Euroscepticism is unfolding as the counterpart of European integration itself and of EU legitimation discourse understood as attempts to lay down the basic purpose and rationale for the Union. Understanding the responsive and public character of conflicts over European integration allows us to propose a typology of six different forms of evaluating the EU polity within the broader discourse on European integration. These vary in the degree of contesting the EU polity in principle, current institutional set-up or future project.

EU polity contestation as a category of political practice

The decisive difference of the period from the mid-1980s onwards to earlier decades is the leap into further political integration and the accompanying public promotion of the EU's basic legitimacy. The citizens of Europe have become more involved in issues of European integration, which are increasingly recognised to be of 'general interest' (Hooghe & Marks 2005, 2009; Imig & Tarrow 2001). This citizen involvement happens most notably through the increased use of popular referenda to decide on membership and treaty revision, but also outside these formal 'constitutional moments'. Citizens have often been a brake on further integration as treaty revisions and membership questions have been voted down in referenda. Rather than a 'permissive consensus' on the benefits of continuous integration, the political climate in Europe has more and more turned towards a 'constraining dissensus' (Hooghe & Marks 2009).

As a starting point, we provide a focus on Euroscepticism as a range of discursive practices of contesting the EU as a political entity and/or the project of European integration in its past, present or future. The emphasis on discursive practice underlines the behavioural and temporal nature of EU polity contestation. It is not dormant attitudes we are gauging, but rather contributions to public opinion formation that are by definition time- and place-specific.

Following Mair (2007), contestation surrounding the EU often does not oppose particular *policies*, i.e. the contents of actions taken by the EU, but the *polity*, i.e. the competencies and constitutional settlement of the EU. EU polity contestation, in this sense, is different from 'normal' politics, understood as the regular conflicts among actors and institutions about the distribution of benefits and burdens *within* the political system. Rather, it affects the basic purpose or rationale of the political system, what sort of principles, procedures and institutions are seen as appropriate for it, or why we should (not) want to have it. In line with this understanding, an argument that the Common Agricultural Policy is not fair, not efficient or not environmentally friendly enough would not be counted as contributing to EU polity contestation. However, an argument in favour of renationalising agriculture – i.e. decreasing EU competencies in this field – would, as this directly affects the nature of the institutional arrangement of the EU in competencies laid down in the Treaties.

Here, we have to acknowledge that contentious practices sometimes escape the schematics of conceptual analysis. The distinctive line between policy contestation and polity contestation is analytically drawn and not to be confounded as a category of political practice. It is indeed one of the distinguishing features of the EU that opposition to certain policies regularly feeds into Euroscepticism. For instance, opposition to financial transfers to the EU has fostered Euroscepticism in the UK, the Netherlands and Germany precisely because the underlying conflicts could not be limited to negotiations on the amount of the national contribution but always incorporated arguments against the EU having substantial financial means in general (Petter & Griffiths 2005; Scheuer 1999). Primarily, our definition of EU polity contestation covers arguments concerning the 'deepening' of the EU in terms of level and scope (Lindberg & Scheingold 1970) as well as the 'widening' in terms of people and nations affected by and influencing the EU. EU polity contestation can thus target the institutional and constitutional design of the polity and/or the project of taking further steps in European integration. Finally, EU polity contestation may also problematise the principle of European integration, which concerns the basic idea of pooling sovereignty among European nation states to solve common policy problems, as opposed to national independence (Morgan 2005; Vasilopoulou 2008).

We expect discursive challenges of EU legitimacy to correlate with discursive defences thereof. The EU is not only opposed in a particular way, it is also supported in a way that is different from the ways nation states or their policies are generally legitimised. The EU is neither an international organisation, nor a nation state, and has therefore been regularly described as the intermediary result of a unique – sui generis – process, or as an '*object politique non-identifié*' (Delors, cited in Schmitter 2000: 2). To be able to capture this uniqueness, EU polity contestation should be analysed in relation to political practices and discourses that evaluate the legitimacy of the EU as a novel political entity against the relatively taken-for-granted reality of the nation state.

Denouncing the EU polity: The responsiveness of Euroscepticism

The legitimacy of the EU is debated in a sphere of multiple and diversified publics, in which rationality and emotion, information and misinformation, support and opposition always co-occur (Schlesinger & Kevin 2000). In this context, we understand Euroscepticism as a collection of counter narratives in which the legitimacy of European integration is denounced. In this sense, its emergence correlates with the initiation of a process of democratic legitimation of the EU.

Understanding Euroscepticism in the form of polity contestation provides a stepping stone to emphasise the responsiveness of EU opposition to the on-going attempts of promoting the legitimacy of the EU. In many cases, Euroscepticism is not singular, isolated and exceptional, but rather responsive. This volume builds on the assumption that Eurosceptic opposition is expressed in response to both the continuing European integration process itself and the pro-European arguments deployed by political actors to legitimise this unfinished project. In turn, Eurosceptic mobilisation may provoke an intensification of justification efforts and pro-European responses by those actors and institutions who wish to defend the legitimacy of the EU.

Euroscepticism 'responds' first of all to the substantial growth of powers and competencies of the EU. The decisions made at EU level have effects on citizens in the Member States both directly and indirectly through transposition and enforcement of EU regulations at the national level, in what is known as a process of Europeanisation (Börzel & Risse 2000; Olsen 2002). This significant political influence of decisions made at European level inevitably provokes responses from affected citizens. It feeds national politics and new forms of transnational alliances. These forms of *politicisation* of European integration may function to stimulate or inhibit particular policies or they may result in more critical scrutiny of the performance of political actors and institutions (De Wilde 2007, 2011). In the unsettled constitution of the EU, public contestation is frequently also about the allocation of competences and legal authority. It concerns institutional and constitutional design, questions of membership and of the 'deepening and widening' of European integration. In its most general and accumulated form, Euroscepticism is bound to these evaluations that go beyond 'regular politics' to oppose the existence of the EU polity as such, or membership thereof. This implies that Euroscepticism is not a marginal phenomenon, but rather stands at the heart of the more recent dynamics of 'post-functional' integration (Hooghe &

Marks 2009). Euroscepticism refers to a kind of contestation that is only possible in absence of polity consensus.

Besides substantive reactions to European integration that feed into Euroscepticism, we assume that Eurosceptic responses are often motivated by pro-European propositions found in the general discourse of debating the EU. Since continued European integration, and particularly the continuous formal constitutionalisation process in the form of Treaty revisions, requires a change of the political status quo, advocates and those responsible for the changes engage in the persuasion of citizens to accept these changes (see Morgan 2005). These pro-European arguments may provoke domestic opposition in the form of Eurosceptic counter-arguments in quite a number of different ways.

Firstly, Euroscepticism can be responsive to the substantive arguments raised by pro-European actors. This opens the possibility of contesting the form and content of the EU constitutional settlement. Secondly, Euroscepticism can challenge the integrity of the political actors and institutions advancing pro-European arguments. This opens the possibility of contesting the attitudes and performances of European elites and asking for their possible replacement. Arguments against single politicians cannot be understood as polity contestation, but arguments against the entire (political) elite can, as they form a more structural part of the regime (Hurrelmann *et al.* 2009). Last, but not least, Eurosceptic arguments may be a response to the *lack* of justificatory arguments provided by European actors and institutions. Thus, a Eurosceptic claim may consist of a demand for accountability in terms of providing sufficient justification for further integration.

European integration has opened a vicious circle in which the discursive building of legitimacy correlates with its own delegitimation. This implies that Euroscepticism is not simply unfounded or unreasonable and as such could be defeated by arguments or overcome by more 'rational' forms of communication. Instead, we draw attention to the possible correlation between pro-European and anti-European lines of argumentation. Attempts to forge rational debate and 'democratic justification' of the EU may create a favourable environment for the spread of Euroscepticism. In this last case, the constant and increased efforts to provide public justifications for European integration, would provide the breeding ground for Euroscepticism. Consequently, we may see EU polity contestation as a response – and therefore inextricably linked – to the modes of arguing in favour of European integration and the EU. Pro-European and anti-European arguments interrelate with each other and with actual developments in European integration and effects thereof on the nation state.

Varieties of evaluating the EU polity

Moving away from the restricted use of the term Euroscepticism as a label in public opinion or partisan competition towards a more comprehensive analysis of the discursive positions that can be taken to either defend or challenge the legitimacy of the EU, the operational task is to arrive at a more comprehensive categorisation of forms of both positive and negative evaluations through which the EU polity is debated. To this end, we propose a critical matrix for the analysis of EU legitimation discourse that takes account of the correlation between opposition and support.

According to Morgan (2005: 17), the structure of legitimation discourse over European integration unfolds along three dimensions. The proponents of European integration provide justifications with regard to 1) why we should support European integration in principle; 2) what institutional and constitutional design should be given to the EU and; 3) what future trajectories of integration should be chosen. Disagreements about the principle, institutional set-up, and project of European integration run deep in contemporary Europe. Thus, the dimensions of support of European integration also mark the dimensions of possible resistance. The opponents of European integration or of EU legitimacy denounce 1) the legitimacy of the underlying principle of integration; 2) the consistency or applicability of its concrete institutional/constitutional form, and; 3) the viability or desirability of future integration.

Rejections of the principle of integration undermine by their very nature the legitimacy of the currently existing EU polity. If one understands integration as a more or less linear process of 'ever closer union', contributions to discourse that reject the current form/state of the EU polity are likely to denounce future plans for even more integration as well. However, based on our typology of argumentation provided in Table 1.1, other 'non-linear' forms of EU polity evaluation are possible. It is therefore necessary to distinguish two additional evaluative dimensions with regard to 'institutional set-up' and 'project' that interact with the evaluation of the principle of the polity.

In order to further demarcate targets of EU polity evaluations, we follow the classic distinction of Lindberg and Scheingold (1970) between *level* and *scope* of integration (*see also* Börzel 2005). 'Level of integration' refers here to the powers of supranational institutions in relation to the Member States, or *how much* influence the EU has. Scope refers to the different policy fields in which EU institutions have competencies, or *on what* the EU has a say. In addition to this scheme, we introduce the *inclusiveness* of integration as a third relevant category as this features largely in the recent debates about the democratic legitimacy of the EU. Inclusiveness refers to constituencies affected by the EU polity, or *about*

Table 1.1: Typology of EU polity evaluations

Project of integration	Principle of integration			
	EU institutional set-up		EU institutional set-up	
	Positive	Negative	Positive	Negative
Positive	Affirmative European	Alter-European	–	–
Negative	Status-Quo	Eurocritical	Pragmatic	Anti-European

whom the EU has a say and *who* has influence on the EU. It might refer to nations, occupational groups, minorities or such broad categories as 'ordinary citizens'. Membership and enlargement questions also fall into this category. Combining the dimensions with targets of EU polity evaluation, statements denouncing European integration could address the principle of integration, the level, scope or inclusiveness of the EU institutional set-up and/or the level, scope or inclusiveness of the project of integration.

Table 1.1 provides six possible lines of argumentation on the EU polity based on our three dimensions of polity evaluation.[2] We find Affirmative European contributions where neither the principle of integration nor the current EU institutional set-up and further plans for integration are contested. On the other side, we find Anti-European statements that denounce all the three polity dimensions. In between these two poles, we find on the more pro-European side statements in favour of the status quo, in which the principle of integration and the current institutional set-up are defended, but further integration is rejected. On the Eurosceptic side, we identify Eurocritical statements supporting the principle of integration but denouncing both the current institutional set-up and further plans of integration. These four categories can thus be understood as scaled from complete legitimation of integration to complete delegitimation.

Two other categories of contestation do not fit this linear scale. Pragmatic statements indicate the seemingly paradoxical position of legitimating the current EU institutional set-up, while at the same time denouncing integration in principle (Kopecký & Mudde 2002). In these statements the EU is often understood as a *fait accompli*, which might be undesirable in principle but deserves support nevertheless, since other alternatives are either unrealistic or too costly. Alter-Europeanism is characterised by a denunciation of the current institutional set-up combined with a favourable stance towards further integration. These statements often criticise certain characteristics of the polity, while at the same time offering a pro-European 'solution' to perceived problems. Statements criticising the EU as a neoliberal project combined with an argument in favour of a European-wide welfare state would fit this category. Another example would be criticism of the EU as undemocratic, combined with an argument supporting the extension of European Parliament powers or a direct election of the Commission President.

Interestingly, Alter-European – and to some extent Eurocritical – statements reflect the discursive grey zone between polity contestation and 'politics as usual'. Their criticism is often founded in ideologies well known from politics as usual, targeting 'neoliberal Europe', 'secular Europe', 'elitist Europe', 'socialist Europe' etc. (e.g. Crespy & Verschueren 2009). However, as our typology aptly shows, these two categories differ fundamentally as Alter-European statements portray a supranational solution to deficits of the EU polity, while Eurocritical statements do not.

---

2. Two categories are ruled out, because for logical reasons integration cannot be rejected in principle, while calling for further steps in the project of integration.

In discursive practice, however, the three dimensions of evaluation are unlikely to be addressed simultaneously. That is, in on-going media debates, for instance, we may often encounter contributions to discourse that evaluate one or two dimensions of European integration only. Most of these can be logically included in one of the six ideal types modelled above (see Appendix III). However, stand-alone negative evaluations of the institutional set-up or the project of information do not provide sufficient information to be categorised in our typology. In other words, arguments that 'the EU does not work' or 'Turkey should not be allowed to become a Member State' could be either anti-European, Eurocritical, status quo or alter-European dependent on missing information. We might even expect that such negative evaluations of the EU on the basis of missing justification might become frequently used in certain types of public and media discourse (e.g. in user comments or in tabloid style news formats where contributors are less trained to provide justifications for their arguments). We label such contributions which escape categorisation as 'diffuse Euroscepticism'. They are interesting as they will prove to be very frequent, and thus influential in opinion-making but insufficient from the perspective of qualifying EU discourse in terms of providing the necessary information about the preferred allocation of political authority and the application of solutions to voiced concerns.

In this last sense, our categorisation of EU polity evaluations can be also used as a quality indicator of justificatory discourse of European integration measuring deviations from the requirements of justifications that contestants of European integration must meet to fully qualify the legitimacy of the EU (Morgan 2005: 17) in terms of principle, institutional/constitutional set-up and project. Abbreviated justifications can be part of the rhetorical strategies of contestants or result from the selective bias of media debates to either focus on particular dimensions of EU polity evaluation or to renounce justification in negatively evaluating the EU. In both cases, we can discuss them as indicative of the quality of debate in terms of facilitating informed opinion-making of the citizens.

For the foreseeable future, the EU will remain a moving target of polity contestation. Discursive manifestations of Euroscepticism are frequently related to opportunities (e.g. referenda), constitutional moments (e.g. Treaty reform) or particular turning points in history (e.g. enlargement, Eurozone crisis) that prompt political entrepreneurs to both legitimate further steps in integration and challenge elite choices and justifications. During attempts to constitutional settlement or enlargement, a struggle for the qualification of EU polity legitimacy is triggered off, which may diminish again when major decisions on integration are removed from the political agenda. The analytical question of interest to us is not how these conflicts can be settled through institutional design, but rather how they are discursively sustained over time during and beyond such explicit opportunities.

Studying the full range of arguments that appear in debates on EU legitimacy, rather than just negative evaluations, enables us to put the responsiveness of Euroscepticism in context and thus to enrich our understanding of the different driving forces of resistances to European integration. In the proposed critical matrix of EU polity evaluation, Euroscepticism is not fully idiosyncratic, but partially scaled on a dimension from affirmative Europeanism to anti-Europeanism. That is, four out of six categories range from challenging none of the dimensions of EU polity evaluation (affirmative Europeanism) to challenging only the future project (status quo), to challenging both the project and the current institutional set-up (Eurocritical) to finally challenging all three dimensions (anti-European). Yet, the categories of pragmatic and alter-European evaluations do not fit onto this ordinal scale. Evaluations of the EU and European integration vary not only across time and space but can also embrace several dimensions of this matrix. The conceptual task here is limited to pointing out the possible varieties of EU polity contestation. The question of how Euroscepticism is constructed in ongoing debates on European integration, i.e. the question of how principled evaluations of EU legitimacy are combined with possible evaluations of the institutional design of the EU and of the future project of integration, will be empirically investigated in the subsequent chapters of this book. With the help of the analytical framework presented here, we are able to capture the full range of EU polity contestation, including wide ranging topics such as the bureaucratic nature of the European Commission, the EU's powers in the field of Justice and Home Affairs, and possible Turkish accession in a way that allows for mapping not only national differences in discourse but also the extent and form of EU-wide commonalities.

The European Parliament Elections of 2009

Instances of polity contestation that may be endogenous to single Member States can only be meaningfully interpreted by capturing the wide range of evaluations that may occur throughout Europe. This book therefore proceeds to apply our discursive understanding of EU polity contestation in a comparative framework to a range of big and small as well as new and old Member States. Yet, the political cycles of EU Member States differ strongly. Discourse in the public sphere may be highly influenced by country specific events that either amplify or crowd out EU polity contestation. National elections, political scandals or other country-specific events could easily distort both the intensity and nature thereof. To measure contestation at any random point in time therefore carries a risk for the generalisability of the substantive findings. In order to minimise such measurement errors, this volume proceeds to study EU polity contestation at the time of an event, which occurred in all EU Member States at the same time with the same relevance: the European Parliament elections of June 2009.

By focusing on the 2009 EP election campaigning in twelve Member States we can systematically analyse variances in the shape and scope of EU polity contestation across the European political space. EP election campaigns provide us with an 'episode of contention' (Tilly & Tarrow 2007) that mobilises relevant partisan actors within the Member States and beyond to compete for public and media attention. As such, EP elections create a transcultural and cross-national media event (Dayan & Katz 1992) that breaks the normal routines of media broadcasting over the EU. As a media event, the EP election attracts the largest possible number of audiences (voters and non-voters). In this quality, the episode of contention has a potential in terms of media power over the EU political system. The mass media become the principal arena for activating the norms and symbols, narratives and cultural codes that are used in contesting the legitimacy of the EU.

By their nature, Parliamentary election campaigns address the audience in its quality as the electorate that exerts political control and through its choice mandates political representatives. Democratic representation via the European Parliament is, however, limited and the EU has other channels of democratic representation, including via the national parliaments (Crum & Fossum 2009). In addition, the European Parliament is not a fully sovereign legislator. In the EU, Member State governments remain the official masters of the Treaties (Hix 2005). They decide, through Treaty revisions, how the EU is formally constituted. This includes all major decisions on the level, scope and inclusiveness of the EU polity. The EP thus has no formal power over the institutional and constitutional set-up of the EU or the process of integration. As a result, issues that would directly load onto EU polity contestation are not formally at stake during the EP elections. EP elections have therefore only an indirect bearing on the legitimacy of the EU polity itself or the process of integration (Blondel *et al.* 1998; Hix *et al.* 2007).

The powers of the EP are further limited in that it is not authoritative in appointing a 'government' for the EU, like the national parliaments in most EU Member States are. As a consequence, turnouts systematically lag behind those for national elections and strategic protest voting in favour of minority, often extremist, parties becomes more prominent (Hix & Marsh 2007; Weber 2007). This, in combination with the fact that EP campaigning is conducted predominantly by prominent leaders of national political parties and not by the MEP (Member of European Parliament) candidates, underlies the 'second order' status of EP elections (Reif & Schmitt 1980; Van der Brug & Van der Eijk 2007). That is, EP elections tend to reflect domestic political conflicts and both parties and voters are inclined to see them as mid-term popularity contests of the national government, rather than as important in their own right with regard to EU policy making.

This particular feature of 'second-order' EP elections allows us to analyse 'ordinary' Euroscepticism as it pops up in moments of regular politics and not in moments of constitutional reform, when the normative foundations and the design of the polity are at stake. We can thus expect EU polity contestation to be less present in EP elections than, for instance, in referenda on Treaty revisions. EU referenda are sometimes linked to exceptionally high levels of political contestation like in France, the Netherlands and in Ireland (De Vreese 2007a; FitzGibbon 2010). It may be expected that questions directly addressing the EU polity would be most salient during Treaty ratification referendums. There are, however, three problems with referendums that bring us to discard this option in favour of EP elections. First, referendums on Treaty change are only held in a small minority of Member States. They thus provide very limited possibilities for comparative mapping of EU polity contestation. Secondly, they rarely occur simultaneously. In the time between different referendums, the EU wide situation, such as its economic performance or functioning of the Commission, may change significantly, altering the background against which contestation unfolds. Thirdly, referendums are not necessarily repetitive. It is unclear if and when there will be another EU Treaty change prompting ratification referendums or which Member States will then opt to hold referendums rather than parliamentary ratification. The periodic recurrences of EP elections simultaneously throughout the EU provide interesting time intervals that facilitate the possible longitudinal extension of this study. For these three reasons, we consider EP election campaigns as superior media events to referendums for the purpose of mapping EU polity contestation in a comparative perspective.

Book Outline

This volume provides a combination of qualitative country case studies and quantitative comparative analysis of debates on the EU polity based on a single overarching research design. Instances of EU polity contestation are contextualised against the background of the more general tone of EP elections campaigns and pro-European statements, in the framework of a cross-country comparison and in the context of different public arenas where this discourse unfolds.

To provide a broad overview of EU polity contestation and a thorough exploration of the usefulness of the above developed analytical framework, the media event of the 2009 EP elections is studied in twelve EU Member States: Austria, French speaking Belgium[3], the Czech Republic, Finland, France, Germany, Greece, Hungary, the Netherlands, Poland, Sweden and the United Kingdom. These countries arguably provide a rich encompassing sample as they incorporate big and small; new and old; northern, southern, eastern and western Member States. Some of these countries are widely known for their critical stances towards European integration, like the UK, whereas others have a reputation to be pro-European, like Germany. Our case sample also includes the debates in the three most powerful EU Member States (Germany, France and the UK) (Moravcsik 1998) thus not just providing a broad picture of EU polity contestation, but also an overview of the most consequential debates. By varying country size, geographic location and history of EU membership the sample represents a most different system comparative research design (George & Bennett 2005). The chance for observing divergence across and within Member States and media outlets as well as between citizens and elites is thereby maximised. This research design thus lends credence to the generalisability of observed convergence. Furthermore, Europe-wide debates in transnational online media have been included as a thirteenth, control case. Transnational online media in Europe address a niche

---

3. Although French-speaking Belgium is not a member state, it is here included as a case of a confined political public sphere in which the EU polity is contested in a distinguished way with a particular constituency/electorate as the addressee of EP electoral campaigning. As Belgian websites in the French language may easily encompass inhabitants of the city of Brussels and Flanders, we use this term throughout this book instead of 'Wallonia'.

audience, mostly comprising policy-makers and lobbyists operating in Brussels, as well as EU correspondents, academics and students of EU affairs. As they address an international audience, they have to operate beyond the confines of the narratives found in the national public spheres. Additionally, trans-European online media are elite spaces, in that their audience is largely formed by individuals with knowledge and interest in EU issues. For this reason, it is important to map the debates taking place in these media, as this will enable us to check if there are any differences in the way that the EU polity is contested by general and elite publics, but also whether the context provided for the debates (transnational or national media spheres) impacts on how the EU is contested.

Several cases are explored more in depth in detailed country case studies. These qualitative contributions serve to further illustrate the context-specific meaning of EU polity contestation by investigating individual instances of contestation against the background of the overarching analytical framework. The qualitative studies also serve to map the prominence of EU polity contestation in different national political discourses and to provide an overview of nation-based Euroscepticism and the way it comes to the fore in our data.

Chapter Two sets out to discuss in detail the research design and methodology. As we argue there, the internet provides a highly promising arena for studying EU polity contestation. Not only because it is occupying an increasingly important place in the mass-media landscape, but also because of its opportunities for interaction between news producers and news consumers. The chapter proceeds to present our sampling strategy of news websites and political blogs and our adapted form of claims-making analysis as a specific form of rigorous quantitative content analysis including the operationalisation of key variables.

The comparative agenda to map convergence and divergence is explicitly taken up in Chapter Three of the book. Here, we discuss the aggregated data set and can thus rely on a unique record of debates that are representative in the double sense of comprising twelve EU Member States and largest possible numbers of audiences (electorates). By focusing on the most salient news sites in each country, we arrive at a reliable indicator of impact of the media in shaping public perceptions of EU legitimacy.

This is followed by an in-depth analysis of eight selected country cases from our overall sample of twelve countries (Chapters four to ten). These country chapters are informative in the sense of providing a state-of-the-art review of member-state specific EU polity contestation including the context of citizens' attitudes and party positions. The chapters are also original in their approach of addressing the role of the media in general and of online media, more specifically, in the propagation of Euroscepticism. The cases selected encompass the three most influential countries of the EU: Germany, France and the UK and a selection of Eastern and Western European countries, namely: Austria, Hungary and the Netherlands, where, together with the UK, Eurosceptic parties have gained significantly high shares of the vote. In the UK, the anti-European UK Independence Party came in second. In Austria, three Eurosceptic parties, the Alliance for the Future of Austria, The Austrian Freedom Party and the Liste Martin gained 35 per cent of the votes. In Hungary, the right-wing extremist party *JOBBIK* gained three seats in the European parliament and 15 per cent of the votes. In the Netherlands, Geert Wilders' Freedom Party took four seats with 17 per cent of the votes. These cases contrast with other countries discussed here, like Germany, France, Belgium and Poland, where the 2009 EP elections either saw a significant drop in support for Eurosceptic parties or where anti-EU discourse did not gain ground altogether. In Poland, for example, all MEPs from Eurosceptic parties lost their seats, whereas in France and Germany, pro-European parties like the Greens, which explicitly campaigned in favour of integration, came out as the winners of the election.

Our qualitative country-case approach allows us to delve into country-specific EU debates as well as to identify concerns that are of relevance to all the Europeans. The volume cannot directly predict impact of media on voters' choice and preferences but concludes with demonstrating clear overarching patterns in the presence and strength of EU polity contestation in mainstream online media in the countries analysed.

Chapter Two | A Comparative Mixed-Methods Approach of Online EU Polity Contestation

Given our conceptualisation and operationalisation of EU polity contestation dynamically unfolding in the public sphere, how might we go about measuring it? This is the challenge of empirical research resulting from the introductory chapter. We argue in this chapter, that this conceptual operationalisation involves three methodological challenges when it comes to empirical measurement.

To start with, the challenge arises how to capture the interactive dynamics of EU polity contestation. In order to assess the extent to which different contributions to EU polity contestation relate to each other and 'provoke' or 'invite' responses, and positive counter arguments, we need to study this phenomenon in a surrounding where such interaction may come to the fore. Of particular interest here, as argued in the introduction, is public resonance or the direct feedback from citizens to arguments by politicians and other prominent actors in the public sphere. Secondly, how can we demarcate individual contributions to unfolding discourse on EU legitimacy? This involves, in particular, the extent to which EU polity contestation addresses the three dimensions of evaluation outlined in the introductory chapter: the principle of European integration, the institutional set-up of the EU polity and future plans for further integration. In going beyond the content of EU polity contestation to include its meaning, our methodological approach, furthermore, needs to include justifications articulated to support, explain and contextualise EU polity contestation. Thirdly, the challenge is to combine precise and reliable data gathering with in-depth analysis of context and meaning. If we are to generate comprehensive empirical insight into EU polity contestation across different EU Member States, our methodology needs to be accurate and generate reliable, comparable data. At the same time, in order to fully capture the meaning and prominence of EU polity contestation in different national contexts, our methodology needs to be able to accommodate specificities of particular debates, including the precise targets, connotation and direction of contributions.

To meet these three challenges, the empirical research project presented in this volume, employs a mixed methodology that includes quantitative content analysis using a rigorous coding scheme generating comparable data cross-nationally. To capture possible interaction in debates on EU legitimacy and public resonance in particular, we target the online news media sphere. We understand this to comprise both professional news websites (usually the online version of established offline mass media) and political blogs, written either by professional or amateur (citizen) journalists. Whether blogs can be classified as a form of journalism or not is a highly contentious issue (e.g. contributions in Ludtke 2003), but in our definition of the online mass-media sphere we follow Lasica's approach, whereby blogging is accepted as a form of journalism (participatory or citizens' journalism), distinct from, but also complimentary to, professional journalism (Lasica 2003). In light of the growing significance of micro-blogging (as represented by the main platform in this field, Twitter), we have extended our definition of the online news media sphere to also include this snippet-like form of communication as a third strand of online reporting, distinct both from professional journalism and traditional blogging. Professional or amateur, what the online news media sphere offers is interactivity: whether we look at professional news websites, political blogs or Twitter entries, it is the reactions of readers that matter as much here, as the original posted articles or text. In addition to the formalised opinions carried forward by professional journalists and political actors, our study of the online news media sphere allows us to capture the spontaneous, unsolicited views of the public and, thus, gain an insight into the meanings attributed to European integration in everyday 'political talk'.

Studying data collected from the online news sphere through a comprehensive sampling strategy, we present a coding scheme measuring EU polity contestation quantitatively by including two levels of analysis. It is in the application of a rigorous quantitative content analysis to cross-country internet data that our methodology is highly innovative. Relatively few studies have so far targeted news websites and political blogs in multiple countries in such a manner (Jankowski and Van Selm 2008; Strandberg 2008; Vergeer and Hermans 2008). In order to further develop our understanding of Euroscepticism beyond the quantitative data generated through our content analysis, we discuss, in detail, the online coverage that the EP elections received in several Member States included in our study, as well as the background of Eurosceptic discourse in these countries (main narratives, key political actors and public opinion trends).

This chapter sets out first, to argue why we consider the online media sphere to be a particularly promising arena for studying EU polity contestation in a cross-national comparative project. Subsequently, we discuss specific challenges for comparative, reliable and replicable empirical analysis of ensuing web-based material. This includes, in particular, challenges related to the sampling, monitoring and gathering of ephemeral data. Following on from this, we outline our quantitative content analysis aimed at capturing both the nature of the debates in EP election campaigns and the specific content, justification and meaning of contributions to EU polity contestation. A brief discussion of operationalised variables is included.

The case for studying EU polity contestation online

Taking our public sphere perspective to EU polity contestation, as outlined in the introduction (*see also* Michailidou and Trenz 2010), intermediation of the political process follows a particular normative script: it relies on transparent political institutions; an active (or at least attentive) citizenry and the creation of a collective will (Fraser 2007; Habermas 1989). Political intermediation through the so-called 'traditional' media (press, television, radio), however, is found to be deficient in many ways. It is inherently linear, highly selective and exclusive, in the sense that citizens remain, with few exceptions, mere observers of the political game. In the case of the EU, the 'traditional' media have also repeatedly been found to re-affirm the nation state and the legitimacy of contextualised national politics (Gerhards and Schafer 2010; Trenz 2004).

The internet is changing the dynamics of public political communication, as this has thus far been channelled by traditional media, in at least three ways:[1] 1) its establishment as an integral source of political news/information that is made salient for a large proportion of the voting population (Eurobarometer 2009a; Smith 2009); 2) the engagement of the users, rise of 'citizen journalism' and establishment of political discourse and action, also outside the realm of the strictly defined public sphere of political institutions (Stanyer 2009); 3) the shaping of political attitudes and opinions, including those of otherwise disengaged and hard-to-reach audiences, particularly young people (Esser and De Vreese 2007; Karlsen 2010; Lusoli 2005b).

Research on the role of the internet in political communication on EU matters, has primarily focused on the internet performance of the input providers of political communication, such as national and transnational political actors, EU institutions and/or social movements, during election campaigns or 'neutral' periods of governance (Foot *et al.* 2009; Lusoli 2005a; Michailidou 2008; Zimmermann *et al.* 2004); and on the 'quality' of online political debates, measured against deliberative democracy standards (Carlson and Strandberg 2005; Jankowski and Van Os 2004; Strandberg 2008). Nevertheless, the complexity of the online political sphere cannot be sufficiently explained either with one-dimensional analytical approaches, focusing on online party politics and electoral campaigns only; or deliberative democracy approaches, which do not take into account the particularities of online public debating. To begin with, the standards of deliberative discourse do not take into consideration the particularities of online communication, most notably that the etiquette of online interaction – or netiquette (Michael Lerner Productions 2010; Stewart 2010) – is more flexible and accommodating than public debates hosted in conventional media. As such, online communication resembles more the informal interpersonal communication individuals experience in their everyday lives. Furthermore, the online public sphere did not set out to be a deliberative space (in normative terms, or even by offline public talk standards), but a sphere of freedom (freedom from censorship, discrimination and offline government).[2]

---

1. Nevertheless, the extent to which these changes have a qualitative impact on mediated political communication, and can revitalise the normative script of the public sphere, remains a highly contested issue that continues to divide scholars: the so-called 'cyber-optimist/cyber-pessimist divide'. See (Albrecht 2006; Dahlgren 2005; Norris 2001; Papacharissi 2009; Sunstein 2007).
2. Early netizens did not intend to build a Habermasian (in the deliberative sense) e-public sphere. The key aim was freedom: cyberspace (which includes the internet) was heralded by early pioneers, such as John Perry Barlow (Electronic Frontier 2009), as the ultimate space of freedom from censorship, government, socio-economic bias, racial prejudice and educational elitism (Barlow 1996).

Therefore, it should come as no surprise that the primary aim of participants in online debates is to express their view, without too much consideration for the manner in which they do so. Indeed, participants join online discussions, precisely because they perceive them as open (Witschge 2008). This 'open' and 'liberal' nature of the internet, in contrast to both traditional mass media and public opinion polls, provides a unique surrounding for analysing relatively unfiltered and unsolicited contributions to EU polity contestation.

Secondly, in search of the elusive deliberative e-sphere, researchers have, thus far, deployed a multitude of deliberative communication models devised to assess online political debates (Albrecht 2006; Fuchs 2006; Gerhards and Schafer 2010; Surel 2000; Trenz 2007). However, the abstract nature of the subject of measurement (deliberation), and the complexity of the models, reduces both the comparability of the results and the reliability of the measurements. This is primarily because these models allow for high levels of inter/intra-coder bias and arbitrary interpretations of the participants' intentions, particularly with regard to qualitative indicators such as 'tone of message' and type of content. In addition, it is necessary to consider that the contributions of online participants are only evaluated within the context of a specific debate. Due to the nature of online communication, this evaluation cannot be corroborated with offline interviews of contributors before, and after, their partaking in the online debate. Consequently, it is not possible to assess whether online political debating leads to mutual understanding and shifting of positions (both key prerequisites of deliberation), or not.[3] Instead, we argue that the online media offer an ideal environment for analysing contestation of EU legitimacy, precisely because they allow us to systematically link political contestation and citizens' participation, with public salience and media framing (Michailidou and Trenz 2010). Bringing together an analytical matrix that maps the different degrees of EU contestation (De Wilde and Trenz 2012), and an investigative model that encompasses the multiple elements of the online public sphere (Michailidou and Trenz 2010), we propose a research design that maps the contours of contestation at national and trans-European level.

---

3. Mei (2008) attempted to gauge the extent of 'periphery participation', or the number of people who visit and follow an online debate without contributing (also known as 'lurkers'). By looking at the number of hits per discussion article post on Chinese forums and comparing them to the number of contributions per article, Mei was able to determine the amount of users who were 'silently' following a debate. To gain some insight into the impact that an online debate has on these silent users, Mei then tested the hypothesis that 'lurkers' would be interested in the same debates as active contributors and, therefore, an article with a high number of hits would also have a high number of contributions. Interesting as this attempt may have been, the methodological and operational problems of testing out this hypothesis, did not allow the author to offer a plausible explanation with sufficient confidence.

Three operational challenges

The operationalisation of our analytical model presents us with three challenges, pertaining to the sampling, gathering and analysing of data. More specifically, the first challenge is to determine, in practical terms, the online public sphere from which to draw our sample. How can we ensure that this sample is representative, and is it even necessary to ensure representativeness, given the fluidity of the online public sphere? Secondly, once our public sphere is defined, how can we address the issue of ephemerality that permeates the online public sphere? Crucially, how can we keep track of the debates across twelve countries, and at transnational level, and shift through millions of webpages with potentially relevant content? Last, but not least, once at the analysis stage of our research, we need a coding scheme that takes into consideration the particularities of online media debates, while enabling us, at the same time, to capture content concerning the legitimacy of the EU polity in a standardised manner. In the following sections, we discuss, in detail, each of these challenges and the ways we have dealt with them.

Web sphere of focus: EU elections 2009

In order to identify our web sphere of focus, we followed Schneider and Foot's definition of a web sphere as 'a hyperlinked set of dynamically defined digital resources that span multiple websites and are deemed relevant, or related, to a central theme or "object".' (Schneider and Foot 2004: 118). The web sphere is part of the Internet media space and is constituted by a single media class (web sites), which are comprised of elements or objects such as links, features and texts (media instances). These, in turn, are combined in larger media objects of web pages or web sites (Schneider and Foot 2004: 118). In contrast to conventional media sources, where the communicator(s) and communicated material remain stable and are easy to identify, the themes and communicators of web content are predicted rather than identified. The degree of 'thematic anticipatability' and actor predictability (Schneider and Foot 2005: 160) determine the degree of confidence the researcher can have of their sample.

As the theme of the web sphere under study is clearly defined and anticipated (EU elections in 2009), it was possible to identify and select relevant websites with confidence. The initial communicators (actors) of our web sphere were pre-determined (professional journalists and independent bloggers) but the overall predictability of the actors in the 2009 EU elections' web sphere remained fluid. This is in accordance with the exploratory nature of our project, which sets out to identify actors who project contributions to EU polity contestation within the European political e-sphere.

In order to define the time boundaries of our web sphere, we followed Schneider and Foot's definition of 'web storms' (Schneider and Foot 2005: 162–3). These are instances when one big event or chain of events (in our case, the EU elections) may trigger a series of inter-actor and inter-site activity online. Because of the brief space of activity, a web storm does not qualify as a public sphere, but it may develop into one over time (Schneider and Foot 2005: 162–3). We anticipated that media coverage of the EP election campaign would peak in the two-three weeks before the election dates, up until several days after the last elections. Our monitoring period was thus limited from 18 May 2009 until 10 June 2009. The sampled and coded threads were then divided into three sub-periods (early pre-election: 18–28 May; late pre-election: 29 May – 6 June; post-election: 7–10 June).

The question that subsequently arises is, how we can locate a web sphere that is not (known to be) there already? We deployed three methods of web sphere identification in our project (as discussed in Schneider and Foot 2005): 1) use of keywords to search for websites that referred to the EU elections; 2) identification of relevant actor types and inclusion of web sites produced by identified actors: in our case, we narrowed our search to content produced by professional journalism websites and independent political blogs; 3) pattern analysis of in-linking to and out-linking from a core set of URLs: This method was particularly useful for identifying the Facebook and Twitter sample of our study, but was also used to verify the popularity of the websites selected at national level. In the latter case, the pattern analysis of in-linking to, and out-linking from, an individual website was not carried out by the researchers but forms part of the rating and ranking engines that assess the visibility and popularity of websites and blogs (Alexa Internet 2009; Technorati 2009).

Website selection

Our aim is to examine EU polity contestation in the online news media sphere and how this contestation is shaped by the new forms of public participation and involvement. Thus, we turn to those online news websites that are most visited by the public in each of our selected countries. In order to create a representative map of the EU elections web sphere, we have looked for EU debates in all publicly available (where no paid subscription is required) online outlets encompassing debates that took place during the last three weeks of the EP election campaign in May–June 2009, as well as the first few days following the elections. Our sample comprises only the most popular political news websites per country and at trans-European level.[4] In total, we have included thirty-six professional

---

4. See Appendix I for all selected websites. Popularity is measured by visitor numbers and influence within the blogosphere, using the Top 100 websites per country listings on Alexa.com (Alexa Internet 2009) and blog aggregator popularity and influence lists, such as Wikio (Wikio 2009a-renamed since then to Ebuzzing). All but four of the professional journalism websites, and four independent blogs, were in the Alexa Country Top 100 websites lists, while the majority of the independent blogs were in the top 500 websites in their country. For Facebook threads, popularity was determined by the number of members subscribed to a group (we only considered groups with a minimum of 2,000 members), while for Twitter threads, we identified the two most popular hashtags linked with the EU elections, and selected all threads ascribed to them for the studied period.

journalism websites and twenty-four independent blogs of national scope.[5] Besides the criterion of popularity, and in order to be able to measure impact in terms of inclusion, news websites were selected based on their potential to open an interactive space between proponents and users. In most cases, this referred to the widespread practice of publicly available user feedback and comments on articles or blog entries. If this commenting option was not available, a website needed to host at least one online debate forum in order to be selected.

At European/transnational level we have included one professional journalism website and two blogs, following the same criteria for popularity and interactivity. To supplement our data from the transnational news websites, which attract a niche, arguably elite, audience, with data from more popular, less elitist online forums, we also included two Twitter threads with EU election-related hash tags,[6] to better capture the more 'popularised' aspect of the trans-European online public sphere. For the same reason we decided to include two Facebook groups and one 'fan page', focused on the EU elections as sources of online debate, even though they do not fall within our definition of the online news media sphere. The selected Facebook sources came up during the analysis of in-linking and out-linking patterns of the trans-European news websites. The European Parliament fan page (not to be confused with the official European Parliament Facebook page) counted over 55,000 members at the time of the sampling (see Appendix I for details), while the two groups were set up specifically for the 2009 elections and counted 5,953 and 2,719 members respectively.

Monitoring

We have given preference to websites where the RSS (Rich Site Summary or Really Simple Syndication) feed application has been available. For the purposes of our project, we used Bloglines Reader (Reply! Inc. 2012) and Google Reader (Google 2012) for collecting the Twitter material.[7] The advantage of RSS feeds is twofold: Firstly, it enabled us to address the instability or 'ephemerality' of web content (Jones 1999; Schneider and Foot 2004), as all material was downloaded upon its appearance online and then filtered for relevancy and archived. This also enabled us to address the dynamic nature of the online public sphere, as we could ensure that we would be able to retrieve selected material, despite the constantly shifting boundaries of the web sphere under study. Secondly, as the dynamism of a web sphere relates also to the way the researcher perceives and defines its boundaries (Schneider and Foot 2004), we ensured consistency and accuracy in the process of website and text selection by establishing a detailed, and rigorously tested,

---

5. Independent blogs are understood here as not sponsored, or run by, EU or national institutions.
6. Hashtags are a 'Twitter community creation', invented by users to easily group tweets and/or add extra data (Twitter 2009).
7. Since 2011, it is no longer possible to access Twitter material through RSS feeds.

sampling manual. In other words, we opted to 'fix' the boundaries of the web sphere under study early on in the process, in order to ensure the representativeness of our sample and replicability of analysis across countries (*see also* Schneider and Foot 2005). Using RSS feeds with pre-determined filtering keywords[8] to automatically select the material for analysis, ensured that there were no changes or diversions of the selection keywords during the monitoring period, while the element of coder subjectivity ('is this article relevant or not?') was eliminated from this stage of the article selection process. Ensuring relevance of the Twitter material was more straightforward, as the hashtags we used played the role of filtering keywords. Similarly, as we only selected Facebook groups that had the EU elections as their topic, relevance was automatically ensured at a general level. We subsequently excluded from coding any discussion threads that concerned group-administration matters, to maximise the relevance of the coded end material.

Selection of articles (threads) for coding

In total, our website monitoring through RSS feeds resulted in the 'clipping' (selection) of 4,815 webpages (threads) that covered the EU elections in the selected websites. A thread is here defined as a single entry online – often comparable to a newspaper article – and all directly attached comments. In other chapters of this volume, they will be referred to with the less technical term, 'online articles'. Figure 2.1 illustrates the amount of threads collected from the five websites per country.

Due to limitations in the coding resources available to us, we had to take a sub-sample from these articles. We decided on a stratified strategy for this part of our sampling process. Firstly, we opted for a sub-sample that would give us a confidence interval between ±3 and ±4 and set our confidence level at 95 per cent. This meant that as a minimum, we would have needed to select 534 threads for further coding. We wanted to ensure representation of all countries in our sub-sample; however we did not opt for a proportionally representative sampling strategy, even though Figure 2.1 clearly shows that the amount of threads collected varied widely among countries. Our decision to not implement a proportionally representative sub-sample, was based on the fact that our analysis of the 2009 EP online news sphere would be of general qualitative nature, i.e. the selected threads would not be used for direct quantitative analysis. Opting for a non-proportionally representative sub-sample would produce a qualitatively richer sub-sample, would also allow us to maximise the use of our coding resources and ensure that, from each country included in our study, the maximum possible amount of threads would be coded and analysed.

---

8. Keywords were tested in the weeks before our monitoring period commenced, to ensure that they captured the maximum amount of relevant articles and were, of course, adapted linguistically for each country included in our study.

Figure 2.1: Total number of articles covering the 2009 EP elections in each country, period: 18 May–10 June 2009

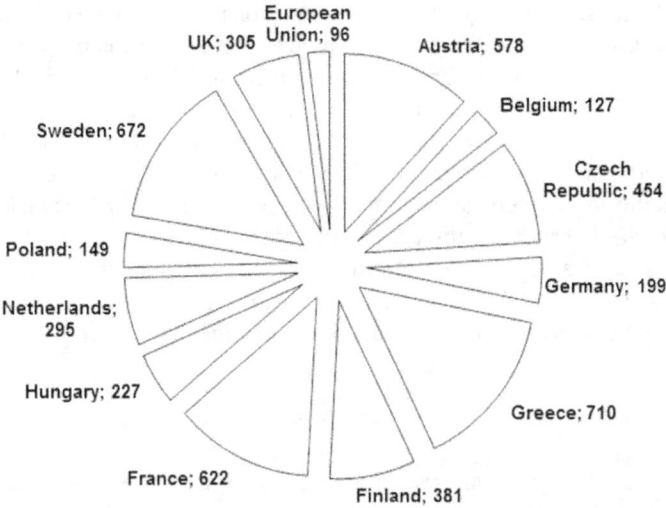

The minimum sub-sample of 534 threads required to meet our confidence standards could not be equally distributed across our thirteen news website groupings[9] (41.07 threads per group), so we increased the amount of articles we would select per country to fifty. This would have given us a final sub-sample of 650 articles for analysis. We further stratified our sub-sample by website and time period during which a thread appeared (18–28 May 2009; 29 May – 6 June 2009; 7–10 June 2009). Specifically, we selected ten threads per website/blog, so that in the end we would have fifty threads in total per country. The selection was random and followed a 3-4-3 pattern corresponding to *the three time periods* (18 May – 28 May; 29 May – 6 June; 7 June – 10 June), i.e. we selected three threads from the first period, four from the second and three from the third period, for each of the five websites in each country. Randomness was achieved by counting the total number of clippings we had per website, per period and dividing that number by three or four (depending on the period). We then used the fraction generated to select our threads. If there were less than ten clippings for a particular website, we picked all available clippings regardless of period and divided the remaining required amount of threads randomly over the other four websites so we would still end up with fifty threads in total. If a selected thread did not provide the possibility to leave comments, then it was removed from the list and replaced by the next clipping on the list.

---

9. Twelve country groups and one group of transnational websites.

In the end, 638 threads were drawn for further coding instead of 650. In the case of Belgium – where, due to lack of resources, we only clipped articles from French-speaking websites – technical problems beyond our control (several threads became inaccessible shortly after our monitoring period expired) meant we could only select twenty-five articles for further coding in the end. At the same time, because in certain countries some news websites located their interactive pages separately from the thread with the main article text, we had to sample extra threads (two in Greece, five in Finland, one in Germany, two in Austria and three in Hungary). The final amount of threads that were selected for coding was, nevertheless, well above our minimum threshold of 534, thereby ensuring the reliability of our sub-sample. Due to the nature of the Twitter material (very short entries – tweets, resembling more the style of contributions in online debates rather than news articles), we treated all tweets in each of the three time periods as one thread, i.e. we had three Twitter threads in total. For the Facebook material, we treated each discussion topic as a thread and classified it accordingly.

Coding

Our quantitative content analysis involves coding at two levels. At the level of the more overarching debate, we use the variable of 'topic' to map the thematic categories under which the EP elections received coverage in online media (domestic, foreign or European issues; political, economic, cultural matters). This variable allows us to capture the context within which the EU polity is contested online and, as such, is measured at the 'thread' level of analysis (Jankowski and Van Selm 2008; Strandberg 2008). For the three Twitter threads, each tweet was then coded as a message, following the same coding rules as for messages found in news articles. After an initial scan of all the tweets included in these, we determined the topic as 'EU politics', to reflect the fact that over 96 per cent of all the collected tweets had a European or transnational approach to the topic of EU elections. For the Facebook material, we treated each discussion topic as a thread and classified it accordingly. Secondly, we use three (sets of) variables at the 'message' level. A message is here defined as 'one or more evaluations on European integration made by a single (collective) actor in a single time and space'. At this level, we measure first who participates in EU polity contestation online (EU, foreign and/or domestic actors, state and non-state actors, citizens, mediators and/or politicians). In the comparative and individual country chapters, we will use the less technical term of 'evaluations' rather than messages. We then record the kinds of evaluations that are made on the three identified dimensions of EU polity contestation. This entails the coding of each contribution to EU polity contestation– our basic unit of analysis – along one, two or all three of the following: principle of integration, institutional set-up of the EU and project of integration. A contribution can be positive or negative and, in the latter two dimensions, it can further address the level, scope or inclusiveness of integration.[10] Lastly, we code the justification given, if any, by the actor for the presented evaluations of EU legitimacy.

Analysis

A mixed-methods design is applied, which combines the measurement of online platforms of communication (how? where?) with the content of public communication (what? by whom?). This is done through the quantitative content analysis of public messages (message level of analysis) and the quantitative profiling of the selected websites in the same coding scheme (thread level of analysis). In the resulting coding model (for the Codebook, see Appendix II), evaluative statements concerning EU legitimacy were identified and categorised in a standardised manner, thus allowing for the identification of transnational trends of public opinion formation and crucial qualitative variations at national level (De Wilde *et al.* 2009). However, qualitative and/or mixed coding comes with the potential risk of different coders interpreting the same text differently, thus increasing the danger of low reliability of measurement. To limit this risk, we provided all coders with a detailed codebook and a week's intensive coding training. Moreover, we conducted satisfactory inter-coder reliability tests, both in the beginning and the end of the training session. We used Krippendorff's alpha to measure inter-coder reliability before, during and at the end of the coding week (eight coders involved). All variables had a score between 0.7 and 1, with the exception of the EU Polity evaluation dimensions, where the score was 0.62. Although this is slightly below the usually recommended minimum measurement of alpha (0.667), we have accepted it as a valid and reliable score, due to the complexity of the EU polity evaluation dimensions (seven values).

Units of analysis

We focus on the content found in selected threads of specifically chosen websites, thus following a discursive or rhetorical form, or micro-level of web analysis (Schneider and Foot 2004, 2005). This means that the focus is on 'micro-units', such as texts and links, and that structural or feature characteristics of the selected websites (accessibility/navigation, format, design, features) are outside the scope of this study. Similarly, socio-cultural analysis of the EU election web sphere concerned us only to the superficial extent, that cross-site action was taken into account when selecting the most popular websites per country and at European level.

In this context, we have coded two different textual units, or units of analysis, namely threads and messages, as discussed earlier. In Bloglines, which we used for

---

10. We exclude the possibility of 'neutral' evaluations, as adding such a category presents a substantial decrease in the reliability of data. An evaluation could thus only be positive, negative or missing.

the data collection, each thread takes the form of a single 'clipping'. Each thread may contain one or more messages or none at all. The coded threads contained a total of 1,135 messages.[11] The different components of this definition are discussed in more detail below, with the relevant coding variables indicated where necessary.

'One or More Evaluations...'

An evaluation assesses the worth of something (in our case of the EU or of European integration). More specifically, we distinguish: 1) the object of evaluation (in our research, this can be the EU, the process of European integration, or Europe perceived as a political unit); 2) the verb or the adjectives that indicate a positive or a negative evaluation; and 3) the underlying criteria of evaluations (the different levels of worthiness, based on which the judgement is given).

In order to enhance the reliability of the coding scheme and reduce ambivalence, we coded evaluations as either positive or negative, dropping the 'neutral' category used in previous projects on Euroscepticism.

'... on European Integration...'

That an evaluation has to be 'on European integration' means we did not code evaluations that have to do with either the content of EU policies (as opposed to the level and/or scope of EU policies), or the election campaign as such (unless it reflects back on the EU polity), or domestic politics only.

We further identify different degrees of contesting EU legitimacy, as well as supporting it, either in a principled, categorical and unconditional way or as a qualified judgement that only focuses on particular aspects of European integration, or takes a balanced view on assets and drawbacks. Thus, we distinguish whether an evaluative statement assesses the principle of European integration, the institutional and constitutional design of the EU, or the project of integration in terms of future development. A single message may or may not hold an opinion on all three types of evaluative dimensions, but must at least hold an evaluation on one of the three; otherwise it did not qualify as a contribution to EU polity contestation.

'... made by a single (collective) actor...'

An evaluation needs to have an actor 'making' it (De Wilde and Trenz 2012). In other words, narratives about European integration have to be 'performed' in the public sphere to contribute to a Eurosceptic discursive formation on European

---

11. Regarding the commenting area of threads, only the first twenty comments visible on the webpage were examined for EU-polity evaluations.

integration. A single actor can only make one message in a given time and space. Moreover, an actor may transmit his or her opinion directly by actually 'saying' it, or indirectly if its opinion is featured by the writer of the text (See Appendix II for all categories).

The territorial level the actor is acting upon (particularly applicable to politicians), is measured by the actor's scope. Thus, if the actor is the European Commission, or a Member of the European Parliament, the scope will be European. The nationality or scope of office of an actor might be explicitly given or it may be deducible from the rest of the message, so we provided all coders with clear instructions and examples to enable them to identify an actor's scope.

'... in a single time and space.'

A single actor can only make one message in a single time and space. Even if an actor made elaborate evaluations in one entry, this would still be counted as one message. This is because, in our public sphere approach of EU polity contestation, the emphasis lies on what the audience 'receives' in communication, rather than on what the actor 'transmits'. However, if the same actor – say the journalist having written the blog – replied later to one of the comments made on his/her original blogs, this would be a separate message from the original one as it takes place in a different time. It would thus be coded as a separate message. Similarly, if the same actor made the same evaluation in different threads, this would be counted as several messages (equal to the amount of threads in which the evaluation is found) as they take place in a different 'space'. Finally, if a thread reports on an actor transmitting an opinion on European integration at different time points, this would also result in multiple messages.

To capture the dynamics of the EP election e-debates, we also created two variables that indicate the location where most evaluations were found within a thread, and the mode of exchange, respectively. Specifically, through the variable 'Location', we identified whether an evaluation was in the main text or in the comments area, further classifying the latter as 'comment in response to main text' or 'comment on [another] comment'. With the variable of 'Transmission', we measured whether the actor actively makes the message with the purpose of it being publicly transmitted, or whether the evaluation is introduced by another actor (usually the journalist writing the blog or the commentator making the comment) to support, illustrate or contradict their own message.

Topics

The topics of threads provide us with a more general image of major issues coming up during EP election campaigns. In our coding scheme, we distinguish between nine topics as follows: 1) domestic party politics, including focus on candidates, polls and election results. This would be the predominant expected topic in light of EP elections generally being considered to be 'second order elections' (Reif and Schmitt 1980; Van der Brug and Van der Eijk 2007); 2) other Member-State party politics; 3) European party politics; including news on party federations in the EP and European wide elections; 4) national economy; 5) European economy; 6) European integration, including such topics as the Treaty of Lisbon which was under ratification at the time, allocation of competencies within the EU, or more generally, the process of pooling of sovereignty of European nation states; 7) Membership/Enlargement, discussing that particular Member State's membership of the EU or Eurozone, or the accession of another country to the EU; 8) democracy, including the legitimacy of the EP, importance of the election, citizens' voting weights, turnout; 9) other. The topics give us an indication of the terms in which the EP elections were debated online, the extent to which the campaigns can be characterised as 'second order election', reflected in debates dominated by domestic politics, and which kind of topics in news items would tend to feature specific kinds and degrees of EU polity contestation.

Dimensions of evaluation

The content of EU polity evaluation is separated into three variables, as outlined in the introductory chapter. In order for us to identify part of public discourse as a 'message', or contribution to EU polity contestation, at least one of the three dimensions needed to be evaluated. Each of the variables could thus be positively, negatively or not evaluated, with the exception of no evaluation on all three dimensions. Furthermore, we distinguished between targets of evaluation (level, scope or inclusiveness) in the dimensions of the institutional set-up of the EU and the project of integration. The variable, 'evaluation of principle of integration', thus has three values: positive, negative or not available. The variables of institutional set-up of the EU, and project of integration, each have seven possible values: level – positive; level – negative; scope – positive; scope – negative; inclusiveness – positive, inclusiveness – negative and not available.

This operationalisation of EU polity contestation provides for both the detailed analysis of complicated lines of argumentation, as conceptualised in the introduction, that address all three dimensions of evaluation and can thus, be placed in the typology presented in Table 1.1. However, it also allows for capturing less 'complete' lines of argumentation that only address one or two dimensions of evaluation.

Justification of worth

Evaluations of EU legitimacy can be given further meaning through justificatory practice. We assume that there is a limited range of constitutional principles that can be used in public discourse to qualify polity worth. Orders of justifications are historical constructs; they provide the grammar for the critical activities of social actors that confine their arguments, frame their interpretations, and establish rules of acceptance (Boltanski and Thévenot 2006). In EU justificatory discourse, we apply the classificatory scheme loosely based on Boltanski and Thévenot (2006), and assume that five justificatory orders are sufficient to describe the vast majority of critical arguments in which actors evaluate EU polity worth: 1) the democratic order based on the higher common principle of government for, by, and of the people, 2) the cultural order based on the higher common principle of tradition and other group commonalities, 3) the necessary order based on the higher common principle of efficiency allowing for functional problem solving and effective governance, 4) the economic order based on the higher common principle of maximising economic prosperity and welfare, and 5) the secure order, based on the higher common principle of safety in the face of existential or less serious threats. A sixth category is included, to capture justificatory practices of either substantially different or ambivalent nature.

These six justificatory orders are not meant as an exhaustive list but as one that is most applicable to ongoing EU justificatory discourse.[12] Accordingly, EU legitimacy can be defended on the basis of claims that 1) European integration increases democracy, 2) European integration serves the purpose of preserving a shared cultural heritage and Europe-wide shared values, 3) European integration is necessary to cope with modern policy problems or in light of previous commitments, 4) European integration increases economic prosperity through stimulating economic growth and general welfare, or 5) European integration is regarded as protecting Europe from internal and/or external threats of various nature. In turn, EU legitimacy can be denounced by claiming European integration/ the EU is 1) undemocratic, 2) not conducive to dominant and treasured culture, 3) not needed or redundant, 4) hindering or not affecting economic growth and general prosperity, 5) not contributing to the safety of Europeans and European nation states.

The practice of justification is here understood in an encompassing way. That is, an actor need not necessarily purposefully link a reason, or commonly shared value, to the advanced argument in order for us to code a justification of worth. Such a case would count as a clearly present justification, yet we would also code a justification in the case of a less clearly, or purposefully transmitted, reason. What is of importance here is not the action of the one making a contribution to discourse, but the message that reaches the audience. Thus, in case a common value, based on which the contribution inclines us – the audience – to consider European integration and/or the EU, is transmitted in connection to the evaluation presented, we would code this as a justification of worth. As such, our analysis approaches frame analysis (De Wilde 2010; Díez Medrano 2003; Entman 1993;

---

12. The underlying assumption is further, that the classificatory scheme for the evaluation of the EU polity is identical, or at least not substantially deviating from the one that is used for the evaluation of the national polity. This also does not mean that the ranking of order in cases of clashes of polity worth is identical. In equal terms, we do not exclude the possibility of a redefinition of worth, or even the emergence of a new justificatory order in relation to the evaluation of EU polity worth. One can wonder, for example, whether sustainability in relation to climate change is currently being set up as a new justificatory order of the EU polity.

Gamson 2004; Surel 2000), with the restriction of applying a set of abstract common values only particularly involved in the justification of polity worth.

Discussion

This chapter has set out a comprehensive and advanced, mixed methodology research design. This serves the dual purpose of capturing both cross-national commonalities, and patterns in EU polity contestation, in a comparable and reliable fashion while at the same time facilitating in-depth qualitative analysis of the context, interactivity and meaning of this contestation, in the context of national EP election campaigns. Our research design and methodology is innovative, first in studying Euroscepticism and other forms of EU polity contestation, as unfolding in the increasingly important medium of the internet. We develop a replicable sampling and monitoring strategy to deal with the ephemeral online data. Furthermore, the combination of quantitative content analysis and qualitative discussion, provides for rich understanding of EU polity contestation in the context of a range of different national political climates. Chapter Three reports on the comparative findings, after which Chapters Four to Ten discuss EU polity contestation in selected country cases.

Our research design is not without limitations. Differences in online communications infrastructure across the countries we have included in our study have meant that, in some cases, the monitoring of online debates has not yielded sufficient material for claims analysis. Similarly, cultural diversities regarding public debating and the use of the internet for political contestation constitute two other factors which may limit the intensity of online debating concerning political issues. We address this challenge by combining a quantitative analysis of comparative data, with country specific qualitative interpretation and contextualisation thereof. Besides these, like all types of public discourse, it is not possible to escape the self-selection issue that permeates online public exchanges.

Nevertheless, these limitations concern more the degree of generalisation that can be applied to the findings, rather than the quality and reliability of the latter. As long as the data is interpreted in relation to the specific object of public evaluation (in our case the legitimacy of the EU polity), then our analytical and methodological model allows us to capture several dimensions of any media sphere (here the EU elections e-sphere) in a systematic manner, and to contextualise the type of contestation that the debate topic (the EU polity) invokes. This, in combination with coding the manner of interaction according to online communication standards, has resulted in a mapping of e-debates that is closer to the reality of online communication than to normative public sphere standards.

Chapter Three | Contesting Europe: Towards Convergence?

At the beginning of this book, we asked to what extent can we find convergence in the nature, intensity and dynamics of EU polity contestation across, and within, Member States. We started with the premise that the polity of the EU has increasingly become an issue of political contestation throughout Europe. In this process of the politicisation of European integration (De Wilde 2011; Hooghe and Marks 2009; Zürn 2006), citizens' attitudes and opinions are, to a considerable degree, shaped through public conflicts and debates. Critics and supporters of the EU and of the project of European integration, can have an impact on public opinion and ultimately, also on voters' choice, by contributing to public and media debates that reach the people of Europe. Political contestation thus accounts for the dynamic aspects of public opinion formation, as filtered through the mass media.

From the outset, the idea to hold general elections for the EP, was meant to lay the grounds for the equal representation of the citizens who should become engaged in a process of collective will-formation across the European space (Rittberger 2003). EP elections have, however, been found to systematically miss this aim and, instead of expressing a European collective will, involve the voters primarily in debates of national relevance (Reif and Schmitt 1980; Van der Brug and Van der Eijk 2007). One question to be addressed at this point, is whether the new salience of EU issues linked to patterns of enhanced politicisation of the EU, has changed this 'second order' character of EP elections. Furthermore, does EU polity contestation lead to a convergence in public opinion formation on the legitimacy of the EU across the European space? As discussed in the introduction, this convergence may take place along the following dimensions: 1) the intensity with which EU polity contestation takes place; 2) the aspects of the EU that are contested, and the ways in which this contestation takes place; 3) whether there is a gap between citizens and political elites; and 4) the ways in which evaluations of the EU polity are justified.

Patterns of convergence and divergence in EU polity contestation, measured along these four dimensions, can be considered as pivotal for the possibility of a European democracy. By careful comparison of the evidence from our twelve country cases, we can chart the process of public opinion formation on the EU, and the potential of EP elections to forge a collective will. Given the fragmented nature of the European political space that is served by different national media, we do not expect that European election campaigns will result in a true 'European debate', as would be manifested in a transnational exchange of arguments among collective actors who justify themselves in front of a European audience. Instead of the emergence of such an encompassing European public sphere, we rather expect EP election campaigns to contribute to the Europeanisation of the existing national public spheres. This would be manifested in the expression of parallel concerns with European integration, underpinned by similar patterns of evaluation and justification within national media debates (Koopmans and Statham 2010).

As outlined in the introduction, we emphasise the dynamic interaction of negative evaluations of European integration, commonly identified as Euroscepticism, with pro-European arguments in public opinion formation. To emphasise this responsive nature of EU polity contestation, our project has focused on professional journalism websites and political blogs that explicitly allow readers to leave comments on news stories. By monitoring EU polity contestation on the most prominent sites of political news-making, we were able to systematically reconstruct how opinions on European integration are made salient and accessible to a mass audience, as well as how members of the mass audience respond publicly. Through such public responses, citizens, in turn, contribute to further shaping of public opinion.

This chapter brings together the quantitative data from all twelve national debates and the trans-European debates included in our study. It identifies patterns and trends across national public spheres. There are four questions, in particular, that our comparative analysis addresses in order to capture the four dimensions in which convergence of EU polity contestation might occur. To begin with, the question is to what extent online news media are used as a platform for public opinion formation on European integration in the context of EP elections. We particularly focus on the degree of prominence of EU polity contestation in online news coverage of the 2009 EP election campaign. This provides us with a clue as to what extent we are dealing with existential debates where the EU polity, as such, dominates EP campaigning (see Chapter One). Following on from this, we ask what the targets and content of online EU legitimacy evaluations are. That is, what aspects of the EU or European integration are contested in national debates? Thirdly, the question is to what extent such online EU legitimacy evaluations are justified, expressing concern for public goods. Together with the discussion on targets, possible commonality in reference frames across nation-state borders allows us to assess convergence in the nature of EU polity contestation. Last, but not least, our data provides unique opportunities to study differences between opinions expressed by political elites and citizens. Claims in support, or in opposition to, European integration by (party) political actors reported in online news media are captured in the same coding scheme as the direct, unsolicited, responses by readers. Comparing the evaluations of political elites and citizens, furthermore, adds insights into patterns of content and justification. In short, we analyse empirically the prominence, content and justification of elite and citizen EU polity contestation.

Categorising varieties of EU polity contestation

To answer these questions, this comparative chapter draws on the complete original quantitative database, constructed through web content analysis of online news during the three weeks prior to the European Parliament elections of June 2009. Data has been sampled and coded from professional journalism websites and political blogs in twelve EU Member States and from transnational European websites.[1] The countries included in the study are Austria, French-speaking Belgium, the Czech Republic, Finland, France, Germany, Greece, Hungary, the Netherlands, Poland, Sweden and the UK. In addition, five transnational websites have been included in our study, namely one professional news website (EUObserver 2010); two blog platforms – BlogActiv (Blogactiv 2012) and BabelBlogs (CafeBabel 2012); and two social networking platforms – Facebook (Facebook 2012) and Twitter (Twitter 2012).

To provide insight into the prominence, content and justification of EU polity contestation across all online media spheres in our study, a number of indicators will be discussed and analysed in this chapter. The prominence of EU polity contestation is operationalised in terms of the frequency of evaluations per country. This indicator allows us to comparatively assess the extent to which EP elections can be considered as existential debates (focusing on the EU as polity) characterised by many evaluations.

The content of EU polity contestation is analysed along the three dimensions of evaluation that relate to Morgan's (2005: 17) ideal typical justification to fully qualify the legitimacy of the EU. As outlined in Chapter One, contestants of the European Union could provide justifications with regard to 1) why we should support European integration in principle; 2) what institutional and constitutional design should be given to the EU and; 3) what future trajectories of integration should be chosen. Media discourse, however, can be expected to operate through abbreviated evaluations, in which single dimensions of what can be considered the full standard in an argumentative practice are left out and meaning is implied more often than not. We, therefore, start our comparison with discussing the intensity with which the three conceptualised dimensions of EU polity contestation – the principle of integration, the institutional set-up of the EU and the future project of integration – came to the fore in the various country cases included in this study. Furthermore, in order to determine the degree of divergence, it is relevant to analyse how mediated debates deviate from these ideal requirements of EU polity justification, selectively highlighting concerns with single dimensions of European integration. We also systematically compare the degree of responsiveness of the debate, measured in the co-occurrence of positive and negative evaluations of the same evaluative dimension within single country cases. This type of comparison brings to the fore the extent to which national media debates evaluate single dimensions of European integration in an equilibrated or biased (evaluations in predominantly negative or positive terms) manner.

---

1. See Chapter Two for a more elaborate overview of the methodology. A concise version of the codebook is included in Appendix II and the complete codebook can be found at <http://www.reconproject.eu/projectweb/portalproject/CountryReports_Euroscepticism.html> (accessed 1 August 2011).

Our empirical findings point to combinations of arguments typically addressing one or two dimensions of contestation. These can be classified along our typology of EU polity contestation assuming that missing information can, to some extent, be filled in by logical extrapolation. By doing so, we are able to reconstruct implicit meaning that often guides public opinion and will formation in media debates. For instance, the statement 'European integration is undemocratic and therefore, we should leave the EU' contains a negative evaluation of the principle of integration and of the current institutional set-up of the EU. We can safely classify this statement as Anti-European since, although information on the future trajectory of integration is missing, the message implicitly excludes the possibility of democratic reform. Yet, apart from the six specified types of EU polity contestation conceptualised in the introduction, our data also points out a number of truncated evaluations, which remain under-specified.[2] Statements like 'the Common Market dismantles the welfare state' or 'EU enlargement is a threat to security', clearly express dissatisfaction in some form with the EU, yet do not specify the full extent of this dissatisfaction or possible remedies. We are thus left with a frequent residual category of evaluations that are placed outside the scheme of polity contestation elaborated in Chapter One. We label such contributions to discourse as *diffuse Eurosceptic*. They are indicative of the extent to which media debates of EP campaigning are conducive to *uninformed opinion-making*. Media recipients are exposed to plainly negative evaluations, which remain inconclusive in political terms, because they lack sufficient information about how the EU or European integration in terms of principle, institutional set-up and project can be evaluated. Such 'truncated' evaluations are nevertheless important to stir emotions in the debate and might be used frequently in practice to express legitimate concerns with the EU.

Following a 'civic engagement' line of thought, instead of the more standard rational discourse parameters, we can classify the diffuse Eurosceptic evaluations as an indicator of political talk, which differs from formal political deliberation (Dahlgren 2009: 89–92). Unspecified negative evaluations of the EU thus become part of the informal exchanges among political actors and citizens. For Bohman, this type of political talk is important for maintaining 'a constant and vibrant interaction among cultures and subpolitics in a larger sphere of common citizenship' (Bohman 1996: 145). In his view, the character of such 'civic talk' is reflexive: self-creation takes place in part via such interaction. One could say that as 'messy conversation' begins to take political connotations, it becomes in some sense 'civic' and activates the weak, non-decision-making public sphere. The way we have captured diffuse Eurosceptic evaluations in our project points to such a

---

2. In detail, this category of 'truncated' or 'unspecified' evaluations encompasses messages containing no evaluation of the principle of integration, no evaluation or a negative evaluation of the current institutional set-up of the EU and no evaluation, or a negative evaluation of the project of integration.

type of 'protopolitical' public talk, in that there is less reason and more passion, in the arguments presented, but that doesn't make them any less political. This public talk has the potential to bring together a new public, that of dissatisfied and disaffected, European citizens. This type of public certainly requires new strategies on behalf of formal political representatives to recapture its approval.

We then continue to approach the question of justification through the 'orders of worth' that underlie legitimacy contestation of the EU (Boltanski and Thévenot 2006). In order to operationalise this question of polity worth, our interpretative scheme relies on the distinction between five types of justificatory order that can be used to defend, or to challenge, the legitimacy of the EU, as outlined in Chapter Two. A legitimacy claim can be based on the value of 1) citizens' rights and self-determination (democracy); 2) shared history and tradition (culture); 3) complying with functional needs or criteria of technical efficiency (necessity); 4) providing material well-being (economic prosperity); or 5) on the value of safeguarding personal or collective integrity (safety). We thus assume that the register of justifications of European integration on which situated actors can draw is limited because critical practices follow particular scripts and guidelines, which are de-contextualised and generalised as part of the cultural repertoire of modern societies (Wagner 2008). Following this classification scheme, justifications were coded as the explicit *reasons* given by the actor of the evaluation for his or her evaluation. By including the category 'other', it was further acknowledged that particular justifications could fall out of this matrix.

The intensity of contestation

Recall that we distinguish between 1) existential, 2) domestic, and 3) substantial debates to characterise the prominence of EU polity contestation during the EP election campaigns (see Chapter One). A debate can be labelled 'existential' when it concerns evaluations of the EU polity in fundamental terms. In contrast, 'domestic' debates reflect a status of EP elections as second order elections (Reif and Schmitt 1980; Van der Brug and Van der Eijk 2007). Rather than contesting European integration in fundamental terms, these second-order debates are relatively oblivious to the EU as polity; debate would focus instead on domestic party politics and electoral horse races. Finally, a debate can be labelled 'substantial', if a significant focus is on EU policies at stake during the EP elections. That is, debate centres on which policies, candidates for the European Parliament, oppose or champion. In this case, we can speak of the EP elections as approaching the type of first order elections in equal terms with national elections. In terms of our coding scheme, the quantity of evaluations of EU legitimacy, i.e. the amount of evaluations that concern the EU in terms of principle, polity and project, is the primary indicator for existential debates. The more evaluations are made, the more the EU polity is politicised.

The UK stands out as the case where EP election debates were the most existential, reflected in the large amount of evaluations made. The density of EU polity debate in the UK is high with an average of five evaluations per coded online article. On the

Figure 3.1: Intensity of EU polity debate by country

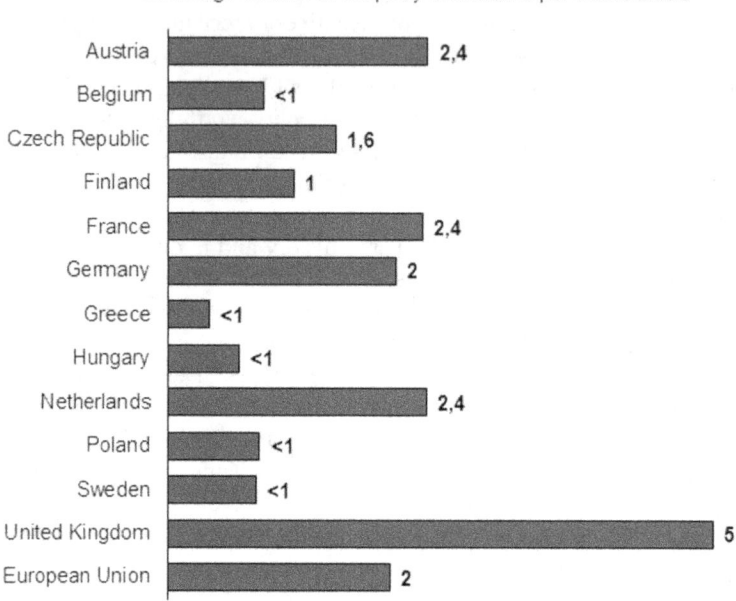

other extreme, we find that the EU polity is hardly contested in Belgium, Greece, Hungary, Poland and Sweden. There was on average less than one evaluation per article in each of these five countries. Austrian, Dutch, French, German, and EU-wide debates might be labelled as 'semi-existential', with approximately two evaluations per article on average. Finland and the Czech Republic fall in between the two groups of no polity contestation and semi-existential debates.

Yet, an absence of evaluations of EU legitimacy in fundamental terms does not tell us whether we are faced with a domestic debate focusing on politics in the Member States or a substantial debate contesting EU policies. To proceed with our analysis, we draw on a comparison of domestic campaigning in terms of salience of issues and debates in the countries analysed. The qualitative country chapters that follow indicate the eminence of domestic debates, with domestic issues and actors featuring most prominently in the online debates. Topics of common concern to Europeans, like the coordination of the financial crisis or of environmental policies, are debated to a much lesser extent than domestic party politics. Also EU politics in terms of candidate profiles or positioning of European-wide parties in the European Parliament are rarely discussed, as apparent in the low profile of European actors as participants in the debates. In other words, supranational actors hardly engage in evaluating the EU.

What emerges from the above is that online media do not provide one encompassing space for contesting EU legitimacy. Instead, debates continue to unfold within the different national online media spheres in which the scope of debates, and degrees of contestation, vary widely. This variance is insufficiently explained by the patterns of support and opposition expressed in Eurobarometer opinion polls. Only in the case of the UK, do we find the generally acknowledged low public support for European integration reflected in large amounts of critical comments online.

Dimensions of EU polity evaluation

In order to analyse the dimensions of polity contestation, we assume that the logics of public discourse lead those contesting the legitimacy of the EU, to provide a sufficient justification for their advocated alteration in the European integration process (Morgan 2005: 38ff). The core understanding underlying this assumption is that both pro-Europeans and Eurosceptics advocate a change in the political status quo of the EU, as it currently exists and has come into being. Their arguments will have to convince others to go along with this course alteration and they, therefore, portray their proposal as furthering a particular public good through justification. We have argued in the introduction, that EU legitimation discourse embraces evaluations in terms of principle, institutional set-up and project. The exchange of arguments and justifications must be organised in such a way, that it shows 1) the principle of transnational integration to be defendable, i.e. whether or not there is a justifiable reason to believe that we are better off in doing things together; 2) the institutional arrangement fits, i.e. whether or not there is a justifiable product in terms of guaranteeing the general compliance with the principle; and 3) the project is ideationally or materially supported, whether or not there are shared goals that drive the process of future integration.

We now continue to discuss first, evaluations of the principle of integration. That is, opinions about the idea or practice of cooperation among European nation states in general. We then examine evaluations of the institutional set-up of the EU polity which may address either the division of power in the EU (level of integration), the extent of its competencies (scope of integration), or membership and influence of particular countries or other societal groups (inclusiveness of integration). Subsequently, our focus turns on evaluations of the integration project which propose alteration in the level, scope or inclusiveness of the integration project in future. Lastly, we consider the extent to which evaluations on these three dimensions load onto the conceptual typology of EU polity contestation, developed in the introduction.

The principle of integration

Evaluations of the principle of integration comprise judgements on the value of cooperation among European nation states in the most basic form. As such, they consist of categorical or principled statements on why European nation states need to collaborate together, or should not do so. Slogans and branding like, 'The EU is good for you' are categorical statements on EU legitimacy. Usually, these are combined with some form of justification by reference to a generalised principle or public good: 'European integration helps to promote peace and prosperity'.

In our study, only a minority of evaluations in all countries and transnational debates concerned evaluations of the principle of integration (Figure 3.2). The fundamental principle of European integration was evaluated mostly in the United Kingdom, transnational debates, the Netherlands and Austria. Evaluations were largely positive, with the notable exceptions of Austria, where the principle of integration received more negative evaluations than positive ones. Finland, Poland and the Czech Republic featured an equal amount of positive and negative evaluations or a very slight majority of negative evaluations.

Figure 3.2: Online media users' evaluations of the principle of European integration (values indicate the number of positive and negative evaluations by category)*

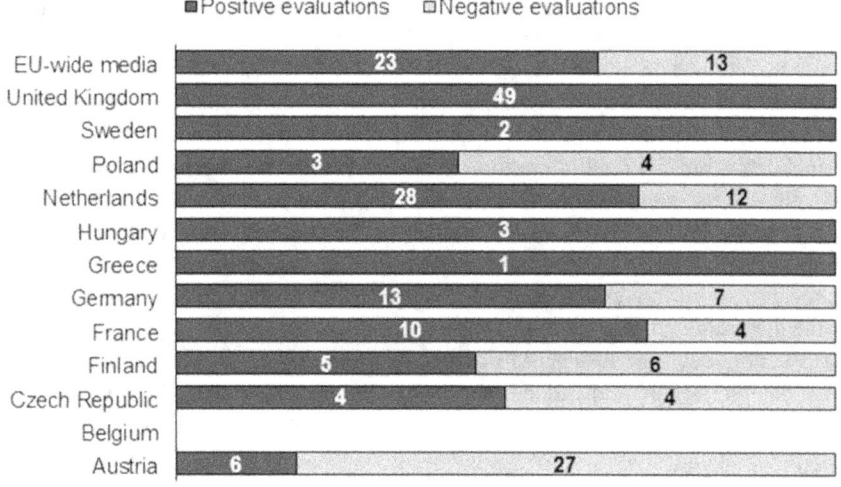

*No evaluations on the principle of European integration were found in the selected Belgium debates.

The marginality of this form of polity evaluation points to a certain degree of familiarity with European integration as a kind of reality taken for granted, within which many Europeans have been socialised. In other words, cooperation among European nation states is a kind of background knowledge that cannot easily be challenged. Positions that express principled support for European integration are therefore, often deemed unnecessary and positions that challenge the dogma of post-war European integration are difficult to justify. Consequently, we can assume that Euroscepticism in the media sphere needs to find a more nuanced expression. In our findings, support or opposition of European integration in principle is usually expressed as part of a more complex argumentation and needs to be contextualised within the broader discursive field of EU polity contestation. One correlation found is that positive evaluations of the principle of integration regularly go together with negative evaluations of the institutional set-up dimension. That is, participants in the debates argue against some aspect of the current institutional or constitutional set-up of the EU, but at the same time demonstrate their principled support of cooperation among European nation states. We will continue to discuss each of the other two dimensions of evaluation separately, before analysing their correlations as part of the justificatory practices of contesting EU legitimacy. Still, as demonstrated by the plurality of positive evaluations of the principle of integration over negative evaluations, the audience of EU online debates is likely to get a positive message about cooperation among European nation states. The convergence on the acceptance of the principle of integration – whether implicitly by not actively challenging it, or explicitly through positive evaluations – presents the basis for legitimating European integration as a process, and the EU as a distinct political entity. To the extent that these public debates structure collective will-formation, there is no reason to doubt the legitimacy of collaboration between European nation states.

The current institutional set-up of the EU

The second dimension of evaluation of EU legitimacy, refers to the current constitutional and institutional set-up of the EU. Here, evaluations were more targeted, comprising aspects of the legal infrastructure and institutional apparatus in place. More specifically, we can discern evaluations of the functioning of the EU polity in terms of level, scope or inclusiveness. Evaluations of each category are found to target the powers of the European Commission, and the European Parliament in particular. Evaluations of the level of integration range from references to 'the extent of EU powers', to precise arguments concerning the need for unanimity voting in the Council of Ministers. Evaluations of scope were found to address policy competencies that have recently been more prominent, such as Justice and Home Affairs in the wake of the September 11 attacks and the continuing threat of Islamic terrorism, as well as growing concerns for illegal immigration. Inclusiveness evaluations particularly concern the voting power of one's own country in relation to that of other EU Member States (generally evaluated negatively) or the broader control and voice ordinary citizens have in relation to European political elites.

Overall, the current institutional framework of the EU is predominantly evaluated in negative terms (Figure 3.3). Participants in online media debates tend to support European integration in principle, but are rather critical concerning the procedures for cooperation that are in place and the institutions that shall support and implement it. This disapproval of the current institutional set-up of the EU was manifest in all Member States that were included in this analysis. Negative evaluations of EU legitimacy prevail over affirmative ones, with online debates being predominantly critical of the achievements of the EU and its

Table 3.1: Online media users' evaluations of the level, scope and inclusiveness of the current institutional set-up of the EU by country*

Country	Current EU set-up					
	Positive evaluations			Negative evaluations		
	Level	Scope	Inclusiveness	Level	Scope	Inclusiveness
Austria	5	2	6	**13**	**8**	**32**
Belgium	3			10	1	2
Czech Republic	9	2	3	**33**	2	**19**
Finland	8	7	4	9	2	**16**
France	5	2		**25**	3	**27**
Germany	8		2	**27**	**14**	**22**
Greece		1	1	7		10
Hungary	1		5	4	4	**12**
Netherlands	8	4	5	**31**	4	**18**
Poland	2	2	2	**10**	**12**	5
Sweden	4	2	2	**12**	**5**	**14**
UK	23	5	9	**124**	5	**52**
EU-wide media	15	6	6	**20**	**10**	**28**

* Numbers in bold indicate the current EU set-up dimensions with highest number of evaluations in each country.

performance. Interestingly, this pattern does not confirm conventional knowledge of Euroscepticism, based on Eurobarometer data. Countries known for their pro-European stance, like Belgium, France and Germany, nevertheless generate highly critical debates. This confirms our initial proposition that conventional indicators to measure Euroscepticism in terms of partisan contestation, or public opinion, are insufficient. Citizens can be exposed to negative evaluations of the EU in the media, even when partisan mobilisation on fundamental issues concerning the principle, scope and future of integration remains limited.

Further unpacking EU legitimacy evaluations in terms of level, scope and inclusiveness, we find that the balance of power between the EU and the Member States, as well as the inclusiveness of the institutional set-up of the EU in terms of membership and participation, are more often targeted than the scope of policies and competencies that are covered by the EU (Figure 3.4 and Table 3.1). This indicates a concern not only with the distribution of power and influence, but also with democracy as well as with belonging and identity, all of which are more pronounced than the concern with the problem-solving capacities within particular policy fields. The allocation of political authority and the sharing of power within the EU are more contested than the efficiency and expansion of the scope of governance.

Figure 3.3: Online media users' evaluations of the current institutional set-up of the EU (values indicate the number of positive and negative evaluations by country)

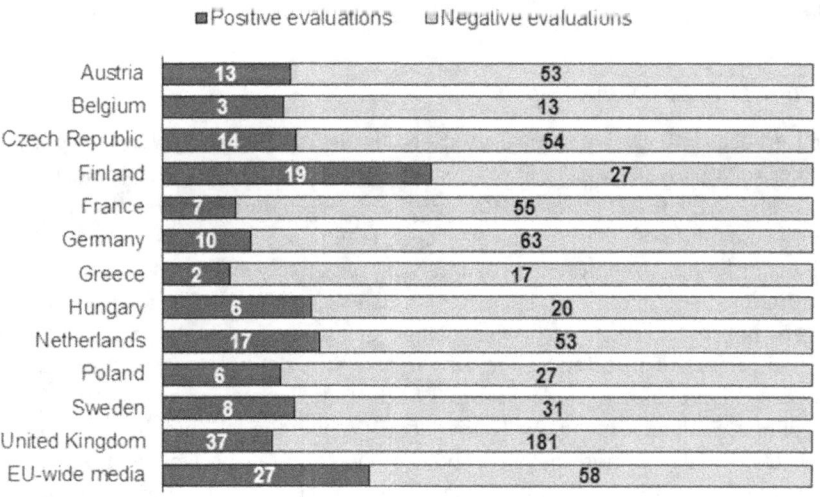

Figure 3.4: Online media users' evaluations of the level, scope and inclusiveness of the current institutional set-up of the EU

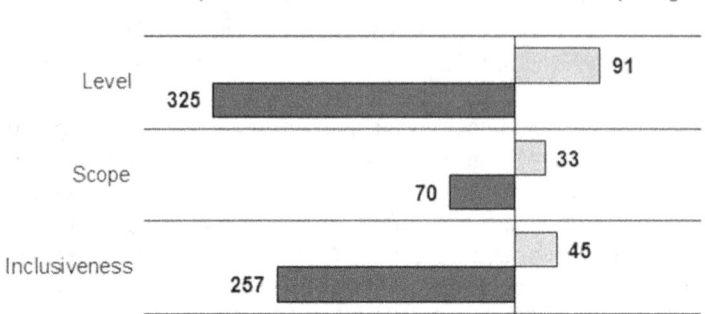

To sum up, the current institutional and constitutional set-up is at the heart of EU polity contestation in online debates, during the campaigns for the European Parliament elections of June 2009. In all observed country-based and transnational debates, the majority of these evaluations were negative. Furthermore, these evaluations particularly target the powers of supranational institutions, questions of membership and influence of certain countries, or complaints about the lack of influence of citizens in comparison to political elites. This convergence across countries towards highly critical appraisal of the current institutional set-up of the EU, suggests public opinion supportive of treaty change. In what ways the treaties ought to be changed would be reflected in the third dimension of evaluation: on the future of integration.

Future prospects of integration

If European integration is evaluated predominantly positively in principle, but rather negatively in terms of the current institutional set-up and performance of the EU, how do the future prospects for integration fare in the observed online debates? While the future of the European project certainly raised concerns in the debates in all countries analysed, it was on average less negatively evaluated than the current institutional set-up of the EU. There was also strong variation among the country cases, not just in terms of the percentage of evaluations containing evaluations of the project of integration, but also in terms of the balance between positive and negative evaluations. As Figure 3.5 illustrates, most cases – Austria, Czech Republic, Finland, France, the Netherlands, Poland, the UK and the transnational debates – featured more negative evaluations of the project of integration than positive ones, while Belgium, Germany, Greece, Hungary and Sweden contained more positive than negative evaluations, or an equal number of both. In other words, the convergence observed in the evaluations of the current institutional set up was not confirmed for the future of European integration.

Delving deeper in our analysis of 'future EU project' evaluations, we find that the future of European integration was not only contested along ideological lines but also along lines of diverging national interests. As can be seen in Figure 3.6 and in Table 3.2, this divide can be further substantiated by unpacking the targets of polity contestation in terms of level, scope and inclusiveness. Table 3.2 indicates the co-occurrence of positive and negative evaluations with regard to each of these three targets. For instance, if a debate in a country promoted many arguments in favour of delegating supranational authority, these tended to be counterbalanced by many negative evaluations of the level of integration. This finding is important because it substantiates our discursive understanding of EU polity contestation as a dynamic and responsive process through which the legitimacy of the EU is negotiated. In many instances, a strong presence of Eurosceptical argumentation provokes pro-European responses and vice versa. The online media thus provide a platform that can be used for spreading both pro-European and Eurosceptic voices, and that facilitates interaction between them.

The promotion of EU legitimacy provokes resistance, and this resistance is likely to be countered again by positive evaluations. Media debates consequently appear balanced in making both pro- and anti-European arguments visible, and facilitating discursive exchange between proponents and opponents of European integration. The targets of debate vary when it comes to evaluations of the future project of integration, with the Austrian, Belgian, Finnish, Hungarian facilitating

Figure 3.5: Online media users' evaluations of the future of European integration project (values indicate the number of positive and negative evaluations by country)

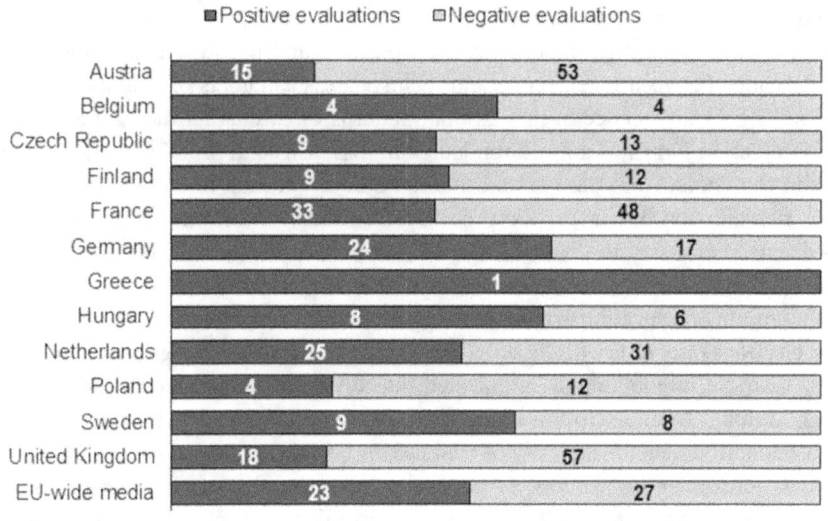

Figure 3.6: Online media users' evaluations of the level, scope and inclusiveness of the future of European integration project

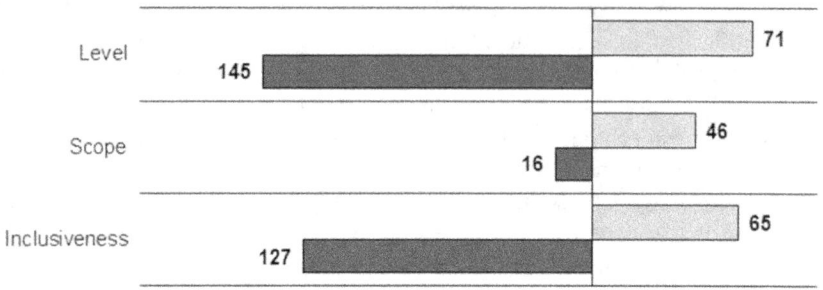

discursive exchange between proponents and opponents of European integration. The targets of debate vary when it comes to evaluations of the future project of integration, with the Austrian, Belgian, Finnish, Hungarian and European debates dominated by evaluations of the inclusiveness of the project of integration; the Czech, French, Polish and UK debates dominated by the level of integration, and the German and Swedish debates featuring the scope of integration more prominently.

Clearly, the third dimension of polity contestation – the project of integration – is the one where most variance is found among the thirteen cases included in our study. Not only does the amount of evaluations containing an evaluation on this dimension diverge, the balance between positive and negative evaluations, and the balance between level, scope and inclusiveness as targets of evaluation, vary as well. This divergence in the national patterns of evaluating the future project of integration indicates a more fundamental dissensus and principled uncertainty about the choices for Europe and the paths of integration to follow. In light of this fundamental dissensus, the process of citizens' reflection, which for many is deemed necessary to give a clearer indication to political leaders about how to reform the EU and tackle its democratic deficit, is difficult to organise.

Summing up our comparative findings, participants in online debates of the 2009 EP elections only rarely discussed the principle of European integration and those few who did, predominantly confirmed that European integration is, notionally, a good thing. Contrary to this, the current institutional set-up of the EU received most attention with the majority of evaluations containing a negative evaluation of this dimension of the EU polity. Also evaluated, in mostly negative terms, was the future project of integration which was the most divergent of the three evaluation categories in terms of amount, positive or negative balance and target of statements.

Table 3.2: Online media users' evaluations of the level, scope and inclusiveness of the future of European integration project by country

Country	Future of the European integration project					
	Positive evaluations			Negative evaluations		
	Level	Scope	Inclusiveness	Level	Scope	Inclusiveness
Austria	1	1	13	6	2	45
Belgium			4	1		3
Czech Republic	3	6		9	1	3
Finland	4		5		1	11
France	17	5	11	34	1	13
Germany	3	13	8	4	4	9
Greece			1			
Hungary	2		6	2		4
Netherlands	10	8	7	16	1	14
Poland	3		1	10	1	1
Sweden	3	6		4	3	1
United Kingdom	17		1	52	1	4
EU-wide media	8	7	8	7	1	19

Evaluations of EU legitimacy

Our comparative analysis, thus far, encompasses the dimensions of EU polity contestation that are selectively taken up in media discourse. In the introduction we further categorised positive and negative arguments on EU legitimacy expressed along six categories of EU polity dialectic: affirmative European, status quo, alter European, Eurocritical, pragmatic and anti-European. The purpose of this categorisation is to enable us to measure variation in the degrees of support with the EU/European integration in principled terms, in terms of present institutional arrangements or in terms of future project. Opinions expressed in the observed online media debates were, however, frequently found to be incomplete as they did not provide the full information of polity evaluation for all three dimensions. Nevertheless, these 'abbreviated' evaluations can often be logically subsumed under one of the underlying categories. For instance, arguments in support of European integration in principle, but critical of the current institutional set-up of the EU, can be safely categorised as 'alter-European', even if information about desirable steps for reform is lacking. Or, alternatively, arguments that categorically reject supranational integration and criticise the excess of authority of the European Commission need to be considered as anti-European, since information on possible future trajectories of integration would become redundant.

Even so, we were still left with one residual category of negative, but underspecified legitimacy evaluations, in which only insufficient information is given to inform the media recipient about the reasons for opposing the EU. In the introductory chapter, we call this underspecified category of negative evaluations, 'diffuse Eurosceptic'. Table 3.3 displays the un-weighted frequencies of all seven types of polity contestation. Positive evaluations of EU legitimacy in one or several dimensions – the polity contestation types, Affirmative European, Status Quo, Alter-European, Eurocritical and Pragmatic – are only found in 36 per cent of all evaluations. Yet also, the openly Anti-European contributions to discourse – those categorically opposing the principle of integration and possibly the current institutional set-up and/or project – remain rather marginal (6.7 per cent of all evaluations). Clearly, the argumentatively incomplete category of under-specified 'Eurosceptic' evaluations is the most numerous, reflecting 57.1 per cent of all evaluations. This echoes the strongly negative tone in the media debates, which more often than not unfolded through slogans, categorical statements and emotions.

Aside from their unmistakably negative connotation, it is hard to establish in what sense and direction EU legitimacy is challenged by under-specified Eurosceptic evaluations. That is, the missing information resulting from evaluating only one or two dimensions makes it impossible to determine which of the six lines of argumentation is advanced. There is thus an inbuilt ambivalence in these negative evaluations of EU legitimacy. Such diffuse Euroscepticism could load onto either Status Quo ('no further steps'), Alter-European ('a different Europe') or Eurocritical ('not this Europe') type of arguments. This would assume some form of support for cooperation among European nation states despite the criticism voiced. Alternatively, Eurosceptic contributions could reflect Anti-European ('no Europe

Table 3.3: Critical matrix of EU polity contestation: frequencies of specified and under-specified evaluations

EU polity contestation		Percentage
Specified evaluations	Affirmative European	15.4%
	Status Quo	10.4%
	Alter European	4.7%
	Eurocritical	5.5%
	Pragmatic	0.1%
	Anti-European	6.7%
Under specified evaluations	Diffuse Eurosceptic	57.1%
	Total	100.0%
	N	1,127

at all') arguments, opposing any form of cooperation. The point is: we simply lack the information to conclude which of these evaluations the actor is trying to convey.

The conclusion is that only a minority of the participants in the observed media debates came close to the normative template of a sufficient evaluation of the legitimacy of the EU/European integration in terms of principle, institutional design and project. The majority of contributions voice diffuse discontent by rejecting single dimensions of EU legitimacy, without clearly demarcating political standpoints or alternative visions that could remedy the expressed discontent. In other words, EU polity contestation dominantly spreads an under-specified negativism about the EU and European integration. We are witnessing many unfocused expressions of discontent, rather than precisely formulated and substantiated evaluations of EU legitimacy and we get only little information on the kind of European polity that would be supported, or that is opposed, by the participants in the examined online media debates.

A gap between citizens and elites?

A main observation of public opinion research on European integration has been a gap between citizens and political elites, with the latter being found generally more pro-European than the former (Binnema and Crum 2007; Franklin and Wlezien 1997; Ross 2008). The question we turn to now is to what extent this citizen–elite divide is reflected in online media discourse. In other words, to what extent is there convergence between citizens and elites in EU polity contestation? If the elite–citizen divide thesis holds, we would expect the elite voice supportive of integration to become dominant on professional news sites, since governments and mainstream political parties retain a strong position as main communicators on Europe in traditional mass media (Koopmans 2007). Citizens, on the other hand, could be expected to dismiss the elite consensus on European integration. As argued in the introduction, the predominantly pro-European voice of elites amplified by the media could create Eurosceptic counter-reactions. Euroscepticism could thus spread independently of the mobilisation by political parties as a negative response of the audience to the predominance of pro-European elite discourse. Online media are the ideal place to explore the relationship between elite propositions of EU legitimacy and citizens' reactions. Our aim was to establish if political elites evaluate European integration differently in online media debates about the European Parliament elections than citizens do.

Our aggregated media data of mainstream professional news sites and political blogs confirms the existence of a citizen–elite divide in media discourse on Europe. Political party actors clearly are more prone to support European integration than citizens. They are also less inclined to make diffuse Eurosceptic contributions, as they tend to underpin their arguments in favour, or against, European integration with sufficient information. It is the strong presence of citizens' voice in media discourse which increases the share of unspecified Eurosceptic arguments in the debate, as shown in Table 3.4.[3] Online news media mark here a clear difference in the quality of EU justification discourse compared to traditional news media, which offer only limited space for citizens to voice their concerns. There is thus partial evidence that diffuse expressions of Euroscepticism are frequently spontaneous reactions by citizens to pro-European elites. Even in cases where European integration is supported by a broad coalition of political parties and elites (Germany, France and Belgium), negative evaluations become highly salient in citizens' comments. Nonetheless, almost half of the statements made by political actors across Europe in the context of EP campaigning, display diffuse Euroscepticism. This shows the role of abbreviated evaluations as an important component of publicly contesting EU legitimacy. EU legitimation discourse, as an element of EP election campaign reporting, is in this sense not conducive to informed opinion-making of the citizens. Still, it could be argued that these patterns of diffuse Euroscepticism during the 2009 European Parliament elections campaign, are less pronounced than those reported during many of the referendums on EU Treaty change (e.g. Aarts and Van der Kolk 2006).

---

3. This table includes all contributions to EU polity contestation made by party actors and citizens (1,018 out of 1,128 or 90.25 per cent of all messages). Not surprisingly, there is a clear association between the actor and the type of contestation advanced (χ_2 (df 6, N = 1,018) = 64.362, p < .000, Cramer's V = 0.252).

Table 3.4: Critical matrix of EU contestation: EU polity evaluations by party actors and citizens

Categories of EU legitimacy evaluations	Actor	
	Party actor	Citizens
Affirmative European	26.9%	8.6%
Status Quo	7.8%	10.7%
Alter European	5.8%	4.1%
Eurocritical	5.8%	5.1%
Pragmatic	0.0%	0.1%
Anti-European	6.5%	7.3%
Eurosceptic	47.2%	63.6%
Total	100.0%	100.0%
N	309	709

Table 3.5: Justifications of EU polity worth by actor type

Principles of justification of EU polity worth	Actor	
	Party actor	Citizens
Democracy	20.1%	43.4%
Culture	9.7%	4.8%
Necessity	6.5%	12.4%
Economic Prosperity	6.8%	8.1%
Safety	7.8%	4.5%
Other	1.0%	0.4%
N/A	48.1%	26.4%
Total	100.0%	100.0%
N	308	715

Principles of justification

Further exploring the citizens–elite divide, we examine the type of justifications that are brought forward by different actors to contest the EU polity. On the basis of which general principle is the EU polity publicly contested? In the following, we cross tabulate both the evaluations and the main actors with the seven categories of justification of worth used in our study (Table 3.5).

We find a substantial association between actors and justifications [χ^2 (df 6, N = 1,018) = 81.751, p < .000, Cramer's V = 0.283]. Surprisingly, party actors provide justifications to support their evaluations of EU legitimacy less often than citizens do. This is related to the dimensions of evaluation. Partisan actors evaluate the principle of integration more often than citizens do and do this with categorical statements providing no justification. Citizens are much more likely to evaluate the EU or European integration based on a concern with democracy than party actors are. As will be demonstrated below, there is a correlation between the dimensions and targets of evaluation and the justification given to support this evaluation. We proceed to investigate to what extent different principles of justification are invoked to support either an affirmative European argument, a support for the status quo or an alter-European, Eurocritical, pragmatic or diffuse Eurosceptic argumentation about the EU.

Table 3.6 below shows first how certain justifications – particularly those concerning democracy and necessity – are more often invoked than others, irrespective of the type of argument made. Yet, there is also a clear correlation between references to democracy and negative evaluations of the EU or European integration. In other words, actors measuring the legitimacy of the EU with standards of democracy tend to be critical. The EU's democratic deficit is thus one of the main interpretative patterns for arguing that the EU is not legitimate. On the other hand, arguments relating to necessity or safety provide typical justifications in support of European integration or the EU. Put differently, actors contesting the EU polity on the basis of standards of necessity or safety tend to be more positive. Two other principles of justifications – culture and economic prosperity – are invoked both by those evaluating the EU positively and those who give a negative assessment.

Conclusion

Our findings point to the high salience of EU polity contestation as an element of EP election online media coverage. Media debates are thus partly detached from partisan contestation providing a central arena for public opinion formation. This confirms our initial understanding of Euroscepticism, as a form of opposition that relies on media infrastructures for salience and amplification. The patterns of polity contestation in the context of the 2009 European Parliament election online media debates, further support our argument that Euroscepticism needs to be discussed in relation to the unfinished character of the EU and the salience of its so-called democratic deficits (De Wilde and Trenz 2012). Our discourse approach to political

Table 3.6: Polity contestation and justifications

Justifications of the EU's worth	Affirmative European	Status Quo	Types of Evaluation				
			Alter-European	Euro-critical	Anti-European	Diffuse Eurosceptic
Democracy	18.8%	31.4%	38.5%	47.5%	43.4%	41.7%
Culture	8.0%	3.4%	7.7%	4.9%	3.9%	6.6%
Necessity	17.0%	19.5%	21.2%	14.8%	6.6%	6.9%
Economic Prosperity	9.1%	14.4%	5.8%	8.2%	7.9%	6.2%
Safety	8.5%	10.2%	13.5%	3.3%	2.6%	3.4%
Other	1.7%	0.0%	0.0%	0.0%	0.0%	0.5%
N/A	36.9%	21.2%	13.5%	21.3%	35.5%	34.8%
Total	100.0%	100.0%	100.0%	100.0%	100.0%	100.0%

contestation in the EU has proven highly valuable in demonstrating how positive and negative evaluations of EU legitimacy are often mutually reinforcing. Efforts to argue in favour of EU legitimacy in terms of principle, institutional set-up and project evoke counter arguments and vice versa. Eurosceptics and pro-Europeans do not occupy radically different spaces in the online media public sphere. Instead, websites paying attention to the political system of the EU in the context of the EP election campaigns, in many instances featured lively debates with a plurality of arguments, where both positive and negative positions regarding the legitimacy of the EU appeared in the same online articles and discussions. Yet, this dynamic co-occurrence that comes to the fore through our public sphere perspective on EU polity contestation remains under-accentuated in studies of public opinion or political party positions.

From a European comparative perspective, the unfinished character of the EU and the perceived deficits of its current institutional set-up were at the focus of attention when the legitimacy of the EU was debated in online news media during the 2009 EP election campaigns. There was, however, only little debate with regard to possible paths of institutional or constitutional reform or future trajectories of integration. On the other hand, there were also only few instances that the EU was attacked in fundamental terms in the debate. The lack of contestation on the principle of integration points to general acceptance among European netizens that some form of collaboration among European nation states is warranted, due to given interdependencies and historically grown relations. Furthermore, after the anticipated completion of the ratification of the Treaty of Lisbon, grand scale future plans for further integration may have (temporarily) disappeared from the public agenda. The strong criticism of the current institutional set-up of the EU, in combination with a lack of contestation on the project of integration implies a stalemate, in which polity opposition frequently remains detached from a discussion on possible reform. The analysed online debates converge on the notion that the EU as it currently exists is problematic, but they diverge regarding where to take European integration from here and how to remedy observed problems.

The citizens–elite divide is clearly shown to be present by our data and thus is to be considered as one of the central vectors structuring public discourse on European integration. Citizens are evidently more critical of the EU than party actors. Citizens are also most likely to employ diffuse Eurosceptic arguments. This reflects the use of a more emotional language. We also find an apparent difference in how party actors and citizens justify their evaluations, with a principled concern with democracy frequently underlying citizens' negative evaluations of the EU. Partisan actors, in turn, apply a more technocratic language and promote, on average, more positive visions in support of the EU on the basis of arguments relating to necessity and safety.

Interestingly, the content of evaluations does not vary substantially among the countries involved in our study. Rather, what differs is the intensity of debates which contest the legitimacy of the EU political system. In the UK, Austria or the Netherlands, where European integration is more salient and public opinion is more critical, the design of the EU polity and its basic underlying legitimacy are more regular campaigning issues. In contrast, in Greece and Belgium, where European integration was relatively uncontroversial, the EU polity is contested with much less frequency. Yet, this conclusion requires further corroboration as the observed phenomenon may be the result of differently developed online discussion facilities and internet habits in the countries under study. Still, the observation draws our attention to EU polity contestation as a specific form of oppositional politics in the EU. Pro- versus anti-European cleavage lines that divide political contestants, public opinion and debates have gained salience over the last years and are likely to find expression in EP elections even in absence of explicit partisan mobilisation on the issue (Mair 2005, 2007).

In light of the prominence of negative evaluations over positive evaluations found in all countries analysed, we conclude that the dynamics of online news media debates tend to support opposition over affirmative voice. What might also count here is that media debates are in general found to be predominantly driven by those critical or dissatisfied with the political status quo (Gamson 1968: 48). Actors supportive of European integration and satisfied with the status quo have fewer incentives to voice their opinions online than disgruntled actors do. Especially citizens, who mainly account for the high salience of EU critical evaluations in online news media, display a strong tendency towards expressions of dissatisfaction with the EU and European integration. By providing a platform for citizens to leave comments that reach wider audiences, online media gives voice to those normally excluded from public discourse. The predominantly critical evaluations of European integration and the EU in citizens' comments amplify diffuse Euroscepticism as the most salient form of expressing discontent with the EU and the course of European integration during 2009 EP elections. Because of their prominence, these expressions of diffuse Euroscepticism are analysed in more detail through country case studies in Chapters Four to Ten. The purpose here is to ground 'diffuse Euroscepticism' in the historical and socio-political contexts of the Member States within which it finds expressions. This includes a closer look not only at patterns of discourse, but also at the carriers of Euroscepticism in the form of civil society organisations, political parties and media organisations, as well as their targets in the form of social groups, electorates and varying degrees of public attention.

The fact that the most prominent online media platforms in the observed countries mirror the mainstream offline media structures – i.e. websites linked to offline newspapers, broadcasting companies etc. – means that it is likely that our conclusions are relevant for offline media too. As can be expected in situations where online media are closely connected to offline media, we find that the websites under study reproduce the narratives and framings of long-running EU debates in the countries under study, as we know them from other sources. With the exception of debates unfolding on the commenting sections, our survey can claim to be representative for mainstream media voice in Europe, as it includes the online coverage of many of the most influential newspapers that are specialised in European news-making in the offline public sphere (Trenz 2005).

Chapter Four | The Mainstreaming of Euroscepticism in Austria: EP Campaigning Between Media Populism and Far Right Extremism

As indicated in the quantitative comparative data provided in the previous chapter, the Austrian debate fields a disproportionate amount of critical remarks. This may not be much of a surprise, given that Austria belongs to those Member States of the European Union where a substantial part of the population is generally categorised as 'Eurosceptic', expressing low degrees of support towards European integration and its institutions (Eurobarometer 2009b). The Austrian political climate is further affected by the permanent anti-system mobilisation of the late Jörg Haider and his party vassals in the FPÖ (Austrian Freedom Party) and BZÖ (*Bündnis Zukunft Österreich*, Alliance for the Future of Austria). Developing a style of 'modern populism' in symbiosis with the mass media, these parties have been successful in mobilising substantial parts of the electorate. Over the last two decades, the FPÖ has consolidated as a 'hard' Eurosceptic party that fundamentally and regularly opposes European integration in terms of principle, institutional set-up and project (Fallend 2008). In this regard, Euroscepticism in Austria is strongly institutionalised and organised. This chapter will flesh out how media populism and far-right extremism can dovetail to amplify EU polity contestation.

Expressions of Euroscepticism in Austria are not unique and marginal but penetrate the core of the political system. Since 1999 there has been a stable percentage of around one quarter of the Austrian population supporting explicit Eurosceptic parties in EP elections. Governmental parties, instead, were regularly defeated in European elections for not being able to mobilise the electorate and losing on issues such as national sovereignty, borders and foreigners. European parliamentary elections are also found to be different from first order national elections in the sense of drawing attention to political outsiders, who mobilise protest votes against political parties and the established system of political representation (De Vreese 2009; Szczerbiak and Taggart 2008a). In the Austrian case, the mainstreaming of Euroscepticism is manifested in generalised patterns of resistance mobilised against the deepening of European integration and enlargement. In the following, we first give a brief historical account of Eurosceptic mobilisation in Austria. Secondly, we explain the strong symbiosis between party mobilisation and media amplification as the principal explanatory variable for the enduring success and impact of Austrian Euroscepticism. The quantitative content analysis data will be shown to reflect this symbiosis of media populism and far-right extremism.

The historical roots of euroscepticism in Austria

There is a notable shift in discussing European integration and Austria's role in an integrated Europe over the last two decades, which is related to Austria's peripheral position of forced neutrality during the Cold War and its unexpected return to European centrality after the fall of communism. After regaining sovereignty back in 1955, Austria stood apart from the process of Western integration. In contrast to the pre-war period when the majority of the population still wished a Union with Germany, the post-war, truncated Austrian state became more than a practical arrangement. As a way of dealing with the guilt of the past, the Austrian *Sonderweg* was welcomed as a detachment from Nazi Germany and fostered the re-interpretation of German regionalism into Austrian national culture (Lepsius 1989). The new post-war Austria did consolidate itself as a democracy and became established as a liberal market economy but, in contrast to Germany, did not develop a strong Western identity. Supranationalism, as linked to the project of European integration, was seen as an infringement of neutrality being at the heart of Austrian post-war identity (Pelinka 2002).

After the end of the Cold War, Austria's new central geographical position with open borders towards the East, and its own capital only a few miles away from Bratislava and Budapest, created mixed feelings among the Austrian population and an attitude of economic opportunism, paired with cultural protectionism and strong reactions against unwanted migrants from the East (Haller 2008a). The country's post war position in the periphery of Western Europe was not the only pretext for displacing the Nazi past. It also shielded Austria from its former 'colonies' at the East of Vienna, which were not exactly an 'unknown territory', as many were made to believe after the end of the Cold War, but became rather associated with the re-discovery of a specific historical and cultural burden. During the Cold War, Austria's negative attitudes towards the project of (West) European integration were nourished mainly by the negative stance of the left (including the governing Social Democrats, *Sozialdemokratische Partei Österreichs-SPÖ*), which officially defended neutrality and anti-militarism behind the curtain of cultural closeness. After the Cold War, neutrality as the official alibi for social and cultural closure soon lost its impact in public debate, shifting towards a more offensive and exclusive rhetoric. Euroscepticism turned from an issue of the political left into the favourite topic of right-wing nationalism (Pelinka 2004).

The historical justification for not joining the European Economic Community (EEC) in the fifties was still held valid, and, in fact, can be found in many of the discussions evolving around the accession of the country to the European Union in 1995 (Pelinka 2004: 211). After the fall of the iron curtain, the SPÖ quickly turned from a defender of Austrian neutrality to a supporter of membership in the EU. In turn, the extreme right, represented by the FPÖ, discovered the issue of Austrian neutrality to justify their hostility towards the opening of the borders towards the East and the sharing of sovereignty with Brussels. This takeover of the Eurosceptic issue by the Austrian right went hand in hand with the reframing of Austrian post-war history. The rejection of Western integration was now justified with a revisionist reading of history, the negation of Austria's guilt of the past and a rapprochement to Nazism and all-Germanism (Pelinka 2004: 211).

The populist strategy to mobilise EU opposition by reference to popular sentiments is facilitated by some particularities of the Austrian political system, which give a strong standing to direct elements of democracy through national referenda[1] and, so-called, popular initiatives (*Volksbegehren*)[2]. The accession referendum in 1994 made clear that in spite of anti-European campaigning from both the right and the left, a stable majority of 66.6 per cent of the electorate (more than in any other country joining the EU in 1995) supported EU membership. In this sense, the referendum still reflected the consensual style that characterised Austrian post war politics. The electorate was (still) on the side of the political establishment and acknowledged the need for a reorientation of Austria and its rapprochement to Europe.

Although anti-EU campaigning during the accession referendum of 1994 was largely unsuccessful, the Eurosceptics succeeded to occupy important issues like resistance against deeper integration and enlargement. The possibility of popular initiatives gives the opposition, even though in a minority position, a powerful tool to oppose official governmental policies and guarantees high public attention and mobilisation. Four popular initiatives took place: *Österreich zuerst* (Austria first) in 1993, the *Volksbegehren Neue* EU *Abstimmung* 2000, the *Veto gegen Temelin* (veto against Temelin, a nuclear power plant in the border area with the Czech Republic) in 2002 and the popular initiative *Österreich beibt frei* (Austria remains free) in 2006 launched with the intention to incommode the Austrian Council Presidency (Wikipedia 2010)[3]. Even though these popular initiatives failed to attract substantial voters' attention, they contributed to the mainstreaming of anti-foreigner and anti-EU discourse, often with openly racist contents and frequent reminiscences to Nazism.

Besides popular moves with anti-EU undertones, anti-system and anti-EU opposition in contemporary Austria is dominated by the FPÖ and its offshoot, BZÖ. Unlike neighbouring countries like the Czech Republic or Hungary, where we can observe a mainstreaming of Euroscepticism as part of governmental strategies, the Austrian case is characterised by a strong system-people confrontation. Euroscepticism has become an opposition strategy to support demagogues like Haider, Strache or Martin and minority parties' claims to side with the people. Pro-

---

1. National referenda are obligatory in the case of a total revision of the constitution and facultative or consultative in cases of substantial or minor revisions. The Constitutional Referendum is initiated by the Parliament.
2. Popular initiatives can be initiated by one-tenth of the Austrian population (approx. 8,000 people) and, once accepted, needs to mobilise support in the form of at least 100,000 signatures to be further proceeded by the Parliament. However, the national government or the Parliament cannot be compelled to change legislation or to take action based on the initiative.
3. A list of all thirty five popular initiatives held in Austria since 1964 can be found at Wikipedia (Wikipedia 2010).

European attitudes are instead associated with a corrupt governing elite that betrays people's genuine interests. The FPÖ learned to combine the anti-foreigner and the anti-EU agenda, which allowed them to hold the EU responsible for the incessant flux of foreigners pervading the country and to be particularly outspoken against enlargement (Pelinka 2006). Euroscepticism of the right is further nourished by the historical animosity against the Czech Republic and the unsettled question of the expulsion of German-speaking minorities after the Second Word War (the so called Benes Decrees), as well as the issue of a nuclear power plant in the Austrian border area.

Right-wing extremism in Austria progressively expanded during the nineties, luring substantial parts of the voters away from the two majoritarian parties *Österreichische Volkspartei* (ÖVP) and SPÖ. In the October 1999 national elections, the FPÖ came in at second place for the first time (coming within 290,000 votes to the first-placed SPÖ) and, to the dismay of Austria's European partners, entered into negotiation with the third placed ÖVP to form a governmental coalition. This right-wing turn of Austria was perceived by many as a breach of European values and, as such, provoked indignation and reactions against Austria in other Member States (Van de Steeg 2006; Wodak and Pelinka 2002). In a joint declaration, the fourteen governments of the EU Member States appealed to their colleague, Schüssel, to not enter a coalition with the FPÖ and threatened with sanctions in case the FPÖ would be placed in government. After the presentation of the new Schüssel government in January 2000, the governments of the EU Member States could, however, only agree to take diplomatic measures which excluded Austrian delegates from informal Council meetings. Nevertheless, these measures were generally referred to as 'sanctions' in the Austrian debate, as well as in debates in other Member States (Van de Steeg 2006). The adequacy of these 'sanctions' was heavily debated in Austria and in other Member States and a Committee of three wise men was put in place to check whether the new Austrian government would infringe EU laws. The wise men evaluated the sanctions as counterproductive and concluded, in September 2000, that Austria had not violated any EU legislation. Despite this, political commentators in other Member States were still ready to declare Haider a Nazi and Austria a revisionist country, that violated the core of European values (Van de Steeg 2006). A campaign against Austria was fought by the media and by political commentators in other Member States, treating the 'Haider case' as an issue that concerned the whole Europe.[4]

---

4. Risse (2010) and Van de Steeg (2006) have investigated the Haider debate as a case for an evolving European public sphere, in which debates about shared values, identities and normative projects are made possible. Their results show that indignation against Euroscepticism and the breach of shared values remains a strictly European phenomenon. The Haider debate was clearly confined to Europe with US commentators taking a much more distanced stance.

The extent to which the Haider debate contributed to the mainstreaming of Austrian Euroscepticism and strengthened the Euro-hostile attitude of a significant proportion of the Austrian population, is discussed controversially in the literature. On the one hand, the impression that the EU sanctioned Austria (and the electoral choice of the Austrian people) prevailed and foreign reactions against the Austrian government had mainly negative repercussions within Austria, solidifying the solidarity of the Austrian population with its government (an experience which prevented European governments to take similar measures against unwanted governmental coalitions in other Member States, notably in Italy). In response to the foreign sanctions, the national allegiance was strengthened whereas the left opposition was blamed for being disloyal to Austria (Fallend 2008: 212).

The Haider case notwithstanding, Pelinka (2004) points to Eurobarometer figures which show that support of European integration has not significantly fallen in the aftermath of the 'sanctions'. One could also argue that with regard to the FPÖ, Euroscepticism had become majoritarian even before the new right-wing government of 2000 took office. The ÖVP–FPÖ coalition government, on the other hand, sought normalisation with the EU: Haider himself dampened down his anti-EU rhetoric and stepped down as the party leader in spring 2000, in an attempt to appease the conflict. The monitoring of Austria by its European neighbours thus brought about the domestic ceasefire of Eurosceptic campaigning and the FPÖ shared the destiny of many populist opposition parties, who, once in government, lost their appeal to the voters. The decline of the FPÖ also continued in the European elections in 2004, when Haider's party was reduced to 6.4 per cent of the general vote. Internal quarrels about leadership eventually resulted in the schism of the party, with the new BZÖ competing for right-wing voters.

Nonetheless, the crisis of the nationalist right in early 2000 does not indicate its defeat. In programmatic terms, there has been little change in Eurosceptic rhetoric and mobilisation. In organisational terms as well, the new populist right soon regained its former strength (Pelinka 2006). Both the FPÖ and BZÖ continue to present a right-wing programme campaigning against Europe[5], against foreigners and with reminiscences of Nazism. The electoral success of both parties in the 2006 and 2008 national elections shows that right-wing populism is firmly established and rooted within the electorate.

The 2009 EP election turnout showed further radicalisation, with the right extremist and Eurosceptic parties back in favour with the electorate, and 35 per cent of the electorate giving the vote to an explicitly Eurosceptic party.[6]

---

5. The argumentative repertoire of both parties is very similar. In the last national elections the FPÖ propagated the exit of Austria from the EU, while the BZÖ campaigned against the 'paternalism from Brussels'.

6. Hans-Peter Martin got 17.6 per cent, the FPÖ got 12.7 per cent and the Alliance for the Future of Austria got 5 per cent.

Media populism and the mobilisation of the electorate

How can the repeated gains of populist, anti-EU parties in EP election turnouts be explained? The post-war Austrian consociational model of democracy has been traditionally characterised by a low salience of class politics and a tendency to define the political community in terms of ethnic, exclusive criteria (Pelinka 2002). On the basis of longitudinal public opinion data, the Austrian electorate has been characterised as strongly obsessed with 'cultural anxiety' and particularly predisposed towards right-wing-extremist or xenophobic attitudes (Strasser 2008). This has laid the ground for the revival of 'old politics of identity', deeply rooted in the ethnocentric and culturalist orientations of the Austrian population and now given organisational form in the emergence of an extremist party beyond the consociational model (Arwine and Mayer 2008; Pelinka 2002).

The Austrian case can only be fully understood through the impact of media discourse as accounting for the high salience of exclusive nationalism and Euroscepticism (Wodak and Pelinka 2002). In the Austrian case, mass media provide a necessary and permanent soundboard for populism and Euroscepticism (Plasser and Ulram 2003: 40). News coverage is filled with anti-EU stories and EU bashing takes place as part of the regular campaigning of political parties and the media.

The case of Austria thus provides an outstanding example of media populism that can be held responsible for the growth of neo-populism there and also in other parts of Europe (Mazzoleni 2003). As reflected in the different contributions in this book, different media structures and practices of news-making are also a good indicator for variances in expressions and organisational forms of Euroscepticism. With regard to the media's role in European integration, the media account for the public salience of the EU, its actors and institutions and provide the basic knowledge that enables people to relate to, and to evaluate, the EU (Trenz 2008). Varieties in EU polity evaluation are in this sense related to particular modes of expressing support for, or opposition to, the EU and European integration in the media (see Chapter One).

One particularity of the Austrian case is the strong standing of popular and populist mass media in reinventing the concept of an exclusive national identity and amplifying the direct voice of the people against the political establishment (Plasser and Ulram 2003; Wodak and Pelinka 2002). Austria's media populism is found to be mainstream, not marginal. Already, ten years ago, Plasser and Ulram (2003: 30) spoke of the consolidation of the populist newsroom, characterised by an editorial logic that tends to pick up anti-immigrant and anti-elitist topics and to amplify popular prejudices. In a populist newsroom, tabloids contribute to the polarisation of the audience. In terms of content and quality of political news, the tabloidisation of the Austrian newspaper market is a strong constraint. Tabloid newspapers have established market monopolies giving low and highly selective salience to European and foreign news and emphasising mainly conflict and national interests (Mokre and Bruell 2006; Sauerwein *et al.* 2006).

From the popular, anti-elitist stance of tabloid newspapers, Europe is a prime target of anti-system campaigning. In the case of news coverage about the European

Union, newspaper populism strongly correlates with the anti-Europeanism of the tabloids, which works across the ideological divide and traditional party cleavages. The *Kronenzeitung*, for instance, does not take a clear ideological stance in terms of partisan affiliation but has regularly expressed a strong anti-Europeanism. Among the quality newspapers, *Der Standard* is the only EU friendly newspaper in Austria. Others, like *Die Presse* or regional newspapers, are neutral with regard to daily EU coverage but critical towards enlargement (Trenz 2005: 242f.; Sauerwein *et al.* 2006). When circulation is taken into account, newspapers with a more or less openly Eurosceptic agenda reach approximately 60 per cent of the Austrian population, while European friendly newspapers are read by just five per cent of Austrians.[7]

In light of the above, we expect that EU polity contestation will take place in the dimension of defining the inclusiveness/exclusiveness of the polity and less in scope and institutional or constitutional design. In terms of actors, we expect a dominance of Eurosceptic party actors in alliance with citizens evaluating the EU/ European integration in a dominantly negative way. When it comes to justifications of Eurosceptic evaluations, we expect that the populist frame is mainly supported by references to democracy, the demarcation of 'we the people' against 'the others'. These 'others' will be variably defined as the 'traitors of the political left' and their cosmopolitanism (domestic) and/or as the EU-elites, Islamic, Turkish or Eastern European (external). Finally, we anticipate the dominance of a tabloid style of reporting about the EU with frequent breaches of the maxims of providing sufficient information, limited coherence of debates and transgressions in style or violations of netiquette. To account for the election turnout, we thus expect that online news and campaigning dominantly replicates the patterns of media populism, systematically damaging the image of mainstream political parties and supporting an anti-system mobilisation of the electorate.

Dimensions of EU polity evaluation

To quantify the hypothesis that the Internet replicates mainstream media populism in relation to European integration, this analysis of the Austrian online public sphere relies on a representative sample of news articles from the two most prominent professional journalism websites (derStandard.at and Krone.at). The two professional news sites are run by two of the most widely distributed offline newspapers in Austria, however, indicating a reverse order in popularity: quality news distributed by *Der Standard* are more popular online than offline (alexa rank 14) whereas tabloid style popular news distributed online by the very powerful offline newspaper *Kronenzeitung* rank only second (alexa rank 32). To account for the specifics of political communication online, the sample includes both main news articles and user comments for the three campaigning weeks of May

---

7. For regularly updated figures of circulation of Austrian print media see Media-analyse (2010).

18 to June 6, and the week immediately following the elections. In addition, the two most popular independent political blogs were identified and included in the sample (Politikblogs.at 2012; Rigardi.org 2012).[8]

Who contests EU-legitimacy?

In a first approach to our data, we identify the campaigning actors who became salient in EU polity debates either opposing or supporting the legitimacy of the EU (see Figure 4.1). Results point to a low intervening role of the journalists who do not take part actively in debates. This is expected with regard to the traditional understanding of journalists as neutral brokers of the political process. Also, journalists of the populist *Kronenzeitung* do not become active in campaigning against the EU, but either leave the floor to partisan actors or take a more passive role in selecting negative news on the EU. Opinion-making in both quality and tabloid news outlets is found in the citizens' comments sections. Also more surprisingly, political bloggers do not take an active part in EP campaigning. The explanation for this is to be found, on the one hand, in the low salience of the EU issue in political blogs, and on the other hand, in the dominant use of political blogs for anti-populist campaigning. The blogging community used the context of EP elections not for a discussion of EU legitimacy but as a pretext to open a battle against the populist right in Austria. Blogging is seen as the antidote to populism as expressed by mainstream tabloids exposing EU hostility. In most blog entries, EU polity evaluations appear as indirect quotations with the intention of the blogger to express outrage or irony against the leaders of the Austrian populist right and their style of campaigning.

In terms of participants, we observe a strong symbiosis between media populism and party campaigning. Media populism is not self-standing and running against political parties but constantly fed by national opposition parties who campaign for voters' attention. Journalists, especially of the tabloid *Kronenzeitung*, are not actively writing against the political elites, they are even passive in framing debates and do not step forward as active opinion-makers against Europe. Media populism is thus linked to an editorial policy of selecting and amplifying political messages and contention, rather than to the active role of journalists in contention. It consists of painting a political reality, not of substantial policies and choices, but of protagonists fighting for power, emotions and credibility.

Both newspapers (quality and tabloid) use party actors as their main source of information and as the reference for evaluations of EU legitimacy. EP election campaigns on the internet are fought by domestic parties. The only visible EU actor was the independent MEP candidate Hans-Peter Martin who defended his seat successfully through explicit anti-EU campaigning.

---

8. The basic unit of analysis were evaluative statements in which the legitimacy of the EU polity is contested (support or opposition). These were taken from a representative sample of fifty-two articles, each article comprising both news articles and user comments). For details of the sampling procedure see Chapter Two of this volume.

Figure 4.1: Distribution of EU polity evaluations across countries: Austrian contributions per actor

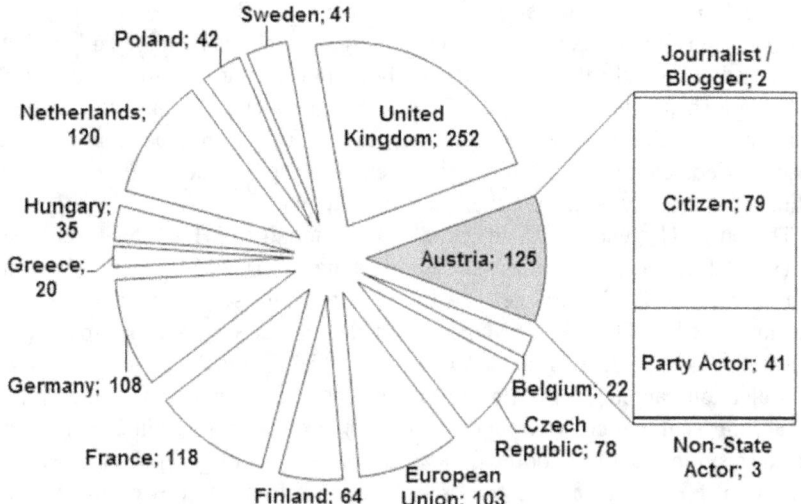

was the independent MEP candidate, Hans-Peter Martin, who defended his seat successfully through explicit anti-EU campaigning. Non-partisan actors or other EU actors and institutions remain marginal. Also news coverage of election campaigns from other Member States is restricted and foreign political actors are only given voice in exceptional circumstances.

The tabloidisation of political discourse had a clear exclusive effect, affecting mainstream political parties and rational arguments that were not framed in tabloid style. Especially, the Social Democratic SPÖ and the Green party became targets of populism in the news and commenting sites of Krone.at and had few opportunities to step forward as agenda setters in their own right. The forums of debate provided by quality sites such as Standard.at or political blogs were overall too small to adjust this imbalance, to the effect that the 'populist, anti-European voice' is largely overrepresented in our sample.

In terms of actors' dynamics and grouping, the agenda of the EP elections of June 2009 was largely set by the aggressive campaigning of the two right-wing populist parties (FPÖ and BZÖ) and the campaign of a single person, Hans-Peter Martin. The populist opposition parties took the opportunity to raise fundamental questions about the EU. They chose an 'essentialist strategy' leading straightforwardly to a Eurosceptic agenda: raising the existential questions about membership, the rationale of integration, and the scope, authority and inclusiveness of the present and future EU polity. Among the essentialist topics raised by the two right-wing extremist parties, the question of the borders of Europe and the inclusiveness towards new members ranked highest. Resentments against the new Member States survived, especially in user comments where the Eastern Europeans were encountered with hostility and made generally responsible for economic decline, crime, and public disorder. The exclusive and populist rhetoric was also found in the debate on Turkish membership. Since all political parties, except for the Greens, expressed themselves against membership of Turkey in the EU, a further radicalisation of the debate became necessary for the populist right to distinguish its own position on Turkey. The distinctive feature was found in islamophobia. Like in other European countries, Turkish membership instigated a general debate on Islam as an imaginary enemy that was seen as threatening the political community both from the inside and the outside.

This anti-EU agenda was also central in the campaign of Hans-Peter Martin but with a different focus. Martin was the leader of the Austrian ESP group in 1999 and after the break with his party defended, successfully, his seat in the 2004 elections with his own list 'Hans-Peter Martin – For genuine control and transparency in Brussels' (*Liste Dr. Hans-Peter Martin – Für echte Kontrolle in Brüssel*). In the 2009 election campaign, Martin presented himself as a 'populist of the middle' and a 'long-standing crusader against EU money wastage' (Martin 2012). Martin became a symbolic figure for the fight against elites and alleged power abuses and corruption. His call to defend the ordinary people from the power abuse of the Brussels bureaucrats got decisive media support with excerpts from his book 'The European Trap', published in a weekly column of the *Kronenzeitung*.

How do mainstream political parties respond to the varieties of Euroscepticism mobilised by populist parties and leaders? Media debates in both newspapers leave no doubt that these campaigns were not well received but instead were condemned by the political establishment for their blatant right-extremist, racist and anti-Semitic contents. However, governmental parties did not campaign with positive EU evaluations in defence of European integration. There is no explicit pro-European campaign that provides substantive arguments in defence of EU legitimacy. The anti-populist response is not a defence (in the sense of endorsing the value of European integration and the legitimacy of the EU) but a counter attack, which challenges the personal integrity of the populist as a legitimate participant of debate. Since the populist right has placed itself beyond the pale of civilised public discourse, any response in substance would mean accepting the company of a demagogue. That is why mainstream politicians shun, so far as they can, a debate on the 'essence'. They ignore the existential questions raised by the demagogue as inappropriate or politically incorrect and attack, instead, the personal credibility and integrity of the political opponent. While anti-EU evaluations are essential, i.e. directed against the EU polity, the counter mobilisation is personalised, i.e. defaming the political opponent on the basis of style and tactics. This leads to a highly polarised debate of fundamental dissent: the political adversary is not recognised as a legitimate actor with whom to enter into a debate about substantial policy issues and solutions. The opponent is defined as racist and xenophobic and therefore excluded from the community of democratic parties.

This refusal by mainstream political parties and government to enter into a debate about essence has fatal consequences for the media representation of EP election campaigning. The re-setting of the terms of the EU debate from 'essence' back to 'substance' does not take place. The exclusionary strategy of the political establishment is not successful to break the hegemony of the populist voice in the media. As a consequence, media reality is detached from political reality. The European Parliament is discussed in terms of corrupt and overpaid MEPs, who are seen as the betrayers of national interest, elitist and fundamentally undemocratic. With this, the basic legitimacy of the European Union as a political entity is negated. The European Parliament is not seen as the palladium of European democracy but quite the opposite, as the quagmire of corruption and even crime. MEPs are personally attacked and portrayed as criminals and not as representatives of the people.

In the Austrian case, this aggressive form of EU polity contestation turns into the main voice that represents Europe in the media. Our data confirms that the FPÖ populist strategy was highly successful in setting the media agenda and imposing the topics and style of debate on other actors. More balanced judgements or positive evaluations of EU polity worth have little news value (20 per cent as compared to 80 per cent negative evaluations of the EU). By making extremist statements, the populist right thus precludes further debates on European Integration. The populist parties maintain the monopoly of interpreting the EU and throughout the debate, and across the news sites, are rewarded with high media attention.

Finally, our data allows us to gain an insight into the users' perceptions of Europe and patterns of interventions in the debate. Citizens are the most frequent actor category that expresses opinions in EU online debates. Our survey indicates that a substantial part of the users were ready to take up the topics raised by the populist opposition and to debate the EU in essentialist terms. EP election campaigns are thus not merely about domestic politics. Citizens are ready to debate the EU and political opposition parties successfully raise EU topics in campaigning. The electorate is thus generally motivated to become engaged in EU debates and, as the following section shows, makes use of this opportunity to express primarily negative attitudes and discontent with the EU and its performance.

Evaluations of the EU polity

In a second step, we categorise the targets of EU evaluative statements in Austria, which can contain a positive or negative evaluation of the EU in principle, in terms of its present institutional or constitutional design or in terms of future projects. One recurrent feature of the Austrian debate is, first of all, the almost complete absence of positive evaluations of the EU polity (Figure 4.2). The principle of integration is not defended, just barely contested. In terms of polity and project, the EU finds few defenders but many opponents. Austrian debates are further characterised by low levels of contestation within one medium but a strong polarisation between different media and their audiences.

This addresses two interdependent aspects: On the one hand, EU polity evaluations are based on democracy, defined not in terms of rights but in relation to the populist idea of defending the sovereignty of the people against the EU and political elites in general. There is the widespread feeling that European integration has gone too far in terms of deepening and widening. The Lisbon Treaty is generally rejected without going into details of its provisions. Past rounds of enlargement are seen as the main cause for the malaise of the EU. As a general remedy, popular sovereignty should be reinstated by re-nationalising the EU. The projects for democratic reform of the EU are often not perceived as a potential solution, but rather, as an amplification of the problem.

Figure 4.2: Evaluations of the EU polity in Austria

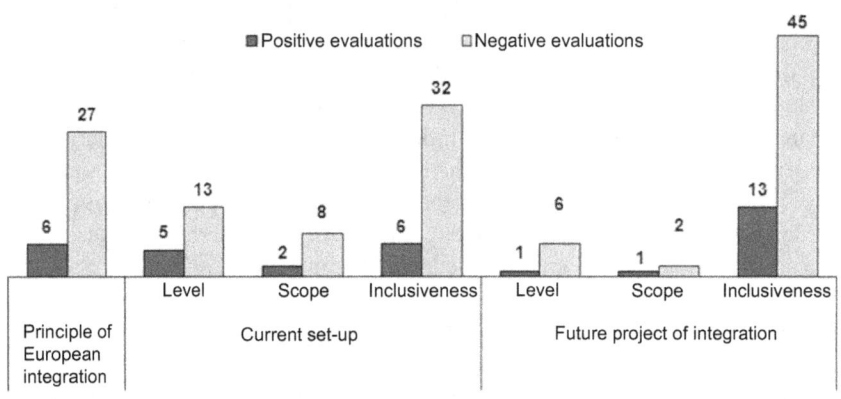

On the other hand, the inclusiveness of the EU is contested on the basis of membership that should remain restricted to the core, exclude the periphery and draw strong borders with the outside. This explains the strong correlation between anti-EU discourse and anti-Islamism. The focus of this debate is on a potential membership of Turkey, which is fiercely opposed by all political parties (except by the Greens) but also on illegal immigration, crime associated with foreigners and security. The borders between anti-Islamism and racism are fluid, transgressions in the form of explicit racist statements by political actors and candidates are frequent.

In terms of internal coherence, the results point to the low complexity of the debate, in which arguments relating to principle, polity and project are not interrelated but isolated and self-standing. Evaluative statements are typically organised in a way to maximise the effects of publicity at the cost of sufficiency of argumentation. For that purpose, the main message needs to be focused and typically embraces only one of the three dimensions of evaluating EU legitimacy. There is also no difference between positive and negative evaluations of EU legitimacy in meeting the requirement of sufficiency. On the contrary, the defence of EU legitimacy tends to be even less complex than the denunciation. Only in seven instances, a complex evaluation is delivered comprising all the three dimensions of EU legitimacy in terms of principle, polity and project and all these instances are categorised as Eurosceptic. The main reason for this low complexity of EU justificatory discourse is given by the specifics of user commenting. These are frequently self-standing and not supported by a more sophisticated argumentation or justification of EU legitimacy in the main news article.

Justifications

After having reconstructed the targets of EU polity contestation, we need to analyse more closely the repertoire of justifications that informs the critical practices of contesting EU legitimacy in online media discourse. From the hypothesis of media populism, we would expect an emphasis on elements of national sovereignty, community and solidarity. This is clearly reflected in Figure 4.3 with a dominance of evaluations relating to democracy (though slightly below the European average) followed by culture and, to a lesser extent, economic prosperity. A more in-depth analysis of the evaluative statements justified in terms of democracy, reveals that democracy is not defined in inclusive terms of personal rights, good governance and justice to be promoted by the EU but in terms of inclusion/exclusion of the political community and the restitution of popular sovereignty against the EU. What concerns participants is not the democratic design of the EU polity or its scope of action but the defence of the national political community, its borders and integrity.

Political actors and citizens converge in their use of justifications of evaluating EU legitimacy. This indicates that the concerns and expectations are shared among the partisan actors who lead the election campaign and the potential voters, who comment upon European integration in the discussion forums of the news sites. There is, however, a noticeable discrepancy between the official discourse of legitimation employed by EU elites and the domestic EU debates unfolding in the online media. Attempts to legitimise the EU as a functional arrangement, or as a welfare and security community in times of global crisis, are not reflected in media discourse.

One recurrent pattern of Eurosceptic evaluations justified in terms of democracy, is the expression of the will of the people against the elites. To understand the particular ways this citizen–elite divide is activated, we need to reconstruct the mythical notion of the people that is underlying such conceptions. Following the dominant logics of media populism, the Austrian people are portrayed as the suppressed majority who suffer from foreign rule. Anti-Europeanism is an intuition, which does not need to be grounded in sophisticated argumentation. The 'genuine' sentiments and emotions of the people have a higher standing than the 'artificial' arguing of the intellectuals and the elites. The populist leader is not expected to enter into a political debate that tests different options, is open to new information or seeks understanding. The leader is supported precisely because she rejects the logic of rational debate and fair game.

Figure 4.3: Explaining opinions – how EU polity evaluations were justified in Austria and in all countries

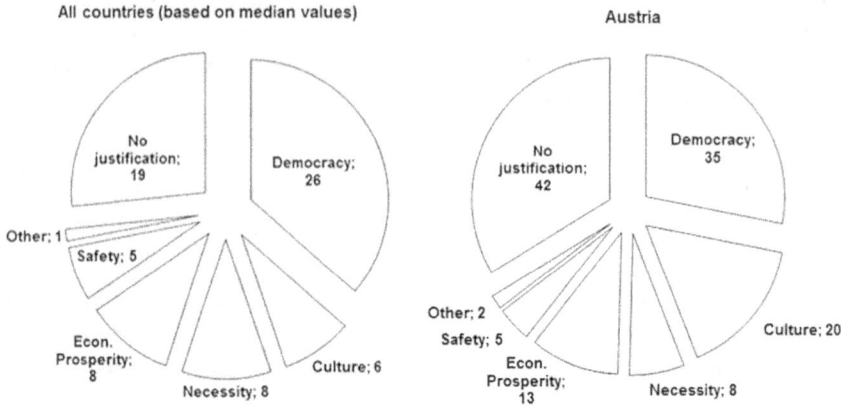

Following the populist logic, the meaning of leadership consists in giving voice to the speechless. It consists of representing and advocating those who are not able to express their diffuse fears and emotions. The kind of trust and charisma the populist leader builds, relies entirely on the image of being 'one of us', not distinguished by office, higher education, elite attitudes or extravagant life styles.[9]

The two right-wing populist parties added to these elements of anti-elitism, an exclusive and xenophobic rhetoric that replaces complex justifications with simple symbols and slogans. The FPÖ's style of campaigning consisted of vilifying other religions and serving anti-Semitic prejudices (the possibility of EU membership of Israel). The 2009 campaign has also focused on religion on several other occasions. The party's leader, Strache, drew media attention by waving a crucifix at a party rally meant as a sign of protection against the threat of foreigners and Islam. Another campaign slogan on posters and newspaper ads, 'The West in Christian hands' (*Abendland in Christenhand*), also drew high public and media attention and was strongly rejected by high authorities of the Catholic Church, emphasising, in turn, the inclusiveness of Christianity.

The possibility of membership of Turkey in the EU was regularly combined with the expression of fears of the islamisation of Austrian society. In analogy to a Schmittian conception of Europe, Islam as the mythic enemy, is found both as an open threat and as secrecy and conspiracy (McCormick 1999: 93). It allows further, political entrepreneurs to make use of both liberal-progressive (defence of free speech, equality, anti-discrimination) and conservative-culturalist

---

9. The leader of the BZÖ, Stadler, a lawyer of profession, used the title 'advocate of the people' in campaigning and addressed the voters with 'mails from the advocate of the people'. After an Austrian court proclaimed an injunction against his abuse of title, he clarified that he would only assume this function as the 'advocate of the people' in Brussels (*see Der Standard* 2009).

(Christendom) arguments that found a broad resonance within all strata of the population (Schneiders 2009). In similar terms, Turkish membership is often not taken up as an issue of debate but merely a reference point to mark a position in partisan contestation. To insinuate that someone is in favour of Turkish membership disqualifies the political opponent as an enemy (*Volksverräter, Nestbeschmutzer*) of the Austrian people: 'Opting to vote for a party which supports accession of Turkey and the new asylum law can only be explained by some level of stupidity'.[10]

Following the same populist logic of argumentation, EU bureaucrats and representatives are also seen as dissociated from the people and allied with the enemy. This corresponds with the general anti-elitist and anti-parliamentarian tone of media populism, which emphasises the legitimacy of the direct voice of the people over representation in the Parliament. Especially, the European Parliament is regularly portrayed as a breeding ground for corruption, not as a site for democracy. On the commenting pages, users call for *Echte Volksvertreter* (genuine representative of the people), instead of *EU-Verräter* (EU-traitors).

Of further particular interest is the type of self-justificatory rhetoric unfolding on the commenting pages through which users reassert the rightfulness and authority of their opinion. By placing the comment on the public site, the user claims to speak for the people as a whole, to be just one of the crowd, who stands up to express the genuine feelings of the commons by the use of simplified language, the expression of outrage and emotions and the rejection of rational argument. Therefore, opinions expressed on the commenting page do not need to be sophisticated; they are legitimate and representative precisely because they are articulated through emotional language and spontaneous thought. In line with this, users are also found to strongly identify with the newspaper, which they chose for their encounters. Other readers are seen as like-minded and potential allies who distinguish themselves, e.g. from the audience of another medium. Part of this imagination of the audience is also the attribution of legitimacy in numeric terms: '3 million readers cannot get it wrong' as one user at Krone.at claims.

The commenting of the users is elevated here to the daily plebiscite of the people. The 'We' of eight million Austrians is put on stage against 'alienated elites' and 'foreign rule'. This is populism in its pure form, which endorses the absolute value of popular sovereignty that is not compromised by representation, universal rights and justification. Media populism is in this sense more than a successful market strategy to create strong reader identification. It is also an exclusive nationalist ideology which aims to appeal to the readers' patriotic sentiment and to put them centre stage as the avant-garde of the people empowered to fight for the restoration of Austria, and against the multiple internal and external threats to its unity.[11]

---

10. 'Eine Partei an die Spitze zu wählen die für einen Türkeibeitritt und für das neue Asylgesetz ist, da gehört schon ein bißerl Blödheit dazu.' Here and in the following, extracts from user comments at Krone.at are quoted by free references (dates and user names are not retrievable).

11. This is often articulated in a manner directly reminiscent of the *Deutschland erwache* slogan

Conclusion

The Austrian 2009 EP election e-sphere is found to offer a platform for the placement of negative news and opinions on the EU. In particular one main news site (Krone.at) is divulging EU hostility through the campaigning messages of Eurosceptic parties and the active promotion of one single candidate (Hans-Peter Martin) as the main commentator on the EU. Anti-EU campaigns amplified by this tabloid newspaper unfolded on the basis of clichés and prejudices against the European Parliament and the EU in general, often enriched with the additional flavour of insults and accusations against EU protagonists or political representatives in general. Another main news site (derStandard.at) is principally promoting quality news and covers EU election campaigns in an impartial way, keeping distance from emotional language and strong evaluations. By adopting professional journalistic standards of truthfulness and proof, *Der Standard* guarantees high coverage but contributes little to ongoing debates and evaluations of EU legitimacy. Quality journalism is therefore not only insufficiently prepared to counterweight media populism but rather accentuates existing cleavages between the public.

Apart from anti-elitism, a further characteristic of the EU debate in Austria is a strong expression of xenophobia. In the case of the EU as a foreign actor, an additional threshold of civicness of public discourse is overcome, in the sense of focusing on the EU as the external enemy that lacks recognition as a political entity. EU-hostile audiences largely coincide with xenophobic ones and anti-European discourse is often also xenophobic, with popular tabloids printing racist and anti-Semitic content. In spite of this strong overlap between xenophobic and anti-European discourse, a manipulation of the newspaper by right-wing extremists did not take place and the link between the media and political parties remains mostly indirect. The newspaper maintains its autonomy and is rather ready to serve the EU-hostile audience on its own account. It serves and at the same time creates a market of populism, anti-Europeanism, xenophobia and also anti-democracy.

Further, symptomatic of the Austrian debate is the indifference of key actors towards political facts and the truthfulness of their assertions. The dynamic of campaigning is driven by the constant and systematic invention of political facts by the populist opposition parties and the denunciation of these lies by the governmental coalition. Public discourse is structured in a way that the EU-critical actors have a license to exaggerate and to simplify, which is seen as legitimate in order to reduce the complexity of the issues and to explain the EU to the voters. In contrast, EU proponents who stick to complex facts and details appear non-transparent and elitist. To invent news like the accession of Israel to the EU can, under conditions of media populism, be more successful to raise voters' attention than sophisticated exploration of the borders of Europe. Lies or exaggerations become a systematic element of a particular form of polity contestation, which is primarily concerned with essence and identity, not with contents and experience.

---

which was used by the NSDAP to win the 1933 elections.

Overall, these findings confirm our hypothesis of a strong correlation between expressions of Euroscepticism and media populism. Media populism is crucial for understanding the success of Eurosceptic parties in elections and the polarisation of Austrian society. The Austrian EP election e-sphere largely reproduces the offline populist newsroom dominated by a tabloid style of news and opinion making. It reaches a mass audience that is made up of substantial parts of the Austrian population and that is already used to consume right-wing populist messages and negative, anti-elitist news (Plasser and Ulram 2003). The critical point is that apart from its scope and impact on opinion making, online media populism also empowers the audience through more direct forms of participation and involvement in online debates. The tabloid readers find in the online newspapers, not only the confirmation of their opinions but also the opportunity to actively express their negative attitudes and to exchange opinions with like-minded individuals. The internet offers a forum for this audience to express their negative views and to unfold hate speech against the EU, and against political elites in general.

The counter strategy of established political parties against populist, anti-EU campaigning is to cover different topics and to use different media channels. *Der Standard*, the first online news site in terms of salience, but only the eighth most sold newspaper in terms of print copies, is used for placing an anti-populist agenda and raising quality standards against the tabloidisation of the Austrian news market. Comparing the online presentation of derStandard.at and Krone.at, the impression prevails of a divided society. Both newspapers stand for two irreconcilable camps of the audience which do not debate with each other in any meaningful sense but treat each other as enemies. European topics and debates are one field where these strong conflicts and the incommunicability between the readers of different media products are sharpened.

The online public sphere amplifies existing differences within Austrian society, contributing to the formation of an EU-hostile and xenophobic user community that is almost exclusively addressed by the right-wing political parties and that can no longer be reached by the political establishment. The 2009 EP campaign thus effectively divided the electorate. It results in a situation of non-recognition between the political adversaries that is translated into a situation of non-recognition between two opposing camps within the audience.

Chapter Five | EU Polity Contestation in France and French-Speaking Belgium: The Bounded Impact of a Referendum

Amandine Crespy and Olga Fimin

France has always had an ambivalent stance towards the project of European integration with shifting attitudes both at elite and mass level. In the course of its history as a founding member of the European Community, France has known spectacular episodes of hostility towards integration, such as the rejection by the *Assemblée Nationale* of the Treaty on the European Defence Community in 1954, the 'empty chair crisis' when General de Gaulle refused to apply the rule of majority voting in the Council, and, more recently in 2005, the rejection of the Constitutional Treaty by 54.7 per cent of the French electorate. The French case is also interesting for the development of outside mobilisation strategies against the political establishment. As in other European countries, EU opposition can become mainstream by successfully exploiting the citizen-elite divide in campaigning. In the 2005 referendum campaign, such ad-hoc mass mobilisation was carried, above all, by the political left and amplified primarily through the online media (Fouetillou 2007). For these reasons, France is an interesting case for exploring further the scope of EU polity contestation on the internet. In contrast, Belgium is widely seen as one of the most Europhile Member States. The main Belgian political parties have consistently called for 'more Europe' and Belgian public opinion has been highly supportive of European integration over time (Delwit *et al.* 2005; Pilet and Brack 2009). Euroscepticism remains confined to the Flemish nationalists and the marginal radical left-wing parties.

These two contrasted cases are particularly interesting in light of the purpose of this book, to test a non-substantialist definition of Euroscepticism as part of the general dynamics of EU polity contestation. Rather than being considered as the property of given actors or countries, EU-resistance is identified here through the discursive positions that are taken in denouncing the legitimacy of the European Union or of European integration. As such, EU-opposition is linked to the performance of particular actors who position themselves in the field of political contestation (see the introduction to this book). In that sense, it is consistent with the approach of EU resistance as developing through strategic framing and conflicting normative models of European integration beyond the framework of traditional party politics (Crespy 2010b, 2011). In previous research, such a more dynamic analytical framework of EU-resistance was useful to reconstruct the confrontation between Neoliberal Europe and Social Europe that was carried by a loose transnational coalition, composed of left-wing associations, trade unions and political parties, against the EU directive for services liberalisation, also known as the Bolkestein Directive. EU polity contestation does not, therefore, constitute a separate discourse to which a fixed meaning can be attributed; it is rather intrinsically linked to the contentious nature of integration, constitutive of both its future and its democratisation.

Of particular interest in analysing the causal path of EU polity contestation in France and French-speaking Belgium is the resonance of the 2005 referendum on the Constitutional Treaty. This event temporarily amplified EU polity contestation. The question remains whether this discourse resonates beyond the particular event. The comparative character of this chapter not only captures possible resonance beyond 2005 in France, but also in the Member State with arguably the closest cultural, political and linguistic proximity to France: Belgium. To the extent that we find resonance, this points to the lasting impact of highly contentious episodes on EU polity contestation and to the connectivity of discourse across time and space. Such discursive resonance across time and space can be an important causal mechanism to explain convergence and divergence in EU polity contestation. We start with a contextualisation of EU resistance in the two countries based on a review of the existing literature and on a general presentation of the main issues raised in the 2009 EP election campaign. We then turn to the analysis of the relevant actors, and the main dimensions of EU polity contestation as it became salient during the 2009 EP election campaigns in both countries.

Contestation of European integration in France and French-speaking Belgium: A historical overview

While France was one of the main driving forces of the European integration project in the immediate post-war period, the major move towards federalism was actually already heavily contested in the founding years of the European Union. Both of the two most influential political forces of the political right and the left, the Gaullists and the French Communist Party, were alarmed by the threat of a loss of French sovereignty but for quite different reasons. In the context of the Cold War, the Communist Party was the main Eurosceptic political force in France, rejecting the project of market integration and viewing the political integration of Europe as a betrayal of international solidarity (Callot 1988; Hivert 2009). The empty chair crisis provoked by de Gaulle in the 1960's in rejection of majority voting in Brussels, contributed to a re-direction of the Community from functional integration to intergovernmental cooperation (Ludlow 2006; Palayret 2006). In the 1980s' and 1990s', Euroscepticism became increasingly marginalised at the fringes of the political spectrum. Europe, nevertheless, continued to divide the French political landscape as well as public opinion across the traditional ideological cleavage. This resulted in the creation of splinter parties both on the left and on the right. With the decline of historical Gaullism, the main right-wing party, the RPR (*Rassemblement du peuple français*), became fully supportive of European integration. Even so, hostility towards the transfer of competences to the European Economic Community remained vivid among some prominent figures of the party, such as P. Seguin, who actively campaigned against the Treaty of Maastricht, and C. Pasqua, who joined forces with the far-right leader, P. de Villiers, and founded the *Mouvement pour la France* (Ivaldi 1999). Right-wing Euroscepticism was also boosted by the rise of the *Front National* (Kriesi *et al.* 2008), which first made use of a pro-European rhetoric accompanied by a Eurosceptic practice and then adopted a much more aggressive discourse emphasising the defence of French sovereignty.

On the left, the dramatic decline of the Communist Party was accompanied by the turn of its traditional French-sovereignist ideology to an alter-European or 'euro-constructive' position close to the global justice movement (Heine 2009; Milner 2004; Santamaria 1999). Under the leadership of François Mitterrand from the 1970s until the early 1990s, the Socialist Party (PS) took a strong – although somewhat ambiguous – European turn. While criticising the liberal market policies and the lack of a social dimension of the European Economic Community, the Socialists advocated the deepening of integration with President Mitterrand as the prime advocate of the Treaty of Maastricht's ratification (Delwit 1995). In the post Mitterrand era, Lionel Jospin took over the critical pro-European stance, which left little room for internal dissent and gave the impression of a consensus with the conservative party of President Chirac under the regime of 'cohabitation' (Bergounioux and Grunberg 2005). The internal divide over European issues, however, dramatically resurfaced during the 2005 referendum campaign over the European Constitutional Treaty.

Euroscepticism or 'Eurocriticism' has also emerged as an epiphenomenon in research on the alterglobalist – or global justice – movement (Della Porta 2006), which considers the EU as the Trojan horse of neoliberal globalisation. From the 1995 great strike, the 'Europe of Maastricht' was the target of leftist discourse (Contamin 2005: 125–30; Gordon and Meunier 2002) and *Attac*, which was founded a few years later, played a major role in conveying a specific leftist critical discourse about the EU in the public sphere (Wintrebert 2007). The eurocritical alterglobalist discourse had spread out into the entire French political radical and moderate left, including trade unions (Hilal 2007) and was very efficient in mobilising against the European Constitutional Treaty (ECT) in 2005 (Crespy 2008; Heine 2009). As far as French public opinion is concerned, it is difficult to draw clear-cut conclusions. Like in other European countries, Eurobarometer data point to a divide not only along income-related but also along cultural educational lines: better-off, more educated and culturally liberal citizens tend to favour more integration (Belot 2002; Percheron 1991; Reungoat 2010). Social issues and the perception of an elitist bias as a feature of European integration play a crucial role in France (Belot and Cautrès 2004; Cautrès 2000; Cautrès and Denni 2000; Costa and Magnette 2007). All these crisscrossing vectors came to play in the dynamics that led to the rejection of the European Constitutional Treaty by 54.7 per cent of the French on the 29 May 2005. Socio-economic issues were identified as the main driver of the campaign (Crespy 2008; Ivaldi 2006; Perrineau 2005; Sauger *et al.* 2007; Sauger and Lauret 2005). Trade unions have also stepped forward as protest actors against EU policies, in particular as far as liberalisation directives are concerned (Hilal 2007), as for instance in the protest over the Bolkestein Directive dealing with services liberalisation (Crespy 2010a). Overall, the impact of civil society and collective action on contention over EU integration, has increasingly attracted the attention of French scholars (Balme and Chabanet 2008; Sanchez Salgado 2009).

Contrary to France, Belgium has the reputation of being one of the most Europhile countries. Broadly speaking, European integration can be considered as a 'non-issue' in Belgian politics (Crespy 2011; Deschouwer and Van Assche 2008). Since the origins of European integration, Belgian support of EU integration has been strong, not only because the country was able to profit economically from the Common Market, but also because of the strength of the federalist movement (Verbeke 1981). Similar to the French case, the political left in Belgium, mainly represented by the Wallonian and Flemish Socialist party, was originally divided over the integration project in the immediate post-war period (Delwit 1995). In the 1950s, under the leadership of Paul-Henri Spaak, socialist elites moved towards a favourable stance towards integration and supported the Treaty of Rome (Belle 1968). In later years, Belgian politicians left their imprint on the integration process through actions of such political actors as, for instance, the Christian Democrat Léo Tindemans who advocated a common currency, a common foreign and defence policy and the strengthening of the European assembly in a famous report as early as in 1975. Today, Wallonia and Brussels, on one hand, and Flanders, on the other hand, display two different faces of Euroscepticism.

Negative instrumental evaluations of the benefits related to EU integration and distrust in the European institutions have been identified as the main elements of Eurocritical discourse in Belgium (Abst *et al.* 2009; Duchesne *et al.* 2010). In French-speaking Belgium, similarly to France, resistance to liberal market Europe has also gained ground as an element of left-wing politics. Echoing their early criticism of the liberal and intergovernmental bias of the Rome Treaty (Verschueren 2010), trade unions – especially the socialist *Fédération Générale du Travail de Belgique* (FGTB) – are cooperating with *Attac* and leftist civil society within the *Forum social de Belgique*. While no party called for the rejection of the 2005 European Constitutional Treaty (ECT), leftist circles, including fringes of the *Parti Socialiste* (PS), strongly resent the 'neo-liberal EU'. However, except for marginal left radical parties such as the *Parti des travailleurs belges* (PTB), the *Ligue communiste révolutionnaire* (LCR) or the *Parti communiste* (PC), the main parties' critical stance consists of calls for a more 'social Europe', a more 'federal Europe' or a 'greener Europe' (Delwit *et al.* 2005; Pilet and Brack 2009; Pilet and Van Haute 2007). In Flanders, Euroscepticism is essentially used by nationalist parties, who have meanwhile acquired a central position in the regional political spectrum. However, the nationalists of the *Vlaams Belang* and the *Nieuw-Vlaamse Alliantie* (N-VA) have avoided frontal opposition to European integration: rather, they have combined criticism at the costly bureaucratic EU with calls for ethnic homogeneity and regional autonomy in the framework of the so-called 'Europe of the regions' (De Winter 2001). All in all, Euroscepticism in Belgium remains relatively weak, especially in the French-speaking part of the country and confined to rather marginal actors. Given the co-existence of two separate regional political cultures, it is not possible to identify a specific Belgian pattern of contesting

European integration. We will therefore, in the following, focus on media contestation during 2009 EP election campaigning in French speaking Belgium, where, as we will be able to show, media coverage interacts strongly with French debates, with domestic actors playing only a marginal role in contesting European issues.

Issues of partisan campaigning

The 2009 EP election was far from an important political moment. In both countries, the campaign started late, and remained at low levels of public and media attention. In France, the campaign strategy was very much focused on President Sarkozy. The President's party, *l'Union pour un mouvement populaire* (UMP), mainly boasted about the success of the French presidency, for instance about the agreements over the climate change package and over the conflict in Georgia. The UMP reproduces the Gaullist discourse about Europe as an enlarged theatre for the French politics of the *grandeur* while glorifying the French leadership in the EU. The *Parti Socialiste* pursued an ambiguous strategy wavering between personal attacks on Sarkozy (*Le Monde* 2009a) and more substantial arguments on European issues. In spite of the progressive nature of the manifesto of the European Socialist Party and its efforts to coordinate national campaigning, the topics and arguments provided by the European party platform remained marginal in the campaign. EU polity contestation on more substantial issues was, instead, monopolised by the smaller parties on the fringes, which expressed a strong desire to change Europe and, with this, had a strong resonance among the French electorate.

On the right, the traditional nationalist and sovereignist parties raised an overtly Eurosceptic agenda but were internally fragmented. The *Front National* (6.3 per cent) was mainly represented by Marine Le Pen. The EU was pictured as a failed enterprise and was accused of ideological bias towards ultra-liberalism and unbridled free trade, undermining the solidarity of the French people. Uncontrolled immigration and Turkish membership were also major topics. The small neo-Gaullist party, *Debout la République* (1.77 per cent) campaigned on similar themes, although in a less aggressive manner. According to its leader Dupont-Aignan, the 'Europe of Brussels' has failed and should therefore be replaced by a system based on intergovernmental cooperation over concrete projects between sovereign nations. Philippe de Villiers' *Mouvement pour la France,* and the traditionalist hunters' movement *Chasse, Pêche, Nature et Traditions* (CPNT) even entered a pan-European Eurosceptic alliance, which was founded under the label *Libertas* by the Irish businessman D. Ganley. Arguably, these attempts of transnational cooperation among Eurosceptics might be read as an effort to improve their credibility towards the electorate while improving their image and softening the anti-European label. *Libertas'* discourse rests on populist arguments denouncing the EU as an undemocratic, technocratic, unaccountable and too costly governance system. The undemocratic European super-state, the European Commission and Turkey were their main targets.

On the left, the fragmentation of the Eurosceptic actors was even stronger. *Lutte Ouvrière* (LO) grounded its campaign on a classic – if not old-fashioned – anti-capitalist rhetoric. It painted the picture of an EU dominated by the dictatorship of bankers unable to cope with the economic crisis and growing unemployment (*Le Nouvel Observateur* 2009b). The *Nouveau Parti Anti-Capitaliste* (NPA), under the leadership of O. Besancenot, used a similar discourse but epitomised better the renovation of anti-capitalism. Its main argument was that more money should be put into the wages and not into the banks and shareholders' profit. The 2009 EP campaign witnessed the constitution of a new EU critical actor: the *Front de Gauche*, composed of the Communist Party (PC) and the *Parti de Gauche* (PG). The PG is a splinter party from the PS; it was founded by J.-L. Mélenchon, a well-known left-wing critic of the European common market, who advocates the uniform implementation of a classical Keynesian agenda throughout the EU. Again, the campaign was mainly targeting President Sarkozy and the government's measures to cope with the financial crisis. As the unity of the French far-left[1] became the dominant theme in the debate, the agenda for 'changing Europe' came only as a secondary issue in the campaign.

In contrast, the green list *Europe-Ecologie*, led by the very popular Daniel Cohn-Bendit, was the most successful new grouping in the 2009 European election campaign. This list is a good example of how difficult (and perhaps misleading) it is to seek to qualify actors according to the binary category of being either Eurosceptic or pro-European. *Europe-Ecologie* rallied various streams of the environmental movement in France, including those who had campaigned against the ECT in 2005, such as José Bové, a leading figure of the peasant movement. While *Europe-Ecologie* did not use an anti-European rhetoric stigmatising the EU in terms of principle, it nevertheless expressed a strong criticism of its current institutional set-up and advocated radical reforms towards a new ecological and social deal in a more federal Europe, thus reconciling the *'France du oui'* and the *'France du non'* (Zappi 2009a, 2009b).

To a larger extent than in France, Europe was conspicuously absent from the Belgian election campaign (Dandoy and Pauwels 2009). The low level of campaigning is mainly explained by compulsory voting. In addition, the EP elections coincided with regional elections, which distracted voters from European topics. EP candidates had a low profile, partly because of prominent bogus candidates who were highly listed but not expected to take their seat in the European assembly. The *Vlaams Belang* campaigned on its favourite theme: Flemish identity, which involves claims for a 'Europe of the peoples' and against Turkish membership to the EU. However, the *Vlaams Belang* came considerably weaker out of the 2009 EP election, since it had to compete with a new Eurosceptic actor, the *Lijst Dedecker* (LDD). This new party developed a different, ultra-liberal style of Euroscepticism, which was critical of the inefficient EU bureaucracy, of the democratic deficit and of the 'green fundamentalism' of the EU.[2]

---

1. Website of the French left-wing party *Front de gauche*: www.frontdegauche.eu.
2. Electoral Manifesto of the *Lijst Dedecker* for the 2009 European election: 'Europees Programma

Data

The three French sites selected are the online portals of the three main, traditional quality newspapers in France: *Le Monde, Le Figaro* and *Le Nouvel Observateur.* As far as blogs are concerned, *Plume de Presse* and *Sarkofrance* were selected from a list ranking political blogs in France (Wikio 2009c), and their popularity was crosschecked on *alexa.com* (Alexa Internet 2009).[3]

Although all the websites created a special section dedicated to the European elections, *Le Monde* published by far the most articles mentioning the elections (around 340) with twice as many articles than *Le Nouvel Observateur* (155) and even three times more than *Le Figaro* (100). Also in relative terms, EU polity contestation was made most visible on *Le Monde* (around 50 per cent of all polity evaluations analysed, compared to 25 per cent for *Le Figaro,* 15 per cent for *Le Nouvel Observateur* and just 10 per cent for the two blogs). To this extent, there was a significant disparity between the news websites and the blogs, with the latter focusing almost exclusively on domestic issues.[4] This favoured domestic debates over European ones: none of the articles coded from *Sarkofrance,* for instance, contained any evaluation of the EU, although they touched on the topic of the EP elections. Articles from *Le Monde* and *Plume de Presse* were regularly and intensively commented, while *Le Nouvel Observateur* and *Sarkofrance* had the least number of interventions from the public. This reflects the fact that the two former sites have a larger readership. The EU polity was mostly contested by citizens and not by journalists or political actors, with the most evaluative statements to be found on the commenting pages of the selected news sites.

For Belgium, the two most popular websites selected were www.dhnet.be, the electronic version of the tabloid *La Dernière Heure* and www.lesoir.be, the website of the daily *Le Soir* which is referred to as quality press in the French-speaking part of the country. Although only at the sixth place in the Alexa ranking, *Le Vif-L'Express* had to be selected over more popular websites – such as the website of the public television broadcaster RTBF (www.rtbf.be) – which did not provide features of interactive journalism through user commenting. The two political blogs selected – *Le Pan* and *Le Blog Politique* – were the most popular ones from the ranking created by the Belgian website www.politique.belgoblog.com. Overall, the Belgian websites displayed few articles related to the European elections and most of them appeared in the last period of our sampling, discussing

---

LDD: "LDD: De Eurorealisten'", available at <http://www.lddwvl.be/docs/2009-LDD_EUROPEES_PROGRAMMA.pdf> accessed 11 June 2013. I would like to thank Teun Pauwelsfor his precious insights on LDD.
3. Alexa does not, however, always measure the popularity of individual blogs, but that of the blog platform they are powered by (for example *over-blog* or *canalblog).*
4. In this sense, the distribution of topics among the selected articles is relevant: many of the articles published by the online journals were about 'European integration' or 'Democracy', while most of the entries from the blogs concentrated on 'Domestic issues'

the election results rather than campaigning issues. Moreover, the contrast between the news websites and the blogs was significant: *Le Blog Politique* published only five entries in the first week of the campaign and nothing else until the 10 of June, although the results were already released on the 7 June. *Le Soir,* on the other hand, contained the highest number of EU polity evaluations of all news sites. The Belgian articles on the elections were mainly neutral presentations of facts, events etc. and not opinion articles, leaving therefore little space for manoeuvre to the journalists for making judgements on the EU.

On the basis of these data sources, three hypotheses can be tested. Firstly, starting from the general observation of the campaign as well as from the existing literature, a very low salience of EU polity contestation is expected, both in the French and the Belgian public spheres. This shall be explained by suboptimal conditions for the mobilisation of EU opposition in the period under investigation. After the political earthquake provoked by the 2005 referendum campaign, all mainstream political parties, and especially the PS, were keen to de-politicise European integration, to restore the pro-European image of France and, more crucially, to benefit from the election at the domestic level. Secondly, we hypothesise that identity-based explanations and the fear of the loss of sovereignty are not so much at the heart of anti-European or Eurocritical discourses in France and French-speaking Belgium. Interactive communication and editorial contents, rather, reflect citizens' generalised distrust toward European elites along with a concern with liberal market Europe and its effects on social protection and the welfare state. The third hypothesis investigated is that the justifications given to oppose or support European integration are converging rather than diverging. In particular, democracy and social security can be invoked by political actors and citizens to either support or oppose a deepened integration. This confirms the idea underlying the theoretical framework of this book, that Euroscepticism is part of the contradictory democratisation of Europe rather than an anti-democratic practice.

Participants in EU online debate: Who contests the legitimacy of the EU?

All across Europe, the 2009 EP election campaign was pervaded by the fear of a high level of abstention. Like in other countries covered by this survey, the French and Belgian debates mainly dealt with the EU's response to the crisis, the inaccuracy of the solutions provided, the 'no' vote in the 2005 referendum and Turkey's accession to the EU. In the French debate, party actors accounted for just forty-five of the 118 evaluations coded. The partisan campaign was to a large extent focused on President Sarkozy. This reflects a typical pattern of the French presidential system, where even regional and local elections tend to focus strongly on the national executive. The UMP insisted on Sarkozy's achievements as a head of state, and its role as a European leader in relation to the French presidency of the EU, and mainly addressed themes of the political right such as, internal security or immigration. The PS, by the voice of its First Secretary, M. Aubry, attacked the government in more substantive terms criticising controversial decisions such as the suppression of the milk quotas or the security measures proposed for combating youth violence in schools. Against this domestically focused style of campaigning of the two main political opponents, the small parties at the margins targeted both the government and the EU. The latter was depicted either as an undemocratic construction infringing on the nation states' competences by far-right parties (*Mouvement Pour la France*; *Chasse, Pêche, Nature et Traditions*; *Front National*) or as an ultra-liberal system built for the benefit of the economic oligarchy, at the expense of ordinary citizens by the radical left parties (*Lutte Ouvrière, Nouveau Parti Anti-Capitaliste*).

Accounting for only one comment, journalists and bloggers did not actively contribute to EU polity contestation. *Sarkofrance*, in particular, was intentionally created as a means for targeting the French President – and his party, the UMP – and none of the articles sampled from this blog contained any evaluation of the EU, although they sometimes touched upon the topic of the EP elections. We can thus conclude that, unlike other countries such as the UK, the pro-and anti-European cleavage leaves no imprint on the French media landscape. Rather, the editorial contents reflect the mainstream party consensus in favour of the EU while remaining vague on substantial policy choices. More clear-cut opinions on the EU, expressed by political parties at the margins, are instead reported with editorial distance. The absence of EU issues on blogs brings further evidence of the fact that European integration does not generate much debate among citizens, or at least among the well-educated and engaged citizens who run a blog on the e-sphere.

The French campaign appears to be unarguably very national, i.e. it involves little or no participation by actors from other countries or the EU: out of seventy evaluations, only two were made by foreign actors and one by an EU actor (Figure 5.1). These evaluative statements are also insignificant in terms of content, as they comprise very short, indirect quotations which do not provide any justification for their criticism.

Figure 5.1: Distribution of EU evaluations across countries: French contributions per actor

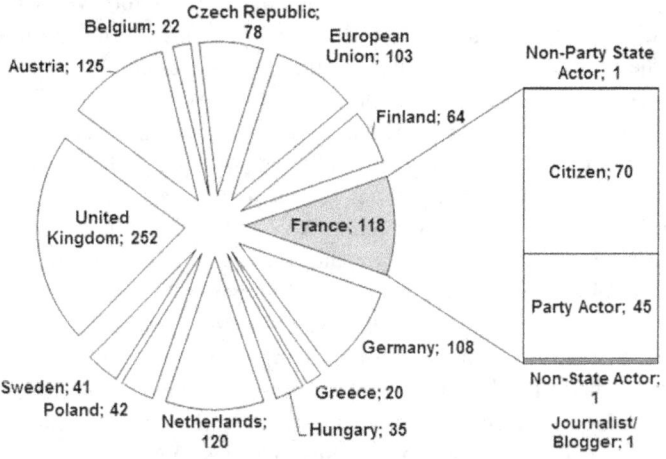

With seventy out of 118 statements, citizens are the most visible category of actors involved in online debates. Few of them, however, take the initiative to launch contentious debates about the EU in independent blogs. Rather, citizens use the existing infrastructure of professional news sites to express support or discontent with the EU. Citizens' attitudes regarding the EU are expressed in response to inputs provided by professional journalists and are not self-generated in the form of alternative online or participatory journalism. Nevertheless, while editorial contents conveyed by professional journalists remain neutral with regard to the evaluation of the EU, citizens' comments are strongly evaluative.

Figure 5.2: Distribution of EU evaluations across countries: Belgian contributions per actor

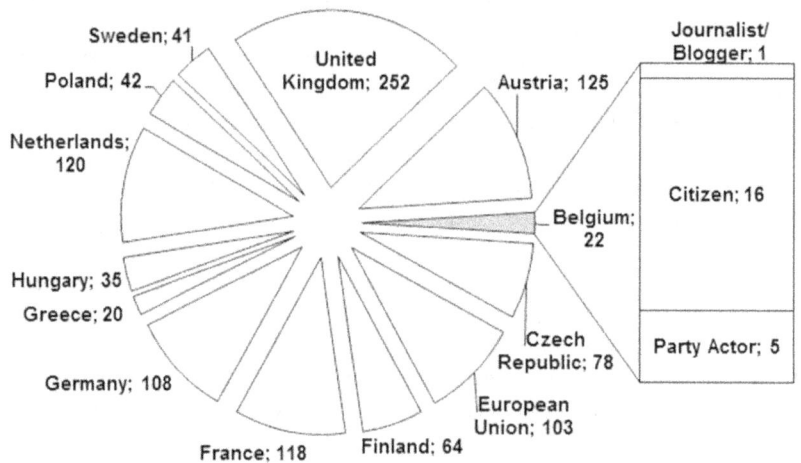

The involvement of the various actor categories is relatively similar in French-speaking Belgium (Figure 5.2). Politicians only account for five of the twenty-two evaluations coded. The fear of high abstention proved unwarranted, partly because the political parties could rely on the system of compulsory voting, and partly because the election for the European Parliament was concomitant with the elections for the regional Parliaments. As a result, the character of EP elections as second-order elections was even reinforced. In light of the great uncertainty about the future of the federal state, the campaign was clearly dominated by domestic issues. The European election was quite frequently mentioned in the news coverage, but mainly related to the power play between French speaking and Flemish elites. As a consequence, the Belgian 2009 election campaign was characterised by the almost complete absence of debates that evaluated the EU or European integration in terms of principle, polity or project. Furthermore, journalists and political bloggers barely expressed an opinion on the EP election. In political blogs, EP elections were a non-issue while journalists mainly focused on neutral presentations of facts and events in professional news sites.

Belgium's atypical profile as a Europhile Member State is further corroborated by the origin of claimants in the e-sphere, which, in sharp contrast to France and other countries covered by this survey, in almost half of the cases (ten out of twenty-five) relate to evaluations made by foreign actors. The Belgian debate can, in this sense, be said to be strongly Europeanised, even though these statements were largely indirectly transmitted opinions expressed by French actors commenting mostly on Turkey's accession to the EU. This type of comment was disseminated, for instance, by Belgian readers who copied them into their comments, quite often to heighten a more Eurosceptic view, which was absent from the domestic debate on the EU. Overall, this accounts for the influence of the French debate on the Belgian campaigning and the difficulties to demarcate an independent public and media sphere in the case of French-speaking Belgium.

As in the French case, the most substantial part of EU polity evaluations was made by citizens (sixteen out of twenty-two comments). Whereas the political establishment and the journalists have a rather positive or neutral stance towards European integration, citizens express criticism to a certain extent. More specifically, they react to issues raised by foreign political actors, in particular the Eurosceptic Dutch or French politicians. Arguably, this means that the e-sphere responds to the representative gap of EU politics: it provides a citizens' forum to discuss contentious aspects of integration which are left out in the parliamentarian and partisan arena of representative politics. However, the findings presented in this section clearly support our first hypothesis on the low salience of European integration in online communication, both in France and French-speaking Belgium.

Dimensions of EU polity contestation: The future of the EU as a main concern

Our analysis of the evaluations made in the online news and blogs distinguishes three main dimensions of Euroscepticism: their stance towards the very principle of cooperation, the evaluation of the current 'state of the Union' and of its institutional and constitutional set-up, and the evaluations of the EU in terms of project and future paths of integration. It is assumed that this threefold dimension helps to better understand the EU as a moving target in time. It also avoids simplification and binary analysis in terms of being either in favour or against the EU.

As accounted for by the very low values on the category, 'principle of integration' (only fourteen in France and absent in Belgium), existential debates on the *raison d'être* of the EU and the purpose of integration, remained marginal in both countries (Figure 5.3). There exists a diffuse support in both countries in the sense that the EU and European integration are taken for granted.

The absence of an existential debate contesting the principle of integration and the focus of criticism on current EU polity or integration as a project in the future, supports our second hypothesis: EU polity contestation in France and French-speaking Belgium is driven by institutional distrust and intertwined social and democratic concerns, rather than by the defence of national identity and sovereignty. In France, approval of European integration is often associated with

Figure 5.3: Evaluations of the current EU polity set-up in France and French-speaking Belgium

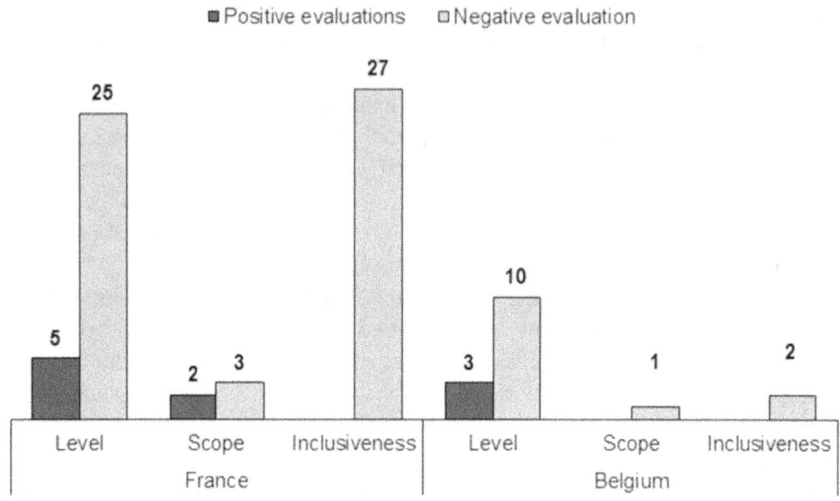

a critical stance towards its present performance: nine out of the ten evaluations that explicitly take a stance in favour of the principle are correlated with negative evaluations of the current status of the EU and/or with its projects of future development.

We find here a common rhetorical figure, in which the expression of principled support of European integration is used as a prelude of criticism: 'I think most of the abstentionists are pro-European, but the Europe that is proposed to us has nothing to do with the Europe we expect'[5] (*Le Monde* 2009b). One main argument invoked to criticise the EU polity, is its failure with regard to social inclusiveness (twenty-seven cases). It consists mainly of critiques of the neo-liberal nature of the EU which is seen as a 'market space that laminates the social conquests and has nothing to offer for the life of its citizens'[6] (*Le Monde* 2009b) or as an entity that 'protects the liberalism, the deregulation and the big businessmen while claiming the contrary'[7] (*Le Figaro* 2009a). A further aspect emphasised by the anti-liberal critics is the EU's submission to the different lobby groups: MEPs are being accused of bowing before lobby groups that 'only represent selfish financial

---

5. 'Je pense que beaucoup d'abstentionnistes sont proeuropéens. Mais l'Europe qui nous est proposée n'a rien à voir avec celle que nous attendons.'
6. 'L'Europe [...], un espace marchand qui lamine les conquêtes sociales, n'a que faire du sort de ses citoyens.'
7. 'Une Europe qui protège le libéralisme, la dérégulation, les grands patrons tout en clamant le contraire.'

interests, hidden behind principles of competitiveness, acting at our expense, to ensure their "profitability" against all common sense, because outrageous benefits are their only aim'[8] (Jennar 2009). The anti-liberal discourse claiming the harmful consequences of both globalisation and European integration on the integrity of the national economy and the welfare state, has been a recurrent discursive pattern since the revival of the left-wing criticism of Europe and the rise of the alter-globalist movement in the mid-1990s (Contamin 2005; Crespy 2008). The anti-liberal discourse has mainly been fed by peripheral parties, both on the left and the right. *Lutte Ouvrière*, for instance, denounces the 'dictatorship' of financial and industrial groups that 'lead whole regions to unemployment and poverty'[9] (Arthaud 2009). The anti-liberal discourse is usually combined with the denunciation of the essentially undemocratic nature of the EU, especially among those citizens who voted against the Constitutional Treaty in 2005 (the 'nonistes'): 'I am hostile to the Europe that some are trying to sell us, those who have ignored our opinion expressed at this referendum [2005]'[10] (*Le Monde* 2009c). In fact, evaluations expressing a general discontent with the EU were often motivated by the feeling of disregard of the French 'non' in the 2005 referendum. In this respect, citizens announce their intention of electoral abstention as a form of protest against the undemocratic way in which the Lisbon Treaty was pushed forward:

> We massively voted in 2005 and politicians brutally ignored it. What's the purpose then to vote if one can just violate the citizens' choice whenever it is not convenient? There are a lot of us who have chosen to abstain rather than to participate in a mascarade. They deny our choices on fundamental aspects and, even more, they want us to elect people that would apply what we have democratically refused[11] (*Le Monde* 2009b).

Furthermore, the democratic argument for criticising the EU is very often associated with distrust towards the institutions of the EU and, in the first place, of the European Commission: '[T]he Commission doesn't want to democratize, it is the government of experts against democracy […] The problem is that this technical Europe has forged very liberal policies that go against the European

---

8. '[Ces groupes] ne représentent que des intérêts financiers égoïstes qui se cache derrière des principes de compétitivité pour toujours agir à nos dépends n'assurant que leur "rentabilité contremiste" envers et contre tout bon sens car seuls les bénéfices à outrance sont leur seul objectif.'
9. '[…]la dictature des financiers [...] ils plongent des régions entières dans le chômage et la misère.'
10. 'Je suis hostile à l'Europe que certains veulent nous vendre, ceux qui ont fait fi de notre opinion exprimée lors de ce référendum.'
11. 'On a voté largement en 2005 et les politiques sont passés en force après. Alors quel intérêt à aller voter si lorsque le choix des citoyens ne convient pas, on le bafoue? Nous sommes nombreux à avoir choisi l'abstention plutôt que de participer à une mascarade. On renie nos choix sur les aspects fondamentaux et on voudrait en plus qu'on élise des hommes pour appliquer ce que nous avons démocratiquement refusé.'

model that they are supposed to promote'[12] (*Le Nouvel Observateur* 2009a). Other evaluations target the 'absence of real powers of the EP'[13] (*Le Monde* 2009b), point at the 'helplessness' of MEPs, who have only 'a minor'[14] (Jennar 2009) say in the European legislative process or allude to the EP's powers as those of a 'XVIIIth century monarchy rather than to a real democracy'[15] (*Le Figaro* 2009b).

In Belgium, the current status of the EU is also criticised, especially with regard to the dispute on the level at which political authority should be allocated. Yet, since the Belgian debate was less path dependent and pre-structured by the legacy of referendums, the proponents and opponents of European integration picked up more random issues to focus public attention on European integration. As a consequence, instead of unfolding explicit arguments in support or in opposition to the EU and of European integration, the Belgian debate displays a more classic, anti-establishment pattern of argumentation. Most evaluations under this category were generated by an article raising the issue of outrageous MEPs' wages:

> Personally, I think our MEPs are useless (except for drafting texts that are 'idiotic' most of the time, for example to define the length of a banana or the diameter of a kiwi). As anything that is useless, they are by definition too expensive[16] (*Le Soir* 2009).

Criticism targeted both the lack of real power of the MEPs: '[T]hey can't do any harm [...] given that they have no power', as well as their personal incompetence: '[They are] rather well paid for some former TV presenter, exhausted sportsmen or retired politicians'[17] (*Le Soir* 2009).

The positive evaluations of the EU polity are frequently given as responses to these accusations, defending the importance of the EP in the European institutional architecture: '[...] the Commission is far from being able to pass anything it wants

---

12. '[...] la Commission ne veut pas se démocratiser, c'est le gouvernement des experts contre la démocratie [...]. Le problème c'est que cette Europe technique a développé des politiques très libérales qui affaiblissent le modèle européen qu'elles sont censées porter.'
13. '(C'est là le point de vue d'un Euro-béat qui ne veux pas admettre la composante anti-démocratique et en catimini de la construction européenne actuelle, ainsi que) l'absence de pouvoirs réels du parlement Européen.'
14. 'Qui fait les textes européens ? Surement pas le parlement, qui n'a qu'un rôle mineur dans l'affaire, donc oui, les textes européens régissent nos vies, et oui un parlementaire est impuissant face à cela.'
15. 'Ce parlement a des pouvoirs beaucoup plus proches de ceux d'une monarchie du XVIII siècle que de celui d'une vraie démocratie.'
16. 'Personnellement, je trouve que nos eurodéptutés sont inutiles (à part pour nous pondre des textes la plupart du temps «crétins», genre pour définir la longueur d'une banane ou la taille d'un kiwi). Comme toute chose inutile, ils sont d'office trop cher."
17. '(Le PE c'est du vent et on y envoie des moulins à vent). Plutôt bien payé pour quelques anciennes speakerines, sportifs épuisés ou politiciens à la retraite.'

[in the Parliament]'[18] (*Le Soir* 2009), or arguing that the monthly salaries MEPs are entitled to are legitimate 'if these MEPs are really competent this wage is justified'[19] (*Le Soir* 2009). Similarly to the French debate, the lack of respect for the citizens' voice is also a motive for discontent.

The third dimension of Euroscepticism explored in this analysis, relates to the future project of integration. It is more salient in France than in Belgium and, being mentioned in eighty-one out of 118 coded evaluations, constitutes the major issue of concern in the French 2009 EP campaign. Overall, evaluations of the prospects of European integration are negative. Distrust towards the future deepening and widening of the EU dominates the debate. Here, statements target the new balance of power brought about by the Lisbon Treaty and express preferences over the maintenance of the status quo and consolidation, instead of further transferring competences to the EU level (thirty-four negative evaluations) or incorporating new members (fourteen negative evaluations). It is remarkable that the future of European debate is mainly carried by peripheral parties on the left and right fringes of the political spectrum. The far-right leader, Philippe de Villiers, was one of the most important representatives of the anti-federalist camp, who rejected the Lisbon Treaty and the creation of a European state by invoking both sovereignty issues and democratic concerns. With regard to identity, the legal personality of the EU and the European diplomatic service would, according to him, 'subordinate national diplomacies' and lead to 'an artificial federation' that would be 'the denial of history, but also of modernity, that is of freedom and singularity'[20] (De Villiers 2009). With regard to democracy, the Lisbon Treaty would reinforce the Commission's powers to the detriment of national democracies. Positive statements within this dimension include (mostly unqualified) evaluations in favour of the Lisbon Treaty or arguments for increasing the powers of the EP, as well as stances defending a federal, democratic Europe created on the model of national political systems.

The project of widening European integration (inclusiveness) is mainly opposed by reference to Turkey's possible accession to the EU (Figure 5.4). Turkish membership is mainly rejected for religious reasons or for its putative negative impact on democracy (recurrent references are made to the risk of 'Islamist drift' or to the possibility of violations of human rights, namely of women's rights). In an interview with *Le Figaro*, former Prime Minister Alain Juppé[21] explains his

---

18. '[...] la Commission est loin de pouvoir y faire passer n'importe quoi.'
19. 'Si ces députés sont réellement compétents, ce salaire est justifié.'
20. 'Je refuse cette évolution, qui conduirait à une fédération artificielle, parce qu'elle est la négation de l'histoire, mais aussi de la modernité, c'est-à-dire de la liberté et de la singularité.'
21. 'Pour revenir à la Turquie, mon opposition est d'abord d'ordre économique. (L'Europe n'est pas l'Aléna ni le Mercosur, c'est une zone de solidarité dans laquelle les plus avancés aident les plus faibles. Nous l'avons fait avec la Grèce, le Portugal et l'Irlande, et en ce moment pour la Pologne et les pays d'Europe centrale et orientale). Mais il y a une limite: nous n'avons pas la capacité

opposition to the Turkish accession 'first of all for economic reasons', emphasising that the EU doesn't have the 'capacity to absorb a country like Turkey' for which it could not provide sufficient structural and cohesion funds, as it did for its previous members (Rousselin and Paoli 2009).

Figure 5.4: Evaluations on the future project of integration in France and French-speaking Belgium

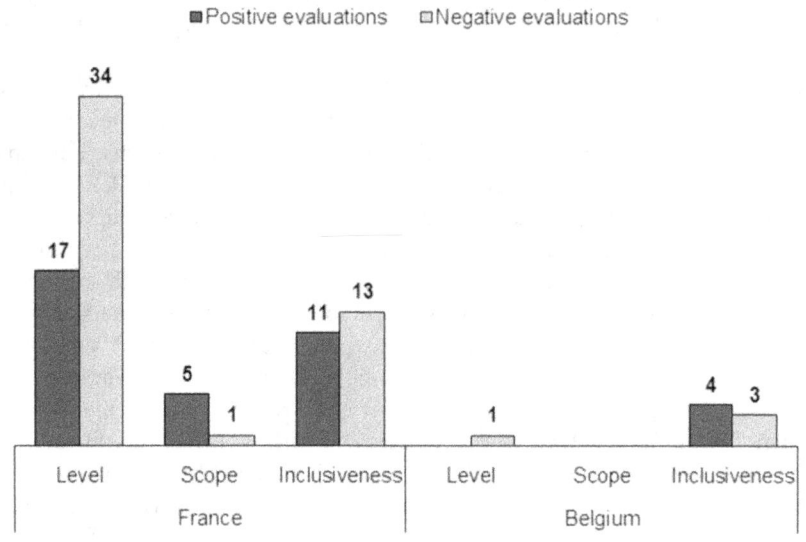

He further mentions cultural reasons and views the EU as 'an original civilization project' which is rooted in Christianity. The debate on Turkish membership is also used to expose the political opponent at the domestic level:

> By defending Turkey's accession to the EU, Lutte Ouvrière in fact supports capitalism in its efforts to deregulate the circulation of the workers'[22] (*Le Monde* 2009d),

---

d'absorber un pays comme la Turquie. Ensuite ma réticence est aussi politique. (Si l'Europe n'a pas de frontière, elle n'est plus l'Europe. Et si on fait entrer la Turquie, au nom de quoi refuser l'Ukraine, la Moldavie, le Maroc ou Israël ? Ce serait une Europe américaine.) Or je continue de penser que l'Europe peut être porteuse d'un projet de civilisation original.'

22. 'En défendant l'entrée de la Turquie en Europe, Lutte Ouvrière soutient le capitalisme dans ses efforts de dérégulation des flux de main d'oeuvre (et est ainsi un allié objectif de la bourgeoisie européenne).'

[...] as President of the Commission he has done everything to bury the political Europe – fervent supporter of Turkey's accession, of the doubtful pipeline Nabuco, etc.[23] (*Le Figaro* 2009c).

Against these highly emotional arguments mobilised by the opponents of enlargement, the accession of Turkey is mainly justified for security and geopolitical reasons. In an interview for *Le Figaro*, Michel Rocard claims that Turkish membership would help create a stable peace in the Asian region and would prevent the country from drifting to radical Islam (*Le Figaro* 2009d). Similarly, the Turkish accession to the EU was the main issue in the debates about the future project of integration in Belgium, with rather balanced positions expressed in favour and against a possible membership of Turkey. However, similar to the French debate over the (un)democratic nature of the EU, this proves to be a surrogate debate, which is *de facto* led by French actors and is merely reproduced by the Belgian media. For instance, it is reported that the UMP politician Michel Barnier, and the socialists, Pierre Moscovici and Michel Rocard (former Prime Minister) support Turkey's accession, the last two even underlining its necessity ('We need Turkey in Europe').

In sum, the debate over the EU as a project corroborates our previous findings, that concerns about the development of the EU institutions and their democratic nature are main concerns. However, the project dimension brings some nuance to this hypothesis, since identity issues emerge as an important theme with respect to the further enlargement of the EU and, more specifically, in connection with Turkish membership. The focus on the justifications invoked for criticising the EU in the next section, sheds more light on the respective importance of the issues of institutions, democracy, social justice and identity.

Justifications: Democracy as a central issue

Democracy is the most recurrent justification for contesting the legitimacy of the EU in French online debates (Figure 5.5). References to the general value of democracy are used, above all, to blame the citizens–elite divide, as exemplified in the extensive power of lobby groups and the exclusion of ordinary citizens from the EU decision-making process. Democracy and social justice in Europe are often treated as interrelated themes. Citizens also frequently use the commenting pages to complain that their voice is not taken into account by EU decision-makers. Especially the perceived disregard of the French 'no', is referred to as a constant reminder of citizens' exclusion. Users accuse, for instance, the 'ultra-liberal' Europe, which provides benefits exclusively to the elite while doing harm to the mass of citizens. The democratic argument also justifies the rejection of the Lisbon

---

23. '[...] en tant que Président de la Commission il a fait tout pour enterrer l' Europe politique, fervent supporteur de l' adhésion Turque, du douteux pipeline Nabuco, que des intérêts américains essaient d'imposer à l'Europe.'

Treaty, which is imposed upon the citizens as a duplicate of the Constitution, in disrespect of the negative vote in 2005. At the same time, the democratic argument is also used to legitimise a federalist vision of Europe with a Commission as a democratic government and a fully empowered European Parliament. This supports our third hypothesis about the convergence of justifications that are used by the proponents and opponents of the integration project.

A significant set of positive claims justifies the legitimacy of European integration in functional terms as a necessity to face collective problems. Most of them advocate a strong and centralised Europe and justify their stance with the need for cooperation in the current era of globalisation. The erosion of nation states' sovereignty by the EU is thus welcomed as the only means to maintaining the decision-making and problem-solving capacities on the world stage:

> In a context of globalization, it is completely unreasonable to want to detach ourselves from an organization that can enable us to have a say on the world stage. Because we have to stop deluding ourselves: the French hegemony is a myth (*Le Soir* 2009),

> It is through a federal pact, defining who does what and engaging all the partners, that, thanks to the subsidiarity principle, we will be able to preserve a certain sovereignty, of course limited, but controlled and guaranteed at the European level, through a federal pact that Europe will be able to function[24] (*Le Figaro* 2009b).

Justifications in terms of necessity can further correlate with positive evaluations of the current state of the EU and of the progress it has brought about (peace, democracy, economic prosperity). The justification based on safety, in contrast, corresponds mostly to negative evaluations highlighting the exclusivist nature of the EU and advocating for a more protective and social Europe. Understood in terms of security and peace, safety is also the main motivation for Michel Rocard's support of Turkish accession which, in his view, will contribute to the stabilisation of peace in the region.

Belgium is the only country covered by our sample where the concern with democracy, as part of the justificatory practices of contesting EU legitimacy, is only secondary. Instead, necessity is found to be the most recurrent justification in contesting EU legitimacy. In the debate on MEPs' wages, for instance, the necessity justification is used to criticise the high expenditure and as admonishment for a more reasonable use of tax money, or conversely, to defend high salaries as a reward for outstanding achievements or as a safeguard from bribery. We explain this functionalist vision of European integration with the specifics of a divided

---

24. 'C'est par un pacte fédéral, définissant qui fait quoi, engageant tous les partenaires, que, grâce au principe de subsidiarité, nous pourrons conserver une souveraineté, certes limitée, mais contrôlée et garantie au plan européen, par le pacte fédéral, que l'Europe pourra fonctionner.'

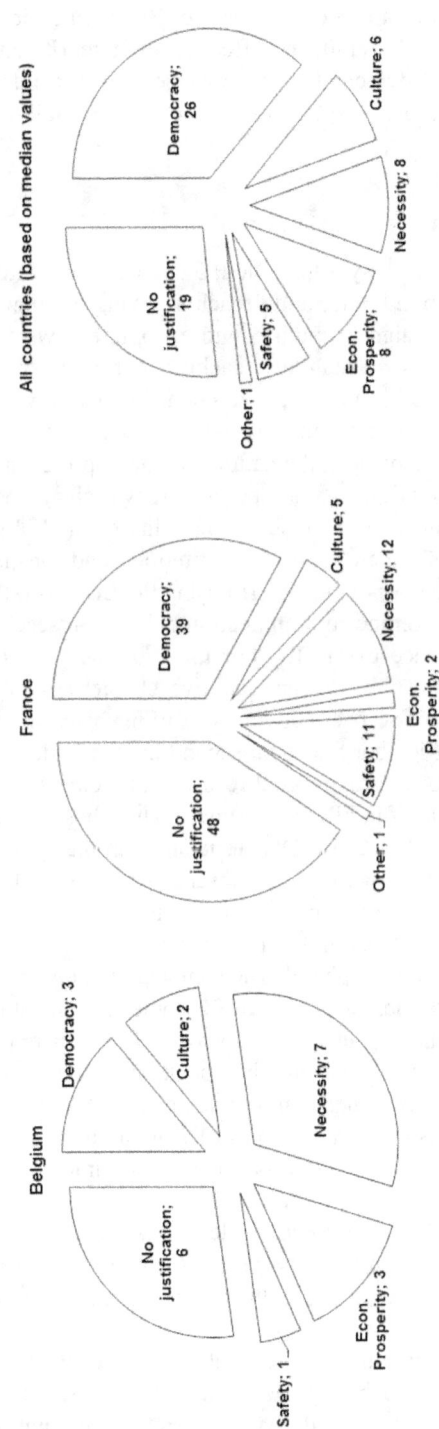

Figure 5.5: Explaining opinions: How EU polity evaluations were justified in France and Belgium

country that, in addition, hosts the capital of Europe. For Belgian politicians and citizens alike, the EU has a tangible stabilising effect on the integrity and well-being of their own country and democratic concerns become secondary. Our sample of French-speaking news sites and blogs is, however, too small to further corroborate this thesis.

Conclusions: the memory of the public sphere

The purpose of this chapter was to analyse how the EU and European integration are publicly contested on the web in France and French-speaking Belgium during the 2009 European election campaign. In both countries, online news coverage concerning the EP elections was substantial, reaching not only small user communities but a mass audience in the respective countries. The investigation of the most visited information websites and political blogs supports three main hypotheses regarding the public resonance, the nature and the implications of EU online debates. The first main finding is that although there was significant news coverage of the election campaigns and its results, the polity of the EU was not significantly contested in terms of principle, current institutional and constitutional setup, and future project. The number of claims criticising the EU was rather low and the analysis of the content of online communication points at a 'second order debate', since neither the existence of the EU nor the substance of European policies were discussed. As shown in the comparative chapter, Belgium and France reflect the low and high end respectively in terms of intensity of debate of a convergence across most EU Member States on second-order election debates. This confirms the findings of focus group-based research that citizens, in Paris as in Brussels, display an attitude of indifference rather than of hostility towards European integration (Duchesne *et al.* 2010; Duchesne and Van Ingelgom 2008). As far as the 2009 EP election is concerned, the absence of strong polarisation over integration could be explained by suboptimal conditions for the advancement of Eurohostile or Eurocritical discourses. In France, so-called Eurosceptic parties were numerous, but fragmented and peripheral. The campaign mainly turned into oppositional politics with the President at the mirror of domestic contention. The low frequency of criticism of the EU in French-speaking Belgium reflects the peripheral role of Eurosceptic actors. Their marginal position within the political spectrum also accounts for their low salience in public debates. As confirmed by the election results, Euroscepticism in France and in Belgium has a low profile. European election did not offer a favourable political opportunity for smaller Eurosceptic parties, which stepped forward with new groupings but were not rewarded with voters' attention. On the contrary, the clearest winner of the elections in France was the pro-European green list, *Europe-Ecologie*, which campaigned by advocating a more integrated EU at the political, social and environmental level.

Looking more closely at contentious statements about the EU, it appears that the legacy of the 2005 referendum debate plays a crucial role in structuring the campaign over EU integration in France and serves as a reference point for both political parties and citizens (*see also* Chapter Eight on the Netherlands). The Belgian debate contrasts this nicely and shows the difficulties with launching EU debates in a rather apathetic political context. Frequent references to the French debate, then became a substitute for the absence of domestic political contestation. Thus, the French 2005 referendum resonated strongly over time within France, but less so across space to French-speaking Belgium. This chapter, therefore, does not provide evidence that nation-state specific contentious episodes provide catalysts for convergence in EU polity contestation across Europe.

The distinction between the different dimensions of Euroscepticism – the principle of cooperation, the current EU polity, integration as a project for the future – allows for a more nuanced analysis of the targets of EU polity contestation. While the EU or European integration is not contested in principle – but, on the contrary, often welcomed – the nature of the current EU polity, and the future of the EU project, are the object of criticism by political actors and citizens. This supports our second hypothesis that EU debates do not so much invoke questions of identity and the loss of sovereignty, but rather on justifications based on distrust towards the EU institutions, as well as the intertwined themes of democracy and social justice. In France, the predominantly negative evaluations of the EU clearly target market-based integration and the promotion of a neoliberal agenda at the expense of social policies and the exclusion of ordinary citizens. Overall, EU criticism focuses at the exclusive and undemocratic nature of the European integration process. In this respect, the EU Commission and its President epitomise, for many citizens, the bureaucratic and neoliberal face of integration. Furthermore, the 2005 referendum has imprinted a strong mark with respect to the organisation of EU debates in France, in light of which, the Parliamentary ratification of the Lisbon Treaty was often denounced as a negation of democracy. However, social and democratic issues cannot be entirely disentangled from identity themes. The Turkish accession to the EU crystallises the fears related to the boundaries of the future EU polity, which are particularly fuelled by the anti-Islam and xenophobic discourse of the French far right.

In Belgium, controversial debates about the EU were much less present. A Eurocritical voice mainly takes the form of institutional distrust towards the EU and its political personnel. The populist theme of greedy MEPs or EU bureaucrats wasting the tax payers' money, is the most identifiable element of a Eurosceptic discourse. All in all, these themes converge in the diagnosis of an elitist and exclusive EU. These findings are in line with the literature which has emphasised economic and social fears, as well as institutional distrust as the main sources of Euroscepticism in France and French-speaking Belgium. In France, the *Front National* and the sovereignist parties of the far right (such as Philippe De Villiers' party and the traditionalist hunters' party *Chasse, Pêche, Nature et Traditions*) have also engaged massively with the anti-liberal discourse and the advocacy of economic protectionism and the defence of the French social model.

The debates in France and French-speaking Belgium feature similar justifications to defend opposed views on integration. Starting from the criticism of the democratic deficit and the lack of efficiency of the EU institutional arrangement, more – instead of less – integration often seems desirable. Indeed, the EU is both accused of eroding the national sovereignty of its Member States and seen as the only possible way of preserving effective government with regard to globalisation. Its federalisation is denounced by some as the end of national democracies, while being presented by others as the sole means of transforming the EU into a true democracy. Similar criticism might reflect the cognitive difficulty for the citizens to acknowledge the legitimacy of a hybrid political system, which is stuck half way between a confederation of sovereign states and a supranational federation.

Finally, the comparative aspect of the chapter provides for interesting insights. One main difference in the dynamics of the campaign in France and French-speaking Belgium is that visibility, articulation and resonance of Eurosceptic themes, and actors in France, were mainly fed by references to the rejection of the ECT. The ratification of the Lisbon Treaty is seen as defying the 'no' vote in 2005 and thus, became a major issue of resentment among political actors as well as citizens involved in political communication in the electronic public sphere. This is arguably a hint that research should pay more attention to the longitudinal dynamics of EU polity contestation. Present and future discursive constructions and re-constructions of a critical discourse over European integration or, in other words, the various actors' ability to 'perform' Euroscepticism are marked by previous political moments and collective experiences that constitute the legacies of the national public sphere. Such path dependencies explain that the dynamics of EU polity contestation as it unfolds through a new medium, such as the internet, remain nevertheless specific to the political culture of the nation state.

Chapter Six | Contending European Integration in Germany: From Permissive Consensus to Moderate Euroscepticism

Throughout its history, the Federal Republic of Germany has understood itself as the 'motor of integration', the 'prig' of the European Union (Lees 2008: 17). A pro-European attitude was consistent with Germany's post-war understanding as a 'tamed' and semi-sovereign nation state that sought strong European and trans-Atlantic partnerships. Political elites were socialised through an ideology of 'progressive Europeanism', that perceived European integration primarily as a project of free market expansion, and thus as a playing field for the expanding economic miracle (*Wirtschaftswunder*), but secondarily, also as the vehicle for the consolidation of democratic culture within German society (Ash 1993). According to this ideology, European integration assumed a moral value of its own and any further step of deepening or widening remained unchallenged (Trenz 2007b). Progressive Europeanism has also been reflected in school curricula and in the mainstream media, accounting for the broad consensus on European integration that was successfully conveyed from economic, political and cultural elites, to the population at large (Teschner 2000).

Among mainstream political parties, opposition to the project of European integration has been moderate, and has been either motivated by the defence of regionalist autonomy, as in the case of the Bavarian Christian Socialist Union (CSU) or, more recently, by left-wing opposition to liberal market Europe as represented by the Left Party (*Die Linke* – founded as the merger of the Party for Democratic Socialism – PDS, and the Electoral Alternative for Labour and Social Justice – WASG). The checks and balances system of German federalism makes it, however, rather unlikely that extreme political positions are incorporated into government policy (Bräuninger and König 1999). A veto-player-based system between the Bundestag and the Bundesrat ensures consensus-oriented policy. Opposition to the process of European integration has, therefore, been mainly restricted to particular policies but has rarely encompassed the wider polity dimension in terms of the fundamental decisions of widening and deepening of the EU.

In this chapter, we explore whether the German consensus on European integration is still upheld or whether EU politics in Germany, like in other Member States, are becoming more contested. If progressive Europeanism can be considered as an elite ideology that sustains European integration (Haller 2008b), the consensus can be broken up in basically two ways: first, we would expect a growing degree of elite contestation with choices for European integration becoming more conflictive within, and between, political parties. Secondly, and only partially related to this, we would expect a growing contentiousness of European integration in unfolding public and media debates. Media conflicts on

European integration could either correlate with partisan contestation, or, offer an alternative forum for the expression of discomfort with European integration, against the persisting partisan consensus.

By choosing 2009 EP election campaign as our object of analysis, we can investigate the dynamics of partisan contestation in relation to other forms of mobilisation or the expression of political discontent that becomes salient in the media. In doing so, we do not look at the character of EP elections as 'secondary elections' (i.e. contesting domestic issues) but at the forms and degrees of contesting EU-polity choices and the potential impact these may have on the EU's legitimacy. Does Germany's traditional role as a motor of integration still hold valid in public debates evolving around the European project, or do we observe important resistance that could possibly constrain the governmental preferences for deepened integration? To approach this question, we first provide a historical outline of German debates on European integration and the patterns of support of, and opposition to, European integration. The substantial empirical part of the chapter is devoted to the carriers and varieties of EU polity contestation in public debates during the European Parliament election campaigns in 2009. In the concluding part, we assess whether there is a shift towards Euroscepticism in the traditionally pro-European German public discourse, and how this relates to the experiences of public debates in other countries, and the general development of the EU.

Profiling Euroscepticism in Germany

Shifting public opinion?

The turning point of Germany's overall supportive attitude of European integration is usually indicated with the unification in 1990. Busch and Knelangen (2004: 86) show, on the basis of Eurobarometer, that public opinion has shifted considerably throughout the nineties from an overwhelmingly supportive, to a more negative stance. On the one hand, this shift in public opinion would confirm the thesis that Euroscepticism is responsive. It responds to the deepening of integration, the empowerment of supranational institutions that cannot easily be held accountable by national electorates and, in particular, the introduction of the single currency that was perceived as a threat to economic stability in the country (Teschner 2000). On the other hand, the German case also indicates the impact of domestic change on perceptions of European integration. Euroscepticism would thus reflect the new self-confidence of a unified Germany. Traditional justifications of European integration, as a protective shield against communism, have lost significance. For a new generation of Germans, the European project is no longer needed as a 'substitute identity', while at the same time, the financial burden of unification has affected the willingness to unconditionally support European integration.

Following Eurobarometer, the decline of support of European integration commenced after an all-time peak in 1990 with the lowest levels of support measured in 2000 and again in 2005. The EU became more unpopular to the extent that it became more salient. The deepening and widening of integration and, in particular, the creation of a common currency and Eastern enlargement generated diffuse fears among the population and did not, as it was envisaged, enhance trust, solidarity and shared identity among the Europeans (Risse 2003). The choice of the EU for more openness and shared responsibilities was not a popular choice in the first place and it was badly communicated to the citizens, justified by functional constraints rather than a democratically legitimate decision (e.g. through a referendum).

Public opinion is thus a reliable indicator for new social and cultural cleavages as they became salient in the course of European integration. The citizens–elite divide was however less pronounced in Germany than in other Member States and degrees of public approval of the achievements of the EU and the general goals of integration remained at a comparatively high level. We also observe strong oscillations of public support with European integration in relatively short time periods. In line with the argumentation of this book, we can explain such fluctuations with heightened public and media attention. In the autumn of 2008, for instance, when EU politics were a low-profile issue, Eurobarometer reports high levels of support with almost two thirds of the respondents evaluating membership of Germany in the EU as a good thing (see Eurobarometer 2009a). Only one year later, in the middle of the financial crisis, support had dropped considerably to about 13 per cent. Nonetheless, there is a stable majority of the population which believes that Germany has benefited from membership in the EU. There is thus no indication that support of European integration will collapse, but rather public opinion indicates the increased contentiousness of European politics that is linked to single events.

Enhanced partisan mobilisation?

Despite the general decline in public support of European integration, political parties have posed no serious threat to European pathway decisions, like the introduction of the Euro or major EU treaty reforms in Maastricht, Nice, the Constitutional Treaty and ultimately Lisbon. Among the parties represented in parliament, only the ex-Communist party, *Die Linke*, voted consistently against all treaty changes (Busch and Knelangen 2004: 88). The pro-and anti-European cleavage structure thus remains latent and is not manifested in partisan contestation. The mainstreaming of Euroscepticism in the form of anti-elitist or nationalist opposition against European integration has not (yet) taken place. Euroscepticism remains a phenomenon of political parties at the extreme fringes of the political spectrum, as far as the national parliament is concerned.

However, hard Euroscepticism has been successfully mobilised in regional elections and has repeatedly helped right-wing extremist parties (National Democratic Party of Germany, NPD; The German People's Union, DVU and *Republikaner*) to pass the five per cent threshold to enter the regional parliaments. The anti-European campaigns were particularly successful in mobilisation against the single currency in the nineties and against enlargement in 2000–2005. The same topics also stipulated the expression of soft Euroscepticism as a minority position within the mainstream political parties, most notably within the Bavarian CSU. *Die Linke* as well, can be classified as soft-Europeanist, rejecting the current structures of market liberalism and campaigning for an alternative social Europe. In ideological terms and in terms of campaigning styles, left-wing and right-wing populism show remarkable similarities, both mobilising against the liberal market Europe and against shared sovereignty (Hartleb 2008: 22).

Media populism

As repeatedly stressed throughout this book, the mass media, more than any political actor, have a potential to shape citizens' attitudes on European integration on a large scale.[1] To improve our understanding of the diffusion of Euroscepticism, we do not only need to analyse the mass media as an amplifier of Eurosceptic campaigning of political parties: in addition, our survey is designed in a way to take into consideration the media's own voice in framing and commenting upon European integration. There is thus, an active role for the mass media in the development of Euroscepticism that needs to be taken into consideration.

Do mass media or specific media segments in Germany account for a spread of Eurosceptic opinion, in absence of significant partisan mobilisation? At a first glance, the case of Germany is rather ambiguous. As a matter of fact, existing surveys have found that the German quality press has remained impartial, for instance, in the coverage of EU constitutional debates during the ratification of the EU Constitutional Treaty (Trenz *et al.* 2009) but, nevertheless, displayed a rather positive framing towards European integration in general (Eilders *et al.* 2004; Trenz 2007b). Tabloid newspapers, on the other hand, have repeatedly stepped forward as campaigners against EU enlargement or against the Euro, representing a popular voice, which is rarely expressed by political parties. The public opinion market, which is delivered by tabloid newspapers, develops a dynamic of EU-contestation which is not part of 'politics' as represented in the Parliaments. At the same time, we observe a high concentration of the power of public opinion-making, which is monopolised by one single newspaper, the *Bild-Zeitung*, which serves almost four million readers and is Germany's most widely circulating newspaper. Since anti-European campaigning is rarely instigated or amplified by mainstream political parties, the *Bild-Zeitung* is rather a lone campaigner, mainly evoking strong emotions through headlines and slogans but providing little substantiated information on EU politics. In fact, the paper is fond of its populist crusades, not only against the European Union, but also against politicians of all stripes, against foreign workers or Islam (Klein 2000).

---

1. See, in particular Chapter One, and, for the case of Germany see Adam 2009.

Impact of online news-making on EU polity contestation

In light of these aspects of German Euroscepticism, we hypothesise that political news-making and commenting through the internet has gained in relevance for shaping public opinion and attitudes on European integration. The impact of online news coverage on EU polity contestation is analysed in terms of two possible effects. One possibility is that we find a replication of the general permissive consensus on EU politics that is found in partisan contestation and that is, partly, also underlying public opinion and offline media coverage. Online debates would thus not substantially deviate from traditional offline media.

The other possibility, however, is that online media contributes to the unfolding of a new contentious logic. This fundamentally challenges the legitimacy of the EU and gives expression to citizen protest. Online media would then provide new participatory and interactive news formats that would be dominantly used for the spread of Euroscepticism.

To test our hypotheses, we drew data from the three most prominent, professional journalism websites (*Spiegel.Online*, *Bild.de*, and *Sueddeutsche Zeitung*) and the two most popular, independent political blogs in Germany (*Bildblog* and *PI-news*).[2] The three professional news sites are run by the most widely distributed offline newspapers and weeklies in Germany and include both quality and tabloid style news formats. In contrast to the offline media market, which is dominated by the very influential tabloid *Bild-Zeitung*, the online news offer is more diversified and dominated by quality journalism. Quality news, distributed by *Spiegel Online*, is the most popular online (Alexa rank 9), whereas tabloid style popular news is distributed online through *Bild.de* rank second (Alexa rank 13). The two subsequent news sites in the ranking (rank 42: *Sueddeutsche Zeitung* and rank 47: *Die Welt*) indicate a clear preference of the average internet user for quality news.

The 2009 EP election campaign in context

With regard to the three ideal types of EU legitimacy debates identified in the introduction of the book, the German debate certainly reflects the main features of a second-order debate. The German European Parliamentary election campaign was characterised by indifference and low-key campaigns on behalf of the political parties. The interest in the EP elections might have further decreased due to election fatigue: 2009 was the 'super election year' (*Superwahljahr*), with no less than fifteen regional and national elections, including the EP elections in June and the National Parliament elections in September. In this context, EP elections ranked only as 'second order' (Reif and Schmitt 1980) and were considered by political parties as a prelude of the Bundestag election campaigns. On the other hand, the particularities of the 2009 EP elections in Germany might have enhanced partisan contestation but certainly did not help to put EU politics central stage.

---

2. The representativeness of the sample was checked using site rankings and blog rankings using alexa.com (Alexa Internet 2009) and wahlradar.de (Linkfluence 2012).

The second-order character of the elections is largely reflected in the content of online campaigning. With just 108 evaluative statements found through random sampling, the salience and density of EU polity contestation is low compared with the other countries in our survey. In contrast to countries like Austria or the UK, the legitimacy of European integration is not fundamentally challenged in EP election campaigns. Not existential debates, but second-order debates are dominant in the German context. More specifically, around 60 per cent of all German articles examined covered domestic party politics while the topics of European integration and European party politics featured in just 10 per cent of the sampled material. There was also no clear difference between quality and tabloid news-making in covering EU politics. As Table 6.1 illustrates, the professional journalism websites of *Der Spiegel* and *Sueddeutsche Zeitung*, and the tabloid *Bild-Zeitung*, cover approximately the same range of issues. Political blogs do not present any substantial difference in terms, for instance, of addressing more plural topics but rather mirror the offline debates. The salience of EU news and the density of debates in political blogs is, however, considerably lower than in professional news media. Blogs offer only a limited choice of selected EU news and cannot guarantee a full coverage of the election campaigns. Specific EU issues and debates are thus predominantly published by professional quality news sites. The most renowned newspapers reproduce online the full range of news provided offline and offer free access to their products.

While patterns of news consumption remain identical, the tabloid *Bild.de* is more engaged in journalistic opinion-making on European integration and also, user interaction is more frequent than on professional journalism news sites. This tendency of tabloid newsmakers to raise the popular voice and provoke respective responses by the population on the internet, accounts for the overall more negative tone of debates on *Bild.de* and an affinity with moderate Euroscepticism. *Bild.de* is successful in activating the largest number of users to comment on the EU. In this sense, the user forum of *Bild.de* becomes a public site to express discontent against the EU and against political elites in general. Media populism, as an amplifying factor for Euroscepticism is, however, less pronounced in Germany than in the UK or in Austria, where it is constantly fed by political parties. This qualifies our hypothesis of online news-media as an alternative platform of anti-European mobilisation.

Apart from the presentation of national parties' platforms, two issues stand out in regard to Euroscepticism. Firstly, all German news sites provide substantial coverage on EP campaigning in other EU Member States (see Table 6.1). Looking more closely at the content of such foreign news, the electoral success of nationalist and extreme right parties in other EU countries, is of special newsworthiness. All three main news sites critically evaluate the rise of Euroscepticism all over Europe. They report on the campaigning of the *Liste Hans-Peter Martin* and the FPÖ in Austria, of the UK Independence Party (UKIP) and the British National Party (BNP) in the United Kingdom and of Geert Wilders' *Freedom Party* in the Netherlands. Euroscepticism and right-wing nationalism is thus discussed as an external problem, to which Germany should nevertheless pay close attention. A

Table 6.1: Debating the EU online: Topics of the German articles

Number of articles referring to the EP elections	Website					
Topic	Spiegel Online	Bild.de	Sued-deutsche.de	Bildblog	Politically-Incorrect	Total
Domestic party politics	9	8	7	1	5	30
Other Member States' party politics	4	3	2	1	4	14
European party politics	-	1	1	-	2	4
National economy	-	-	-	-	-	-
European economy	-	-	-	-	-	-
European integration	-	-	2	-	1	3
Membership/ enlargement	-	-	-	-	-	-
Democracy	-	-	-	-	-	-
Other	-	-	-	-	-	-
Total number of articles	13	12	12	2	12	51

new understanding is developed here which sees Germany in a role as a critical observer of the integration process, with a mission to prevent extremism and the spread of anti-democratic sentiments all over Europe.

As German politicians (especially EU politicians) sometimes directly intervene in the debates in other Member States,[3] the media monitor Germany's neighbouring countries and warn against the threat of extremism. In this respect, Germany turns from being the motor of integration to the saviour of the European idea. By externalising Euroscepticism, it is nevertheless accepted that the choices of the electorates in other Member States matter.

---

3. The MEP and leader of the European socialists Martin Schulz commented on the Austrian campaigns in an interview with the *Financial Times* by stating that 'the "FPÖ" speaks the language of the Third Reich' (*Financial Times* 2009).

Secondly, the all-time low turnout in Germany drew considerable attention in the media and gave rise to the expression of concern with the state of democracy in Europe. Journalists discuss possible reasons for this indifference by the voters and interpret abstention as a possible expression of latent Eurosceptic attitudes of large parts of the population. Here, Euroscepticism is seen as resulting from insufficient campaigning by domestic and European actors, who do not reach the electorate and behave in an elitist way. Poignantly, the tabloid *BILD* (Blome 2009) asks: 'Europe is not sexy – but why?' The 'whose fault' debate is one of the few examples of internalising Euroscepticism, which is no longer seen as a problem that primarily affects other Member States but more as a systemic problem of EU legitimacy. The reasons for voters' indifference are searched in the deficits of Parliamentary democracy and can, therefore, not be attributed to single parties.[4]

The campaign, as well as the connected debate, made it clearly visible that the upcoming election for the German Parliament had already cast a shadow on the election for the European Parliament: 'For the first time since 1994 [the European election] takes place in the same year as the election to the Bundestag. The European elections are obviously more overshadowed than usual; it is a test vote for autumn' (*Süddeutsche.de* 2009).[5]

In the shadow of the German Parliamentarian elections, the debates in the context of EP elections did rarely touch European topics in substance but clearly focused on national issues. Only the international financial and economic crises, its effects on the European economy and the financial market as well as alternative ways out of the crisis were discussed with some frequency. Chancellor Angela Merkel underlined the importance of a united Europe to overcome the crisis: 'If someone wants to prevent that such debacle ever occurs on the European financial market again, eighty million Germans only have a little influence, the Chancellor said. In contrast 500 million Europeans have a strong voice in the world [...]'[6] (*Bild.de* 2009a). 'The economic crisis is of course [...] the main topic in Chancellor Angela Merkel's campaign speeches, which she holds normally alongside with the President of the European Parliament Hans-Gert Pöttering'[7] (*Bild.de* 2009a).

---

4. The *Süddeutsche Zeitung* (Winter 2009), for example states: 'The EU is in acute danger to perish due to indifference and egoism.'
5. Translation from the original: 'Denn zum ersten Mal seit 1994 findet sie wieder im gleichen Jahr mit einer Bundestagswahl statt. Noch eindeutiger als sonst ist die Europawahl deshalb eine Wahl im Schatten, sie ist ein Stimmungstest für den Herbst.'
6. 'Wenn man verhindern wolle, dass sich solch ein Debakel an den Finanzmärkten wiederhole, könnten die 80 Millionen Deutschen allein wenig ausrichten, argumentiert die Kanzlerin. Die 500 Millionen Europäer hätten dagegen zusammen eine starke Stimme in der Welt.'
7. 'Die Wirtschaftskrise ist natürlich auch das Hauptthema in Merkels Wahlkampfreden, die sie in der Regel an der Seite von Europaparlamentspräsident Hans-Gert Pöttering (CDU) bestreitet.'

The German debate further reveals a self-reflective potential, in which media and political analysts critically reflect the nature of the EU in light of the low salience of the elections. In this context, quality journalists step forward with a more thorough analysis of the causes of the voters' indifference. This can be interpreted as an attempt to popularise scientific explanations such as second-order elections, the scapegoating of the European Union or the lack of participatory elements. The European public sphere deficit acquires its own news value as a catchphrase for commenting upon the course of European integration. In some instances, also solutions are discussed like the proposal of the Commissioner Verheugen for the enhanced use of direct democracy in order to involve citizens in EU politics (Bolesch and Gammelin 2009). MEP Schulz bemoans the disappearance of a 'European gut feeling' which could be strengthened by the use of European symbols (Beste and Kurbjuweit 2009). After the elections, *BILD* postulates: 'Low Turnout. Introduce Compulsory Voting!' (Ronzheimer 2009a).

As in all other countries covered by our sample, a substantial debate, i.e. a focus on the EU issues at stake in the elections, is lacking. Milestone decisions like institutional reform of the EU and the new role of the European Parliament within the institutional architecture of Lisbon are rarely mentioned as part of electoral campaigning. In equal terms, references to European party politics, to manifestos of the European party coalitions and their campaigns during the elections are absent.

The primary campaigning strategy of the two main competing parties, the CDU and the Social Democratic Party of Germany (SPD), was to bring their candidates for the Chancellorship in position. Both parties campaigned with the portraits of their leaders, Chancellor Angela Merkel and her SPD-challenger Frank-Walter Steinmeier – also Minister of Foreign Affairs and Vice-Chancellor of the grand coalition of CDU and SPD. MEP candidates who actually stood for election, remained in the background; even the two German front persons of the European People Party and of the European Socialists, Hans-Gert Pöttering (CDU) and Martin Schulz (SPD), were barely mentioned. In line with this strategy to use EP campaigning as a prelude to the general elections to be held in September the same year, the dominant contestants in the German 2009 EP online campaigns were – unsurprisingly – national political parties. Other collective actors, such as economic interest groups or civil society organisations, did not appear as contestants of EU legitimacy. EU actors and institutions remained equally invisible. The German tabloid press wrote to this effect:

> Do you know this man? Two kind gentlemen take a walk. One of them is the Minister of Foreign Affairs Frank-Walter Steinmeier (53) – but who is the other one? The SPD delegate Martin Schulz (53) is already member of the European Parliament since 1994. Anyway, hardly anybody knows him![8] (*Bild. de* 2009b).

---

8. 'Kennen Sie diesen Mann? Zwei nette Herren gehen spazieren. Einer von ihnen ist Bundesaußenminister Frank-Walter Steinmeier (53) – aber wer ist der andere? Der SPD-

Figure 6.1: Distribution of EU polity evaluations across countries: German contributions per actor

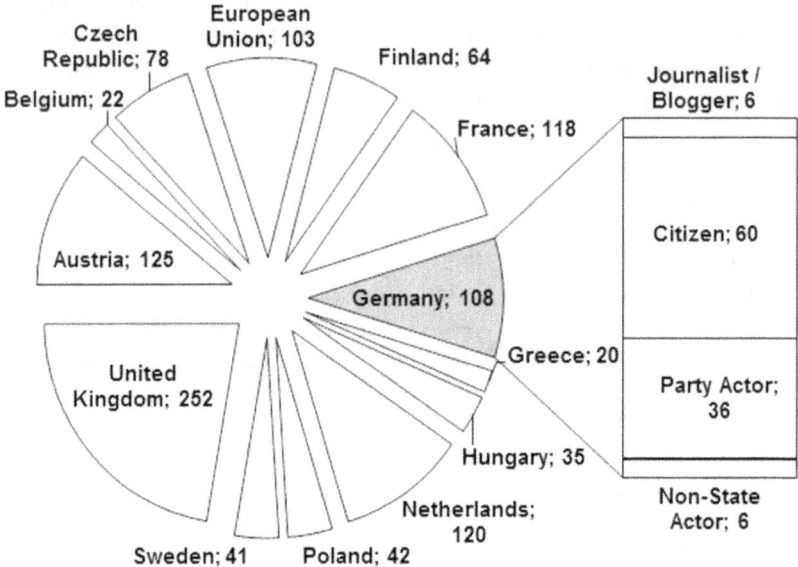

The most regular contestants of EU legitimacy in the online public sphere were, however, not political parties but individual citizens and EU evaluative statements were mainly found on the commenting pages of the news sites, and not in the main articles (see Figure 6.1). This is in line with the findings from other countries comprising our survey and indicates the potential of online media to enable the citizens' voice, which is largely absent from offline media debates. In addition, citizens use the online forums predominantly to raise fundamental concerns over EU legitimacy which are not taken up by mainstream political parties. Online debates thus convey the image of a situation of misrepresentation between political elites and citizens. In the next section, we analyse more closely how these online forums were used to express dissatisfaction with the EU and to spread Euroscepticism.

Europaabgeordnete Martin Schulz (53) gehört bereits seit 1994 dem Europäischen Parlament an. Trotzdem: Kaum einer kennt ihn!'

Dimensions of EU polity evaluation

The 'principle of integration' as the widest, most fundamental and most general way of transmitting an opinion on European Integration, is only exceptionally put into question in the German debate. The majority of the actors (thirteen) defended the principle of integration in a way that confirms the permissive consensus: 'Many people basically support the idea of European Integration. We live in an area of peace, security and wealth'[9] (Helmes 2009). Yet, a small number of statements (seven) could be found, which opposed European integration categorically.

The 'project of integration' is discussed less critically in the German context than in other countries included in our sample. German actors were still more optimistic with regard to the possibilities for the future development of European integration. The deepening of cooperation by the Lisbon Treaty was generally welcomed (scope positive: thirteen statements), especially with regard to the expansion of social policies and the new framework for security and foreign policies. In response to the financial crisis, the regulation of the financial market was also regarded as an important future task for the EU. Future enlargement, and, in particular, a possible accession of Turkey, were strongly opposed (inclusiveness negative: nine statements), while the improved possibility of citizen participation under the forthcoming Lisbon Treaty was welcomed (eight statements). Only a few EU polity evaluations contested the level of future integration (three positive and four negative), indicating that the delegation of sovereignty and the distribution of power within the EU polity were not seen as problematic.

Dominantly negative evaluations can, however, be found with regard to the current EU institutional set-up, which is most heavily contested in EU debates in Germany. Like in other countries covered by our survey, the way the EU is currently governed gave rise to the expression of deep dissatisfaction by both political actors and citizens. The vast majority of participants expressed negative opinions about the way decision-making power is distributed between EU institutions and national governments, as well as among the different EU institutions (twenty-seven evaluations). Contributors to this debate underlined the undemocratic features of the EU and saw themselves confronted with an abstract political power cycle, which was not accessible for ordinary citizens. Especially in citizens' comments can such negative evaluations be found. The European Parliament was described as an undemocratic and powerless institution with a low level of citizens' trust. 'A parliament without a governing party, an opposition or a government'[10] (Helmes 2009); '[...] the EU Parliament a puppet, final depot for scrapped politicians [...]' [11] (Politically-Incorrect 2009a).

---

9. 'Sehr viele Menschen in Europa stimmen der europäischen Idee grundsätzlich zu. Wir leben in einem Raum von Frieden, Sicherheit und Wohlstand.'
10. 'Ein Parlament ohne Regierunsparteien, keine Opposition, keine Regierung.'
11. '[...] das sg. Europarlament ist ein Popanz, Endlagerstätte für abgehalfterte Parteifuzzis [...].'

In contrast to debates in the UK, for instance, this criticism is often expressed with the intention to further strengthen EU authority. Here, the target is not the EU as a superstate with power-hungry officials (see Chapter Ten for the UK case) but the national governments, who are not ready to delegate further competences to the EU and to empower the European Parliament. This shows that EU contestation can be salient in different contexts and even target the same processes, but nevertheless, reflect contrary visions of EU legitimacy. Following our categorisation of EU polity contestation, we would qualify this debate as alter-European.

Another recurrent pattern of EU-criticism focused on the exclusive character and the elitist bias of EU decision making. The inclusiveness of the current EU institutional set-up was evaluated negatively in twenty-two cases. Contrary to other countries in our sample (e.g. Austria), where such criticism frequently questioned the belonging of the new Member States as full and equal members of the European club, the German debate mainly focused on the lack of opportunities for citizens' participation. Especially, the European Commission became a target for citizens' commenting, on the one hand bemoaning its elitist character (example of a negative evaluation on inclusiveness), on the other hand complaining about excesses of bureaucratisation, or the single focus on market liberalisation that was not balanced by social policies (negative evaluation on scope, altogether fourteen statements): 'Bisky views the EU as the motor of neoliberalism' (Fischer 2009).[12]

Cross tabulation of these three dimensions of EU polity evaluation reveals the low argumentative complexity of EU legitimacy debates. In most cases, EU evaluative statements remain one-dimensional, i.e. only focusing on single aspects like criticising the democratic deficit but not pointing at possible reforms. Contributions to the debate therefore frequently transmit an image of fatalism, of citizens being exposed to the arbitrariness of EU power. Exit (i.e. abstention) and not voice, is then seen as the only alternative: 'These political puppets see in each vote just a legitimation for their pseudo-parliamentarianism. That is why I don't vote!'[13] (*Spiegel Online* 2009a). 'What should you vote for? They just squander our taxes and the result is just rubbish. Nobody cares whether the cucumber is sold 24 or 25 cm long. You don't need to support this idiocy!'[14] (Ronzheimer 2009b).

---

12. 'Bisky sieht die EU als "Motor des Neoliberalismus".'
13. 'Jede Stimme wird von diesen Politdarstellern nur als Legitimation ihres Pseudo-Parlamentarismus verstanden und deswegen kriegen sie auch keine von mir.'
14. 'Was soll man da wählen, die verprassen doch nur unsere steuergelder und sonst kommt doch nur müll raus.das interessiert doch keinen ob die gurke mit 24 oder 25 cm verkauft werden soll, da muss man doch diesen schwachsinn nicht noch fördern.'

Qualifying Euroscepticism: Justifications

As in all countries in our survey, the primary concern driving online evaluations of the EU in Germany is democracy. Almost half of justifications were based on democratic values and governance. In distant second place, we find justifications pertaining to safety (20 per cent) and economic prosperity (8 per cent). This slightly deviates from the overall pattern of justifications at cross-national level, where the EU is recurrently justified in functional terms or with reference to the efficiency of governance arrangements (see Figure 6.2). Germans are more concerned with the economic performance of the European common market and the single currency, than with the scope of regulatory policies and well-functioning administrations. We further find a relatively high share of non-reasoned arguments, which we interpret as an indicator of the low contentiousness of the German debate. In most cases, contestants, who put the legitimacy of the EU into question, remain unchallenged.

Figure 6.2: Explaining opinions: how EU polity evaluations were justified in Germany

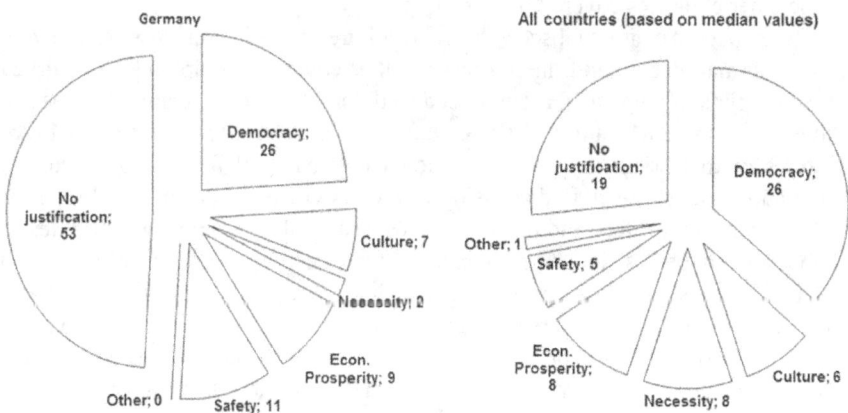

In light of the traditional framing of European integration as a way to mark a distance to the nationalist past (Bude 1992; Díez Medrano 2003), one would expect that German media debates back a federalist vision of EU-democracy while, at the same time, dismissing an exclusivist notion of culture and national identity. The overall dominance of justifications relating to democracy supports this interpretation. Debates about the democratic deficit have a long tradition in Germany and have been a driving force of journalism in interpreting the EU. As part of the dominant attitude of progressive Europeanism, this criticism was mainly paired with support for proposals of deep democratic reform, delegation of competences of democratic control to the supranational level and a promotion of federalism (Jachtenfuchs 2002; Trenz 2007b).

In the 2009 election campaign, political claimants, including MEP candidates, who campaigned around this issue spread optimism with regard to the possibility of implementing democratic reform and signalled their hope for a more democratic EU with the coming into force of the Lisbon Treaty. This hope was particularly linked to the new possibility for citizen referenda. The prime candidate of the Free Democratic Party, Silvana Koch-Mehrin, for instance, tried to raise her profile with the promotion of more direct forms of democracy (Fischer 2009). This emphasis in the campaign on participation as the primary way of democratic reform can be also interpreted as a disregard of representative (Parliamentarian) democracy, which the EP elections ultimately stood for.

Concerns with democracy were expressed, above all, in citizens' comments. In general, citizens hold a less nuanced and also a less optimistic view on democratic reforms and base their complaints on some commonly held clichés about the undemocratic character of the EU: '[…] powerless European Parliament, which only serves as overpaid façade for the virtual dictatorship of the EU Commission'[15] (*Spiegel Online* 2009a). In similar terms, mistrust in the representativeness of European governing institutions was also given expression in citizens' comments in the other countries covered by our sample.

References to contextualised values and culture, instead, figure less prominently in the German debate and, in contrast to other countries comprising our survey (e.g. Austria and Hungary), are not used to defend the nation against Europe but rather to promote a cultural vision of Europe (e.g. references to the plurality of cultures or to Christianity). The traditional post-national framing of European integration thus survives in dismissing an exclusivist notion of national identity. The concern with safety and economic prosperity reflects some particularities of the German debate. It is also explained by the effects of the financial crisis and the Left Party's agenda of protective socialism. *Die Linke* campaigned against the dismantling of the welfare state and a turn from 'market radicalism' to more interventionist and regulatory state policies, to be implemented at European and (preferably) at national level. This campaign found particular resonance in the East of Germany. 'Economic Prosperity', instead, is a typical Western concern and reflects mainly the obsession of many Germans with economic stability and the mastering of the economic and financial crisis. Interestingly, both debates converge in a sovereignist vision of a strong and regulatory state and remain ambivalent with regard to the prospects of European integration. As this debate took place before the Euro entered into crisis, the European Monetary Union was still seen as a guarantee of economic stability in times of economic and financial turmoil. Political actors used references to economic prosperity to advertise the European Union and a strong economic community as a harbour of stability in times of crisis

---

15. '[…] das EU Parlament de facto keine Entscheidungsgewalt hat und stattdessen als überbezahlte Fassade der quasi diktatorischen EU Kommission dient.'

(Puhl 2009)[16]. In line with this, the financial crisis was used to promote an even deeper economic integration: therefore, Chancellor Merkel postulated the need for '[…] a true regulation of the European financial market […] to serve as a model for others'[17] (*Spiegel Online* 2009b).

The notion of Europe as a cultural Union was not used in the inclusive sense, as it is part of the official slogans of the EU (Backhaus *et al.* 2009)[18], but in an exclusive way to campaign against the opening of borders, immigration and diversity. In line with other countries in our sample, this debate focused mainly on Turkish accession. Although we know that political parties on other occasions made frequent use of an exclusive rhetoric against Turkey and against Islam (Vobruba *et al.* 2003; Wimmel 2006)[19], this topic was less prominent in the EP election campaigns and remained restricted to some blog entries at *PI-news* (Politically- Incorrect 2009b).[20]

Conclusion

What does our survey of online media contestation during 2009 EP election campaigning in Germany tell us about a possible Eurosceptic convergence in debates about European integration and modes of contestation of EU legitimacy? Summing up, our findings indicate that Germany's traditional role understanding, as a motor of European integration, is slowly replaced by a new critical distance. However, different from most other countries in our sample like Austria, the Netherlands, the Czech Republic, Hungary, Poland and even France, where political stances on European integration were found to be more contentious and polarised – the debate in German online media still mirrors the traditionally broad societal consensus on European integration. If at all, the analysis can track soft traces of Euroscepticism (Szczerbiak & Taggart 2008c). Not even the *Bild-Zeitung*, the best known daily tabloid, which often takes a rather populist stance on the EU, kept true to its image. Moderate Euroscepticism slowly gains ground in user commenting, while political elites and commentators display a new

---

16. '[…] das es gut ist, gerade in Zeiten der Krise zu einer größeren, starken Gemeinschaft zu gehören.'
17. '[…] eine echte Regulierung der Finanzmärkte […] [so]dass Europa Vorbild für andere ist.'
18. The fact that the EU promotes diversity and peaceful coexistence of different cultures was only mentioned once in our sample in an interview with Chancellor Merkel.
19. An illustrative case is the so-called 'Sarrazin debate' of 2010 that was triggered as a reaction to a book published by the former Bundesbank board member, Thilo Sarrazin. 'Europe' in this context is used as a substitute of the ethno-cultural nation and political entrepreneurs campaign in defence of the 'judeo-christian civilization' against Islam as the external other.
20. 'The ideological foundations of predominantly Islamic states cannot be reconciled with the traditions and roots of the contemporary EU' ('Die weltanschaulichen Grundlagen von vorwiegend islamisch geprägten Staaten lassen sich nicht mit der Tradition und den Wurzeln der heutigen EU verschmelzen').

role understanding of Germany, as the saviour of the European idea against the Eurosceptic threat. Euroscepticism is thus externalised as a problem that is mainly manifested in other Member States but, nevertheless, affects the whole of Europe.

In light of the scarce literature on German Euroscepticism, we would suggest that further research efforts are necessary – not so much concerning the phenomenon of party based Euroscepticism but a general re-orientation of the 'culture of public discourse' around European integration. The impulse for ever deeper integration, which has been underlying Germany's self-understanding as a motor of integration has weakened. Germany has not turned Eurosceptic but it also no longer takes European integration for granted. Dissensus on fundamental questions concerning European integration is no longer categorically excluded but increasingly accepted as a legitimate position in public discourse, not least through the diffusion of anti-EU rhetoric from neighbouring countries. German media closely observe the mainstreaming of Euroscepticism in other Member States. Political extremism and populism of the kind of Geert Wilders and other like-minded political actors across Europe has high news value. In facing Euroscepticism as a foreign phenomenon, political journalism also domesticates and critically reflects some of the arguments taken by foreign actors.

This new critical stance towards European integration is reflected in several parallel discourses, which, as a common denominator, blame the democratic deficit of the EU and call for deep institutional and constitutional reform. We find here the ingredients of a combination of Euro-critical and alter-European discourse, which is also expressed in very similar terms in other countries in our sample, most notably in France (see Chapter Five). A position of moderate Euroscepticism can be recognised on the one hand, in the anti-market rhetoric and the call for a social Europe (mobilised mainly by *Die Linke*), the sovereignist rhetoric and the opposition against the Lisbon Treaty (voiced by both left and right parties, mainly *Die Linke* and CSU) and in the notion of a culture-based nationalism (or alternatively Europeanism) which is underlying the opposition against Turkish membership in the EU.

Euroscepticism in Germany still remains confined to the fringes of the political spectrum. The mainstreaming of Euroscepticism is neither supported by political parties nor by the media. Against our initial hypothesis, mass media, and in particular online news media, do not provide an alternative forum for the mass diffusion of negative opinion about the EU and European integration in the context of 2009 EP campaigning. As in other countries included in our sample, the active participation of citizens turns EU debates more negative. In the German case, this is expressed in a variant of soft Euroscepticism. EU hostility, which is found to be the dominant voice of citizens in countries like Austria or the UK, is less pronounced in the German context. Further, the average online news reader displays a clear preference for quality journalism news and not for tabloids or political blogs. The interesting observation that tabloids are more marginal online than offline makes us conclude that political news, as they are diffused through the internet, are, on average, even more EU-friendly than traditional offline news. The online news sphere is therefore not so much an anonymous place for angry citizens to express their dissatisfaction with European integration and with politics in general. Rather, it is found to be the meeting place for citizens to comment on daily events, to express qualified opinions about ongoing political affairs and to build online communities around the trusted news providers, which are already dominant and firmly established.

Chapter Seven | Reflecting a Morose Political Climate: EU Polity Contestation in Hungary

Maria Heller, Tamás Kohut and Borbála Kriza

The roots of Eurosceptic discourse in Hungary need to be sought in the history of the country's rapprochement to the West. Hungary, like other Central and Eastern European countries, has known a certain delay in economic and social development accompanied by a profound commitment to European – or rather 'Western' – values, culture and civilization. The problem of how to catch up with the West has divided political and intellectual elites since the beginning of the nineteenth century. Three developmental models have been particularly influential in shaping intellectual, public and media debates. The first model advocated by progressive, urban intellectual circles promoted Western patterns of modernisation and the adoption of Western values including individual freedom and rights, liberal thinking and capitalist economy. The second model picked up on social injustices (second serfdom still in the nineteenth century, unequal treatment of ethnic and social groups, extreme poverty, etc.) which enhanced the appearance of left-wing ideologies. These got strong reinforcement later from the Soviet Union and the geopolitical arrangements after the Second World War. The socialist-communist orientation in the escalating competition during the Cold War period set the goal of rapidly overhauling the West and attempted a forced reorganisation of the economy and the society accordingly (Burawoy 2009). The third main option is – as Hungarians often call it – 'the third way': this ideological orientation rejects both Western liberal models and the 'socialist' solution idea, to catch up with the West through centrally organised, forced modernisation. The followers of this option rather advocate an insular orientation: the country has to reinforce its own traditional (national and ethnic) values without being exposed to Western influences. This orientation is extremely inward looking, trying to build on historic values, past glories, ethnic-national values and 'uncorrupted' social forces, such as peasantry and religion.[1]

These three orientations have informed social debates in the nineteenth and twentieth centuries without their proponents being able to find common understanding in goals or methods. As a result, their differences have escalated in large-scale intellectual confrontations in the public sphere. At certain historic periods some collaboration existed among Westernisers and 'populists' (as the nationalist-traditionalist orientation is often called in Hungary) against the common 'enemy': the highly centralised 'socialist' establishment with its coercive

---

1. This type of argumentation is not uncommon in other Central and East European public discourses. See Styczyńska in this volume on the case of Poland.

ruling communist party. It is important to mention that the struggles among the orientations were of symbolic nature, the participants were mainly intellectuals representing various fields of social sciences and humanities (historians, sociologists, lawyers, writers, journalists, teachers, etc.).

The system change in 1990 put an end to the peaceful cultural-ideological debates among intellectuals of the three opposing orientations and quickly dissolved any hope that they would be able to cooperate in putting the country on a new path of development and modernisation. With the implosion of the former political system, the former political class was also swept away and the empty political field was immediately filled up with representatives of all three camps. Yet with the rapid and unexpected system change, public intellectuals found themselves in the middle of the political arena and heavily politicised: the former cultural orientations have, all of a sudden, been reconstructed as political parties and ideological debates have been transformed into fierce political struggles. The public sphere has quickly become a battlefield where debates have increasingly glided to the extremes (Csepeli and Örkény 2002; Heller and Rényi 1996). The climate of political debate is now characterised by extremely violent skirmishes, spreading hate-speech, scapegoat-forming strategies, exclusion and radicalism (Gombár et al. 2006). As such, Hungarian politics have lately degenerated into a morose political climate.

The controversies in the new millennium around the question of joining the project of (Western) European integration have to be understood in this general political and cultural context. The very idea of EU accession was popular in public opinion as this move could be interpreted as a kind of achievement of the country or as reparation for the long historical, unjust fate of Hungary. As a matter of fact, most Hungarians have always considered that the country belonged to the West, even if it was condemned to a situation of periphery for long historical periods. The Hungarian society can be characterised by a complex and intricate construction of collective identity with strong feelings of inferiority mingled with self-pride and disdain of others. The country is often depicted in public discourse (literature, journalism, etc.) as a heroic nation having sacrificed itself to defend the West against enemies coming from the East, such as the Tatars and Turks (Hungary as 'defending bastion of the West'). Public representation of the nation also includes the image of the 'victim': a prey of the strong competing European powers and empires (between Habsburgs and Russians, the Third Reich and the Soviet Union). The country is also often thought of as being a link between East and West ('the ferry-country' or the 'bridge'). The most important item of the identity-complex is constituted by the still vivid wounds of the Treaty of Trianon. Probably the greatest problem of Hungarian politics, inherited from the Austro-Hungarian Monarchy, is the fact that the relationship between minorities in Greater Hungary and the new surrounding nation states in the twentieth century could not be tackled in a harmonious way and mutual grievances have never been settled. EU accession in the light of these popular symbolic constructions was considered as possible reparation for the discriminations of the past but it has also been considered, by emerging and strengthening nationalist political forces, as a means of 'reuniting the torn apart nation'.

The topic of EU membership has, thus, re-opened an old ideological battlefield among intellectual elites. The expectations of the general public related to membership were based, however, mainly on economic grounds as it can be seen both from opinion polls and qualitative research materials (Heller 2010). Political debates of the 1990s tried to emphasise the political advantages of accession: guarantees for solid democracy, participation in EU institutions, freedom of movement and disappearing borders. However, the majority of the Hungarian population, deprived from consumption for long, associated EU membership with economic advantages: the hope for higher salaries, social security, 'Western' lifestyle, increased living standards and the advent of consumers' society. In the early 2000s, public opinion became more realistic, although information and knowledge about the EU, its institutions and its functioning, continued to be extremely low (Hegedűs 2004).

In this chapter, we build on these existing analyses of public discourse about European integration in the period after accession. The question arises how the European orientation of Hungary and its increasingly deteriorating political climate interacted during the 2009 European election campaigns to shape discourse on European integration in general and EU polity contestation in particular. To further substantiate this question, this chapter now proceeds with a more thorough discussion of the political climate in Hungary that led to the expression of Euroscepticism.

Euroscepticism in a morose political climate

As in many other new Member States (see, for example, Styczyńska in this volume), the public expression of Euroscepticism in Hungary has increased in salience since accession. When analysing this phenomenon, it is not enough to point to common European trends; intrinsic domestic developments that underlie the strengthening of Eurosceptic discourse also need to be examined. With regard to the process of European integration in general, the ongoing conflicts concerning the EU's internal functioning (the failure of the Constitution, the negative French, Dutch and Irish referenda, the long parley about the Lisbon Treaty) and the uncertain directions of future development (negotiations with Turkey and Balkan countries) have affected public opinion about the efficiency of the EU. The global financial crisis that found the EU unprepared has also played a determining role in the disillusionment of many Hungarians with the project of European integration.

Besides these common European trends, the rise of Euroscepticism in Hungary is mainly explained by domestic factors. With accession, the pronounced political goal has been achieved and Europe, as a catchword, ceased to play its role of defining the political agenda. On the other hand, as people did not experience any rapid amelioration of their living standards or tangible personal benefits from EU membership, public opinion very soon became indifferent or even disappointed about the EU.

Recently, disenchantment with EU membership has been aggravated by domestic political turbulences, in particular by the deep cleavage and the evolving conflict between the two major political parties, which distanced people even more from public affairs (Szalai 2008). The financial crisis, which has hit Hungary in a particularly strong way, increased this general malaise and depression.

EU statistics (Eurobarometer 2008a, 2008b, 2008c, 2009a) show that the popularity of the EU has been decreasing in Hungarian public opinion (Heller 2010). Euroscepticism has indisputably gained importance in the Hungarian public sphere during the last decade (Horváth 2009). The 2009 EP election campaign would thus offer a context for raising questions and doubts concerning the benefits of EU membership. In the period preceding the elections, political activism increased considerably, with large layers of the population being mobilised in street protests (Ilonszky and Lengyel 2009). The street riots in Budapest of Autumn 2006, mostly by extreme-right supporters, were triggered off by an internal speech of the Socialist Prime Minister of the coalition government asking his party fellows for support of his radical reforms. This speech was later leaked and served as a pretext for the political right to mobilise against the government and its reform policies.

This domestic turmoil contributed to the re-emergence of the far-right, which had already been represented in the parliament between 1998 and 2002 by the Hungarian Justice and Life Party (Hungarian: Magyar Igazság és Élet Pártja -MIÉP), but then slowly disappeared from the political landscape. *Jobbik* (Short for *Jobbik Magyarországért Mozgalom – The Movement for a Better Hungary*), a quickly growing extremist movement, stepped in to become Hungary's new far-right party and formed an alliance with the militaristic *Gárda* (Short for *Magyar Gárda Mozgalom –Hungarian Guard Movement*). The right-wing radicals have been using more and more outspoken racist language especially against the economically and socially marginalised Roma population.

On the basis of these antecedents, it is foreseeable that the 2009 EP election campaign would focus more on domestic political issues than on European ones. Parallel to the political instability, economic downturn and the impact of the global financial crisis stimulated a negative public atmosphere against the ruling socialist-liberal coalition. Even the previously popular European Union lost a lot of supporters (Eurobarometer 2009a).[2] In these circumstances, the EP election, which is usually a second-rate political issue (Elections 2009)[3], became an event to deliver a verdict on the government. Even among the domestic issues, the most frequent discourses were overall criticisms on governmental policies or personal attacks on various politicians of the ruling Hungarian Socialist Party (*Magyar*

---

2. According to the spring 2009 wave of Eurobarometer, only 32 per cent of the Hungarians agree that the EU membership of the country is a 'good thing' and only 36 per cent of the respondents believe that the country has benefited of the EU membership. With these results Hungary is among countries evaluating the EU most negatively.
3. The turnout at the 2009 European Parliamentary elections at 36.31 per cent was below the European average of 43 per cent, and it also slightly underscored the turnout of the 2004 European Parliamentary elections.

Szocialista Párt- MSZP). As the campaign was taking shape, it became more and more evident, that most of the campaign events were organised against the rival political actors or groups. As a consequence of the realignment of the whole political arena into a merciless battlefield, the campaigns were characterised by domestic conflict, while the EU and related topics were rarely mentioned.

On the basis of this overview, we can advance the following hypotheses:

1. Substantive and informative debates about EU policies are rare in 2009 EP campaigns.
2. EP election campaigns are organised around 'second-order' debates putting domestic affairs, party politics and strong negative discourse centre stage.
3. The EU and the EP elections are interpreted from a restricted, national interest perspective.
4. EP election campaigns emphasise the special geopolitical situation of Hungary between East and West, thematising the possibility of a specific role to the country.
5. Euroscepticism gains momentum in the form of insular, extremist discourses.

EU polity evaluation in the 2009 EP election campaigns

Following the common methodological framework laid down in Chapter Two, three professional journalism platforms ([*origo*], *Index* and *Figyelőnet*) and two independent blogs (*W – For a Better Magyarland* and *Reakció – polgári underground*), were selected.

By far the most well-known web platforms in Hungary, [*origo*] and *Index*, offer a wide variety of services. The high rankings of Alexa.com for these two websites – sixth most visited website in Hungary for [*origo*] and tenth for *Index* – illustrate the wide impact of the sample. [*origo*] is a website employing around sixty journalists, offering political, business and sports news. It includes sections dealing with lifestyle, tabloids, cars, women's pages and scientific topics. Remarkably, in the context of other professional journalism websites included in this volume, [*origo*] is an exclusively online platform, with no links to any traditional print or electronic media. The political stance of [*origo*] is moderate, and it could not be affiliated with any of the Hungarian parties. The option of comments at the end of politics-related articles, at the time of the sampling period, was seldom available, however, separate user-generated forums were provided through the [*origo*] website.

Quite differently from [*origo*], *Index* is a firmly political website with a very distinctive political worldview and tone. It is politically independent and cannot be affiliated with any of the Hungarian political parties; however, it is politically much more active than the measured and neutral rival, [*origo*]. But similarly to [*origo*], *Index* is also an exclusively online platform. Its style represents a younger and more independent tone. Being outspoken is one of its most typical characteristics. It could be argued that the originally liberal website turned much to the right in the last few years, parallel with the general electorate. Having said that, *Index* cannot be characterised as traditionally conservative. This type of independent tone is hardly visible elsewhere in Hungarian mainstream media. To add further complexity to its political profile, *Index* can be strongly tabloid at times, though it is presenting tabloid news with outsiders' irony. A direct commenting function was not available at the time of sampling. However, user-generated discussion forums, separated from the main news page of *Index*, were very popular. According to Alexa.com, they attracted about a quarter of *Index* readers. The third most popular professional journalistic website was *Figyelőnet*, the online version of the weekly *Figyelő*. The offline *Figyelő* focus on economic and business news is reflected in the online version, but it also offers some entertainment sections, including blogs. Its political platform can be categorised as liberal. Comments were allowed only in the separate opinions, section of the homepage and at its own blogs.

The selection procedure for the independent blogs was less clear cut, since Alexa.com only ranks the popularity of the blog generator sites and not of single blogs. From the most popular blog provider *Blog.hu* (Alexa ranking 17th in May 2009) we, therefore, selected the two most popular Hungarian independent blogs of political content (*W – For a Better Magyarland* and *Reakció – polgári underground*), which ranked 12th and 26th in the list provided by Blog.hu.

W – For a Better Magyarland is run by the young columnist Árpád Tóta W., a former journalist of *Index*. He has an unconventional mix of liberal and conservative views based on liberal economic and social values, which are hardly popular themes in the Hungarian political public sphere. Tóta W. is a member of the new generation of journalists who try to shake journalistic routine and traditions; his blog is outspoken, ironic, witty and sometimes radical in its language use. The topics of the posts include human rights, moral issues and internal political power struggles, as well. Comments are always numerous and the new posts are usually listed among the recommended links at *Index*.

The group of young conservative bloggers at *Reakció – polgári underground* independently criticise the whole political spectrum, including those that are affiliated to the conservative political parties. However, its name gives a clear signal of the group's political roots: the term *'polgári'* is one of the most well-known political PR words invented and used by the main central-right political party *Fidesz* (Short for *Fidesz – Magyar Polgári Szövetség*; *Fidesz* – Hungarian Civic Union)[4] to label its political vision, values and main electoral base. *Polgári* might best be translated as 'bourgeois', but without any negative ideological connotations. The blog's tone can be described as radical, though it is more outspoken and explicit in its criticism than in its suggestions. Comments were

---

4. When the party was founded in 1988, it was named simply *Fidesz* (*Fiatal Demokraták Szövetsége*, Alliance of Young Democrats). 'Hungarian Civic Union' was added in 1995, following the turn of the party's ideology from liberal to conservative.

numerous at every post, which included a lot of campaign videos throughout the sampling period.

On the whole, we can conclude, therefore, that the sample reached its main goals in creating a database representing the most salient Hungarian websites and weblogs of political content. In the sampling period (18 May – 10 June 2009), there were altogether 245 articles available mentioning 'EU elections'.

Already in 2004, the EP campaigns centred on the question of who will better represent Hungarian national interests in the EU (Hegedűs 2004; Koszta 2009). In line with our hypotheses, domestic party politics was also the most important topic of the EP election campaign, with nearly half of the selected news articles coded under this category. The second most popular topic was 'European Party Politics', followed by 'Other Member States' Party Politics'. The 2009 EP elections in Hungary were thus organised around second-order campaigns. This reflects a limitation regarding convergence on Eurosceptic discourse which we also find in most other Member States. Debates were also rather instrumental, focusing on current domestic affairs and rarely opening a broader interpretative context, for instance, by emotional references to history or remembrance of the drama of the former domination of Hungary by foreign powers (which otherwise play a significant role in Hungarian collective memory and also in the far-right websites). Issues not related to partisan contestation were only marginally taken up in the campaign. Even the economic crisis did not figure prominently as an independent issue of campaigning but, as we shall see in the following, was rather instrumentalised by political parties. It is thus noteworthy, that substantial debates about EU policies, or the development of European integration, are missing in EP campaign coverage in Hungary (Table 7.1 below).

The only issue that had a historical bearing was the relationship between Hungary and ethnic Hungarians living in neighbouring countries. The Trianon Treaty, the peace treaty after the First World War, that caused huge territorial and population losses to the country, is usually thematised by the populist right-wing and the far-right, but the support of ethnic Hungarians is a general political topic which has been part of the agenda of every government since the transition. This topic continues to be broadly debated along political, ideological and social cleavage lines of the different party groups. The debate directly relates to the problem of redefining national identity and affects the country's relationships with its neighbouring countries, and its relation to Europe. Right-wing and central-right parties have long been accusing the liberal and socialist parties of not doing enough for the ethnic Hungarians.

The issue of ethnic Hungarians had been closely connected to debates on EU membership for years. In the 2009 campaign, Viktor Orbán, the president of the main opposition party, the conservative nationalist *Fidesz*, declared that the EP elections would measure the weight of Hungarians in the forthcoming European Parliament. He maintained that if ethnic Hungarian politicians from neighbouring countries gain seats in the European Parliament, Hungarian national interests would get stronger representation in Europe. This campaign caused an outrage among Slovakian politicians and added to the already tense relationship between

Table 7.1: Debating the EU online: Topics of Hungarian articles

Number of topics referring to EP elections		Website				
Topic	[origo]	Index	Figyelőnet	W – For a better Magyarland	Reakció – Polgári underground	Total
Domestic party politics	5	9	5	4	3	26
Other Member States' party politics	3	2	3	-	1	9
European party politics	3	2	3	-	2	10
National economy	1	-	-	-	-	1
European economy	-	-	-	-	-	-
European integration	-	-	-	-	-	-
Membership/ enlargement	-	-	-	-	-	-
Democracy	-	-	-	-	-	-
Other	3	2	2	-	-	7
Total number of articles	15	15	13	4	6	53

the two countries. The campaign of the nationalist right-wing presents strong evidence of how national interests in Hungary are defined in a way that reaches beyond the country's geographical and political borders. Such trans-border activism of the political right is, however, not to be confused with a European or possibly even cosmopolitan perspective, because it is grounded in the nineteenth century ethnic, primordial, nationalist-populist conception of Greater Hungary.

As part of domestic partisan contestation, the slump of the national economy was a topic taken up by all political parties in the campaign. There was also consensus among the oppositional parties of the right and the left, that the socialist government was to be blamed for the bad economic performance. This is hardly surprising, as the economy was particularly affected by the global financial crisis, which forced the Hungarian government to negotiate an agreement with the International Monetary Fund to refinance the huge national debt. The issue of economic crisis was a major topic in the campaign, emphasised by the main opposition party, *Fidesz*, to call for early general elections. The European Parliamentary elections were thus depicted as a verdict on the socialist government and a possible turning point towards the empowerment of a new right coalition. The strategy of instrumentally using EP elections in order to demolish the ruling socialist party and to request early national legislative elections further demonstrates the second-rate importance of EU issues in Hungary's morose political climate, where the main stake was the struggle for internal power.

The other main set of issues in the campaign was linked to the emergence of the far-right movement. A counter campaign against the looming of right-wing extremism was initiated by the ruling socialists and especially the liberal party. The message of this campaign was focused on a set of worrying incidents, among others, the long series of street riots since the autumn of 2006, the establishment of a paramilitary organisation, called Hungarian Guard, and several attacks on the Roma population, in six cases homicidal. *Jobbik* made increasing use of xenophobic and racist discourse, strongly attacking the government for the 'incomplete transitions' and the, supposedly corrupt, 'sell-out' of Hungary that benefited 'foreign interests' (*Jobbik* 2009a). The political enemies in their discourses were not only elites, the establishment and foreign interests, but first and foremost the Roma population. The main slogan of their campaign was '*Hungary belongs to the Hungarians*' with racist connotations against foreign and domestic enemies: Roma, Jews and foreigners in general (*Jobbik* 2009b). In more indirect terms, this slogan could also be interpreted as Eurosceptic since it connotes nation state independence from all foreign influences, but a possible demarcation of Hungary against the EU, was rarely made explicit.

Due to the particularities of the Hungarian websites for professional journalism, there are only few comments in the Hungarian sample. Most of the available comments tackled domestic politics. Comments were often personalised, targeting prominent political figures and not substantial policies. Comments were also used to express dissatisfaction with the political system in general. The most visible type of comments, however, contained far-right, racist ideologies mostly aimed against the political mainstream and the Roma population. One can conclude that extreme right-wing activists were strongly present and creative in online media during the campaign.[5]

> The slogan '*Hungary belongs to the Hungarians*' does not mean any kind of exclusion from the nation. It only expresses that the last two governments have been collaborating with the foreign, international capital, and they have been selling out the resources of the nation. Based on false left-liberal ideology, they provided the foreign big capital total control over our country (Nádori 2009).

Another commentator denies the extremism of *Jobbik*, and attacks the lifestyle of the Roma:

> It shows the moderation of the Hungarian citizens, that they lawfully voted for the new force, which intends to create order lawfully, especially in the field of public security and more importantly, in the field of living costs. Why, would it have been better, if they got their scythes and hacks, and finish off the criminal Gypsies, themselves?? So that a civil war would have started? 'Cause in Italy, they had burned the dumps long before, instead of voting. Therefore the 15 per cent[6] is the success of democracy. Because *Jobbik* is not extreme but the situation is! And only radical change can be effective. Because if it does not happen, then in 30 years time this beautiful country will be degenerated to the level of African countries (Nádori 2009).

Besides being reflected in the topics of online coverage, the hypothesis that the Hungarian EP election campaign was first and foremost a campaign of domestic party politics is also reinforced by the type of actors contributing to EU polity contestation. Most often, EU legitimacy was contested by political party actors, as Figure 7.1 below shows, although citizens also contributed to the debates on domestic topics with almost as many evaluations. The political party actors represented in the Hungarian online media are usually members of a small circle of familiar faces: the politicians in the spotlight are the selected few leading candidates, party chairmen, spokesmen and Hungarian MEPs.

About two thirds of political actors and three quarters of citizens contributing to the EU campaign are Hungarian, as opposed to foreign or European. This information provides further support for our hypothesis that the Hungarian campaign was, first and foremost, occupied by Hungarian political actors.

We can thus conclude that a mainstream partisan consensus on European integration survived in the Hungarian debate. The legitimacy of the EU was not fundamentally contested in Hungary in the context of EP elections. Instead, campaigning evolved almost exclusively around 'secondary debates' that reflected the morose political climate of Hungarian domestic politics.

---

5. This is corroborated by the extremely high number of professionally produced political clips of *Jobbik* at various video-sharing websites. See among others: *Jobbik* 2012a; 2012b.
6. The score of the extreme right-wing party at the EP elections.

Figure 7.1: Distribution of EU evaluations across countries: Hungarian contributions per actor

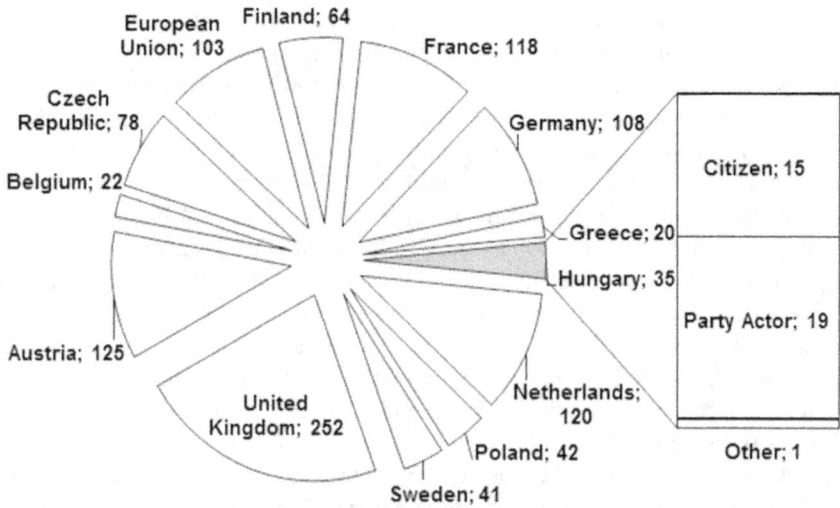

Following the categorisation of Euroscepticism as forms of public discourse developed in the introductory chapter of this volume, contesting the 'principle of integration' is the widest, most fundamental and most general way of transmitting an opinion on European integration. It concerns the idea and/or act of cooperation among European Member States in any form. If the very notion of European cooperation is rejected, this can be considered as the hard case of Euroscepticism.

Even though it is quite clear that there are political parties on the extreme left and right (the far-right *Jobbik* and the communist *Munkáspárt* (short for *Magyar Kommunista Munkáspárt* – Hungarian Communist Workers' Party) which see the EU as a hostile, globalising power, a hard Euroscepticism, that fundamentally rejects the project of European integration, was not part of the online political discourse in the context of the EP campaign. Opposing Hungary's membership in the EU mainly remained a taboo, even for the aforementioned Eurosceptic parties, and risked becoming counterproductive for those political actors who tried to enter the difficult terrain of fundamental EU opposition. In the case of *Jobbik*, for instance, the party built the image of a radical outsider, yet nevertheless sought to send MEPs to the European Parliament. However, one should not take this finding as a proof of a general acceptance of European integration. As it was previously argued, public opinion in the last decade has shifted significantly from pro-EU to Eurosceptic opinions (Heller 2010). Thus the lack of negative or positive evaluations on the very notion of European integration indicates the ambiguous state of opinions on these issues and only demonstrates the dominance of the domestic political issues in the Hungarian EP campaigning.

While negative evaluations of the principle of integration were absent in our representative sample, we find occasional affirmations of the positive value of European integration as part of the rhetorical strategies of campaigning by mainstream political parties. Such references to the benefits of past or recent events concerning integration, can be utilised to create a political identity for a party or to set the ideological borders of a political agenda. This strategy seems to have been the case when Frank-Walter Steinmeier, German Minister of Foreign Affairs, was cited, who said that 'Germany once again acknowledges the Hungarian nation for its role in the reunification of Germany. The German unification was the premonitory sign of the unification of Europe' (fn24 2009c).

Another example for this affirmative rhetoric is a statement by the chairman of the Slovakian Party of Hungarian Coalition, Pál Csáky, in response to the diplomatic row between Hungary and Slovakia caused by the aforementioned campaign speech of Viktor Orbán. The principle of European integration was evoked here as a model that the Hungarian and Slovak patriots should follow. It was seen as an example of civilised European cohabitation, and the European Union was called in to help establish mutual respect among Hungarians and Slovaks (Origo 2009c).

While the principle of European integration was rather confirmed in online debates, EU polity contestation in the Hungarian debate focused mainly on the present institutional and constitutional arrangements of the European Union. This category is without question the most salient in measuring Euroscepticism in Hungarian online media and encompasses the majority of all evaluations.

Most of the assessments of the present institutional set-up are critical. The most frequent point of criticism is the powerlessness of the European Parliament, which is seen as democratically weak. Also, the unbalanced, asymmetric relationship between the EU and Hungary is often criticised. In a comment on the possible consequences of the EP elections, a reader reflects on the status of Hungarian MEPs in the European Union as powerless.

> If the EP wants to help us, then it is going to happen, but if it does not, then it [the Hungarian MEPs' group] does not make any difference. Very little is going to be entrusted on the representatives elected by us. Like a drop in the ocean (Antal 2009).

Those who share similar interpretations tend to regard EP elections as meaningless and would most likely abstain from voting. As one commentator puts it: 'I think we shouldn't have entered the EU. […] it has to be acknowledged that the dictate comes from above, and here it is only implemented' (Árpád 2009). This widespread apathy of the voters is however open to different interpretations. At one point, the lack of interest of the European voters is used as an argument to turn down the Lisbon Treaty, while the 'supporters of the Reform Treaty' would argue, at the same time, that the apathy of the voters means that the 'EU needs indeed a "shake-up" that might be brought by nothing else than the Lisbon Treaty' (*Index.hu* 2009a).

As the above mentioned examples show, most of the negative evaluations of the EU institutional set-up point towards alter-European arguments. They criticise existing deficits in the democratic design of the EU but remain principally open to reform. More fundamental Eurocritical statements were found with less frequency and remained confined to the fringes of the political spectrum. As such, they were expressed by the far-right *Jobbik* and the communist *Munkáspárt*. Both question the benefits from EU membership for Hungary in the only televised political debate during the EP election campaign. The arguments put forward, in this main television debate, were also commented upon in the online media. One journalist of *Index* reported that the leading candidate of *Munkáspárt* told the audience that, 'European membership brought nothing good to Hungary, therefore the question of staying in should be raised'. The candidate of the extreme-right *Jobbik* was also quoted, saying that 'Hungary's membership in the European Union ruined the country and brought success only to a small circle' (Hírügynökség 2009).

As was the case for negative evaluations, the few positive evaluations of the EU polity were mainly put forward by political actors. About half of them were connected to the MSZP. A journalist of [*origo*] acknowledged that this political party had good reasons to emphasise the huge success of European membership, as the country had received vast amounts of subsidies and development aid (Origo 2009d). This argumentation was repeated twice in the sample by the leading candidate of MSZP, Kinga Göncz, who stated that if Hungary had not been a Member State, it would not have reached the level where it was now (Hírügynökség 2009). At another occasion she was quoted stating that Hungary had not been alone in the crisis thanks to its membership in the EU, and she warned of the dangers of not being a member: 'We have seen how fast a highly developed country, Iceland, which is not a member state of the European Union, has collapsed' (fn24 2009b). EU membership was also interpreted by the government-friendly mainstream as a useful protective shield against the threat of a right-wing takeover of the country. One commentator writes that 'Thank, thank God that we are part of the EU [...]' assuming that the country's EU membership would prevent forthcoming possible future right-wing governments from abolishing democratic standards, such as general elections (AliceCsodaországban01 2009).

Despite the existing positive evaluations, it can be concluded that the polity of the European Union is addressed mainly in a critical way. This criticism is mostly connected to the topic of the relationship between Hungary and the European Union and it is made mostly by Hungarian political actors or citizens, as opposed to foreigners.

The 'future of Europe' debate, as the third dimension of EU polity contestation highlighted in this volume (see Chapter One), was not highly topical in the Hungarian campaign. In the few contentious moments found in online debates, the EU's future is seen in a rather positive light. In line with the alter-European criticism, most statements were supportive of future steps of integration.

These supportive arguments were, above all, evaluating the future relation between Hungary and the EU. The leading candidate of MSZP, Kinga Göncz, declared that the turnout of the elections has special importance, as it determines the future legitimacy of the Hungarian MEPs in the European Parliament (Hírügynökség 2009). Ibolya Dávid, leading conservative politician from the Hungarian Democratic Forum (Magyar Demokrata Fórum, MDF), said she wanted a strong European Union as a way to strengthen the national economy (*Index*.hu 2009b).

As already mentioned earlier, a speech by Viktor Orbán, the leader of the main conservative nationalist right-wing party *Fidesz*, became an often debated reference in the campaign. In a joint rally with ethnic Hungarian politicians from Slovakia, Orbán solicited ethnic Hungarian voters from Slovakia to support only ethnic Hungarian candidates in their own country, in order to increase the number of 'Hungarian' MEPs and the weight of Hungarian interests in the EU. 'The European Parliamentary elections will decide how many MEPs will represent the Hungarians of the Carpathian basin' (fn24 2009a; Origo 2009b, 2009c). This remark, as mentioned before, became one of the main campaign events in Hungary, also sparking heated reactions from Slovakia, the Czech Republic and Germany. The project of European integration is tied here, by Orbán and his party, to the future of the nationalistic project of the resurrection of Greater Hungary and its allegedly fifteen million Hungarian inhabitants. Indeed, in the current Hungarian context, the European Union with its fading internal borders is interpreted by the right-wing and the extreme right as a symbolic revision of the Trianon Treaty and the possible 'reunification' of the nation. A similar nationalism is also found in the sensitive responses from Slovakia to this type of campaigning. EP campaigning is thus one further instance of the frequent ethno-nationalist conflicts between Hungary and its European neighbours, and the lasting dominance of ethno-nationalist politics in this part of Europe.

On the other hand, radical political parties had mostly a negative stance towards the future projects of the EU. Gyula Thürmer, leader of the communist party *Munkáspárt*, criticised the European Union saying that Hungary sold itself to the West, and affirmed that

> the stake of the elections is whether Hungary can strengthen its positions in the European Union, whether it can find a solution to the actual crisis which reinforces the opportunities of the Hungarian economy or we continue to sell ourselves to foreigners (fn24 2009e).

In the extreme right side of the political spectrum, contributors often aligned with positions that were taken in other parts of Europe. In particular, Dutch far-right politician Geert Wilders found resonance in the Hungarian debate and his view on blocking Turkey's accession to the EU was supported (fn24 2009d). Wilders' views were also discussed in some of the extreme right-wing websites that did not get into our sample but which attracted strong extremist and radical online activism.

As in all countries covered by our survey, 'democracy' was most frequently used to assess EU legitimacy in EP online campaigns. In Hungary, evaluations based on democracy were closely followed by references to economic prosperity and culture (*see* Figure 7.2).

Although numbers are too low to generalise, negative evaluations of EU legitimacy in our sample are often justified in terms of the malfunctioning and lack of efficiency of the EU system. A typical example is the case of a commentator at the discussion forum site of [*origo*], who wrote that the European Union is 'hardly functional' after Eastern enlargement. He argues that this failure is caused by the old members of the European Union because they supposedly 'lobby among each other and for themselves, excluding the new members!! In the long run, the EU is "doomed"!' (*Origo* 2009a).

Figure 7.2: Explaining opinions: how EU polity evaluations were justified in Hungary

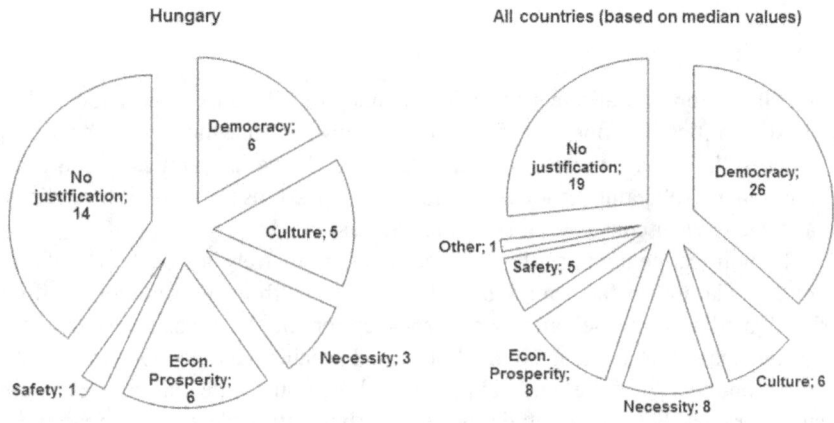

The category of 'Economic Prosperity' is evenly divided between positive and negative assessments. A frequent example is the aforementioned reference to the expected economic benefits of membership. One of the most visible representatives advancing economic reasoning was Lajos Bokros, a well-known economist, the leading candidate of the small centre-right conservative MDF. Throughout the campaign he advocated liberal economic reforms. At the last campaign event before the elections, he was quoted saying that 'The strengthening of Europe is a common interest, and this is the right way in order to strengthen Hungary, as well' (*Index*.hu 2009b). Economic justifications were also given in arguing against the EU. Gyula Thürmer, the chairman of communist *Munkáspárt*, using a partly xenophobic, partly anti-capitalist argument, said that the main stake of the European Parliamentary elections was whether Hungary can strengthen its positions, or 'we will keep on selling out to foreigners' (fn24 2009e). These types of justifications were equally distributed over the political spectrum and were used to blame either the performance of political actors or the system qualities of the EU. On the one hand, democracy justifications were used by citizens to accuse political representatives, or elites in general, for the low level of adequate representation. For instance, a commentator at the opinion section of [*origo*] talks of the failure of democratic representation in the European Parliament because the Hungarian MEPs are unqualified for their jobs: '[...] these people, sitting in the European Parliament, cannot even explain the situation of Hungary. [...] One should not go there only to read newspapers and have a rest or a little nap after the late night parties' (Antal 2009). On the other hand, we also find remarks by politicians which discuss the 'democratic deficit' in relation to the polity type of the EU and with reference to inappropriate procedures, or a lack of democratic culture. Nevertheless, references to democratic values can also be turned positively to support deeper European integration. In an article on European politics, promoters of the Reform Treaty were quoted in favour of the Lisbon Treaty, on the basis of their hope that it would make political decision making more democratic and thus convey more trust to the voters (*Index*.hu 2009a).

Conclusion

The 2009 European Parliament election campaign in Hungary mainly focused on domestic politics. The findings of the present study of online media debates widely testifies to the general morose atmosphere of the Hungarian political climate and public sphere, reflecting its identity complex, its pessimism and lack of readiness to achieve a wider consensus on common affairs.

The political contents of the selected mainstream websites of the Hungarian online media are, in fact, not significantly different from the traditional offline printed media, with the only possible exception of the website *Index*. As a consequence of this, coverage of the European Parliamentary elections was mostly focused on the role of the political parties and internal political affairs. European issues were hardly present in the European Parliamentary elections campaign.

The most frequent Eurosceptic contributions focused on internal politics and asserted that the capacities of domestic parties, and their leaders to represent national interests and values in the European Parliament, were weak. Thus, feelings of national identity and sovereignty, attitudes towards Hungarian minorities in neighbouring countries, the influx of foreign and multinational capital in the Hungarian economy and the fear of foreign ownership of (agricultural) land, were the most recurrent topics in debates on EU legitimacy. This was in line with a populist nationalist argumentation, which expressed a general mistrust in supranational institutions and perceived the EU as a globalising power which threatens national culture, national values and interests (Bóka 2009). Besides well-known Europe-wide Eurosceptic arguments, such as criticising the size of EU-bureaucracy, typical 'small country' arguments also emerged, blaming the supposedly greater influence and unequal treatment of the large Member States.

Populist, nationalist speakers, most of them from the right or even the extreme right-wing of the political arena, thus played the major role as an amplifier of Eurosceptic discourse in Hungary. The anti-market and anti-capitalism rhetoric of the extreme left was much less visible, although similarly Eurosceptic. Pro-European discourse was mainly produced by mainstream centre and centre-left parties. But it has to be pointed out that pro-European discourses were not ideologically backed like the nationalist discourse of the political right, but rather focused on matter of fact politics: ongoing EU policies like agricultural subsidies, road construction and cultural programmes. These arguments were advanced in a rather defensive way and were often criticised even by socialist activists as sheer government propaganda (Gombár *et al.* 2006).

In spite of the fact that the emergent far-right was the central issue of the campaign, the very notion of European integration or the existence of the European Union were rarely rejected. In fact, no single contribution was found that questioned the principle of European integration. The present state of the European Union was much more negatively evaluated by both political actors and citizens. Commentators of online articles were mostly weary of the EU and its institutions, and there was a sense among citizens that Hungarian interests were not well enough represented in the European Parliament. Political actors, on the other hand, differed concerning their evaluation of the EU polity according to their political stance; the mainstream parties were more positive towards the EU, while the far-right and the extreme left were mainly against the European status quo. Future steps in integration were somewhat more welcomed by the political actors, as more than half of the evaluations were positive towards European plans.

Thus, this research on online media debates about the EU presents evidence of the general morose political climate of the Hungarian public sphere. The debates reflect Hungary's identity complex, its pessimism and lack of readiness to achieve a wide consensus on common affairs. As such, the EP campaign points to the impasse of national democracy, rather than to a specific resistance to the project of European integration.

Chapter Eight | The Netherlands: Reliving the 2005 Referendum on the Constitutional Treaty?

For a long time, the Netherlands was generally not known for its Euroscepticism. As a founding father of the EU, it is more often considered a pro-European country. A small open economy and home to one of the world's largest harbours, the Netherlands maintains a self-perception as a country of merchants and trade and has benefited enormously from European integration economically. A pro-European sentiment was especially strong in the early 1990s. When the Netherlands held the Council Presidency in 1991, its government proposed a new Treaty to the other Member States that was so federal in scope that only one other Member State (Belgium) supported it. In the end, the Presidency had to revert to an earlier, less federal, proposal of the previous Luxembourg Presidency that would become the blueprint for the Maastricht Treaty.

The 'no' vote during the June 2005 referendum on the Constitutional Treaty, therefore, came as a surprise to many, both within and outside the Netherlands. Yet, there have been strands of Euroscepticism within the Netherlands throughout the process of European integration that started with the European Coal and Steel Community (ECSC) Treaty in 1951. In fact, rather than perceiving the current Eurosceptic prominence as expressed in the June 2005 'no' vote as exceptional, some consider the pro-European episode of the early 1990s as peculiar instead (Aarts and Van der Kolk 2005; Harmsen 2004; Vollaard and Boer 2005a).

Analysing the specifics of EU polity contestation in the Netherlands, this chapter focuses, in particular, on whether the referendum of June 2005 has left a lasting impression on Dutch discourse about European integration. If so, this may indicate a convergence of the Netherlands from exceptionally pro-European to a more critical stance, known to many other EU Member States (Eichenberg and Dalton 2007). Furthermore, it would point to the more structural effects short term episodes of contention, like a referendum campaign, may have on EU polity contestation in the long run. The referendum debate might be 'relived' during the 2009 EP election campaigns in several ways. First, main topics of the referendum debate – including most notably questions of institutional design, balance of power between EU institutions, the influence of the Netherlands, the Euro and EU enlargement – might feature again in the debates, even if they are not formally on the table for decision making. Secondly, the referendum might be relived through the labelling of political parties and other actors as belonging to either the 'yes' or 'no' side of a perceived political cleavage line on European integration. Finally, more indirectly, the 2005 election campaign might resound in elevated levels of salience of European integration. In other words, the referendum functioned as a mechanism to bring to the fore differences of opinion concerning European integration. The question is to what extent this debate has muted down again, following the formal closure of the opportunity for mobilisation during the referendum.

The chapter proceeds by analysing expressions of Euroscepticism and other forms of EU polity contestation in the Netherlands, as expressed during the campaign on the June 2009 European Parliament elections. The study analyses empirical material from online debates on frequently visited websites connected to professional journalism organisations (Nu.nl, Telegraaf.nl and NOS.nl) and independent political blogs (GeenStijl.nl and Marokko.nl). Deviating from the dominant focus on party politics and public opinion polls within the study of Euroscepticism, the present chapter explores EU polity contestation as portrayed in the media and as voluntarily offered by citizens responding to media stories in online commenting functions.

Euroscepticism in the Netherlands

Euroscepticism in the Netherlands has a long tradition, although it has only recently become a more politically significant influence. In the 1950s, Dutch political parties were not entirely convinced of the necessity to join in the initial steps towards European integration lead by France and Germany. That is, there was both strong opposition to political integration and strong support for economic integration (Haas 2004). In fact, Dutch resistance to political integration has led to delays in the creation of the draft Treaty for Political Union. By the time Dutch resistance had receded, the window of opportunity in France had arguably closed as demonstrated by the failure of the European Defence Community in 1954 (Milward 2000: 186). Also, it was on Dutch initiative, together with the other Benelux countries, that the Council of Ministers was included in the Treaty of Paris as an intergovernmental institution to balance the powers of the High Authority and Common Assembly (Haas 2004: 249). At the same time, the creation of the eventual European Economic Communities can be traced to a proposal by Jan Willem Beyen, then Foreign Minister of the Netherlands (Milward 2000: 196). Thus, the Netherlands has been both a break on political integration and a driving force behind economic integration in the early days of the integration process.

Principled opposition from political parties to European integration could, for a long time, only be found at the political fringes. Orthodox protestant parties, *Staatkundig-Gereformeerde Partij* (SGP), *Gereformeerd Politiek Verbond* (GPV), *Reformatorisch Politieke Federatie* (RPF) and *ChristenUnie*, have always been against European integration. They considered European integration as merely the newest of papal plots in a long history of Catholic attempts to dominate Europe. Furthermore, they argued that integration challenges the divine independence of the Dutch people and their Royal House (Voerman 2005; Vollaard 2005, 2006). On the left, the Dutch Communist Party *Communistische Partij Nederland* (CPN) was against integration which was considered a capitalist project strengthening the position of business at the cost of workers' rights (Voerman 2005). Whereas the mainstream protestant and catholic parties – *Anti-Revolutionaire Partij* (ARP), *Christelijk-Historische Unie* (CHU), *Katholieke Volkspartij* (KVP) and the later union of these three parties *Christelijk Democratisch Appèl* (CDA) – have always been strongly in favour of integration, the social-democrats' *Partij van de Arbeid*

(PvdA) and liberals' *Volkspartij voor Vrijheid en Democratie* (VVD) have shifted positions between the 1950s and today, largely as a result of the preferences of party leaders. Both were generally pro-European in the 1950s, turned towards a more critical stance in the 1970s, became pro-European again up to the early 1990s, and finally turned more Eurosceptic again from the early 1990s onwards (Boer 2005; Koole and Raap 2005; Voerman 2005; Vollaard and Boer 2005b).

For a long time, public opinion and civil society in the Netherlands, including organised business and trade unions, have been strongly pro-European, even in comparison to the other five 'founding fathers' (Haas 2004; Thomassen 2005). More recent developments in European integration have, however, been received more negatively. First, from the mid-1990s onwards, the Netherlands turned from a net recipient of EU funds to a net contributor. By the end of the century, the Netherlands was the biggest net contributor per capita to the EU budget. This was strongly opposed by the VVD party in the 1990s and by Pim Fortuyn and Geert Wilders more recently (Boer 2005; Petter and Griffiths 2005). It has contributed to a 'reassertion of the nation state' in political discourse as the guiding constitutional basis of the EU polity (De Wilde 2009a). Second, the introduction of the Euro in 2002 and the loss of the Guilder as national currency were received very critically and perceived to cause inflation (Aarts and Van der Kolk 2005). Thirdly, the 2004 Enlargement was perceived negatively by the political left who feared that unfair competition from 'Polish plumbers' would put pressure on the Dutch welfare state. Partially in line with the resistance to the 2004 enlargement, there has been growing opposition to possible Turkish membership of the EU, particularly voiced by Geert Wilders and his party *Partij voor de Vrijheid* (PVV). Finally, growing Euroscepticism among Dutch citizens should be understood as part of a more general decreasing trust in Dutch political elites (Aarts and Van der Kolk 2006). This growing gap between elites and citizens eventually came to the fore in the rise of Pim Fortuyn in 2002, and through subsequent populist movements lead by Rita Verdonk and Geert Wilders. Thus, the 'no' vote of June 2005 to the Constitutional Treaty has been understood as a belated no vote to the Euro and Enlargement, as well as a more general denunciation of the political elite (Aarts and Van der Kolk 2006).

The June 2005 referendum on the Constitutional Treaty undoubtedly forms the single most important event in recent history shaping Dutch public opinion, public discourse and party contestation concerning European integration. It has created the general consensus that a federal super state is not wanted by the Dutch people, something only the social-liberal *Democraten 66* (D66) party is still openly in favour of. It has, furthermore, created clear 'yes' and 'no' parties in the political spectrum. Following the referendum, the 'yes' or 'no' question regarding the Constitutional Treaty during the referendum is increasingly considered to reflect general positions on European integration. Thus, parties that advocated a 'yes' vote in the 2005 referendum are now seen as 'pro-European', whereas 'no' parties are considered Eurosceptic. The political mainstream of pragmatic pro-European parties is made up of CDA, PvdA and VVD (Pellikaan and Brandsma 2005). The Eurosceptic opposition consists of the *Socialistische Partij* (SP) on the left and SGP, *ChristenUnie* and PVV on the right. A pro-European opposition exists in the form of the green *GroenLinks* party and the social-liberal D66. In the subsequent national elections of 2007, however, the issue of European integration did not feature prominently. Although the parties that campaigned for a 'yes' vote in 2005 lost in relation to the previous European election, the vote percentage for 'no' parties collectively was much lower than the 61 per cent majority in the referendum that rejected the Constitutional Treaty. The question therefore remains whether the 2005 election was a unique outburst of Euroscepticism that faded away immediately afterwards, or rather an important event in shaping long-term debate on European integration within the Netherlands.

The European Parliament elections of 2009 are an ideal moment to study the remnants of the referendum and Dutch discourse on European integration more generally. We may expect these elections to be 'second-order elections' (Reif and Schmitt 1980) and reflect national issues largely. That is, European Parliament elections are generally found to be fought over domestic issues by national party leaders, rather than over EU policy issues or institutional questions of European integration. Partially, this is because questions of more or less integration are not formally on the table during European Parliament elections as the European Parliament does not decide on such issues. On the other hand, the elections took place at a time when the Lisbon Treaty was still in the process of ratification, which may have presented an opportunity to turn the EP elections into a pseudo referendum on the Lisbon Treaty. There was thus also an opportunity to 'relive' the 2005 referendum, as the Lisbon Treaty is considered by many Dutch citizens to be the Constitutional Treaty in disguise. Highlighting specificities of the Dutch case, this chapter asks: to what extent did the online debate during the 2009 European Parliament election campaign resemble the campaign debate for the 2005 referendum on the Treaty Establishing a Constitution for Europe, in terms of issues raised by participants in the debate, justifications provided to substantiate arguments and difference of opinion between political elites and citizens? As the referendum was such a pronounced event of EU polity contestation in the Netherlands, its possible resounding beyond 2005 may provide key insights into more structural convergence. This chapter asks how Dutch discourse evaluating the project of European integration and the EU polity is structured and how it relates to the discourse expressed in the online campaigns of other Member States included in this study. Convergence in EU polity contestation can possibly come to the fore as a convergence of the tone of debate as a whole, towards a more critical stance known to many other Member States, and as convergence in the way elites and citizens debate Europe.

Data

Based on the ranking of Alexa.com, the three most visited professional journalism websites in the Netherlands were selected (Nu.nl, Telegraaf.nl and NOS.nl). Also, the two most visited political blogs were included in the sample (GeenStijl.nl and Marokko.nl).

As the eighth most visited website within the Netherlands, Nu.nl is clearly the most important political news site in the Netherlands. Founded in 1998, it fields a wide range of news items, ranging from domestic and foreign news, to sports and entertainment. Since the majority and most popular stories come from a national press agency without a clear political profile, it can also be argued that the political profile of Nu.nl is rather neutral. Nu.nl is owned by the Ilse Media Group, which is an internet company that also owns other websites, including a search engine (Ilse.nl), consumer site (Kieskeurig.nl), and Dnews.de, a recently created German version of Nu.nl. The second website, Telegraaf.nl, is the internet portal of the largest Dutch national newspaper *De Telegraaf*. This newspaper is known for its relative conservative political stance on the right of the political spectrum. Unlike countries such as the UK or Germany, the Netherlands does not have clear tabloid newspapers like *The Sun*, or *Bild Zeitung*, nor newspapers particularly aimed at sports reporting, like many southern European countries have. Rather, *De Telegraaf* and its main rival *Algemeen Dagblad* are generally characterised as 'popular' newspapers (Bakker and Scholten 2005), located somewhere in between the quality press and sensational tabloid press known in other countries. Besides sensationalist news, *De Telegraaf* is known for its excellent economics section and wide coverage of sports. The site is owned by *De Telegraaf Media Groep BV*, which owns several more newspapers and magazines in both the Netherlands and other countries. The third site belongs to the Dutch broadcasting company NOS (*Nederlandse Omroep Stichting*). The NOS website provides news both in text and images, as well as blogs featuring stories by both permanent correspondents and guest bloggers. Although it has no clear political profile, the NOS is generally considered to provide news to the higher educated segment of Dutch society and has been criticised by the late Pim Fortuyn, and his followers, as being elitist and leftist ('*De linkse kerk* – The leftist church'), blamed for ignoring 'regular people' and demonising Pim Fortuyn, and even considered an accomplice to Fortuyn's murder by his followers. In the populist blog GeenStijl.nl, which will be discussed below, the NOS political news is regularly referred to as the '*SStaatSS Hoernaal*' or '*NOSS Hoernaal*'. Although hard to translate accurately, these terms carry references to state propaganda, the Nazi paramilitary organisation *Schutzstaffel* (SS), and prostitution. Partially as a result of the Pim Fortuyn revolt against the political elite and the *Linkse Kerk* of elitist and leftist media, the political blog of GeenStijl.nl has become the most prominent blog in the Dutch online public sphere. The blog, whose name can be translated as 'no style' or 'without class', features easy to consume news commentaries by the employed staff of the site. The lack of seriousness, politically 'unacceptable' language, and discussion of political taboos are trademarks of this site. It can be seen as highly populist, right-wing, and aimed at the younger generations. 70 per cent of its visitors are male, between twenty-five and thirty-five years old, highly educated, who enjoy above average income and own a home and car (Van Stegeren 2006). The site is now owned by the *Telegraaf Media Groep*, but remains editorially independent. The final and fifth site in our sample, Marokko.nl, is a blog particularly aimed at young Dutch and Flemish people of Moroccan decent. According to Van Stegeren (2007), virtually all Dutch Moroccans between fifteen and twenty-five years old visit this website more or less often. Although it carries the name of a country of origin, the main uniting theme is Islam and being a young Muslim in a Western country, rather than Morocco. As such, it is not purely a political news site, as it also features social exchange, event calendars, sports, digital meeting places and advice of a religious nature. Although it has a very clear segment of society as target group, it doesn't have a clear political profile, and certainly not a very radical one (Amouch 2006). Rather, it claims to be aimed at furthering understanding between Muslims and non-Muslims in the Netherlands and providing young people with a sense of identity. In the words of the website owners: 'Morocco Media wants to amuse and inform young Moroccans as well as stimulate them to think about society and social relations within the Netherlands'[1].

General nature of the debate

As discussed in the introduction, campaign debates of European Parliament elections could be categorised as existential, substantial or domestic. Existential debates feature strong focus on the EU polity, substantial debates focus on EU policies instead, while domestic debates prioritise national politics and politicians. The prominence of domestic debates, so far, has contributed to the understanding that European Parliament elections can be considered as second-order elections reflecting the domestic political climate (Van der Brug and Van der Eijk 2007). Three indicators serve the purpose of determining the general nature of the Dutch online debate. First, we may consider the topics of the online articles that are analysed. Secondly, we can compare the amount of evaluations of the polity with those made in other Member States. Finally, these numbers need illustration with qualitative findings in order to locate their broader relevance and meaning, as well as to compare coded contributions (inherently of existential nature) with other non-coded text in the sampled articles which might indicate domestic or substantial debates.

As Table 8.1 clearly demonstrates, the most frequent topic of the sampled articles was 'Domestic Party Politics'. Furthermore, we notice a stronger bias towards domestic politics in the two blogs than in the three professional news sites. Of the fifty coded articles, twenty-one (or 42 per cent) fell into the domestic politics category. These articles largely reported on the horse race between parties during the campaign as reflected in opinion polls, as well as the election results and their implication for domestic politics, with a particular focus on the success of Geert Wilders' PVV party (*De Telegraaf* 2009c, 2009d). This provides support for the notion that online political media reflect second order debates, just like offline media do. Nevertheless, several articles in the professional news sites reported on foreign party politics. For instance, there was reporting on the success of the

---

1. Original quote in Dutch: 'Marokko Media wil Marokkaanse jongeren amuseren, informeren en tot denken zetten over maatschappelijke en sociale verhoudingen binnen de Nederlandse samenleving' (www.marokko.nl).

Table 8.1: Debating the EU online: Topics of the Dutch articles

Number of articles referring to the EP elections	Website					
Topic	Nu.nl	De Telegraaf	NOS	Geen Stijl	Marok-ko.nl	Total
Domestic party politics	4	4	3	7	3	21
Other Member States' party politics	1	4	2	-	-	7
European party politics	1	1	2	-	-	4
National economy	-	-	-	-	-	-
European economy	-	-	1	-	-	1
European integration	2	1	1	-	-	4
Membership/ enlargement	1	-	-	-	-	1
Democracy	3	1	-	3	-	7
Other	-	1	2	1	1	5
Total number of articles	12	12	11	11	4	50

Swedish Pirate Party (*De Telegraaf* 2009e), the fact that a Basque separatist party was allowed to participate in Spain (*De Telegraaf* 2009a), and the disappointing election results for Silvio Berlusconi in Italy (Nu.nl 2009a). Despite the dominance of domestic politics, there is clearly attention to European issues too, particularly of an 'existential' nature. These issues often reflected issues from the 2005 referendum. For instance, the leading candidate for D66 argued in favour of removing Member State veto powers in the Council of Ministers (Nu.nl 2009e), and her PvdA counterpart argued in favour of EU-wide referenda on future Treaty revisions (Nu.nl 2009c). Finally, there was attention to the financial costs of EU membership and more general support among the Dutch population for European integration (Nu.nl 2009d; *De Telegraaf* 2009b). The election results were interpreted as a victory for parties with a clear Eurosceptic or pro-European profile, at the cost of more pragmatic parties in the middle (GeenStijl 2009c; NOS 2009c; Nu.nl 2009f), as well as a punishment for the Dutch governing coalition at the time (GeenStijl 2009b; *De Telegraaf* 2009d).

Most of the evaluations on European integration were made on the professional journalism websites, which also featured the most news items and the most diverse range of topics of these news items. Figure 8.1 demonstrates the interactive nature of Web 2.0 news reporting. Contributions to EU polity contestation in the main texts of the news articles on these websites, particularly on Nu.nl and NOS.nl, tend to invoke responses by readers in the commenting function.

Such direct responses on the main text, in turn, invoke responses by other readers. Thus, online news items including evaluations of European integration stimulate debates, which partially directly revolve around the arguments made by politicians and journalists in the main text, and which also evolve into different topics and lines of argumentation.

The existential aspect of the debate is further substantiated if we look at the amount of contributions made in the Dutch debate. The total of 120 contributions to EU polity contestation in the fifty coded articles ranks among the highest of the online debates in the twelve countries involved in this study. This reflects the relatively existential nature of the debates in comparison to other Member States included in this study. Still, based on the distribution of topics, we may conclude that the Dutch online debate was in line with the expectations of the 'second order elections' thesis. The nature of the debate will be further explored in the next section that focuses on the particular contributions made, the actors making these contributions and justifications provided for evaluations of the EU polity.

Figure 8.1: Mapping EU polity evaluations in Dutch online debates

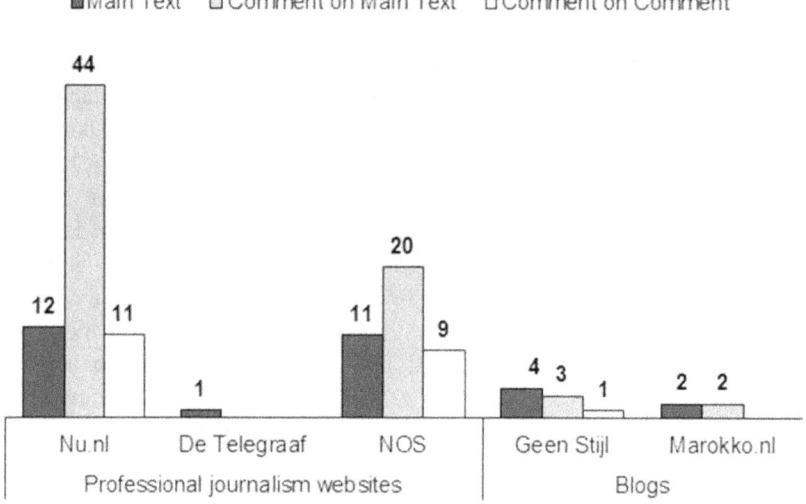

Figure 8.2 EU polity evaluations across countries: Dutch contributions per actor category

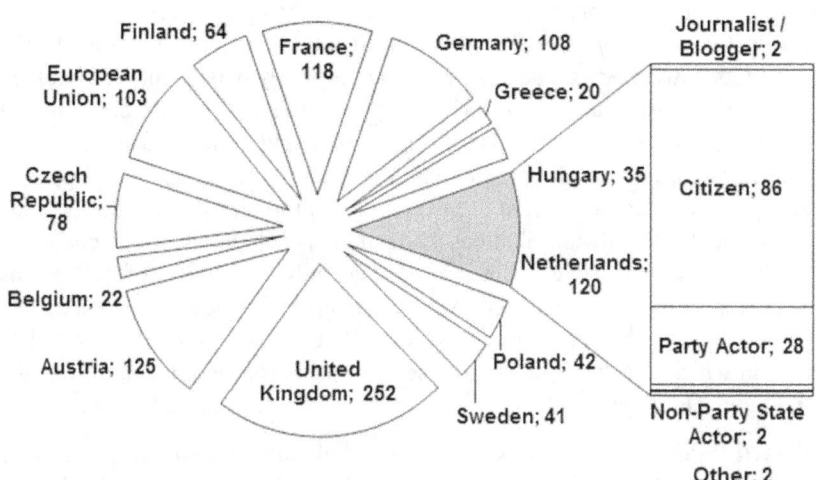

Dimensions of EU polity evaluation

Central in the Dutch debate were questions of how much of a federal 'super state' the EU is and should become, how much cooperation between European countries is needed in such controversial issues as Foreign Policy and Justice and Home Affairs, and how the balance of power between EU Member States and between EU institutions ensures accountability, democracy and political equality in the EU polity. Although these can be labelled as existential issues as they address the EU polity as such, Dutch online debates do not focus on the question of membership of the Netherlands. There is a clear consensus on the issue of membership in the Netherlands. No contributions were found actively arguing in favour of the Netherlands leaving the EU or abolishing the EU altogether, with the exception of one person who argued in favour of leaving the Union should Turkey become a Member (Nu.nl 2009g). On the other hand, the membership of other countries was to a certain extent contested. For instance, some argued the New Member States (countries of Eastern and Central Europe that joined the EU in 2004 and 2007) should not have been allowed to join the EU. Also, the issue of possible future Turkish membership remains highly contested. Figure 8.2 displays the intensity and ways in which the three dimensions of EU polity evaluation conceptualised in the introduction, featured in the Dutch online EP election campaign debates. It shows, first, that many of the 120 contributions did not contain an evaluation on all three dimensions. The principle of integration was the least evaluated dimension, with only forty of 120 contributions addressing this dimension of contestation. Of these forty contributions, twenty-eight were positive. This reflects the basic acceptance of European integration in the Netherlands. Secondly, Figure 8.2 shows that the institutional set-up of the EU was the most evaluated dimension, and largely in a critical way. In particular, the level of integration (thirty-one contributions) and the inclusiveness of integration (eighteen contributions) were negatively evaluated. Thirdly, debate on the future project of integration demonstrates the closest balance between positive and negative evaluations, with level and inclusiveness evaluated slightly more negatively while the scope of integration is evaluated more positively. In other words, Dutch contributors to online debates do not want the EU to expand its powers or include more countries currently outside the EU, but they do want the EU to take up more responsibility in certain policy areas currently not under EU jurisdiction. In particular, foreign policy and police cooperation were mentioned as areas where the EU should become more active.

Analysing the first dimension of integration in more detail, we may conclude that only one third of all contributions made in the Dutch online debate contained evaluations of the principle of integration. Secondly, a majority of evaluations made in this category are positive. A good example of a positive evaluation of the principle of integration is provided by 'DrWouter' commenting on an article in nu.nl in which Dutch public opinion concerning European integration was the central topic. He stated:

> [Geert] Wilders wants to go back to the good old times before the EU existed? That was a period full of war last time I checked my history books. [...] A Europe torn by conflict and ruled by hunger. Again and again, the Benelux countries got sucked into wars we didn't ask for by our powerful neighbours. Be wise and vote for a pro-Europe party (Nu.nl 2009d).[2]

Although citizens opposing the principle of integration are still deemed a minority, NOS reporter Chris Ostendorf assessed their influence would increase in years to come: 'There are a lot of people who don't believe in Project Europe and they promise to become more vocal in Strasbourg and Brussels in the years to come.'[3] In general though, the debates demonstrate a broad consensus within the Netherlands that some form of collaboration between European nation states is required and desired given border-crossing policy challenges, and that the Netherlands should be somehow involved in this cooperation.

Criticism focuses much more on the current form this collaboration has taken in the EU and its component institutions and their powers. This is demonstrated by the plurality of negative evaluations concerning the EU polity. Of all 120 contributions in the Dutch debate, thirty-one contain negative evaluations of the powers of EU institutions over Member States and eighteen contain negative

---

2. 'Wilders wil terug naar de good 'ol times voordat de EU bestond? De laatste keer dat ik mijn geschiedenisboek raadpleegde was dat een periode vol met oorlogsgeweld. [...] Een Europa verscheurd door conflicten waar hongersnood heerstte. Een Benelux die steeds maar weer in oorlogen waar wij niet om gevraagd hadden werd meegesleurd door onze machtige buren. Wees verstandig en stem voor een pro-Europa partij.'

3. 'Er zijn ook veel mensen die niet geloven in het project Europa en zij beloven zich de komende jaren te laten horen in Straatsburg en Brussel.'

evaluations of either the influence of the Netherlands in the EU, the influence of ordinary citizens over the EU, or of membership of the new Member States. After the elections, NOS editor Hans Laroes evaluated the coverage of NOS of the European elections after criticism, voiced by politicians, that the media had not paid enough attention. He argued the NOS had made a major effort to report on the elections. This evoked the following response from 'Marcel':

> I have some more work for you and your colleague journalists. Go check how much of our legislation here in the Netherlands has its origin in laws/rules/directives/etc... of the EU. And please use the same method used by the German Ministry of Justice over the period 1998–2004. I would be surprised if the percentage of 84% hasn't risen further (NOS 2009a).[4]

Responding to a guest column by PvdA Minister for European Affairs, Frans Timmermans, on NOS.nl for more collaboration at European level, 'Douwina' argued:

> The lack of responsibility of this government is 'Zum Kotzen'. As long as the world economy, and with it the Dutch one, is governed by greedy criminals and gambling addicts who are allowed to do as they please while their criminal behaviour creates millions of victims worldwide, Europe has no meaning for me whatsoever. I will not vote for the Devourers of Europe' (NOS 2009b).[5]

A nice example of criticism on the current inclusion of ordinary citizens is provided by 'Liesvan88': 'My opinion is that the EU should become more democratic [...]. And at this stage, Members of the European Parliament don't have enough power. Too much is being decided by unelected people'(Nu.nl 2009d).[6] Also, the influence of small Member States in relation to large Member States is criticised:

> In the European Union, you have hard working countries that pay a lot of money, and you have those who profit. The Netherlands is a contributor and

---

4. 'Ik heb nog wel werk voor u en uw collega journalisten. Ga eens het percentage na van onze wetgeving hier in Nederland die zijn basis heeft in handelen of wetten/regels/directieven/etc... van de EU. En dan graag berekenen op dezelfde wijze als het Duitse ministerie van Justitie dat deed over de periode 1998–2004. Het zou mij verbazen als dat percentage van 84% inmiddels niet gestegen was.'
5. 'De vrijblijvendheid van deze regering is "Zum Kotzen" Zolang de wereldeconomie, en daarmee ook de Nederlandse, geregiseerd wordt door graaiende criminelen en gokverslaafden, die ongestoord en straffeloos hun gang kunnen gaan, terwijl hun criminele gedrag wereldwijd miljoenen slachtoffers eist, heeft Europa voor mij geen enkele betekenis. Ik stem dus niet op de Opvreters van Europa.'
6. 'Ik vind dat Brussel democratischer moet [...]. En op dit moment hebben Europarlementariërs te weinig macht, teveel wordt geregeld door mensen die niet gekozen zijn.'

doesn't have shit to say. The member states that profit are the largest ones and they have all the power (Nu.nl 2009e).⁷

A bit later in the same discussion, 'Upperstream' argued: 'Reinstate the Guilder, close the borders. No more nuisances caused by criminals from the East. Didn't the EEC work just fine?'⁸ With regard to the current institutional set-up of the EU, the majority of arguments made are targeted at political integration. Thus, those negatively evaluating the level of integration in the EU polity, often argue in favour of returning to pre-Maastricht European Communities or limiting European cooperation to trade agreements. Negative evaluations of the inclusiveness of the EU polity specifically argued that 'ordinary citizens' do not have sufficient influence or that the Netherlands, as a country, has insufficient influence.

In the third dimension of evaluation, the target is the possible future extensions of integration. This includes increasing the powers of the European Parliament, but also possible enlargement with Turkey. The level of integration and its inclusiveness are more often the topic of debate than the scope of integration. That is, actors evaluating the EU in the Netherlands are more concerned with the powers of supranational institutions and the extent to which citizens, Member States and different societal groups have influence on them, than they are concerned with the policy fields in which the EU does, or does not, have influence. Furthermore, evaluations of level and inclusiveness are predominantly negative, whereas evaluations of scope are predominantly positive. In short, Dutch debaters online want the EU to become less powerful and stop further enlargement, but they also want the EU to take up responsibilities in more policy fields than it addresses now, particularly in the field of Justice and Home Affairs. A call for expansion of the policy fields under EU jurisdiction was made by Hans van Baalen, leading candidate for the EP elections of the conservative-liberal VVD party. As Nu.nl reports:

> Hans van Baalen argued [...] that the free market is vital for the Netherlands. 'We are merchants and not scared. A free market means open borders. That demands close European cooperation among police and judicial powers. That demands one single European asylum and immigration policy', according to Van Baalen (Nu.nl 2009b).⁹

---

7. 'Binnen de Europese Unie heb je hardwerkende landen die heeeel veel betalen, en je hebt profiteurs. Nederland is een betaler en heeft geen flikker te vertellen. De lidstaten die profiteren zijn het grootst en hebben het voor het zeggen.'
8. 'Terug naar de gulden, grenzen weer dicht. Ook geen last meer van al die criminelen uit het oostblok. De EEG werkte toch prima?'
9. 'Hans van Baalen zei in Rosmalen dat de vrije markt voor Nederland van levensbelang is: "Wij zijn kooplieden en geen bange mensen. Een vrije markt betekent open grenzen. Dat vraagt om nauwe Europese samenwerking tussen politie en justitie. Dat vraagt om één Europees asiel- en immigratiebeleid", aldus Van Baalen.'

A positive evaluation of future integration is provided by another party politician. Reporting an interview with Sophie in 't Veld, the European leader of the Dutch social-liberal party, D66, Nu.nl stated:

> Everyone thinks that veto powers provide power, but it only provides the power to block things. Only criminals profit if Europe is unable to provide adequate answers. According to the D66 leader, it is therefore necessary to remove [Member States'] veto powers as soon as possible. She argues Europe must be strengthened to ensure prosperity, a clean environment and safety (Nu.nl 2009e).[10]

It earned her generally negative responses from readers, like '100days': 'Yet another attempt to further shape the super state. D66 = 66 x STUPID' (Nu.nl 2009e).[11] Considerations of how the European Parliament elections might affect the future of integration were taken into the ballot box, as demonstrated by 'brutus68': 'Have just voted. A solid vote against a big Europe. Hopefully, Madlener [leading European candidate of Geert Wilders' PVV party] will wreak some havoc over there shortly' (GeenStijl 2009a).[12]

This points us to the important question of whether party politicians evaluate Europe differently from citizens. The present study is uniquely qualified to address this question as the evaluations of party politicians (often made directly or reported upon indirectly in the websites) are voluntarily commented upon by citizens in the commenting function. In addition, citizens entered into debate with each other in the commenting function, following party politicians' statements in the main articles. The gap between citizens and elites is not as pronounced as it was during the 2005 referendum, as reflected in the 61 per cent citizen vote against the Constitutional Treaty as opposed to the 85 per cent elected party politician vote in favour. Citizens tend to focus their comments more on the EU as it currently exists, whereas party politicians more evenly address all three dimensions of evaluation. Citizens are also more negative concerning the level and inclusiveness of the EU, whereas party politicians are more negative of inclusiveness (particularly enlargement with Turkey which is a main issue challenged by Geert Wilders). In light of this, the gap between citizens and elites over Europe, so strongly apparent in the 2005 referendum, appears to have become less pronounced in the 2009 European elections campaign. In other words, this chapter documents convergence within the Netherlands between elites and citizens in their evaluations of European integration and the EU.

---

10. 'Iedereen denkt dat je met veto's macht hebt, maar je kan enkel dingen blokkeren. Alleen criminelen hebben er baat bij dat Europa geen adequaat antwoord kan geven. Volgens de D66'er is het daarom noodzakelijk dat de veto's zo snel mogelijk worden afgeschaft. Ze stelt dat een versterking van Europa nodig om welvaart, een schoon milieu en veiligheid te kunnen garanderen.'
11. 'Wederom een poging om de superstaat verder vorm te geven. D66 = 66 x DOM!'
12. 'Net ook mijn stem uitgebracht. Een keiharde stem tegen een groot Europa. Hopelijk gaat Madlener flink schoppen daar straks!'

Justifications

As discussed above, with the exception of a few politicians and the early 1990s political consensus, the Dutch approach to European integration has generally been pragmatic. Politicians and citizens are in favour of integration in light of economic benefits and the recognition that the Netherlands is too small, and too open, to deal with certain policy challenges alone. Figure 8.4 provides an overview of all justifications used. Interestingly, the two justifications expected to dominate the debate in light of traditional Dutch discourse on European integration – necessity and economic prosperity – feature prominently, but not as prominently as the 'democracy' argument. As mentioned earlier, the leading candidate of the liberal D66 party, Sophie in 't Veld, argued in favour of removing Member State veto powers (Nu.nl 2009e). For her, the removal of veto powers would mean quicker decision making and thus a more efficient EU. It sparked a discussion in the commenting space on Nu.nl on whether this proposal was indeed necessary for the well-functioning of the EU. This quickly included a discussion on whether Member State veto powers are democratic and whether the European Parliament is useful, democratic and a cost-efficient counter balance to the Member States. Justifications on necessity, economic prosperity and democracy were all used in this debate. It is further interesting to note that a key topic that featured in the 2005 referendum campaign – the European Parliament's moving up and down between Brussels and Strasbourg – quickly re-entered the debate through citizens' comments, even if the main text of the article did not mention the European Parliament at all. This particular discussion thus neatly illustrates the extent to which existential issues like veto powers and the legitimacy of the EP featured in the Dutch EP election campaign. It furthermore shows how topics of the 2005 referendum resonate, even if politicians or journalists do not actively put them on the agenda again. Finally, it illustrates how justifications of democracy, necessity and economic prosperity are predominantly used in Dutch discourse to evaluate European integration (see Figure 8.3). On a more minor note, it is interesting to see that the justification of safety is nearly absent in the Dutch debate. This is interesting as safeguarding peace in Europe has long been a dominant argument in favour of integration throughout the EU, including in the Netherlands. The argument of peace was furthermore used frequently by the Dutch government during the 2005 referendum campaign, which earned them heavy criticism from the 'no' side and was generally considered to be counterproductive. In a sense, the 2009 campaign debaters have learned the lesson from the referendum campaign, that the argument that European integration is needed to prevent a third World War in Europe is no longer considered valid.

In comparison to the EU-wide debate covered in our comparative analysis, the Dutch debate does not stand out much in terms of justifications. Evaluations of European integration are slightly less often justified in the Netherlands than in the total sample. In particular, the justifications of safety, culture and democracy are less often invoked than in general, whereas the justifications of economic prosperity and necessity are invoked slightly more often. Still, the differences are not striking.

Paradoxically, therefore, there is clear evidence that the 2005 referendum debate in the Netherlands resounded in the 2009 European elections campaign, as topics and arguments can be qualitatively traced. Yet, this resounding of the 2005 referendum has not led to a unique debate in terms of substance, despite the fact that most of the twelve countries included in our study did not have a referendum on the Constitutional Treaty, or any other Treaty for that matter. Rather, the inheritance of the referendum seems to lie especially in the amount of evaluations made, where the Netherlands ranks relatively high among other Member States, such as the UK and Austria where the EU is controversial. Whereas the resonance of the 2005 referendum thus spells convergence of the Netherlands towards the more Eurocritical norm throughout the EU, it also means divergence, as the Dutch EP election debates are comparatively existential in nature.

Although the Netherlands has contributed strongly to European integration after the Second World War as one of the European Union's founding fathers, its Europeanism has mostly been pragmatic. European integration was seen by the majority of Dutch citizens and politicians as economically beneficial and unavoidable, in light of a need to collaborate internationally to address border crossing policy challenges and exploit international market opportunities.

Figure 8.3: Explaining opinions: how EU polity evaluations were justified in the Netherlands

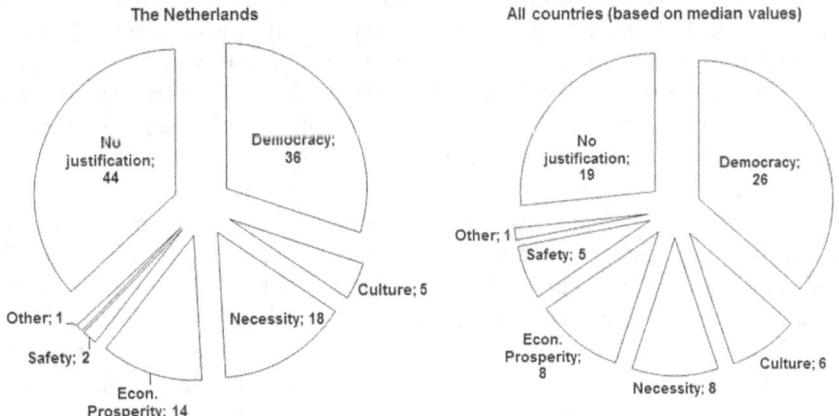

Conclusion

In general, European integration can hardly be called a controversial issue up until the mid-1990s. However, since then, issues like the introduction of the Euro, Eastern enlargement of 2004 and 2007, troubles with the Stability and Growth Pact, and the development towards becoming the largest per capita net contributor to the EU budget have made the Netherlands a markedly more Eurosceptic country. Euroscepticism has, furthermore, been fostered by a growing disillusionment in the established political elites, where populist parties on both the left and right side of the political spectrum have folded the issue of European integration into their more general criticism of 'The Hague' and its ruling political class. All this came to a head in the June 2005 referendum on the Treaty Establishing a Constitution for Europe, which was defeated by a majority of 61 per cent of the voters despite a majority of 85 per cent of Dutch parliamentarians in favour of the Treaty.

The findings presented in this chapter are three-fold. First, the 2005 referendum has clearly left its mark on Dutch politics concerning European integration. All major political parties were clearly recognised by citizens as either 'yes' parties or 'no' parties during the 2009 EP elections. Rather than a specific stance on the Treaty in question, these positions are now generally understood as positions concerning the entire project of European integration. Aside from having created clear profiles, the 2005 referendum also resonates in terms of themes. The Dutch debate might be characterised as 'existential', especially in comparison to the other countries involved in this study. A significant part of the debate addressed the institutional set-up of the EU, the powers of its different institutions, the extent to which citizens and the Netherlands are able to influence what happens in Brussels, and whether other countries (Central and Eastern European countries and Turkey) should be allowed to be(come) members of the Union. On the one hand, this contradicts the 'second-order elections' thesis that European parliamentary elections are about domestic politics. On the other hand, it stands in contrast to 'substantial' debates about what the elections should actually be about: EU policies in which the European Parliament has a meaningful say. Finally, it is different from other existential debates where the question of one's own membership is central. Few in the Dutch debate argued in favour of a withdrawal of the Netherlands from the EU. Rather, discussion focused on several aspects of the institutional design of the EU polity in which Dutch membership is taken for granted.

Secondly, debates about European integration took place, especially, on the three professional journalism websites, in contrast to the two political blogs. As clearly demonstrated by Figure 8.1, the debates on the three professional journalism websites were much more diverse in terms of topics than the ones on the blogs, which focused on domestic politics predominantly. Also, and probably related to this, the articles on the professional journalism websites stimulated many more evaluations of European integration. This was initially the case in the main texts of these articles, but these evaluations, in turn, invoked comments by readers and comments on comments in the discussion forums. There is thus evidence for the responsive nature of EU polity contestation, where arguments by politicians and other societal actors reported in the media trigger responses from citizens which are predominantly negative.

Thirdly, both party politicians and citizens address multiple aspects of European integration in their evaluations and provide both pro-European and Eurosceptic arguments. There was, in other words, a lively and diverse debate on European integration online during the 2009 European Parliament elections campaign in the Netherlands. Although party politicians in general still make more positive evaluations of European integration than citizens do, the huge opinion gap apparent in the 2005 referendum seems to have been reduced. This is so because Eurosceptic party politicians were more vocal in the online debate in 2009 than in the Dutch parliament in 2005. Also, citizens engage with each other in the commenting functions of websites on all kinds of aspects of European integration, including both highly informed and ill-founded arguments, well-argued statements as well as unreasoned outcries, polite comments and distasteful ones, pro-European and Eurosceptic arguments.

Chapter Nine | The European Other: The EU as External Threat in the Polish Online Debate

Natasza Styczyńska

With the collapse of the Iron Curtain and the commencement of economic and systemic transformation, Central and Eastern European countries, Poland amongst them, began the process of the 'return to Europe' – understood not only as a collection of values, but also as a concrete institutional framework. Since the 1990s, accession to the EU has constituted a strategic goal in Polish foreign policy, which was the only policy area conducted in a consistent way by subsequent governments, regardless of their party affiliation (Terry 2000). The fact that Poland is a relatively new Member State may be reflected in the divergence of its EU polity contestation in relation to older Member States. At the same time, its Euroscepticism and wider EU discourse are less historically engrained, which allows for more flexibility towards EU wide convergence. To fully grasp the intensity and meaning of Polish convergence on Euroscepticism, this chapter presents the findings of the Polish quantitative content analysis against the background of the main actors, lines of argumentation and historical turning points in recent Polish history.

The distinct stages of Poland's process of European integration are reflected in Polish public discourse on Europe. Up until the accession referendum in 2003, public debates on the issue were characterised by the assumption of the integration as a normal course of events, due to the 'return to Europe' (Fawn 2003). At the same time Poland's place in Europe was not widely debated among the general public, but mostly among political and economic elites (Góra and Mach 2010). Publicisation of the discourse and the intensification of public debate on membership only coincided with the date of the accession referendum in 2003[1], resulted in an intense campaign and an increased presence in the media both of supporters and adversaries of integration.

Crucially, almost from the beginning of the democratic transformation period the debate on Europe, and Poland's place in the structure of the EU, was determined by three dimensions. The first one is economic: accession in this respect is perceived as profitable for Poland, positively assessed by the majority of society, except radical groups in the fringes of the socio-political spectrum. Democracy is the second dimension, as the EU is seen as a guarantor of Polish democracy. Again, some right-wing nationalistic groups perceive 'the European criteria of democratization as the price to be paid for the economic profits of integration and modernization' (Góra and Mach 2010: 240). Last, but not least, is the axiological

---

1. The accession referendum took place on 7– 8 June, 2003, with the turnout of 58.85 per cent, and among these, 77.45 per cent voted to support Poland's EU membership.

dimension, which captures the extremely strong polarisation visible in Poland. For one part of the society, 'the EU is the embodiment of the Enlightenment, human rights, liberalism and individualistic values', but for the other 'Europe only makes sense when it is Catholic, or at least Christian' (Góra and Mach 2010: 240). The latter group perceives liberal values and the legacy of the Enlightenment as a danger, and destruction for both Europe and Poland (Góra and Mach 2010: 240).

This three-dimensional dichotomy of pro-European versus Eurosceptic arguments has influenced not only the pre-accession debates, but also, when EU membership became reality, the debate on integration and on Poland's place in European structures, as well as the further development and shape of the EU polity (Ziółkowski and Jędrzejewska 2009: 36). The most heated discussion has revolved around the voting procedures in the Council of the European Union and the allocation of votes to particular Member States. Other issues that featured in public debates at the time of accession were the deadlines for lifting the restrictions on land purchases by citizens of other Member States; the opening up of the labour markets to Polish citizens; energy; the EU Constitution; and the Charter of Fundamental Rights (Ziółkowski and Jędrzejewska 2009: 22–3). Since the accession in 2004, the contrast between pro-EU citizens and prominent Eurosceptic political actors has been centre-stage in the Polish political scene. Furthermore, the vast majority of Polish people have started to regard Poland's presence within the EU as a natural thing, even though there remain numerous voices criticising the role of the EU in the modernisation of the country or blaming the EU for all the misfortunes in Polish politics (Skotnicka-Iliasiewicz 2009a: 42–3).

In the following, I first discuss the manner in which EU polity contestation unfolds within this three-dimensional frame of the Polish debate on Europe and Poland's place in the structures of the EU, as well as the actors that carry the Eurosceptic arguments forward in the public debate. Three core characteristics of the Polish Eurosceptic camp emerge from this profiling exercise: the first one is the focus on the issues of the endangered national economy and identity. Secondly, and closely linked to the first element – particularly the endangered identity aspect is the citizen–elite divide, which brings to the fore the deep distrust of Polish citizens towards politicians and resonates with divergence of opinion between citizens and elites, reported in many other EU Member States. Thirdly, even though Euroscepticism enjoys limited support from the public, it is very prominent in the public debate, thanks largely to the high public profile of some of its key proponents, such as prominent politicians, certain high-circulation media outlets and the Catholic Church.

It is in this context that I then discuss the findings from the 2009 EP elections, following a brief presentation of the sources and data, as well as the general nature of the Polish online debate. I revisit the paradoxical nature of Polish Eurosceptic public discourse (marginal public support yet high public profile) and the dual-axis of Eurosceptic argumentation, namely the endangered national economy and identity, in the concluding part of the chapter.

The components of Polish Euroscepticism

To begin with, expressing support or opposition towards European integration requires a certain maturity of society, which is characterised not only by experience in civic activity, but also by a high level of knowledge about social and political processes. In Poland, the general low level of interest in political matters and in civic activity has resulted in weak civic initiatives, both in support of and in opposition to European integration (CBOS 2010a; Osiatyński 1996; Zuba 2006: 239–40). Nevertheless, the entry in the national Polish Parliament of Eurosceptic parties in 2001, followed by the entry of some of these in the European Parliament in 2004, as well as the Eurosceptic rhetoric of prominent mainstream politicians, like the Kaczyński brothers, have certainly compounded Poland's image as Eurosceptic among its EU counterparts (Szczerbiak & Taggart 2008b).

In the Polish academic discourse (Zuba 2006) the term *Eurosceptic* is used to define a person negating integration and the EU as such, whereas those who approve of integration and the EU whilst maintaining doubts about some aspects of integration are defined as *Eurorealists*.[2] Nevertheless, the boundaries between Eurosceptic and Eurorealist rhetoric are often blurred in Polish discourse, largely due to the shift of rhetoric of the same actors in the post-accession era from a Eurosceptic-EU-negating position, to a more realistic EU-membership-with-caveats line of argument. In the following I use the term 'Eurosceptic' to refer to those actors and lines of argument that have been at the forefront of Eurosceptic campaigning and public discourse, and are largely rooted in a basic rejection of the core values and structures of the EU polity – even if in recent times this rejection is adapted to the reality of Poland being a EU Member State.

Before I get into the specifics of the online debates concerning the EU during the 2009 EP election campaigns, it is necessary to address, in greater length, two issues which consistently feature in Polish public contestation of the EU polity, namely the endangered economy and the endangered national identity.

Endangered economy

Societal expectations about Poland's accession to the EU have played an important role in shaping attitudes towards the Union itself. Before 2004, there were two distinguishable types of attitudes; on the one hand, we find very high economic expectations connected to the process of EU integration. On the other hand, there was a total negation of validity of integration connected to the fear of deterioration of the Polish economy, and the situation of farmers in particular. The latter group was convinced that Polish people would be treated as second-class citizens in the

---

2. *See also* the analytical model proposed by Kopecký and Mudde (2002), which allows the distinction between those who constructively criticise the European Union, but do not negate the idea of European integration, from those who reject the very idea of the EU and demand withdrawal from the Union.

first years of membership and that Polish products would not find purchasers in the markets of other Member States. There was also concern about Poland becoming a market for the old Member States, and the slogans of '40-million market' appeared in the campaigns of the populist Self-Defense, the League of Polish Families and the agrarian Polish People's Party (Zuba 2006: 211).

The debate about presumptive economic gains and losses was closely linked to the discussion about endangered identity. On the one hand there was awareness of possible benefits from gaining new investors; on the other, the fear of foreign capital buying out Poland and leading Polish businesses to mass bankruptcy, was a strong feature of the debate. This fear particularly characterised those who lost as a consequence of economic change in time of transformation, in which case their reluctance and aversion towards foreign capital was not entirely unfounded (Adamski 1998). Another controversial issue has been the entry to the euro area, as adoption of the euro requires a change to the Constitution. In 2007, the government of Donald Tusk undertook the first attempts to address this, but both the then-president Kaczynski and the Law and Justice Party wanted a referendum before any changes were to be introduced in the Constitution. To avoid an open conflict with the President, the Tusk government slowed down the reformation process and the issue has stalled since. Recent public opinion polls, which I discuss at greater length later on in this chapter, show that Polish society remains concerned with regard to the pace of the euro adoption process (Więcław 2010). Despite these concerns, support for the entry of Poland into the euro area currently fluctuates at around 60 per cent (Więcław 2010).

Endangered identity

The Polish debate on European integration and the EU polity is historically determined by the issues of Poland's peripheral location and geopolitics, which include the permanent fear of its two great neighbours and 'significant others': Germany and Russia (Góra and Mach 2010: 239; Tazbir 2004). Furthermore, Poland's political history has generated the strong tradition of citizens opposing authority, as in the last 200 years the state institutions have been mainly oppressive to the nation.[3] As a result, Polish national identity has developed not on the basis of state institutions but in opposition to them (Mach 1993). This tradition has led to the creation of a strong conviction among citizens that Polish identity is under constant danger – also from the EU – and there is thus the need to protect it. This embeddedness in the national community, understood as 'we' and being part of the opposition 'us' (the citizens) vs. 'them' (the politicians), is to some extent, also the legacy of communism as felt through a deeply rooted feeling of community under threat, and a rejection of the surrounding system (Ziółkowski and Jędrzejewska 2009: 26–7).

---

3. Poland faced partitions and the rule of Austria, Prussia and Russia in the years 1772–1919, and the communist rule in the years 1945–1989.

The problem of the 'endangered Polish identity' is particularly important for the EU adversaries. The cultural and identity dimensions of EU membership has been one of the most hotly debated and controversial aspects of the accession debate and comes under the axiological dimension of the wider Polish debate on European integration. Eurosceptics have been expressing their concerns that as a result of European integration, a new (European) kind of identity would emerge and might become an alternative to the predominant Polish national identity. These anxieties were reflected in the discussion about the loss of Polish cultural identity as a consequence of accession (Mach and Niedźwiedzki 2002: 10). This type of EU polity contestation draws on a specific perception of the EU, ascribing to it certain (stereotypical) features – the Union is dominating, bureaucratic, colonial, liberal, and secular, and thus diametrically opposite from the Polish identity, which is built on morality and 'healthy', Christian values (Janicki 2009). As Zuba (2006) notes, the threat to national identity in Eurosceptic argumentation refers to a fear of 'dissolving' into the European multicultural space, or domination over Polish culture by the culture of bigger, wealthier and more expansive countries.

One can find here a double-bottom argument, as Eurosceptics marry up political aspects with those of culture and identity. The EU is perceived by its critics as an empire, with accession as irreversible, and integration advancing on an everyday basis in the realisation of federation and the 'absorption' of nation states. Another argument on the part of Polish Eurosceptics is the conspicuous deficit of democracy in the EU, which amplifies the 'imperial' character of the community. EU membership, especially in the rhetoric of the League of Polish Families, or the Real Politics Union, was to weaken the relations between Poland and the USA and undermine Poland's position in the international arena (Nalewajko 2003: 129). Further compounding the fears of colonisation is the rhetoric against Germany and its hegemonic role, as voiced by right-wing parties, both in the margins and in the mainstream of Polish politics. For example, former and current leaders of the Polish People's Party (Jarosław Kalinowski) and of the Law and Justice party (Jarosław and Lech Kaczyński) are no strangers to this type of rhetoric (Zuba 2006). This brings me to one of the key arenas for current Polish Eurosceptic discourse, namely party politics.

Party politics

Crucial for understanding Polish Euroscepticism is the strong correlation between domestic and supranational politics and the fact that Europe is still perceived more as 'them', rather than 'we'. Strong axiological divisions on the domestic political arena have a significant impact on the perception of the EU as such, and also on the support for candidates in the elections to the European Parliament. Citizens tend to cast their vote along the same lines as their national party preferences rather than supranational fractions. Treating the EU as 'them' reflects in the belief that European institutions do not influence citizens' lives (Gajda 2009: 229).

Adversaries of the European integration process were mostly active on the Polish political scene in the years preceding the accession referendum and the signature of the Accession Treaty itself. Among groups opposing the accession, two main trends were observable: the first, comprising predominantly farmers, maintained that joining the EU was detrimental to the Polish economy and agriculture in particular. The second, which emerged within the Catholic Church and its associate conservative circles, argued that the accession posed a threat to Polish national identity and morality (Zuba 2006: 444). These organisations and political parties (and consequently their followers) which claim that the accession to European structures was a mistake, and the Polish presence in the EU is detrimental to the state, currently enjoy much less public support than in the pre-accession period, with the exception of the Law and Justice party, which is the main opposition party in the Polish parliament.

One such political grouping, the League of Polish Families (*Liga Polskich Rodzin*, LPR), was formed in 2001 by small parties and associations organised around the ideology of National Democracy and references to its inter-war tradition, that claimed Poland should be inhabited by the ethnic Poles only (Walicki 2000: 324). Its youth wing[4] considers itself as a reactivation of the anti-Semitic and xenophobic youth organisation established in the late 1920s. The League positioned itself as the main party that opposed Polish membership in the EU and also organised and initiated a series of events, manifestations and conferences in 2002 and 2003, with the aim to persuade Polish people to reject accession in the referendum (Pankowski and Kornak 2005: 159).

The League's core argument against EU membership is that Poland can only develop outside the EU, because the latter is a 'neo-colonial' project, promotes a 'civilization of death' by propagating moral decay: euthanasia, abortion, drugs and sexual perversions (Góra and Mach 2010: 230; Sokolewicz 2003) and also pushes for a 'buyout of the Polish land and annihilation of the Polish raison d'être', which would form the foundation for the 'fourth partition of Poland' (Sokolewicz 2003).

In the 2004 elections to the European Parliament, LPR obtained 15.9 per cent of the votes, and inducted ten deputies into the fractionfaction Independence and Democracy (Słodkowska and Dołbakowska 2006). In the 2005 national parliamentary elections, the LPR gained nearly 8 per cent of the votes and became a part of the government until the accelerated elections in 2007. However, the costs of integration were to be much fewer than LPR predicted and the party neither entered the national parliament in 2007, nor gained the European Parliament mandate in 2009. Nevertheless, LPR-affiliated politicians actively participate in devising new anti-EU political groupings such as the Polish division of Libertas.

---

4. All Polish Youth (Młodzież Wszechpolska) is an organisation referring to the rhetoric of the radical right pre-war National Democratic camp. The organisation was very active between 2002 and 2007, but as a consequence of their failure in 2007 election, their activity has since faded away. All Polish Youth would frequently adduce to anti-Semitic, xenophobic slogans which referred to the tradition of national socialism, provoking storms of protest from public intellectuals, artists and other public figures (Pankowski and Kornak 2005: 159).

Emphasis on the threat the EU poses to the Polish economy was also at the heart of Self-Defense's (*Samoobrona*) rhetoric, which also had a focus on agriculture claiming that Poland would become a 'selling market' for the European Community, which would drag down the unsubsidised Polish agriculture. This party promoted 'tough negotiation conditions' with the EU, and also an almost total ban on land purchase by foreigners (Zuba 2006: 281–2). In the 2004 EP elections Self-Defense received nearly 11 per cent of the votes, which enabled the party to introduce 6 deputies to the European Parliament. Similarly to the League of Polish Families, Self-Defense did not manage to enter neither the national parliament in 2007, nor the EP in 2009.

In contrast to the above two political parties, whose presence in the national and European parliaments has withered in recent years, the Law and Justice Party (*Prawo i Sprawiedliwość*) remains a key player in the Polish political scene. Eurosceptic from its inception, in the pre-accession era it emphasised the need to protect the Polish economy and claimed that Poland should maintain a strong and uncompromised position during negotiations with the EU. However, as Krzysztof Cebul (2009: 168) notes, these claims were characterised by inconsistency, with the party warning of the threat of EU domination on the one hand, and welcoming the prospect of aid and benefits that EU membership would bring to Poland on the other. Since the 2007 election Law and Justice has become the major opposition party, continuing to support a Europe of loosely connected nation states (Europe of Nations) and maintaining a decisive stance in support of Polish national interests and the strengthening of Poland's strategic partnership with the United States (PiS 2010; Podgórzańska 2007: 140–1).

In addition to the above, there are several minor Eurosceptic organisations and associations, which do not enjoy the same support as political parties, but have always been present in public discourse. Among these we find Poland's most extreme far-right organisation National Rebirth of Poland (*Narodowe Odrodzenie Polski*) and the, now-collapsed, self-proclaimed conservative-liberal party, Real Politics Union (*Unia Polityki Realnej*) (Witczak 2009). The latter was founded by Janusz Korwin-Mikke, whose blog was one of the most frequently visited political blogs during the election campaign of the European Parliament in 2009. Korwin-Mikke, frequently declares that Hitler's rule was less oppressive in terms of taxation than the current democratic system, and also that the EU is a creation of Jews and/or masonry (Pankowski and Kornak 2005: 163). Though marginal, the Real Politics Union is a visible player on the Polish political scene thanks to its bold presence and controversial views.

In 2009, the Polish division of Libertas also appeared in the Polish Eurosceptic scene, bringing together anti-EU membership campaigners of the pre-referendum era and focusing on denying further integration, defending 'national values and national identity' and rejecting the Lisbon Treaty (Styczyńska 2009: 141). These formations are active in the online realm, which proves to be the easiest and cheapest way of reaching their potential recipients. Overall, the media have a central role in both facilitating and sustaining EU polity contestation in the Polish public discourse, as I show below.

The media and the Catholic Church

In the years 2005–07, the Law and Justice party, in cooperation with the League of Polish Families, tried to gain control of the media landscape by obtaining partial ownership of dailies with broad circulation, such as *Rzeczpospolita* and *Polska The Times*, as well as by appointing ideologically affiliated members to the board of public television (the board is selected by the parliament and as Law and Justice had a majority in the parliament at the time, they saw an opportunity to ideologically control the public television broadcast). These media outlets frequently adopt Eurosceptic views for their news framing.

However, the most active Eurosceptic voices nowadays, come from the Catholic media group, which includes the weekly Ours Daily (*Nasz Dziennik*) and Radio Maria (*Radio Maryja*). Radio Maria is a nationalistic, xenophobic broadcasting company, established in 1991 by a Redemptorist congregation. Its charismatic director, Father Tadeusz Rydzyk, is well known for his anti-Semitic, nationalistic views. In the period preceding the referendum, the radio station actively supported the view of rejection of the accession treaty and since 2004, the station presents a critical stance towards the EU and the conditions of Polish membership (Markowski and Tucker 2010: 526). The radio supports the Law and Justice party and other minor organisations of national character. The share of Radio Maria in the market amounts to 2 per cent, and its listeners are mainly older people but its online presence is virtually non-existent (Wirtualnemedia.pl 2009). Its case is indicative of the role that the Polish Catholic Church has played in the process of European integration. The attitude of the Catholic Church in Poland towards integration and EU membership has not only been diverse with regard to time, but also with regard to the Church hierarchy. Specifically, the Church has never spoken about European issues in one voice and its stance has been shifting since 1989. Even though the official stance of the Church after 1997 has been pro-European, Eurosceptic fractions factions persist. Officially there is no support for Radio Maria, but part of the clergy still relies on its message in their everyday work (Leszczyńska 2009a). Prior to the referendum, some Church circles emphasised that EU accession brings the danger of implanting in Poland a so-called 'civilization of death', namely access to abortion and euthanasia. Currently, the Church in Poland stipulates that it does not support certain aspects of EU politics, such as financial aid for in vitro research (Leszczyńska 2009b: 216–17).

Civil society and public opinion

Contrary to political and Church actors, Polish public opinion is generally pro-European, and observable benefits of EU membership have convinced a lot of people who had previously been opposed to accession, to change their minds (CBOS 2010b; Pilecka 2009: 353). This applies mainly to farmers, since they are the biggest beneficiaries of the accession. The 2009 autumn Eurobarometer public opinion survey shows that a majority (85 per cent) of the society are content at Poland's membership (Eurobarometer 2009d). More than 74 per cent believe the accession contributed to the strengthening of Poland's position in the world and almost half of the respondents think their material status improved (Szacki 2009). It needs to be stressed, however, that the interest in supranational politics is low, as can also be observed during EP elections, when voter turnout is usually lower than in domestic ones (PKW Państwowa Komisja Wyborcza 2010). Most of the citizens have a 'second-order election' view of the EP electoral process, i.e. EP elections are less important than the national ones (Gajda 2009: 229).

When Eurosceptic attitudes are recorded among citizens, these are linked to a lack of information about EU structures, as well as to the Eurosceptic catchphrases replicated by the tabloid press, which enjoys substantial circulation (Mikułowski-Pomorski and Gawlewicz 2009; Skotnicka-Iliasiewicz 2009b). Scant knowledge about the functioning of the EU generates a lack of trust in effectiveness of negotiations, augmented by a lack of trust in politicians and disappointment with politics in general.

Crucially, those opposing integration base their opinions on 'common knowledge' and, as it was shown in an opinion poll carried out before the accession referendum, 63 per cent of the respondents declared that their opinions are based on 'their own considerations', while 36 per cent on 'conversations with acquaintances', only 16 per cent on public claims by politicians, and just 11 per cent on information derived from newspapers (Skotnicka-Iliasiewicz 2002: 8). A public opinion poll before the referendum revealed that when choosing candidates, 30 per cent of Polish citizens would be guided by their family's opinion, 19 per cent by the Catholic Church's, and 15 per cent by the party which they support (CBOS 2003). Correlation with pro-European evaluations is only observable in relation to domestic politics – specific groups of voters (mainly Civic Platform and Democratic Left Alliance followers) are regarded as Euroenthusiasts by nature, thoughtlessly approving of the Union, in contrast to whom, opposition is created by self-proclaimed realists who tend to notice threats, especially with regard to the process of deepening integration (Jasiecki 2004: 94–5; Wiszniowski 2008: 223–4).

European Parliament elections in Poland

In light of the issues discussed above, Polish Euroscepticism emerges as largely marginal in terms of public opinion, media coverage and party politics, but at the same time, as highly visible in the public arena, mainly thanks to the strong public profile of some of its proponents, who have top positions in mainstream political parties. Eurosceptic arguments made in Polish public discourse are strongly historically determined, focused on national identity and economy but the overall public knowledge and interest in the EU is low, as is also reflected by the very low turnout in the EP elections.

We would, thus, expect online coverage of the 2009 EP elections to at least, partially reflect these tendencies, namely for online EU election debates to unfold along existential lines of argument, i.e. framed in a national context, with frequent references to national identity and sovereignty; and for Eurosceptic arguments to form the minority of arguments but to come from prominent actors. Similarly, given that opinion polls consistently portray Polish citizens as largely pro-European, we would expect online contributions from the public to be also predominantly pro-European, in a pragmatic, substantial way, unless the more deeply rooted 'us V. them' culture of citizens against politicians resurfaces online, where citizens have the potential to directly express their views, as opposed to offline media, which constitute the 'stronghold' of political actors and journalists. The data analysis presented below largely confirms these expectations but also reveals some trends that break away from what we have come to expect of Polish public debates on the worth of the EU.

Online EU polity contestation

The three most popular professional journalism websites of the Polish e-sphere sampled for this study were *Wirtualna Polska* (Alexa rank: 5), TVN24.pl (Alexa rank: 31) and Gazeta.pl (Alexa rank: 10). The two most popular political blogs included were Janusz Korwin-Mikke (Korwin-Mikke 2010) and Janusz Palikot (Palikot 2010a).[5] Of the three professional news websites, TVN24.pl is the online version of the television channel TVN24, Gazeta.pl is owned and run by the newspaper *Gazeta Wyborcza*, while *Wirtualna Polska* (wp.pl) is a web-only platform. All three belong to large media groups that include various media outlets (online platforms, newspapers, TV, radio). As regards the two blogs, both of them are written by controversial and rather eccentric individuals. Korwin-Mikke is a former dissident and monarchist, founder of *The Highest Time* (*Najwyższy Czas*) weekly, where he maintains a column. He criticises the EU as a bureaucratic regime and as 'Europe's backwater' (*eurozaścianek*), and argues that the EU is non-democratic. Korwin-Mikke is also against Poland joining the euro area. His often politically incorrect and controversial opinions are supported only by a marginal number of voters – he was thrice candidate for president and voter support towards him decreased from just over two per cent in 1995, to just over 1 per cent in 2005. UPR obtained 1 per cent of votes in the 2009 elections to EP. Janusz Palikot is an active politician, originally a member of the Civic Platform (ruling party from 2007), who has recently formed his own movement, based on anticlerical and liberal positions, and who is generally considered as a 'court jester' by his opponents (Palikot 2010b). His blog contains different forms of news and gossip mainly about the opposition, especially the Law and Justice party and the Twin Brothers (Kaczyński). Palikot is well known for his 'political performances' and controversial actions in the Parliament.

---

5. As there were no political blogs among the top 100 Polish websites on Alexa, independent political blogs were selected on the basics of Onet political blog ranking (Onet.pl 2010).

Profiling the election in the Polish debate

The campaign before the elections to the European Parliament in 2009 was dominated by political declarations which can be divided into three types: negating the EU and integration, realistic (pragmatic) and Euroenthusiastic. Parties opposed to the EU were represented by the Polish division of Libertas and Right of the Republic (*Prawica RP*) and hardly gained any support from voters (3.1 per cent of votes in total). The Libertas candidate from the Warsaw list, Artur Zawisza, when asked about the dangers the EU poses declared that 'the biggest danger is the antidemocratic and the bureaucratic Treaty of Lisbon' (Wirtualna Polska 2009a). Eurosceptic Law and Justice got the second best result after Civic Platform (27.4 per cent of votes), catering to those who are dissatisfied with the current shape of Poland's membership in the EU, or with the Union itself. The ruling party, Civic Platform, received the best result, gathering 44 and 43 per cent of votes. The pro-European Alliance of Democratic Left and Workers Union received 12.3 per cent of the votes.

Nevertheless, the turnout was only 24.53 per cent, slightly higher than in the 2004 elections (PKW 2009). The election issues were not broadly discussed in the media. The Eurobarometer survey conducted in autumn 2008, revealed that three-quarters of Poles (74 per cent) were not aware when the coming European parliamentary elections were due to take place (Rzeczpospolita 2009). Instead, the media limited themselves to descriptive coverage of electoral lists and prospective alliances in the EP. Some popular Internet platforms created special services devoted to the elections, where they presented the latest news, candidate profiles and their statements. The most popular such service, was offered by Onet.pl portal (Onet.pl 2009). Among the Eurosceptic media, Radio Maria remained active, supporting not only Law and Justice, but also the campaign of Right of the Republic and favourably viewed the creation of Libertas in Poland. The public television channels also criticised the future shape of the Union and favoured politicians representing Libertas.

Main moments and issues during the election campaign

The campaign started in early May 2009, but was not visible in the online media during the first weeks of May. The campaign in public television started on the 13 May, and interest in the elections increased among the public from 30 per cent in April, to 38 per cent by the end of May (Rzeczpospolita 2009). A series of public institutions, independent associations alike, carried out various actions aimed at encouraging Polish people to vote, but also presented the workings of the European Parliament and its influence on the functioning of Member States. One such initiative was the Pro-attendance Campaign Poland, 'The Navel of Europe'. Another, organised by the EP in all Member States, was the information campaign aimed at the youngest voters, for whom these elections might be the first ones in their life (PEBI 2009). At the same time, however, several Polish MEPs, who were initially non-inscrits, have now become members of marginal, Eurosceptic political groupings. An example of this, is the Union for a Europe of the Nations (in 2004–09, Law and Justice deputies constituted almost half of its members).

The issues that dominated during the 2009 EP election campaign, were the entry into force of the Treaty of Lisbon and the chances of the creation of a new fractionfaction in the EP by Law and Justice, together with British and Czech conservatives. Even so, the press and online news services devoted more attention to domestic issues than to the EP elections. Online debates got off to a late start, not commencing until nearly four weeks before the election. This may have been caused by the late start of the main political party campaigns (Szewczyk 2009). General interest in the elections was not substantial, thus in turn, the volume of information on this topic is insignificant. During the whole period under study, 148 articles were recorded on selected sites. It is worth noting, however, that the online news platforms under study do not specialise in political news, and if they focus on politics, it is usually restricted to a domestic dimension.

The presence of election-related articles in electronic media initially boiled down to the presentation of candidates, and then, with the election approaching, was narrowed down to the assessment of the prospects for particular committees or prospective coalitions in the European Parliament. The online platforms under study lacked commentary journalism, or expert analysis, with short, synthetic information being the focus instead. Interestingly enough, coverage of the political programmes was practically non-existent, and the discussion on the future shape of the European Union was limited to underscoring the division into supporters and adversaries of deepening integration. Politicians themselves contributed to this state of affairs. On the website of Zbigniew Ziobro, candidate to the European Parliament from the list of Law and Justice, the programme link led to the domestic political programme of the party rather than his programme on EU issues and policies (Kursa 2009).

In general, online debates about Poland's membership of the EU and further integration were marked by emotions and reflect division lines in the domestic political arena. This emotional character applies mainly to comments posted by ordinary Internet users, since information provided by portals (journalists) in the form of news or articles usually assumed descriptive character. In the rare occasions when journalistic coverage offered any evaluation of the EU, this assessment was supported by the evidence, such as public opinion trends and pools.

Although the selected professional news websites and political blogs offer the possibility for interaction between the core communicators and the audience, being active online is not yet popular among Poles. Currently 53 per cent of men and 45 per cent of women use the Internet in Poland, and only 21 per cent of all Internet users read political blogs. In contrast, non-political blogs are read by more than 40 per cent of Polish internet users (CBOS 2009). The percentage of Internet users who comment increased from 20 per cent in 2005 to 37 per cent in 2009 (Pliszka 2009), but it is still not common behaviour. Of a total of forty-two EU polity evaluations coded within the selected fifty articles, most of the EU evaluations (twenty-one cases) were located in the main article, with just fourteen cases found in users' comments.

The debate mainly reflected domestic politics, and the few articles about the Union's politics were also linked to domestic politics. For example, there was a discussion about the prospects for the future coalition of conservative parties in the European Parliament, but mainly through the prism that Law and Justice could have played an important role there (Gazeta.pl 2009; *Polska The Times* 2009). Coverage of the 2009 EP election campaigns was certainly more balanced in terms of journalistic coverage, particularly on the three professional journalism news websites. Users leaving their comments on the main articles focused consistently – and in one case exclusively (Wirtualna Polska 2009b) – on the domestic dimension of the EP elections, often directing invectives at the domestic party's EP candidates.

Online debates hardly focused on the future development and integration of the EU, but they briefly touched upon the Treaty of Lisbon and its signature. This reflects also the disinterest of Polish public opinion towards the Treaty of Lisbon. Research conducted by the public opinion research centre CBOS, has shown that only 7 per cent of Poles declare distinct interest in the Treaty of Lisbon. At the same time almost 70 per cent of Poles declare that their knowledge about the Treaty is insufficient (CBOS 2008). This lack of knowledge occasionally finds expression in the online debates examined through prejudiced comments, based on aggressive, xenophobic or homophobic attitudes such as calling the Lisbon Treaty a 'lesbian treaty' (PAP 2009a).

Regarding the main topics and issues one can notice a decline in incisive, confrontational rhetoric since the parliamentary elections in 2007, which, however, does not mean a significant change in worldview. The change concerns only the way interests are articulated. Instead of conveying the Europhobic rhetoric of 'derooting', 'buyout of land', 'civilization of death', we find more frequently in the 2009 EP election online debates postulates of 'strengthening nation states', 'restricting integration in non-economic areas', or 'necessity to strengthen Christian values in the EU'. Articles containing evaluations that totally negate Poland's presence in the EU were found only on Janusz Korwin-Mikke's blog (four evaluations).

Dimensions of EU polity evaluation

Out of the forty-two EU polity evaluations coded in total within the selected fifty articles, only five were made by journalists, as Figure 9.1 below illustrates; a finding which reflects the overall descriptive nature of the coverage that the 2009 EP elections received online. As mentioned earlier, the principle of European integration and the EU in general are viewed favourably by Polish society and hardly anyone contests the validity of the very process of integration. Issues of EU structure and activity invoke more controversy and this is also reflected in the online debates examined here: thirty-three evaluations were found concerning the current EU polity set-up, the majority of which were negative. The EU is characterised as 'a façade organization' (Pawlicki 2009), a social democracy with no real power due to its 'democratic deficit' (Korwin-Mikke 2009a) and the only valuable idea is that of rejecting a federal model for the sake of a 'Europe of nation states' (PAP 2009b).

Figure 9.1: Distribution of EU evaluations across countries: Polish contributions per actor

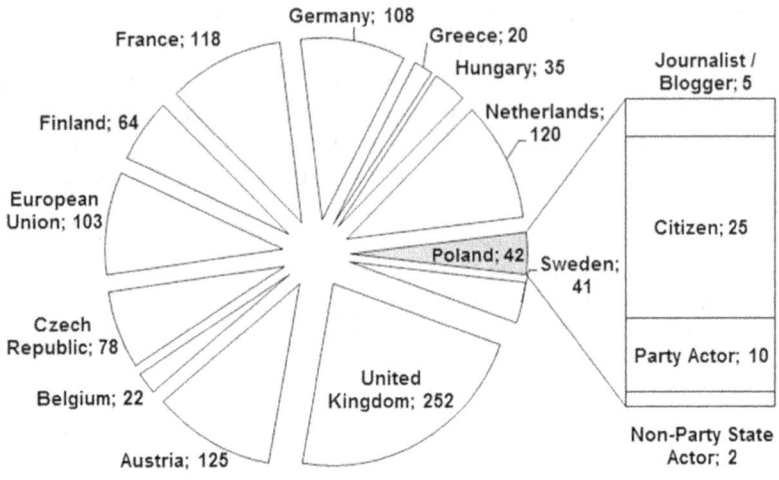

Similarly, users of the online news media examined here were negative towards the future of the EU project, although this aspect of European integration was largely ignored in the online debates analysed here (just sixteen evaluations concerned the future project of integration and twelve of these were negative). Contributors insisted on a 'Europe of Nations' model than what is perceived as EU federalisation. Moreover, the relevant evaluations resonate the fears raised before the 2003 referendum of the loss of independence and national identity, of accepting the so called civilization of death and of losing control over crucial economic branches (Zuba 2006: 194–5). Some of the users identify these threats with the ratification of the Lisbon Treaty, while several commentators agreed with the statement made by Czech Prime Minister Topolánek, that the 'Lisbon Treaty is already dead' (PAP 2009b) and the only solution is an idea of union based on independent states.

The negative evaluations found in the Polish online debates on the EU polity go hand-in-hand with the claims of democratic deficit (in twenty-one cases out of twenty-three where the contributor offered an explanation of their EU evaluation), which concerns not only the distribution of power and democratic virtue of the EU institutions but also, the extent to which the citizens' voice can be heard in the decision-making process. Comments such as, 'The EU is not democratic' (Pawlicki 2009), 'in the European Union ordinary citizens have no say' (*Polska The Times* 2009), 'European politicians and clerks are only using our money, instead of working for us' (Pawlicki 2009), 'it is only about euro-propaganda, but nothing for the citizens' and the 'EU is colonizing Eastern Europe' (Korwin-Mikke 2009a) are indicative of this type of argumentation used to structure negative evaluations about the EU polity.

Justifications of the worth of the EU polity correspond with the main dimension of the Polish debate on Europe in general: democracy and economic prosperity (Figure 9.2 below). As the online debate is not substantial, there was a high rate of statements without any justification. In the majority of cases, comments are about domestic politics and typical Polish experiences. If one is criticising the European Union, they may base their argument on the post-communist attitude – denying every authority, no matter where it comes from, and even if it is democratic. People are emphasising their lack of trust in politicians and not attending the European parliamentary elections, is a way of expressing their mistrust: 'I won't vote, as I don't want them to earn so much money, while I am unemployed' (Wirtualna Polska 2009c, 2009d); 'voting is not going to change a thing, they will cheat on us, as they always did' (Pawlicki 2009); 'the European Parliament is not democratic and does not represent citizens' (Wirtualna Polska 2009d); politicians are only 'pulling the wool over our eyes' (Pawlicki 2009). In the case of the village Bieczyno, people didn't vote at all, explaining it as an act of 'revenge' on the local authorities (Uhlig 2009). Others argued that 'politicians are proving every day that they are not worth our voices' (PAP 2009c).

Besides those using the 'democratic deficit' line of argument to explain their assessment of the EU polity and project of integration, the majority of contributors simply did not offer any justification for their evaluations. Rather they built their views on generic assessments such as, 'The European Union makes no sense' (PAP 2009d) and 'joining the European Union meant acceptance of Germanization' (PAP 2009e). Moreover, coded statements are short, often formed in an emotive way: the European Union is labelled as 'euro-rubbish' (Korwin-Mikke 2009b) or as 'EU=fascism' (PAP 2009a). References to issues present in domestic politics are prevalent, as is the negation of current government activity, which can be noticed in such comments as 'PO (Civic Platform) is doing what Merkel tells them to do' (Pszczółkowska *et al.* 2009).

Figure 9.2: Explaining opinions: how EU polity evaluations were justified in Poland

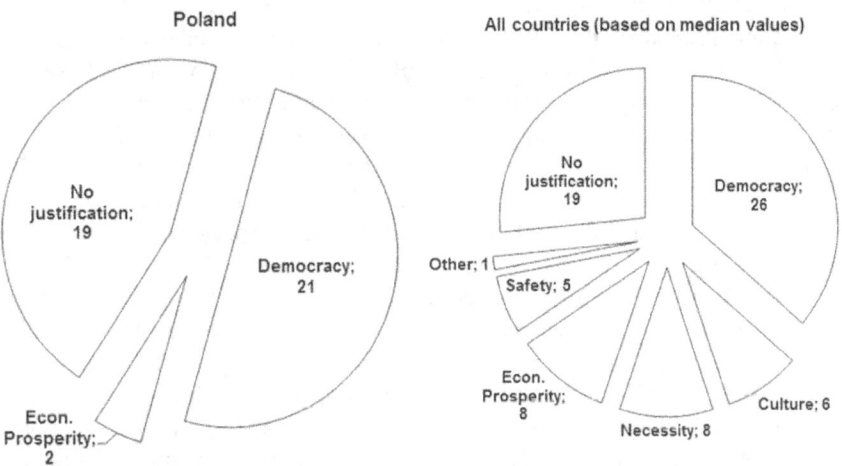

Conclusion

The profiling of Polish Euroscepticism along the three-dimensional frame of economy, democracy and cultural/societal values (Góra and Mach 2010), points to three core characteristics of the Polish Eurosceptic camp that concern both the actors and the manner in which Eurosceptic arguments unfold within public debate on Europe, and Poland's place in the structures of the EU. The first element characterising Polish Euroscepticism is the focus on the issues of the endangered national economy and identity. In other words, the key arguments underlying Polish Eurosceptic discourse are deeply existential. Secondly, and closely linked to the first element, particularly the endangered identity aspect, is the citizen–elite dimension, which brings to the fore the deep distrust of Polish citizens towards politicians. Thirdly, even though Euroscepticism enjoys limited support from the public, it is very prominent in the public debate, thanks largely to the high public profile of some of its key proponents, such as prominent politicians, certain high-circulation media outlets and the Catholic Church.

The analysis of the data from the 2009 EP election campaign e-debates in some of the most popular professional journalism news websites and political blogs, has shown that the deeply rooted 'us vs. them' culture of citizens against politicians resurfaces online, giving more space to the Eurosceptic voices in the online debate. This, however, is not the only factor that explains the prominence of Euroscepticism in the Polish online public discourse. Rather, the latter is a result of a confluence of several factors: lack of interest in European integration, a build-up of historical bias based on emotions and mainly on fears of what is unknown and strange.

First and foremost, the Euroscepticism recorded in online debates is a response to domestic politics and conspicuous social divisions, and consequently it is a counter argument to Euroenthusiasts. The main Eurosceptic voices came from the citizens (anonymous users). It is appropriate to come back at this point not only to the low turnout, but also to the lack of interest in politics on the part of Polish people, and their scant knowledge about it (Skotnicka-Illasiewicz 2009b: 239).

Nationalisation of the EU's politics, i.e. identification of domestic politics with European politics, is also well visible. The soundness of such a linkage is confirmed by the very political parties for whom European parliamentary elections are a litmus test of support in society. However, voters are tired of the style and effects of politics. In online debates, there frequently appeared statements that voting in EP elections would not change anything. This argument has been seen in domestic campaigns and reveals the level of trust society puts in the political elite. What is more, the Polish public lacks awareness of how the European Parliament actually affects their lives (Gajda 2009).

The analysis of the coded material has shown that EU polity contestation often comes from disappointment with domestic politics and the transformation itself, as the current division between supporters and opponents of European integration overlaps with the division between beneficiaries and losers in the Polish transformation (Jarosz 2005; Jasiecki 2004). Poles are disappointed with politics in general, and the lack of interest in European politics was also visible in the low EP elections turnout. Commentators emphasised that they are 'too smart to go to elections' (PAP 2009f) as all citizens know that politicians are not trustworthy. This situation is also influenced by the persevering division of citizens vs. politicians and a lack of trust in the effectiveness of politics in general.

The fact that internet use is not so widespread in Poland is worth noting as one of the explanatory factors of low commenting numbers, but it's not sufficient on its own to explain the low resonance of EU debates online. Although a small number of evaluations were coded, the patterns of the online debate are in line with the wider political climate and public opinion trends towards the EU and politics in general. In the Polish case, every article about Europe, the European Union or European integration, is cast in 'domestic politics' light (e.g. Gazeta.pl 2009), with the clash between Law and Justice and Civic Platform supporters at the core of all reporting. In effect, there was no online debate about European matters in the most popular online Polish media studied here: Poles do not perceive Europe as 'us' – the European Union is still considered an external entity. Even if some statements about the EU polity's worth were found, they were often very basic, lacking further explanation, as the following evaluation exemplifies, 'I don't want the Lisbon Treaty and the United Sates of Europe' (*Polska The Times* 2009). The lack of justificatory statements, in combination with strong language and xenophobic/homophobic characterisations deployed to express disapproval of the EU polity, further point to an overall low quality of debate and tabloidisation of the online media, and also to the strong tradition of opposing politics in general – a tradition which evokes strong sentiment among supporters of one or the other partisan group.

Pessimistic as the above observations may be as regards the future of public debating of the EU legitimacy in Poland, it is worth remembering that the majority of Poles remain firmly in favour of EU integration and Poland's EU membership. Moreover, in spite of the prominence in media discourse of Eurosceptic political and social/religious actors, Polish public opinion appears strongly independent of public actors' views and opinions. Besides this, the online public sphere, which offers citizens the possibility to participate ad hoc (and largely uncensored) in political debating, remains still in its infancy (only 18 per cent of Internet users post comments on political articles or discussion forums concerning politics). This means that online debates on the EU do not reflect the entire spectrum of citizens' opinions. These three factors constitute for the Polish public a fluid case that can be swayed either towards a more firm Eurosceptic stance or towards even firmer support of the EU polity. Which actors will exploit this fluidity better remains to be seen. In any case, the outcome will determine whether the EU will come to mean 'us' for the Polish people, rather than 'them'.

Chapter Ten | The UK: A Case of Extraordinary Euroscepticism

The United Kingdom is arguably a case of Euroscepticism par excellence. Branded Europe's 'awkward partner' (George 1990), the UK has been a reluctant EU member from the outset both in terms of its political choices and in terms of public opinion, as this is voiced through and by media actors, as well as through opinion polls. During the '50s the UK attempted to antagonise the then new-founded EEC, with Whitehall developing an alternative 'Plan G' for a Free Trade area across Europe; a move that not only demonstrated British scepticism towards the Franco-German driven effort for European integration, but also fuelled suspicion and mistrust towards the UK from its continental neighbours (Young 2000). After the UK's EU accession in 1973, scepticism has continued to characterise not only the country's stance towards the Union, but also the way Britain's role is viewed by its continental counterparts, not least because of key events, such as the insistence of the 1974–9 British government to renegotiate the terms of the UK's EU membership just fifteen months after the country's accession (by referendum) in 1975 (Byrd 2008); or the British rebate, which Margaret Thatcher 'forcefully and successfully' negotiated in the 1980s and which remains a recurring topic of heated domestic public debate and intergovernmental negotiations ever since (Daddow 2004). This chapter investigates whether traditional British Eurosceptic exceptionalism in comparison to its continental neighbours endures, and how it is reflected in online EU polity contestation. If exceptionalism is found to persist and Euroscepticism to be very prominent, this would suggest strong limitations in convergence on Euroscepticism. On the flip side, it could still be that the UK provides a template of Euroscepticism on which other Member States converge.

British public opinion consistently comes up in opinion polls as strongly Eurosceptic and largely ill-informed, and/or indifferent towards EU matters. As for the British media, there is a long history of Euroscepticism in parts of the British press, so much so that it can be considered one of the driving forces of Euroscepticism in public opinion (Carey and Burton 2004). It is telling of the influence of certain (mostly tabloid) newspapers on public opinion formation towards the EU, that the EU Representation in the UK has a special service dedicated to rebuffing myths and inaccuracies about the EU circulated by these media outlets. In other words, the UK is a case of consistent historical divergence from the largely pro-EU political rhetoric and public opinion that has characterised most of its continental neighbours for the best part of the last sixty years.

A key feature of British scepticism towards European integration is the focus on sovereignty and national identity (e.g. Nugent 1996; Wallace 1986). The transfer of powers from the UK government to 'Brussels' has consistently been viewed with suspicion and understood as a gradual surrender of national sovereignty, usually on the grounds that the EU decision-making process provides little or no guarantee that the UK has a say on all matters European (Díez Medrano 2003). At the same time, national identity ('what Britain stands for') is commonly perceived as nearly diametrically opposite from what the EU represents, namely opaque, undemocratic, bureaucratic governance that stifles individuals' initiatives and entrepreneurship.

Given that the UK's Eurosceptic stance has been near constant in the past sixty years in terms of both political rhetoric and public opinion (media and opinion polls), it may perhaps, seem superfluous to produce yet another study on what Britons think of the EU. The aim here, however, is not to prove or disprove the presence of Euroscepticism in the UK's public political discourse, nor to measure how much more Eurosceptic the UK is compared to other Member States. Instead, this chapter investigates two rather overlooked elements of UK public debates on the EU, namely 1) the way in which political actors and professional journalists, as well as citizens, choose to formulate their arguments about the EU polity; 2) the way in which these arguments are presented, received and reacted upon by other actors participating in the debates. It is the analysis of this mechanism of public debating that enables the cross-national comparison presented in Chapter Three and allows us to draw conclusions about the nature, as opposed to the intensity, of EU polity contestation within and across countries. In this respect, online debates offer a unique insight into how the EU is debated particularly by citizens, when they air their views in public without any probing from journalists, scholars or opinion poll researchers.

Before presenting the findings, we discuss British Euroscepticism as this emerges from historical accounts and analyses of party politics and opinion polls. This profiling of Euroscepticism in the UK serves as the frame within which we formulate the hypotheses and subsequently, analyse the making of online EU polity contestation. In the final part of this chapter, we revisit the key features of British Euroscepticism, namely national identity and sovereignty, and discuss their role in shaping online public debates of the EU.

Profiling British Euroscepticism

Scholarly approaches of Euroscepticism in the UK vary widely, both in terms of the conceptual framework and the method(s) deployed to measure Euroscepticism. This variation notwithstanding, researchers largely agree on two points: Firstly, that the term 'Euroscepticism' is multifaceted, meaning that there is no one single expression or source of Euroscepticism in Britain. Secondly, expressions of Euroscepticism carry, to varying degrees, an evaluative opinion of the EU as an idea and/or of the EU as an integration project (Daddow 2006; Vasilopoulou 2009). This approach of British Euroscepticism, as a wide-ranging set of attitudes towards the EU based on and driven by the worthiness of the polity as a whole and/or the process of integration, coincides with more general definitions of the term outlined by scholars in order to describe the phenomenon of scepticism towards the EU across Europe (Kopecký and Mudde 2002; Taggart and Szczerbiak

2004). There are two core features of British Euroscepticism, which permeate all its expressions (political rhetoric, media coverage and public opinion), namely national identity and sovereignty. Scholars identify three core manifestations of the 'sovereignty' line of argument, namely popular (legitimacy of decision making derived from a clearly defined citizenry); parliamentary (supremacy of national parliament over any other legal body); and national, which refers to the ability and right of Britons to decide and legislate for Britons without external restrictions (Bulmer 1992; George 1990; Nugent 1996; Wallace 1986). Baker *et al.* (2008) have shown that Euroscepticism is a product of Britain's 'historical geopolitical experiences' (geographical seclusion, imperial legacy, the Commonwealth), which have solidified the country's 'free-trade, free-movement' ideology and led to its establishment as a key actor in the global economy. As a result, British Eurosceptics, most notably among the Conservative political elites, identify the UK 'with a global rather than European volition' (Baker *et al.* 2008: 109). In this case, the EU becomes a hindrance to the UK's ability to exercise its financial hegemony and global entrepreneurship (see, for example, Baker *et al.* 2002 on the Conservatives' 'hyperglobalist ideology'). The EU is thus understood as a threat to Britain's economic sovereignty. Turning this argument on its head, left-wing British Eurosceptics have also been arguing against the EU precisely because its interests and policies are not 'global' enough, in the sense of having a social justice and welfare outlook that encompasses also less developed countries in other parts of the world (Baker *et al.* 2008). Added to this, is the criticism that the EU simply represents the capitalist system of the rich and powerful, with no concern for the welfare of the people – an argument well-known also from left-wing Eurosceptics in other countries.

Similarly, Daddow identifies the source of British Eurosceptic public opinion in the 'modernist approach to history prevalent among British historians and the society in which they work' (Daddow 2006: 66). According to the author:

> The overly reverential attitude to recent history on the part of the British, and an almost total neglect of the peacetime dimensions of modern European history since 1945, both serve to exaggerate the tendency in the country to fall back on glib images of Britain as a great power with a 'special relationship' across the Atlantic with Europe a hostile 'other' across the Channel to be confronted rather than engaged with constructively (Daddow 2006: 66).

This 'peculiarly British' historical approach to Europe means that Eurosceptics tend to view European integration through the lens of British history before 1945, while Europhiles evaluate the European project on the basis of peacetime history, i.e. after 1945 (Daddow 2006; *see also* Díez Medrano 2003 on the narrative of 'loss of empire' as a factor for UK Euroscepticism). Below we examine the different manifestations of Euroscepticism in the British political sphere, starting with party politics and moving on to public opinion and the media.

Party politics

Euroscepticism within the British party system has been thoroughly documented and analysed by a host of scholars (e.g. Aspinwall 2000; Wallace 1995). The term tends to be associated with those politicians within the Conservative party who increasingly contested the project of European integration in the 1980s and 1990s[1], and eventually succeeded in establishing a Eurosceptic policy line for the Conservative party (Gifford 2008). Nevertheless, Forster (2002) traces the history of Euroscepticism in Britain back to the end of the Second World War and Britain's first application for membership to the European community, as 'a particular manifestation of a school of sceptical thought about the value of Britain's involvement with moves towards supranational European integration' (Forster 2002: 2), highlighting that Euroscepticism is, or has at one point or another been, a feature in both of the main British political parties (Labour and Conservatives; *see also* Daddow 2004).

In their historical overview of Euroscepticism in the British party system, Baker *et al.* (2008: 94) identify four distinct periods of British Euroscepticism, starting with the 'Euroscepticism as conventional wisdom' phase, which is dated from the end of the Second World War and up until Britain's entry into the EEC in 1973. At the outset of this period and until 1961, Euroscepticism was 'the conventional wisdom' (Baker *et al.* 2008: 94) among the British political elite. However, once Britain applied for membership and the 'pragmatic economic rationale for membership' became apparent, Euroscepticism gave way to pro-European sentiment among most elite opinion in both the Conservative and Labour party, who presented the UK's membership of an effective European Community as a way of maintaining Britain's international influence (Baker *et al.* 2008; *see also* Lord 1992 and 1994).

Following Britain's accession to the EU in 1972, there came a brief period of 'Euroscepticism in the offence' phase which lasted until the 1975 referendum on Labour's renegotiated terms of UK's membership. This phase saw Eurosceptics fight 'a rearguard action to secure Britain's exit from the EEC' (Baker *et al.* 2008: 94) but without success. Subsequently, the 'dormant' phase came, spanning from the year of the referendum until 1988, when Euroscepticism was not at the fore of political actions and debates in Britain.

This 'dormant Euroscepticism' period gave way in the late 1980s to the current phase of Euroscepticism as, 'fundamental to the contemporary configuration of British politics and general elections' (Baker *et al.* 2008: 94). It is in this period that Baker *et al.* locate the 'catalytic' role of Euroscepticism in current British politics in the acceleration of European political integration, which has fuelled

---

1. The first public use of the word 'Euro-sceptic' was in The Times, on 30 June 1986, in reference to British Prime Minister, Margaret Thatcher (Hooghe and Marks 2007: 127). The Oxford English Dictionary dates the first appearance of the term 'Euroscepticism' to April 1990, in a book review published in the International Affairs Journal (Hyde-Price 1990).

Eurosceptic concerns on issues of sovereignty and national identity (Baker *et al.* 2008; *see also* Evans and Butt 2007; Forster 1998). This, in turn, has accelerated the growth of Euroscepticism within the Conservative party, as both an ideological stance and a rhetorical tool used in factional battles (Lord 1992). As a result, the Conservatives appear to advocate, in recent years what Statham and Koopmans call 'committed Euroscepticism'- a rhetoric which 'reject[s] the value and substance of Europe, ideologically, by mobilizing an anti-European critique that substantively politicizes a cleavage over advancing European integration' (Statham and Koopmans 2009: 452). The Conservatives' Eurosceptic rhetoric is rooted on political grounds, focusing on issues of sovereignty, federalism, democracy and EU centralisation (Statham and Gray 2005: 74) with frequent references to the 'European super-state', and always with a strong economic aspect to it. As discussed earlier, the UK's economic sovereignty has always been a prime concern for the Conservatives and references to federalism and EU centralism often have an economic undertone. At the same time, the acceleration of political integration in the EU has also given rise to new Eurosceptic parties, such as UKIP and the BNP, which have gathered significant electoral momentum in recent European Parliament elections (Lubbers and Scheepers 2007) and follow an anti-EU rhetoric along the same lines as the Conservatives, but going a step further and advocating complete withdrawal of the UK from the EU (Baker *et al.* 2008).

Alongside these 'hard Eurosceptic' parties, a new type of Eurosceptic politician has recently come to the fore, those that Baker *et al.* (2008) call a 'new breed of Soft Eurosceptics', who present themselves as pro-Europeans but strongly oppose the euro. Support of the UK joining the Eurozone has typically been part of pro-European discourse in Britain (Statham and Gray 2005), as the Economic and Monetary Union (EMU) was considered as a step closer to greater economic stability and prosperity across Europe. However, all this changed with the breakout of the current financial crisis in the EU, which has brought the usefulness and viability of the common currency under question, thus further strengthening the 'new soft' Eurosceptic argument.

A key point that emerges from the above is the presence of Euroscepticism not only in the agenda and rhetoric of peripheral or marginal parties, but also on the mainstream political stage. Arguably, the 'factional' nature of the British party system has enabled Eurosceptic voices to become centre-stage in UK politics (Aspinwall 2000; Usherwood 2002). The so-called 'Eurosceptic social voice' found in Member States with power-sharing governments does not make it into mainstream politics, as it gets 'filtered out' through a range of institutional mechanisms (Aspinwall 2000: 433). By contrast, British governments operating in a system of one-party rule have to give greater consideration to backbench Eurosceptic opinion (Aspinwall 2000: 434–6).

More than backbench Eurosceptic concerns, however, political elites appear to take into consideration the political cost or potential gains of a Eurosceptic or pro-European stance and shape their agenda and rhetoric accordingly. Sherrington (2006) notes a strong link between party rhetoric concerning the EU and expected political gains: in the period 2000–05, the 'British agenda' for a 'Europe of states' was consistently promoted by all three main parties. In the aftermath of the Constitutional process (or 'post-Constitutional stalling of the European project', as she calls it), the European issue has become electorally 'damaging' or at least 'unrewarding' for British parties. So much so, that her research uncovered 'almost deafening political silence on the European issue' during the 2005 UK general election, 'underwritten by a silent pact between all the major parties' (Sherrington 2006: 69 and 76). Similarly, Daddow (2006: 76) has pointed out the 'pick-and-choose approach to integration' of the Blair governments, which were largely determined by Labour's internal party politics.

Gifford (2006, 2008) takes this 'pick-and-choose' point further and identifies Euroscepticism as part of populist discourse used by all political parties in their attempt to gain legitimacy, by transcending party politics and appealing to the nation's collective identity. UK party Euroscepticism is, therefore, just one of the many expressions of the 'degenerating' populist approach to international affairs, characterised by 'the centrality of the Westminster parliament' and 'the myth of exceptionalism – a free country confronting an unfree European continent' (Wallace 1991: 29 in Gifford 2006).

Public opinion

At first glance, the UK's EU membership also gathers little support from the public, both in terms of absolute numbers and in comparison to public opinion in other Member States. In the latest Eurobarometer public opinion poll (Eurobarometer 2010a, 2010b) the country's EU membership received a positive evaluation from only 30 per cent of the respondents, when the European average is at 53 per cent (only in one other Member State – Latvia – does EU membership rank lower). The British public is also by far the least trusting of the EU as a polity, with only 25 per cent of respondents declaring their tendency to trust the EU overall (Eurobarometer 2010a, 2010b).

Nevertheless, the public's trust towards institutions increases, the more specifically defined the latter are, i.e. the British are more trustful of the European Parliament, than the EU as a whole (Eurobarometer 2010a, 2010b). Crucially, the British support intergovernmental cooperation at EU level on matters such as the fight against terrorism (63 per cent; EU average: 80 per cent); protection of the environment (56 per cent; EU average: 70 per cent); and defence and foreign affairs (44 per cent, EU average: 67 per cent) (Eurobarometer 2010a, 2010b). These statistics are consistent with scholarly research findings on Euroscepticism in Britain and across Europe (Wessels 2007). There appears to be a link between pro-EU attitudes and level of specificity of EU politics, i.e. the trend for the British public to become more pro-European the more specific the EU aspect they are asked about, as well as the higher and/or clearer the (perceived) benefit this EU aspect brings to the UK. In other words, public opinion polls reveal a 'utilitarian' or 'what's in it for me?' – one could also call it 'pragmatic' – attitude towards the EU, similar to public opinion in several other Member States, such as the Netherlands and Poland (see Chapters Eight and Nine in this volume).[2] Nonetheless, this combination of 'utilitarianism' and national identity discourse is not UK-specific: these are factors that determine public support of European integration and EU institutions across Europe, as McLaren's research has shown (McLaren 2007).

Upon closer inspection, the above figures reveal not so much a Eurosceptic public in the UK, as a politics-sceptic one. The British appear distrustful not only of EU institutions but of their national counterparts too (Eurobarometer 2010a, 2010b). This is in line with Rohrschneider's argument that citizens' trust towards EU institutions is proportional to their trust towards their domestic institutions and political system, i.e. the higher the trust of domestic institutions, the higher the trust of the EU, as citizens feel their interests are being adequately safeguarded by their national representatives in the EU (Rohrschneider 2002).[3] If British citizens are distrustful of their domestic political system, it follows that they will show low levels of trust for the EU too.

Approaching the issue from a rational choice institutionalist theory, Hix (2007) offers a different explanation for the Euroscepticism in British public opinion:

> Where a member state's domestic policy regime is to the left (right) of the European average, voters and parties on the left (right) are more likely than voters on the right(left) to be Eurosceptic, and vice versa (Hix 2007: 137).

Following on from this axiom, his research findings show that the UK fits this rational choice institutionalist framework best of all Member States examined, as with a liberal labour market and service sector, Britain's domestic policy regime is to the right of the EU average (Hix 2007: 142; *see also* Brinegar and Jolly 2005). It is also important to note that insofar as the evaluation of EU membership is concerned, the positive response was lower than the EU average (53 per cent) in thirteen out of twenty-seven Member States, which reflects a more general shift towards Euroscepticism across Europe, in terms of EU polity worth (Eurobarometer 2010b: 34).

Another possible explanation, at least partially, for the high levels of Eurosceptic public opinion in the UK could be the low levels of knowledge about the EU among the British people. Specifically, sixty per cent of UK citizens said

---

2. It is this link between pro-European attitudes and perceptions of benefiting from EU membership that largely drives the Commission's persistence on more information made available to the public about the EU, in as many formats as possible.
3. Conversely, Anderson argues that citizens' attitudes towards the EU are inversely proportional to their attitudes towards the domestic political system (Anderson 1998). The more citizens find that their interests and needs are met by their national government/political system, the less they will agree with a transfer of powers to the European level. In her work on the influence of the nation-state on individual support for the EU, Kritzinger (2003) also found that, in general, the higher the satisfaction with the performance of the nation-state, the lower the support is for further EU integration.

they do not understand how the EU works (Eurobarometer 2010b: 34). Although British citizens are by no means alone in their lack of knowledge on EU issues (across the whole of the EU, 48 per cent of those polled gave a negative response), research suggests that lack of knowledge fuels Euroscepticism (Lubbers and Scheepers 2007; Wessels 2007). In the UK case, support for the EU and the UK's membership increased manifold in the categories of educated to the age of 20 and beyond and those still studying, as compared to those who had finished education aged 15 or less (Eurobarometer 2010b).

Media

Education is not the only factor that determines the level and quality of knowledge about the EU: research across Europe confirms that media reporting has a direct impact on the levels of public Euroscepticism (Hooghe and Teepe 2007; Szczerbiak and Taggart 2008a, 2008b; Trenz 2008). This particularly concerns the national framing of EU issues, which has repeatedly been affirmed by empirical research on content produced by the so-called 'traditional' media (TV, radio, press) (Gerhards and Schafer 2010; Hafez and Skinner 2007; Trenz 2004). Across Europe, media coverage of the EU tends to re-affirm the notion of the nation state and the legitimacy of contextualised national politics. The UK is no different: Statham and Gray (2005) have shown that EU politics is made visible to British citizens primarily as a national affair, with European/supranational actors hardly present in the mediated public discourse (*see also* Pfetsch 2007). EU issues, or the European dimension of an issue, are less likely to find their way in the headlines of articles and generally coverage of EU topics is low to modest, although it tends to increase during European election periods (Kevin 2003).[4]

Framing is crucial in shaping attitudes towards the EU among audiences and readerships. In one of the most recent studies of this issue, De Vreese's research shows that the extent to which the media may feed into Eurosceptic attitudes depends on two factors: 'the pervasiveness of strategically framed news reporting' and individual level characteristics, such as the level of 'political sophistication' (De Vreese 2007c). This means that when EU news coverage is not worded/ framed in a suggestive manner, pointing at winners and losers, using 'war and games' language, focusing on opinion polls and/or specific candidates, then cynicism about EU affairs decreases. Conversely, individuals may have a high level of political sophistication (to be interested and knowledgeable about EU matters) and still be dismissive of politicians and their performance (De Vreese 2007).

---

4. A general problem with studies looking at the salience/amount of coverage of EU issues in national media is that they lack an overall reference frame of what constitutes low, modest or high salience/ coverage of a topic or issue. Therefore, findings concerning EU coverage can only be discussed in relative terms, i.e. compared to past measurements or findings across countries, but always in relation to EU issues only and not in comparison to the overall amount of political news, for example, generated over a specific period or by a particular media outlet.

This is an intriguing finding that flies in the face of the widely-made assumption that it is the sheer quantity of information present (or absent) in the media that affects levels of Euroscepticism. Based on this assumption, an increase in information about the EU in all media channels has been driving the EU's public communication strategy in the new millennium (Michailidou 2008) while the EU's Representation in London has a special section on its website dedicated on dispelling 'Euromyths' invariably circulated in the British press (ERC-UK 2009). Yet, as De Vreese (2007b) argues, it is not knowledge about the EU that generates greater public trust, but rather the way media present EU issues.

Certainly the British press has been repeatedly found to be negatively positioned towards European integration (e.g. Pfetsch 2007; Carey and Burton 2004)[5], although UK journalists' self-perception is that they provide balanced coverage of EU issues and their opinions are based on facts rather than anti-EU bias (Statham 2008). While Euroscepticism is not an exclusive trait of specific UK newspapers, it is generally understood that the 'Eurosceptic tag' applies to the following:

- Tabloids: *The Sun*, the *Mail*, the *Express*
- Broadsheets: *The Times*, *The Daily Telegraph* (Spiering 2004)

With regard to strategic framing of EU issues, the British press often makes references to national identity. Daddow has shown that Eurosceptic press material is directly linked with Britain's history before 1945, i.e. with the times of UK imperial/military glory (Daddow 2006: 81). This arguably points to an existential type of public discourse on European integration and the EU polity. At the same time, however, Anderson suggests that although the British Eurosceptic press indeed frames EU issues in a national-identity context, this discourse is largely a 'façade masking the commercial interests of the newspapers' proprietors' (Anderson 2004: 151). He consequently highlights the (often covert) utilitarian aspect of Euroscepticism in the press (*see also* Inthorn 2006). The press is also closely linked with Euroscepticism in party politics: Gifford, for example, draws attention to the fact that the Eurosceptics within the Conservative Party, who eventually became the dominant voice within the party during the Maastricht Treaty crisis, enjoyed 'substantial backing' from 'significant sections of the press' (Gifford 2006: 861).

---

5. For the role of British TV and radio framing in European integration public discourse see De Vreese 2003; Kevin 2003; Gavin 2001.

British Euroscepticism and the 2009 European Parliament Elections

In light of the profiling exercise presented above, British Euroscepticism emerges as an enduring, certainly prominent and deeply rooted line of political rhetoric, media coverage and public attitude, largely shaped along the lines of existential discourse over European integration. We would, thus, expect online coverage of the 2009 EP elections to be slightly increased compared to coverage during non-election periods (on the basis of relevant measurements from previous studies); but the framing to take place within a national context; and Eurosceptic arguments to prevail both in the journalists' reporting and political actors' claims, with a strong focus on national identity and sovereignty. Similarly, given that opinion polls consistently portray British citizens as largely Eurosceptic, we would expect online contributions from the public to also be predominantly Eurosceptic and equally concerned with issues of national identity and sovereignty. The data analysis presented below confirms some of these expectations but also reveals some trends that break away from what we have come to expect of UK public debates on the worth of the EU.

Sources and data

The three UK professional journalism websites in the sample are the online versions of well-established news outlets, both in the UK media sphere and internationally.[6] At the time of conducting our online EU polity evaluation analysis, first in popularity among professional journalism websites, and seventh most popular website in the UK, was the British Broadcasting Corporation (BBC) (BBC 2009). As the UK's public broadcasting service, it is expected to retain its political impartiality (BBC 2009), which it does more or less successfully and consistently (McNair 2009). The organisation is generally respected for the quality of its broadcasting both domestically and abroad. Moving from audio-visual to print media, the second-in-rank *The Guardian* (21st on the 2009 Alexa ranking) is classified as 'broadsheet' or quality newspaper, priding itself to be independent, and is situated on the centre-left of the political ideology spectrum (Guardian News and Media Ltd 2012). The other newspaper in the sample, the *Daily Mail* is a tabloid newspaper focusing more on social, entertainment and sport issues. Its website (Associated Newspapers Ltd 2009) ranked only a few places lower than *The Guardian* in popularity (27th position). The language used is more sensationalist as are the photos that accompany several of the featuring articles. There is no subcategory of political news, but the Mail Online has four permanent

---

6. For the selection, we used Alexa rankings (Alexa Internet 2012) for the TOP 100 websites in the UK. Rankings as of 17 August 2009. Although rankings may have shifted slightly since May 2009, when the selection of websites took place, the overall order of political websites has not changed. This means that the BBC is still more popular than *The Guardian*, and *The Guardian* is more popular than *The Daily Mail*.

political blogs featuring at the top of its relevant blogs' webpage. The Mail expresses conservative views on most issues and has a clear anti-EU stance (Mail Online 2012). All three selected news outlets enjoy a significant online readership outside the UK, with the BBC ranking among the top 50 websites worldwide.

Moving to citizens' journalism, because there were no political blogs in the UK Top 100 websites listed on Alexa, Wikio rankings were additionally used to identify the top ten most popular blogs (Wikio 2010). The ratings were then cross-referenced with Alexa and the following two blogs were eventually selected, as they were top on the Wikio list at the time (and have remained most popular since ratings were first checked in April 2009) and the most popular by Alexa measurements:

1. Iain Dale's Diary, a leading UK political blog, written by a professional political journalist, party activist and former lobbyist.[7] Dale appears regularly as a commentator on TV and radio programmes and contributes to various press outlets. He stood as a Conservative candidate at the 2003 UK national election (Dale & Co 2011). The quality of the commentary is high for blog standards (anonymous postings, swearing and libel are not allowed), while Dale is also a pioneer in mapping the UK's political blog scene: his magazine, *Total Politics* compiles and publishes yearly awards for best political blogs in various categories as these are voted by users as well as a Top 100 Political Blogs list (Total Politics 2012). In July 2011 Dale was positioned 93rd in *The Guardian's* Media 100 (*The Guardian* 2011b).

2. Guido Fawkes' blog of plots, rumours and conspiracy (Global and General Nominees Limited 2012) is the UK's most popular and influential political blog (see *The Guardian* 2011a; *Total Politics* 2011). Guido Fawkes (Paul Staines in the 'offline' world) aims to uncover 'political sleaze and hypocrisy' but 'doesn't believe in impartiality nor pretend to it' (Global and General Nominees Limited 2004). Guido Fawkes has won several awards and distinctions, while his numerous revelations of political scandals have prompted *The Telegraph* to describe him recently, as the 'blogger who strikes fear into Westminster' (Rayner 2009).

During the 2009 EP election campaign period, we found 305 articles which covered the topic of the EP elections, bringing the UK well below other countries in our study, such as France and Greece, where the amount of relevant articles was twice that of the UK in the same period. This is in line with what we would expect, according to the UK's profile as a country where public opinion shows little interest for EU matters, and therefore, news coverage of EU topics remains

---

7. Iain Dale closed his blog on 8 July 2011 and now blogs from Dale & Co (http://iaindale.com) instead.

low priority. Nevertheless, of the fifty articles that were further selected for coding, half (50 per cent) contained evaluations of the EU polity, which is slightly above the all-country average in our study (47 per cent). In total, 253 evaluations were identified and coded within these twenty-five articles, making the UK the leading country in our sample in terms of intensity of EU polity debates.

General nature of the election debate

To begin with, the majority of articles had a topic that covered domestic politics. Specifically, more than half of all UK articles examined (twenty-eight) covered domestic party politics issues, while the topics of democracy and European party politics featured in just eight articles each. This was certainly expected, especially given that the EP elections were held concurrently with local elections, which turned the whole process into an 'informal' referendum on the government's strength and credibility (and which eventually became one of the worst electoral performances for the Labour party, giving a taste of what was to follow in the national elections in 2010). What is more interesting to observe here is the distribution of topics across the different websites. As Table 10.1 below illustrates, the range of topics covered in relation to the 2009 EP elections coincides with the impartiality and quality indicator of the professional journalism websites and their overall stance towards the EU, as this has been recorded in previous studies. In this respect, the BBC, as the UK's national service, selected articles covering all topics identified in our Codebook. It also appears to be the most broadcast service and among the most popular news websites across the globe, offering plural coverage, with 'European' coverage in all five websites, as the majority of the articles concerned European party politics. In this sense, the BBC provided the most substantial coverage.

There is a clear difference in the overall nature of the debates examined on the BBC and *Guardian* websites, on the one hand, and the political blogs on the other. The latter tend to focus almost exclusively on the specifics of the domestic political process (particular individuals, voting issues, local/regional results, party tactics), while the former emerge as more encompassing, addressing wider aspects of politics. BBC and *Guardian* articles also tend to be more EU and/or Europe focused than the political blogs. Somewhere in between the blogs and the two professional news websites comes the *Daily Mail* (Associated Newspapers Ltd 2009), insofar as style of EU elections coverage is concerned. The extensive factual information regarding the EU elections in the form of feature webpages was absent here. Nevertheless, coverage was more varied than that of blogs, as both news items and debate/commentary articles were available on Mail Online. The overall tone of the articles (and relevant debates) on this website is notably more Eurosceptic than in the other two professional news platforms and a key contributing factor to this is that Mail Online journalists also take a more sceptical (at times anti-EU) stance when introducing the main topic of an article.

The variation in style of coverage is certainly linked to the type of online media each of the selected websites represents. However, there are other factors that may be affecting the overall nature of the debates found in each website, which applies not only to the main articles but also the comments left by readers/participants. The BBC and *The Guardian* have a stricter moderating system in place – with the BBC only publishing select comments from those submitted. Although there is no evidence of bias (all sides are equally represented in the comments, insofar as the EU polity is concerned), this moderating practice could be impacting on the overall quality and focus of the debates that appear in BBC and *The Guardian* articles. The Mail Online also moderates comments left by readers, like *The Guardian*, but the focus of its articles is mostly on domestic politics, in a manner similar to the political blogs, so the comments follow suit and also concentrate on domestic politics issues.

Table 10.1: Debating the EU online: Topics of the UK articles

Number of articles referring to the EP elections	Website					
Topic	bbc.co.uk	guardian.co.uk	Mail Online	Iain Dale's Diary	Guido Fawkes' blog	Total
Domestic party politics	2	4	8	10	4	28
Other Member States' party politics	2	-	-	-	-	2
European party politics	5	2	1	-	-	8
National economy	-	-	-	-	-	-
European economy	-	-	-	-	-	-
European integration	-	1	-	-	-	1
Membership/ enlargement	1	-	-	-	-	1
Democracy	2	4	1	-	1	8
Other	1	-	-	-	1	2
Total number of articles	13	11	10	10	6	50

One key theme dominated the EP election campaign in the UK, virtually eliminating debate on any other issues: UK national parliamentarians' expenses. The revelations on Members' of Parliament (MP) excessive, and at times unlawful, expense claims caused what many have come to consider as the greatest political scandal in Britain's recent history. Although the issue of MPs expense claims has been under public scrutiny for two years, it was not until January 2009 when the case rapidly unravelled: the UK government dropped a motion to exempt Parliament from key parts of the Freedom of Information Act, which could prevent details of MPs' expenses from being revealed. A month later, *The Telegraph* published the first in a long series of detailed expense claims submitted by MPs and furore ensued (*The Telegraph* 2009). Such was the public outcry on the revelations that MPs had been using taxpayers' money to pay for anything from lavish refurbishments in their main homes to movies, toilet seats and outlandish dry cleaning bills, that the House of Commons Speaker, Michael Martin, announced his resignation on the 19 May, an unprecedented move in modern British history.[8]

The implications of this scandal for the EP elections campaign were grave: as Richard Whitaker observed on the day the elections were held in the UK:

> Such is the domination of the campaign by the issue of MPs' allowances that most of the main parties' European Election Broadcasts – a place where they have the opportunity to talk specifically about European issues – made little or no mention of Europe (Whitaker 2009).

In this context, the UK debate on the 2009 EU elections undoubtedly reaffirms the status of EU elections as a 'second-order' event (Reif and Schmitt 1980). This is certainly not a uniquely British phenomenon, as in most of the EU Member States these elections have, so far, generally been about domestic policy issues, with domestic politicians dominating the campaigns.

What little space was devoted to EU issues focused primarily on the Lisbon Treaty and, in particular, the extent to which the treaty is democratic, as well as the potential impact it may have on the UK's sovereignty. From this perspective, UK online debates analysed in relation to the 2009 EP elections contained seeds of an 'existential' type of discourse, whereby discussions prominently feature contestation about European integration. That is, many questions central in the campaign would be about more or less integration, increasing or decreasing the powers and reach of supranational institutions and/or about membership in the EU or Eurozone of one's own Member State, other Member States, or applicant countries.

The Lisbon Treaty was one of the central issues for the Conservative Party, not only in their EP election campaign but also in their national election campaign strategy. The Conservatives' foreign affairs spokesman (and current Foreign Minister), William Hague, was reported to have described Gordon Brown's refusal to hold a referendum on the Lisbon Treaty as 'a betrayal of voter trust which

---

8. The last time a House of Commons Speaker was forced to resign was in 1695, when Sir John Trevor was expelled from the Commons after being found guilty of accepting a bribe.

"debases the coinage of politics"' (Euractiv 2009). The Conservatives' leader, David Cameron, on several occasions made the commitment to hold a referendum on the already ratified by the UK Treaty as soon as his party became government, provided that the Treaty would not have been ratified by then. According to the party's EP elections manifesto, the Conservatives pledged that:

> If the Lisbon Treaty is not in force in the event of the election of a Conservative Government this year or next, we will hold a referendum on it, urge its rejection, and – if successful – reverse Britain's ratification. And if the Constitution is already in force by then, we have made clear that in our view political integration in the EU would have gone too far, the Treaty would lack democratic legitimacy, and we would not let matters rest there (Conservatives 2009: 2).

During the EP election campaign, David Cameron also declared his party's intention to withdraw from the European People's Party (EPP) coalition, where Conservatives' MEPs have traditionally been sitting, and form a new anti-federalist group with allies drawn from other independent (and Eurosceptic) parties around Europe.

Amidst the MPs' expenses scandal and the Conservatives' calls for a referendum on the Lisbon Treaty, the BNP made a dynamic comeback, following a rhetoric strategy similar to the Conservatives on the Lisbon Treaty issue. However, the BNP's overall electoral campaign was far more extreme in the policies it proposed than that of the Conservatives, in line with its overall right-wing, xenophobic ideology.[9] Despite its extreme rhetoric, it became quickly apparent that the BNP was gaining in popularity and speculation about it gaining its first seat in the EP was rife in the days before the elections were held.

As far as strategic media reporting is concerned, both press and online media focused on 'performers' and 'critics', 'candidate style and performance' and opinion polls (components of strategic reporting as per Jamieson 1992), although online media offered extensive factual resources on the European Parliament, EU issues and policies and political parties across Europe (*The Guardian* 2009; BBC 2009). This is where we can locate traces of policy-themed (substantial) debates, which focus on policy issues decided at EU level in which the European Parliament has a say. At the same time, the UK media were largely negatively predisposed towards the BNP, despite its Eurosceptic positions. Rather, its openly racist ideology led even other Eurosceptic politicians to condemn the party's positions, both during and after the elections, in what the BNP itself evaluated as a 'media onslaught' against it.

---

9. It is indicative of the party's ideology that even the meta-description it uses for its website (i.e. the description by which all search engines list the website) declares that 'The British National Party is the only party which opposes mass immigration and surrender to the European Union. Unlike the other parties, we mean it when we say it.'

Professional journalism websites are still the main locus for the unfolding of EU debates and also the principal arena where EU legitimacy is contested. As such, they are also the main reference point for citizens to engage in forms of participatory journalism and express discontent or concern with the EU (Figure 10.1).

The tabloid Mail Online, ranked only third in terms of density of EU evaluations, containing only one third of the evaluations of the BBC and half of *The Guardian*. Blogs do not figure prominently as a contentious arena, neither for political actors nor for citizens. The vast majority of evaluations were located in the comments-area of the websites (211 evaluations), with the largest proportion of these generated as a direct response to the content of the main article/topic of discussion (156 evaluations). Moreover, in line with the cross-country findings, citizens dominated the EU election online debates in the UK (Figure 10.2).

Dimensions of EU polity evaluation

Taking a closer look at how the debate on the EU unfolded in the selected UK articles, we can identify a clear trend of negative evaluations of the EU, which focus on the current political set-up and power distribution between EU and national institutions, as well as among the different EU institutions. More specifically, few participants (forty-seven) expressed evaluations concerning the principle of integration, which is the general idea and/or act of cooperation among European Member States in any form. Moreover, all evaluations recorded under this category were positive, i.e. no participants expressed opposition to the idea of collaboration among EU countries, but were usually quick to clarify what their understanding of collaboration entails and point out that it is different from the way things are currently set up in the EU. As user 'kaybraes' put it (Mardell 2009a): '[...] the EU [...] was intended to be, a group of free trading, cooperating nations living in peace'. Similarly, 'joseph1832' stated in *The Guardian*:

> Of course, European countries should work together. The question is whether you think this should involve majority voting, the supremacy of legal law, a single currency, a common foreign policy, etc. If you really believe that that is the way ahead, then please embrace a fully federal system. That would at least be democratic. [...] The persent [sic] system involves a system of federal law touching important parts of government, yet without a federal government to vote out (Bet El 2009).

The future of the EU (project of integration) also generated a limited amount of evaluations (76). However, unlike the principle of integration, the prospects of the EU polity were evaluated in a mostly negative way, with the vast majority focusing on the level of future integration, i.e. the future distribution of power within the EU polity (fifty-two evaluations). This is encapsulated in the comment left on the BBC website by user 'Freeborn John', according to whom:

> The real objective of EU supporters is to find some excuse, no matter how weak, to justify the creation of EU law in new fields, because it is

the replacement of national law by EU law that is the principle means by which the federal super state is constructed. [...] The remedy now is to permanently break European federalism as a political movement and to restore democracy by taking back powers from Brussels (Mardell 2009b).

This trend of negative evaluations of the level of EU polity reflects exactly the pattern of opinions concerning the most contested of the three EU polity dimensions, i.e. the current EU political set-up. With 222 evaluations, the way the EU is currently governed was at the epicentre of the UK online debates. The vast majority of participants expressed negative opinions about the way decision-making power is distributed between EU institutions and national governments, as well as among the different EU institutions (127 evaluations). The EP is frequently described as a 'gravy train', drawing comparisons with the UK parliamentary body and its expenses scandal (for example, see 'littleredtomahawk' on Juniper 2009), while the EU is likened to a 'superstate' with power-hungry officials. For example, responding to a previous user, 'GMel' expressed the view that the Tories are right to move away from groups (in the EP) that want even more integration than now, because:

> We were tricked by the EU from the very beginning. We were told it would be for greater co-operation and trade, not to become part of some super state like the Soviet Union (look what happened to that!) (Phibbs 2009).

Qualifying Euroscepticism: Justifications

The primary concern driving online evaluations of the EU in the UK is without doubt democracy. Of the 252 evaluations recorded in total, almost half (126) were justified on the basis of democratic values and governance. This is also in line with the cross-national trend, where the majority of evaluations were also justified on this basis (422; 37 per cent of all evaluative statements). In distant second place, we find justifications pertaining to necessity (forty evaluations), i.e. an assessment of the EU polity is made on the basis of efficiency, effectiveness, governability and/or obligations of Member States' and/or EU institutions deriving from the Treaties. In fact, the overall pattern of justifications in the UK is exactly the same as at cross-national level, as Figure 10.3 below illustrates.

Furthermore, justifications are not affected by actors' stance on the EU, i.e. by whether an actor makes a positive or negative assessment of one or more of the EU polity dimensions. In addition, it was not possible to statistically confirm a link between the online source and the type of justifications. Nevertheless, as the majority of evaluations concern the current EU polity set-up and are negative, so most justifications appear in relation to this type of evaluation. What concerns political actors and citizens alike, as this transpires from the analysis of online debates, is the lack of democratic mandate that EU institutions present. The EU polity is perceived as a near-authoritarian, corrupt regime (the 'EU gravy train'), in which the peoples of Europe were lured by their political elites. The latter are accused of having 'miss-sold' the EU membership case to citizens, portraying it as

190 | Contesting Europe

Figure 10.1: Mapping EU polity evaluations in British online debates

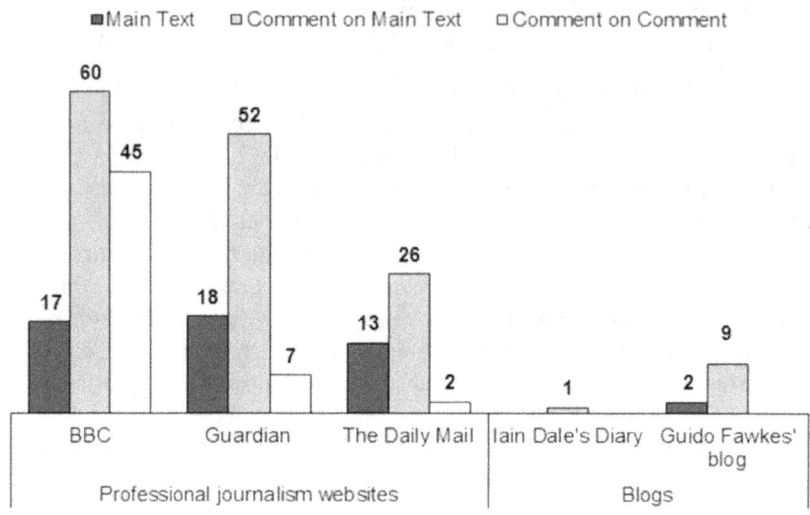

Figure 10.2 EU polity evaluations across countries: UK contributions per actor category

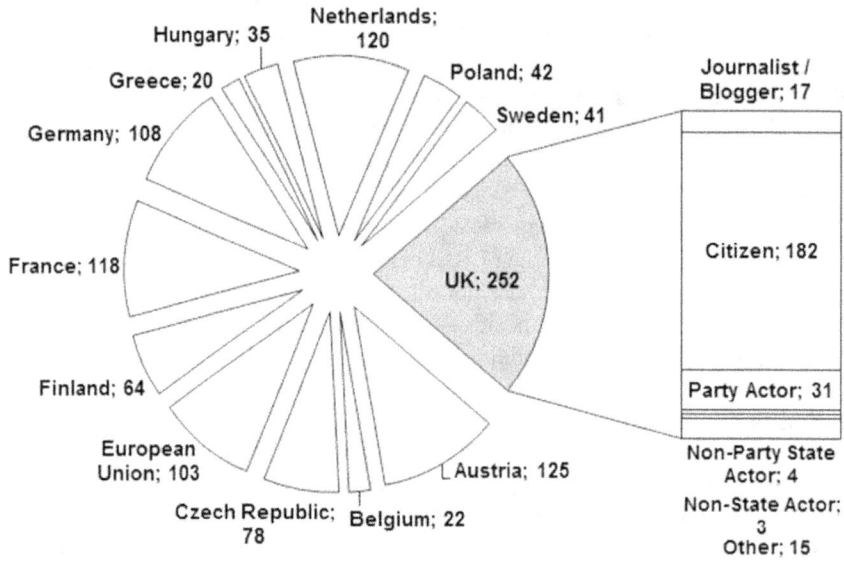

Figure 10.3: Explaining opinions: how EU polity evaluations were justified in the UK

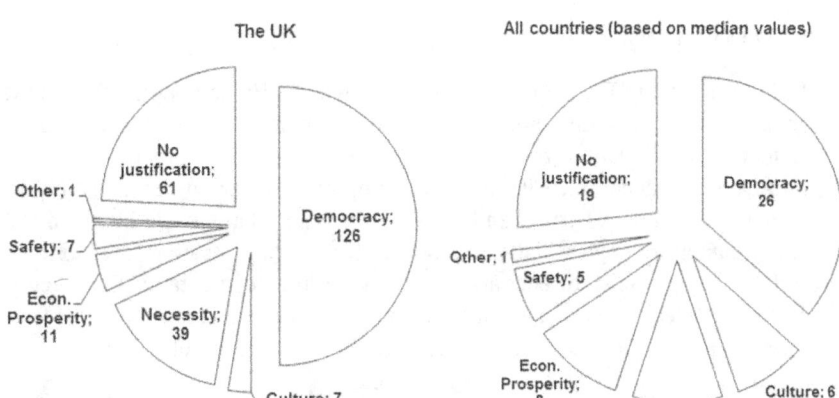

primarily an economic union that would enhance prosperity and market stability, only to increasingly delegate political powers to EU institutions. Once appointed or elected in EU positions, national politicians get their 'snouts' even deeper in the 'trough', i.e. continue squandering public money.

The issues of sovereignty and national identity were present in all websites, more implicitly in BBC and *Guardian* articles, more openly in articles found in the Mail Online and the two political blogs. Sovereignty was more prominently discussed, but nearly always in relation to the two key topics that dominated debates across all five websites, namely corruption and democracy. Support for the Lisbon Treaty is often perceived as support for federalist Europe. It is on this understanding of pro-EU discourse that several Eurosceptic arguments are pinned, arguing for looser ties with Brussels and, implicitly, for regaining the UK's chipped sovereignty, as it can be seen also in the quotes presented earlier, concerning the dimensions of Euroscepticism in the analysed debates.

Comments in the selected UK e-debates invariably point to the gap between citizens and politicians at national and EU level, which is caused by the 'refusal' of the latter to 'listen to the people', thus introducing policies which are unpopular. At the same time, the democratic process at EU level is regularly deemed 'a joke' and 'an insult', since citizens feel their vote is wasted: firstly, the EP is perceived as an institution with no real powers. Secondly, citizens' votes are ignored when they do not fit with the plans of the political elites, with the Maastricht and Lisbon Treaties most quoted as examples. The following comment, posted by 'Johannestannes' on the BBC website, exemplifies the justificatory logic that most EU polity evaluations followed in the UK:

> The lamentable rise of the right is sadly a reaction to millions of Europeans being deprived a say in the new EU post-democratic age. This is still a muted

response however. Imagine American citizens being TOLD that their laws would all originate from an un-elected 'commission' of 17 people, [...] there would be an armed revolt against their masters!

And he continues:

The notion of any EU country's (I refuse to use the EU jargon of 'state') laws being made by its own commissioner and 26 others who perhaps know little of that country's language, heritage and mentality [...] is ridiculous at best. The Dutch, French and Irish made their opinions clear on the Constitution/ Lisbon. Germans, Austrians and Brits also demand that the EU be given less rather than more power. Sadly [...] the un-elected commission refuses to listen and has the audacity to encourage us to vote in a 'democratic' EU election where one German vote has only 1/16th the democratic clout of a voter from Luxembourg. Welcome to post-democratic Europe. ! (Mardell 2009c).

Discussion

Britain has long been considered exceptional as a highly Eurosceptic Member State. The two constants that define UK Euroscepticism are the unswervingly Euro-distrustful British public opinion and the consistent rhetorical link between (loss of) national identity and EU membership. While no longer an exclusive characteristic of British politics, Euroscepticism in the UK constitutes a core feature of public political discourse, both media- and party-driven, as well as a key trait of public opinion, as this emerges through opinion polls and electoral results. Moreover, Euroscepticism in the UK is unique in that it is embedded in the rhetoric of the two dominant mainstream parties, Labour and Conservative, with variation in the strength and prominence of Eurosceptic arguments according to the political circumstances (for example, depending on which of the two parties happens to be in government at the time or on the economic climate in the UK).

The analysis of online debates on the 2009 EP elections adds new layers to the profile of British Euroscepticism. Firstly, and in line with previous research and opinion polls, the EU is a second-order media issue. Throughout the EP election period, the focus of online media coverage and of the debates linked to it, was on national politics. Secondly, British public opinion is not simply Euro-distrustful but rather politics-sceptic. It thus appears that the distrust towards the EU polity is directly linked to the distrust (and disgust) people expressed online for the corrupt ways of national politicians. The unfolding of the EU issue into wider scepticism towards politics is something we also see in countries like Hungary and Poland (compare with Chapters Seven and Nine). The two core themes of British Euroscepticism, national identity and sovereignty, were present implicitly rather than being the focus of EU polity evaluations.

At the same time, the key theme that monopolised the EP electoral campaign, namely MPs expense claims, confirms those scholarly propositions that Euroscepticism is an expression of discontent, directly proportional to the discontent citizens feel about national governments. This could also go some way towards explaining the presence of that other 'elephant in the room': the impressive 57 per cent of Europeans on average (65.5 per cent of Britons) who did not vote. Voter turnout was at just 34.5 per cent, but although this is not a high outcome, it is not the worst to be ever recorded in the UK and also, it does not deviate much from previous years' turnouts (European Parliament 2009; Mellows-Facer et al. 2009).[10] Moreover, it is not much lower than the European average, which hit a record low this year at 43 per cent (European Parliament 2009).

In this context, it is clear that the political issue of European integration is no longer a 'sleeping giant' in most Member States, as the evidence, which enabled Van der Eijk and Franklin (2004: 8) to make this assessment just five years ago, has now been overturned. On the other hand, with European citizens 'turning right' at these EP elections, UK Eurosceptic parties, acting nothing like the 'awkward partners' in the EP, continue to lead and organise their continental counterparts in formal Eurosceptic EP formations.[11]

On the surface, the June electoral results confirmed the UK's leading position as a Eurosceptic country. In total, the UK elected 72 MEPs, of whom 25 are Conservatives, 13 Labour, 13 UKIP, 11 Liberal Democrats, 2 Greens and 2 of

---

10. However, it is necessary to take into account here the fact that the 2009 EP elections took place concurrently with local elections. This could go some way towards explaining the slight increase in voter turnout compared, for example, with the 1999 elections, when EP elections were a stand-alone event and voter turnout was the lowest thus far recorded in the UK.

11. True to their pre-election pledge and despite predictions for the contrary, the Conservatives have formed a new Eurosceptic EP group, the European Conservatives and Reformists group (ECR), after succeeding in gathering the required number of MEPs (minimum twenty-five, from at least seven Member States) from across the EU. The majority of the group's MEPs come from the UK (twenty-five), while the rest are mostly MEPs who formerly grouped either under the centre-right European People's Party/European Democrats (EPP-ED) or the (former) Union for Europe of the Nations group (UEN). In total, seven countries apart from the UK, are represented through fifty-five MEPs in the ECR, namely Poland, Latvia, Lithuania, Hungary, the Czech Republic, the Netherlands and Belgium.

    UKIP has also formed a new Eurosceptic EP group, although more out of necessity, as the previous EP formation to which it belonged (Independence/Democracy, IND/DEM) failed to meet the numbers required to qualify for EU funding and recognition as a formal EP group. Similarly, UEN faced a similar problem so the two groups merged to create what is now called the Europe of Freedom and Democracy group (EFD). In total, thirty MEPs from nine countries (Denmark, Finland, France, Italy, Greece, the Netherlands, Lithuania and Slovakia) belong to this group, with the majority representing UKIP. Ideologically, the new EP group is far more to the right than UEN, to which UKIP previously belonged, as there are no left-wing Eurosceptics in this formation and all other national parties represented here sit on the extreme-right end of the political spectrum. Like the Conservatives, UKIP will head the new EP group, with UKIP's Nigel Farage sharing leadership with Italian Enrico Speroni of Lega Nord.

the BNP, the first in the party's history. But when taking into account the wider political context within which these elections took place, what the results mostly reflected was the public's discontent with Labour, who lost even in what were considered to be core areas, such as the North West and Wales. It is worth noting that, although both parties won an equal amount of seats, UKIP actually received more votes than Labour.

Ultimately, however, the analysis presented in this chapter has shown that citizens in the UK are concerned about the same aspects of the EU polity's legitimacy as are the citizens in all the other countries of our sample. Though the UK retains its exceptional status insofar as the intensity and historical background of British Euroscepticism are concerned, we find evidence to support convergence with other countries in our study regarding the targets and justification of Eurosceptic positions. In light of this, the UK makes for a typical case of the 'constraining dissensus' (Hooghe and Marks 2009: 4) which is taking root across the EU, whereby electoral results confirm the rise of Eurosceptic parties, as well as an overall turn of Europeans to the right (European Parliament 2009).

Chapter Eleven | the limited convergence in EU polity contestation: implications for democracy

The prominence of EU polity contestation as an element of online media debates on EP electoral campaigning, has placed the problem of the legitimacy of the EU under a new light. No longer a formal question of the procedures of EU governance and its performance, the unresolved legitimacy problem of the EU has profound impact on democratic politics at the Member State level and beyond. Political conflicts concerning European integration have intensified and mobilised a wide range of actors including political parties, social movements, interest groups and citizens. Although we observe a certain prominence of EU polity contestation, EP election campaigns are still found to unfold within differentiated national media spheres. The scope of debates and the degrees of contestation vary widely between the countries analysed, and the internet has no visible effect of facilitating processes of transnational opinion and will formation. In these concluding remarks, we wish to discuss the implications of this limited convergence of EU polity contestation for democracy. How do the dispersed practices of mobilising EU support and resistance as an element of national campaigning, affect the democratic functioning of European Parliament elections as the main act of authorisation and control of European citizens? We first summarise the key comparative findings of our research and discuss their relevance in light of the existing research literature. Secondly, we draw the main lessons from the country cases that contribute to an understanding of the variances of political contestation across the European space. In the final part, we draw a tentative normative conclusion on the observed convergence and divergence in EU polity contestation during European Parliamentary elections, and its rather restricted potential to provide the basis for collective will-formation.

Against the background of recent scholarly attention on the politicisation of European integration and the rising prominence of Euroscepticism, this book studies discursive acts of EU polity contestation, including how criticism of EU legitimacy meets with public defences thereof, in online debates during the campaigns for the European Parliament elections of 2009, in sixty-five Member State-specific and transnational websites. The approach is highly innovative in approaching political contestation over European integration from the perspective of public debates and the media, studying online debates where citizens voluntarily and directly respond to journalists' news stories and claims made by party politicians. As such, the contributions of this book and the overarching methodology have been explicitly designed to explore possible interaction in arguments defending and challenging EU legitimacy.

One key finding is that online debates during EP election campaigning tend to be predominantly critical over the achievements of the EU and its performance. Negative evaluations of EU legitimacy prevail over affirmative ones in all countries included in our survey. This confirms our initial assumption that the media are relevant as a forum for opinion-making, partly independent from partisan contestation. Media debates in Belgium, France and Germany, where negative partisan mobilisation is limited and public opinion is generally classified as pro-European, nevertheless expose their readers to highly critical evaluations of the EU. The prominence of Euroscepticism in countries where no significant Eurosceptic parties stand for election can be partly explained by the resonance of Eurosceptic actors and discourse from other Member States. In Germany, for instance, the Austrian and Hungarian debates, which display high levels of negative evaluations, have gained a high news value (see Chapter Six). In turn, debates in countries with a Eurosceptic reputation, like the Czech Republic and Sweden, do not display higher percentages of negative evaluation of EU legitimacy in online debates than less Eurosceptic countries. There is thus much more convergence in EU online public spheres, in terms of Eurocritical debates in the media, than would be expected based on traditional research. As a result, the distinction between pro-European and Eurosceptic countries becomes blurred. This confirms our initial proposition that conventional indicators to measure positions on European integration – especially Euroscepticism – in terms of partisan contestation or public opinion are insufficient. Citizens can be exposed to negative evaluations of EU legitimacy in the media, even when partisan mobilisation on fundamental issues concerning the principle, scope and future of integration remains limited.

Secondly, we find clear patterns of co-occurrence of positive and negative evaluations with regard to each of the three targets of EU polity contestation. That is, if a debate in a country features many positive evaluations of the project of integration in terms of delegating or restricting supranational authority, the same target of contestation is also likely to raise many negative evaluations. This finding is important because it substantiates our discursive understanding of EU polity contestation as a dynamic and responsive process (*see also* Díez Medrano 2003; Díez 1999). The promotion of EU legitimacy provokes resistances, and this resistance is likely to be countered again by positive evaluations. Media debates are balanced in making both pro- and anti-European arguments visible and facilitating discursive exchange between proponents and opponents of European integration.

Thirdly, there is a rather unitary voice across all websites in affirming European integration in principle but opposing its current institutional set-up. That is, most contestants do not question the need for European countries to collaborate and to pool resources and competences, but also, do not actively affirm it. At the same time, the majority of contributions target the current institutional set-up of the EU. Prominent EU institutions, competencies and decision-making processes are heavily criticised and the current state of integration is challenged in terms of allocation of political authority, scope of competences and inclusiveness. The dominant picture conveyed by media contestation is that European integration is in crisis. Yet, there is wide divergence with regard to expressing preferences for future paths of integration and strategies of reform. The rather unitary voice of critique of the EU and its current crisis is not translated into consensual opinion on possible ways out of the crisis. The point here is not that strategies for reform are discussed controversially in the media but that the opinions expressed on the future of the EU remain dispersed in general: some advocate more integration to overcome current shortcomings, others advocate a reversal of previous steps in the integration process, while the third and largest group does not give clear indications as to how EU failures might be addressed.

Fourthly, we find the citizens–elite divide as one of the central vectors structuring public discourse on European integration. Citizens are clearly more critical of the EU than party actors and regularly make use of the new online commenting facilities to express their discontent with European integration, or with political elites in general. We also find a clear difference in how party actors and citizens justify their evaluations, with citizens on the commenting pages frequently referring to the principle of democracy while partisan actors' evaluations, in the main news articles, are less explicit on the underlying principles that justify their arguments. The type of justification further correlates with the expression of support or opposition. The EU institutional set-up or the process of integration are typically challenged by expressing concerns with the EU's democratic performance and are affirmed by reference to necessity and safety. We thus find a powerful confirmation of the analytical value of our discursive notion of EU polity contestation that develops in partial independence of the strategic campaigning of political actors. EU opposition mainly found expression in popular discontent and the deep concern of citizens with democracy.

Contestation in selected Member States

The detailed examination of EU polity contestation during the 2009 European Parliament election campaigns in Chapters Three to Nine, demonstrates the many varieties in which negative evaluations, especially, may come to the fore. On the one hand, this book has succeeded in identifying four overarching patterns in the unfolding of EU polity contestation. On the other hand, the use of a stringent content analysis method has also enabled us to provide a detailed insight into the nation-state specific contexts of EU polity contestation. Each of these chapters highlights different aspects of Euroscepticism, from the extent to which the EU has become internalised into domestic politics to the way the domestic political climate, and recent history in EU politics, shape the national discourse.

Austrian debates, discussed in depth in Chapter Four, clearly demonstrate the activism and the fragmentation potential of online media. The biggest offline Austrian newspaper – *Kronenzeitung* – actively campaigns against the EU. For example, it provided an opinion platform and editorial support for Hans-Peter Martin, an independent Eurosceptic candidate. Partially because of this newspaper's support, Martin was able to secure strong support in the EP election gaining 17.7 per cent of the vote. The online portal of the *Kronenzeitung* reflects this Eurosceptic campaigning. Comments left by readers often combine elements of Euroscepticism with anti-elitism and xenophobia. On the other hand, the online portal of Austria's leading quality newspaper – *Der Standard* – featured a much more balanced debate in its discussion forums. Taken together, these two professional news websites contributed to a growing cleavage within Austrian society onto which the issue of EU legitimacy loads. The comparison of debates in French-speaking Belgium and in France, demonstrates the continued importance of national political culture in structuring EU polity contestation.

In Chapter Five, Crespy and Fimin clearly show how the expression of both Euroscepticism and pro-Europeanism remains very inhibited in Belgium as the EU is not strongly contested by political parties, and concerns with the legitimacy of the EU remain a non-issue. In contrast, the 2005 referendum on the Constitutional Treaty in France still resonated during the 2009 EP election campaign and continued to shape the patterns of online discourse on EU legitimacy. In France, the EU remains highly criticised as a neoliberal market project, while concerns with the democratic deficit are frequently expressed by both citizens and political parties. This finding of divergence between French-speaking Belgium and France is given extra weight in light of the fact that language is not a barrier between these two countries and that the internet potentially facilitates communication across borders. As such, it shows that the importance of national political context for EU polity contestation goes beyond demarcation because of language barriers and factors such as, the continued organisation of democracy and identity around the nation state, need to be taken into account when studying EU polity contestation.

In Chapter Six, the German debate is further explored as a case where Euroscepticism is still confined to the fringes of the political party spectrum but is slowly gaining prominence in media discourse. The key finding here is that the traditional understanding of Germany as a motor of integration, has been slowly replaced by a new critical distance from European integration. This increasing criticism can be attributed to the dual process of European integration proceeding rapidly since the late 1980s – and thus provoking critical responses – and the reunification of Germany, which has supported Germany's more self-confident attitude in recent years. Still, Germans remain rather uncritical in comparison to outspoken Eurosceptics in other Member States. The internet debates during the EP elections of 2009 picked up on several of these outspoken foreign Eurosceptics, such as Dutch far-right politician, Geert Wilders, and the Hungarian *Jobbik* party. In partial contrast to these openly and radically Eurosceptic voices, their reporting by German online media created the image of Germany as protector of European integration in the face of foreign Eurosceptic threats. As such, this chapter demonstrates how debates on EU legitimacy may preserve nation-state specific characteristics, yet respond to debates in other Member States.

The Hungarian case discussed in Chapter Seven by Heller, Kohut and Kriza further clarifies how EU polity contestation may be heavily affected by the prevailing national political climate. Although critical and supportive arguments pick up on specific aspects of the EU polity and European integration process, they cannot be understood without the context of national politics. Specifically, the increasingly morose political climate of Hungary is reflected in highly combative contributions to EU polity contestation. This raises the important question of where the much reported democratic deficit of the EU is located. That is, domestic failures in democracy may have a negative impact on the perceived legitimacy of the EU. Finally, the specific Hungarian context with a large Hungarian diaspora living in neighbouring EU Member States, provides additional support for our argument that EU polity contestation needs to be unpacked beyond the simple pro–anti dichotomy, or 'soft' and 'hard' Euroscepticism distinction. Much of the Hungarian EP election campaign evolved around a speech by Victor Orban, then oppositional leader of the liberal-conservative party *Fidesz*, arguing how European integration may facilitate Hungarian interests as long as Hungarians living abroad vote for ethnically Hungarian candidates. As such, this call could be labelled both pro-European and nationalist at the same time, defying the notion that these two positions are diametrically opposed.

The Dutch chapter discusses the extent to which the 2005 referendum on the Constitutional Treaty was 'relived' during the 2009 European Parliament elections. It demonstrates how the referendum has created a lasting impression on the Dutch EU discourse, as topics of the referendum resounded in the 2009 EP election campaign without being explicitly on the policy-formulation agenda. Furthermore, the referendum has succeeded in creating a clear image of 'yes' and 'no' political parties in the Netherlands in citizens' perceptions. The 'yes' and 'no' positions of political parties on the Constitutional Treaty during the referendum campaign are now increasingly generalised to overarching dispositions towards European integration. That is, parties that advocated a 'yes' vote during the referendum are considered, generally, pro-European and parties that advocated a 'no' vote, are considered Eurosceptic. The election results were also interpreted as a clear vote for the extremes on the pro–anti-European scale, since the Green-Left and D66 parties on the one hand and Geert Wilders' PVV party on the other, won seats in the parliament.

In the Polish public discourse, Eurosceptic arguments are strongly focused on national identity and economy, as Styczyńska has shown in Chapter Nine. The 2009 EP election online debates on the EU reproduce the same contradictions of discourse reflected in offline media coverage, public opinion polls and party politics: EU legitimacy emerges as largely marginal in terms of scope and resonance with the public and political actors, but at the same time as highly visible in the public arena, mainly thanks to the strong public profile of some of the more critical actors, who have top positions in mainstream political parties. Overall, however, public interest in the EU is low online, as is also reflected by the very low turnout in the EP elections. The focus of public political discourse is national politics and this is also reflected in the online coverage of the 2009 EP elections, where both the framing of the election event itself and the (limited) debates that sprung in response to that, were firmly rooted in the national political context, with frequent references to national identity and sovereignty.

In Chapter Ten, the idea that British Euroscepticism is exceptional is investigated. Clearly, the EU is widely contested in British media, with no other country in our study featuring as many contributions of EU polity contestation as the UK. Also, the question of membership of the EU is more frequently raised in the UK than elsewhere. Yet, the overall balance of positive and negative evaluations of EU legitimacy does not deviate strongly from the other countries in our study. In other words, it is the intensity of contestation that is exceptional, not the tone or content of the debate. Finally, even though the membership question is raised more often in the UK case than elsewhere, the larger part of British EU polity contestation does not challenge the EU in principle. Rather, the majority of contributions to the debate target specific characteristics of the EU polity, most notably its decision-making mechanism.

Implications for democracy in the EU

How can we evaluate these findings in terms of possible advances of democratic reform and the status of European parliamentary elections as an element of EU representative democracy? At the heart of the emerging multilevel parliamentarian field, the powers of the European Parliament have increased steadily over the last twenty years, but its modes of implementing the principles of representative democracy, remain ambivalent (Crum and Fossum 2009). The European Parliament is the only directly elected legislative body of the EU and therefore plays a decisive role in the authorisation and accountability of EU governance (Rittberger 2003). Yet, any answer to the question whether the empowerment of the European Parliament would contribute to the solution of the EU democratic deficit is dependent on the type of electoral connections between citizens and the EU policy-making process (Hix et al. 2005).

Arguably, European Parliament elections can best fulfil the democratic functions of authorisation and accountability by fostering debate on EU policies and partisan positioning in substantial terms. That is, the policies at stake during the legislative period should also be subject to campaigns and media debates, thus bringing exposure to different candidate positions, contributing to collective opinion formation on these issues, and providing voters with a meaningful choice (Føllesdal and Hix 2006; Mair 2000). Neither existential debates focusing on the institutional set-up of the EU nor domestic debates focusing on national party politics meet these requirements.

Yet, having European Parliament elections function as a vehicle for public opinion formation on European integration may be considered a second best solution to engage voters and involve them in informed opinion-making (De Wilde 2009b). Existential debates about the rationale of European integration, the institutional and constitutional set-up of the EU and its future trajectory, should ideally be held in the context of national election campaigns, since it remains the prerogative of national governments, national parliaments and national electorates (e.g. through referenda) to decide upon these issues. The fact that it becomes a salient issue in European elections indicates, nevertheless, that there is a critical demand to discuss the EU in fundamental terms and that these discussions cannot be simply confined to the national electoral context. EU criticism is advanced especially by oppositional parties which mobilise the national electorate by expressing similar concerns across the European space (Franklin and Wlezien 1997; Hooghe and Marks 2009; Van der Eijk and Franklin 2004). There is thus a potential to involve the national electorates in parallel processes of informed opinion making and to launch substantial debates on European integration in a European electoral context. Also possible, however, is a potential clash in the expectations that are raised by such campaigns and the restricted competences of the voters, who are not formally empowered to authorise and control EU constitutional decisions, but only the restricted policy agenda that is at stake in European Parliament elections.

Domestic campaigning is in this sense to be considered the least adequate to fulfil its democratic functions in terms of authorising a supranational representative body and holding it accountable. From a purely normative perspective, even existential debates are preferable, since they hold national governments and national political parties accountable for their landmark decisions on European integration. However, such existential debates in the context of EP elections have only indirect sanctioning power. They remain disconnected from the EU policy process since they touch only marginally upon the agenda that is open for electoral authorisation and raise issues that are out of reach of the limited competences of the European Parliament. Finally, substantial debates that evolve around policy issues on which the European Parliament has a direct say, can be said to authorise MEPs in democratic terms and, in turn, hold them accountable for their performance in the past. Through such debates, party positions might be communicated to citizens supplying them with a meaningful choice during the elections and at the same time provide candidate MEPs with an idea of the main concerns of their constituencies (Thomassen and Schmitt 1999). Our findings indicate that such substantial debates online are rare in the context of EP election campaigns. Online media coverage of electoral campaigns is however not simply 'second order' in terms of focusing on domestic politics. It also increasingly raises existential issues concerning the legitimacy of the EU and, thus, concerns the type of polity questions for which only national governments and national representative bodies can be held accountable. Our data therefore confirms a trend in EP elections away from 'second order', through raising the 'polity question' of the EU and sharpening the anti- versus pro-European cleavage as a structuring conflict in mediated debates.

Ways forward

Following the conceptual, methodological and empirical approach developed in this book, we would like to draw attention to three avenues for further research. These include, firstly, a more in-depth investigation of the internet as platform for debates about European and international political issues. How professional news sites, political blogs and social media facilitate, inhibit and structure political contestation of the kind investigated in depth here has not been the main focus of this book. Yet, on the basis of the existing data set, these issues can be explored in more detail.[1] Secondly, we draw attention to additional episodes of contestation beyond European Parliament elections with relevance to debates on

---

1. Research on the scope, content and 'mediatising effects' of online political communication in the EU context will be collected by the authors in a separate volume (*see also* Michailidou and Trenz, 2010a).

the transnational political order. Of particular relevance here, is the investigation of how major shocks to the existing transnational political order – such as the Eurozone crisis starting in 2008 – affect polity contestation. Thirdly, the question is how political elites pick up on EU polity contestation online and thus, to what extent such debates are uploaded towards reforming the European Union and shaping the future process of European integration.

When shifting the focus from the content of EU polity contestation to the way the internet facilitates these debates, the research presented in this book opens up the potential to investigate two opposing scenarios with regard to a possible transformation of the public sphere. On the one hand, online media could support the development of a European public sphere that unfolds through processes of transnational opinion and will formation. Online media have the potential to actively involve citizens in political communication on EU legitimacy through such interactive features as commenting functions and online discussion forums. Debates taking place in these forums could be a key piece of the puzzle of disconnected public opinion from the communication efforts of transnational organisations such as the EU.

On the other hand, the fear has been expressed that online media contribute to a further fragmentation of the public sphere, thus disconnecting public opinion from sources of political authority. The sheer number of online news media and information sources points to the risk of fragmentation of the audiences into niche publics and closed user communities exposed to like-minded opinions only, since users control to a high extent which websites, topics and discussions they expose themselves to and which they avoid (for example, Sunstein 2002 and 2007). Through fragmentation, the internet might function to distance and marginalise citizens' discussions from elite dominated policy-formulation processes and thus reinforce the disconnection between EU citizens and the political elites. Our findings provide only little evidence in support of the fragmentation thesis. EU criticism unfolds regardless of the political positioning of the hosting news medium, involving a plural community of citizens that is exposed to both negative and positive evaluations.

The proposed analytical focus on discursive dynamics of polity contestation is highly applicable to the trans-disciplinary debate on state transformation and the re-configuration of political legitimacy, in a world where fully sovereign and independent nation states are no longer the sole guarantor for welfare, peace and security (Leibfried and Zürn 2005). The signals of a crisis of democratic legitimacy in the Western world are widely discussed and directly related to the mistrust of citizens in many societies towards the ability of both their national institutions of representative democracy and the international political system to deal with global problems, such as environmental challenges or, most recently, the turmoil of the global financial markets. Major shocks to the international political order, such as the 2008 financial crisis that consequently turned into a crisis of the Eurozone, directly reflect on the legitimacy of international and European political and economic order. Since such shocks clearly travel between economically interdependent countries, they immediately raise the question whether more or less international integration and collaboration on such issues may contribute to a return to stability and to prevent future crises. One might thus expect such international shocks to perform a catalyst function on polity contestation about competing visions of the international political order, in the same way that a referendum on EU Treaty change performs this function regarding the institutional design of the EU. Just as the repercussions of the 2005 referendums in France and the Netherlands were still clearly traceable in the 2009 EP election campaigns, the Eurozone crisis will certainly have a long lasting effect on the structuring of public debates and cleavages across the European space. Hence, one key issue is to understand the long-lasting impact of such shocks or turning moments on the legitimacy contestation of the international political order. The first question to ask is how such catalytic moments define political contestation and public expectation, not only within the existing national public spheres but also in building new alliances and cleavages across the European political space. A second question is how such catalysts translate into competing visions of crisis governance (nationally and transnationally) and support or challenge delegation of political authority to international institutions.

Lastly, another avenue for further research we would like to draw attention to, is governmental responsiveness to polity contestation. There is overall agreement that the EU has become increasingly responsive to legitimacy constraints imposed upon it by public debates. Yet, we lack understanding of how political decision making is transformed in light of this increased public scrutiny. That is, the question remains to what extent political elites are sensitive to the arguments presented by citizens in public forums such as the ones reported in this book. To what extent are they aware of such platforms as offered, for instance, by online social media, not just as a way to reach out to citizens and voters, but also as a source for information concerning public opinion? Even if political elites are frequently found to participate in debates and to contribute to public opinion formation through their public communication mechanisms, it remains to be seen to what extent they take up their voters' publicly expressed preferences in the formulation of policy responses, or in the promotion of institutional reform of the European Union and other aspects of international political order. If traces of such 'uploading' of opinions from public discussion forums to political decision making can be found, it would lend additional weight to the importance of studying these relatively new and under-researched platforms of political communication. Yet, even if impact on EU decision making is restricted and mostly indirect, such discussion forums remain highly interesting as a case of mediated public opinion formation in practice.

Appendices

Appendix I: Websites selected per country

Country	Professional journalism websites	Blogs
Austria	*Der Standard*	Politikblogs
	Die *Kronenzeitung*	Rigardi
Belgium (French-speaking)	Le Soir	Le Pan
	RTL	Le Blog Politique
	Le Vif l'Express	
Czech Republic	Novikny	Blogy iDnes
	Aktualne	Blogy iHNed
	Lidovky	
Finland	Iltalehti	Kasvi
	Iltasanomat	Soininvaara
	Helsingin Sanomat	
France	Le Monde	Plume de Presse
	Le Figaro	Sarkofrance
	Le Nouvel Observateur	
Germany	Spiegel Online	Bildblog
	Bild.de	Political Incorrect
	Sueddeutsche.de	
Greece	Ethnos	Press-GR
	Skai	nonews-NEWS
	Ta Nea	
Hungary	Origo	W – For a Better Magyarland
	Index	
	Figyelőnet	Reakció – polgári underground
Netherlands	Nu.nl	Geen Stijl
	De Telegraaf	Marokko.nl
	NOS	

Country		Professional journalism websites	Blogs
Poland		Gazeta Wyborcza	Janusz Palikot blog
		onet.pl	Janusz Korwin – Mikke blog
		TVN24	
Sweden		Aftonbladet	Rick Falkvinge (PP)
		Expressen	Politiskt Inkorrekt
		Dagens Nyheter	
United Kingdom		BBC	Iain Dale's Diary
		Guardian	Guido Fawkes' blog
		The Daily Mail	
Trans-European level	Professional news	EU Observer	
	Independent Blogs	Babel Blogs	
		BlogActiv	
	Social networking	European Parliament' Facebook fan page (unknown owner, 54,686 fans at the time of sampling – no longer available)	
		'Voter registration campaign for European Elections 2009' Facebook group (unknown owner, 5,953 members at the time of sampling – no longer available)	
		'I will vote in the 2009 European Parliament elections' Facebook group, (2,719 members at the time of sampling- no longer available) Twitter hashtags #eu09 and #ep09	

Appendix II: Codebook

Threads

In this project, we code two different textual units, or *units of analysis*. The first of these are generally referred to as *threads* in internet discourse research (e.g. Strandberg 2008). A thread is a single entry into one of our sampled websites, including the main entry of the journalist/blogger and all comments directly linked to this entry. In Bloglines, which we used for the data collection, each thread takes the form of a single 'clipping'.

Messages

Within these threads are an unknown number of *messages*. A message is *one or more evaluations on European integration made by a single (collective) actor in a single time and space*. The four different components of this definition will be discussed in more detail below, to help locate and demarcate messages.

'one or more evaluations...'

We are only interested in evaluations, as opposed to description. That is to say, language in which an actor transmits an opinion to the public. Some of these evaluations are very straightforward, such as when the blogger or commentator writes he/she thinks European integration is a good/bad thing; there should be more/less European integration; the EU has become too powerful/not powerful enough. Note that an 'evaluation' does not necessarily mean it is about something achieved in the past. A plea for something to happen in the future is here also understood as an 'evaluation', since it transmits an opinion and is thereby more than mere description.

The difference between evaluation and description is sometimes very subtle. The mere sentence: 'There will be European elections in June', is clearly descriptive. It doesn't transmit any opinion. However, the sentence: 'A low turnout in the election is expected, because people do not see the importance of the election,' is an evaluation. A negative opinion of the European Union is transmitted through this text by 'people', implying there should be more at stake during the elections.

Secondly, note that an evaluation does not necessarily have to be 'spoken', but rather be 'transmitted' to the public in a wide sense of that word. Thus, whenever an actor 'wants'/ 'would rather have'/ 'opposes'/ 'acts in favour of' something related to European integration, that all counts as a possible evaluation. This means an actor does not necessarily have to 'do' anything literally to evaluate European integration. If a journalist writes: 'Party X is in favour of more integration', that party doesn't really do anything but still transmits an opinion concerning European integration to the public. We include this in our coding because we assume that the journalist, in this case, bases this sentence on previous actions by that party, its manifesto or an interview with a party member, thereby passively reporting a previous action. *We thus code the meaning of the text, rather than what it literally says. Coders are to ask themselves the question: 'is there an opinion of an (collective) actor transmitted by this text?' If the answer is yes, it is coded as a message.*

'... on European integration...'

That an evaluation has to be 'on European integration' means we are not coding evaluations that have to do with either the content of EU policies (as opposed to the level and/or scope of EU policies), or the election campaign as such (unless it reflects back on the EU polity), or domestic politics only. Thus, the evaluation that 'the EU should be willing to threaten Iran with military sanctions if it doesn't stop its nuclear ambitions' is not coded, since it is about an EU policy without saying anything about the range of issues the EU has competencies in, or the balance of power between Member States and supranational institutions. The evaluation that 'political parties are not doing enough to make clear what is at stake during these elections' also is not coded, since it doesn't reflect on the EU. It only criticises national political parties. It is an evaluation, but not on European integration. However, the previous example of 'people do not see the importance of the election' is an evaluation on European integration. This is so, because the meaning transmitted by the text could be reformulated into 'people disapprove of the fact that there is little at stake during these elections'. There would be more 'at stake' if the European Parliament had more powers, particularly if it could elect a European government. Thus, this is an indirect negative evaluation of the European Parliament's current powers.

This example shows two things that we would like to stress. First, it is important to code beyond the literal text. Rather than the literal text, we are interested in the meaning it transmits to its public. Second, this example proves that it may be hard to decide whether an evaluation is on European integration or not. Here it is important to first ask whether the transmitted opinion carries consequences for the principle, polity or project of integration. Keep in mind that Member States and their domestic politics are part of the European Union. An evaluation *primarily* directed at domestic actors may still have a *secondary* evaluation of European integration, in which case we code. Only if it is exclusively directed at the domestic level do we not code.

'... made by a single (collective) actor...'

An evaluation needs to have an actor 'making' it. In other words, narratives about European integration have to be 'performed' in the public sphere to contribute to a Eurosceptic discursive formation on European integration. There are three rules concerning defining the actor and the message. First: a single actor can only make one message in a given time and space. Second: if there is doubt as to who the actor is, prefer one of the non-journalists/bloggers categories. This will be discussed in more detail below, when elaborating on the actor variable. Three: an actor may transmit his or her opinion directly by actually saying it, or indirectly if its opinion is featured by the writer of the text. In the above example of 'people do not see the importance of the election', the actor – people – is not actually transmitting an opinion itself. Rather, the journalist features this opinion to support or contradict her own evaluation. We still code the people as an actor in a separate message, but the message is transmitted 'indirectly'.

If only the blogger presents his or her opinion, there can only be one message irrespective of how elaborate or short the text may be. If the blogger provides a platform for multiple actors, there may be an equal amount of messages included depending on whether all of these actors make evaluations. Thus, if the blogger discusses the opinions of others – e.g. political parties – these actors can each make a message of their own.

There may be times when it is unclear whether a message is made by the blogger or by someone else. For instance, if the blogger writes: 'the European Union has lost much of its legitimacy, as clearly expressed in public opinion polls', one may consider this an evaluation by the journalist as actor, or by 'the people' as collective actor, since 'the people' transmit their opinion in public opinion polls. In such instances, *always prioritise other actors over the journalist/blogger*. This message would thus be attributed to 'citizens' as actor.

'... in a single time and space.'

A single actor can only make one message in a single time and space. There may be very elaborate evaluations in blogs, however, if they are made by the same actor (most often the writer of the blog), it is still one message. If the same actor – say the journalist having written the blog – replies later to one of the comments made on his/her original blogs, it will be a separate message from the original one as it takes place in a different time. It should thus be coded as a separate message. Also, if the same actor makes the same evaluation in different threads, this will be counted as several messages (equal to the amount of threads in which the evaluation is found) as they take place in a different 'space'. Finally, if a thread reports on an actor transmitting an opinion on European integration at different time points, this would also result in multiple messages. Thus, if a text reads: 'The majority of citizens used to be of the opinion that […], but recent polls indicate that there is a shift of opinion towards […],' this will be two different messages, both made by 'citizens'. Although they are made by the same actor in the same space, they are made at different times.

Coding threads and messages

General variables

The first two variables are general. That means they apply to both threads and messages. 'Country' is a variable that is stable for all units, given the coding of a debate in one Member State.
Country [Country]

1.	Austria	8.	Hungary
2.	Belgium	9.	Netherlands
3.	Czech Republic	10.	Poland
4.	Finland	11.	Sweden
5.	France	12.	United Kingdom
6.	Germany	13.	European Union
7.	Greece		

The variable 'Unit of Analysis' provides whether this coded variable is a thread or a message.

Unit of Analysis [UnitAnal]
1. Thread
2. Message

These are two variables that apply to all units of analysis. The rest applies either to threads or to messages (although some thread variables will be copied into messages as well, see elaboration later). To make it easier to remember which variables are thread variables and which are message variables, the labels of all thread variables start with 'T_', whereas the message variables start with 'M_'.

Thread variables

The coding of threads gives us background information on both the campaign itself and on the structure of the digital public sphere. Thus, rather than measuring Eurosceptic discourse (this is done at the message level), the thread level of analysis measures what the main topics are in the campaign and how many comments come to what kind of entrances. There are six thread variables.
Thread Number [T_Number]
This number is composed of both the country and a consecutive numbering to create a unique number for each thread in our entire study. The appropriate number is reached by taking the country number, multiplying it by 100 and adding the number of the thread. So, the first thread from the German case (number 6 in variable Country) is 6*100+1= 601. The 40th German thread is 640. The 12th thread from the UK is 1212.

Website [T_Source]

1. Der Standard
2. Krone
3. Kurier
4. Politikblogs
5. Rigardi
6. Le Soir
7. RTL
8. Le Vif l'Express
9. Le Pan
10. Le Blog Politique
11. Novikny
12. Aktualne
13. Lidovky
14. Blogy iDnes
15. Blogy iHNed
16. Iltalehti
17. Iltasanomat
18. Helsingin Sanomat
19. Kasvi
20. Soininvaara
21. Le Monde
22. Le Figaro
23. Le Nouvel Observateur
24. Plume de Presse
25. Sarkofrance
26. Spiegel Online
27. Bild.de
28. Sueddeutsche.de
29. Bildblog
30. Political Incorrect
31. Ethnos
32. Skai
33. Ta Nea
34. Press-GR
35. nonews-NEWS
36. Origo
37. index
38. Figyelőnet
39. W – For a Better Magyarland
40. Reakció – polgári underground
41. Nu.nl
42. De Telegraaf
43. NOS
44. Geen Stijl
45. Marokko.nl
46. Gazeta Wyborcza
47. onet.pl
48. TVN24
49. Janusz Palikot blog
50. Janusz Korwin – Mikke blog
51. Aftonbladet
52. Expressen
53. Dagens Nyheter
54. Rick Falkvinge (PP)
55. Politiskt Inkorrekt
56. BBC
57. Guardian
58. The Daily Mail
59. Iain Dale's Diary
60. Guido Fawkes' blog
61. Facebook
62. BabelBlogs
63. BlogActiv
64. EUobserver
65. Twitter

Enter the website from which the thread is sampled.

Period [T_Date]

1. 18 May – 28 May
2. 29 May – 6 June
3. 7 June – 10 June

Topic [T_Topic]

1. Domestic Party Politics [party candidates, pollings, election results]
2. Other Member State Party Politics [political parties, results in other Member States]
3. European Party Politics [EP party federations, European wide election results / polls]
4. National Economy [prosperity, growth, unemployment, financial crisis]
5. European Economy [same as previous, but at European level]
6. European integration [Treaty of Lisbon, allocation of competencies, safeguarding or reversing integration, superstate]
7. Membership / Enlargement [own country's membership, enlargement with own or other country, leaving the Union]
8. Democracy [legitimacy of the European Parliament or EU, turn-out, importance of the election]
9. Other

This is one of the more complicated variables, and will require active judgment on your part. We mean to *capture the main theme of the thread only*. This may be indicated by the title, or otherwise in the main text.

Keep in mind here that most of the threads will have some domestic politics linkage or dimension. Thus, the author might compare results of Eurosceptic parties in other countries with those in their own country. Or they may write that the current national government lost in the elections / does badly in the polls. This does not necessarily make it the main topic. This is often a trick used by journalists to make their topic interesting to a domestic public. A teaser, if you will. In doubtful cases, other values are *prioritised over 'domestic politics'*.

Also, see that some values are more specific than others. Values 4 and 5 on economy are more specific than values 1, 2, or 3. One might say that most economy discussions during elections also have to do with party politics, but party politics does not always have to do with the economy. *Prefer value 4 or 5 over 1, 2, or 3 when in doubt*. The same applies to values 6 and 7. Membership / Enlargement

(7) is also about European integration (6), but the reverse does not always apply. *Prefer value 7 over 6* when in doubt.

Amount of Comments [T_Comments]

[Enter the total amount of comments attached to this thread. Apply '0' when there was an option for comments, but none entered. Leave open when there was no option to comment.]

Evaluations [T_Eval]

1. Yes
2. No

The answer is 'yes' if there is one or more evaluations on European integration in the thread and 'no' if the thread is purely descriptive or has evaluations on other topics. This means that any threads where the answer is 'yes' will also contain messages to be coded. Threads where the answer is 'no', will not.

Message variables

There are 8 message variables, which will be briefly discussed below. Thus, if the unit of analysis is a message, a value for each of the following variables is coded. In addition, the values for the variables T_Number, T_Source, T_Date and T_Topic are copied from the thread where the message is located into all coded messages from that particular thread. The thread variables T_Comment and T_Eval remain open if the unit of analysis is a message.

Location [M_Loca]

1. Main Text
2. Comment on Main Text
3. Comment on Comment

This codes the location, and to some extent the direction, of the message. If the message is in the main text of the blog, it gets value 1. If it is in a comment on the main text, it is value 2. It is also value 2 if the target of the comment is unspecified by the author. It is value 3 when the commentator actively addresses a previous comment or responds to something written in one of the previous comments.

Actor [M_Actor]

1. Journalist / Blogger [the main author of the thread]
2. Citizen(s) [either individually – i.e. most commentators – or collectively as people or public]

3. Party Actor [government, Member of Parliament, Members of the European Parliament]
4. Non-Party State Actor [judges, bureaucrats, non-elected heads of state, European Commission]
5. Non-State Actor [civil society, NGOs, trade unions, companies, media]
6. Other

This is the (collective) actor of the message. In case of doubt, *values 2 – 5 are preferred over 1, and 1 over 6*. A party actor is an actor who is in office primarily as a representative of his or her party. Thus, Member State governments count as party actors, since it is political parties in national parliaments that form a government and supply its members. However, European Commissioners are coded as non-party members because they are, in first instance, representatives of their country, with party affiliation secondary. There could be reference to a vague collective actor, which does not fit well into 'citizens', such as 'Europhiles', 'federalists' or 'Eurosceptics'. Code these as 'other'. However, note that such categories as 'tree huggers', 'farmers' or 'capitalists' are a more clear societal group and fall under 'non-state actor'.

Actor Scope [M_ActScop]

1. Regional [sub-national territorial level of action]
2. National
3. Foreign [national in another EU Member State]
4. European [at EU level, supranational institution]
5. International [country outside the EU or international organisation]

This is the territorial level the actor is acting upon, particularly applicable to politicians. Thus, if the actor is the European Commission, or a Member of the European Parliament, the scope will be European. The nationality or scope of office of an actor might be explicitly given. It may also be deductible. For instance, if a commentator on a British website addresses his comment to 'you British people', we may safely conclude that he/she is not British. National politicians, judges, journalists etc. have the 'national' scope. If it is unknown or unclear what level the actor is acting upon, value 2 'national' is the default option. This is likely the case for most journalists/bloggers and individual citizens.

Transmission [M_Trans]

1. Direct
2. Indirect

This variable measures whether the actor actively makes the message with the purpose of it being publicly transmitted, or whether the evaluation is introduced by another actor (usually the journalist writing the blog or the commentator making the comment) to support, illustrate or contradict their own message (see the discussion on actors and definition of message above).

The following three variables concern the evaluative dimensions of the message. They are a combination of topic and opinion, which will be discussed further below. Furthermore, a single message may or may not hold an opinion on all three types of evaluative dimensions, but must at least hold an evaluation on one of the three; otherwise it does not qualify as concerning European integration (see the definition of message above).

The 'Principle of Integration' is the widest, most fundamental and most general way of transmitting an opinion on European integration. It concerns the idea and/or act of cooperation among European Member States in any form. We are not interested here in forms of collaboration outside EU framework. Thus, an evaluation of NATO membership or the Council of Europe does not count as being on 'European integration'. However, a general argument that economic collaboration between European countries is a good thing does count, since this area is exclusively dealt with by the EU and its direct competitors (EFTA, EEA, 'Europe of Nation States'). In case the opinion gives more detailed information on what kind of cooperation is preferred/opposed and in what institutional format, the evaluation is likely to fall into either of the next two categories: 'EU Polity' or 'Project of Integration'.

The category 'EU Polity' concerns the current institutional makeup of the European Union. It may be about any of its institutions – i.e. European Commission, European Parliament, Court of Justice etc. Secondly, it may be about decision-making rules – i.e. codecision, open method of coordination, unanimity voting. Thirdly, it may be about competencies in certain policy fields – i.e. trade, foreign policy, justice and home affairs etc. Fourthly, it may be about the membership or constituencies of the EU. This last one includes individual member states, but also societal groups such as farmers, 'the poor', 'ordinary citizens', or big business. If it concerns who decides in the European Union, including the division of power between Member States and supranational institutions, it concerns the level of integration. Thus, arguments for more powers to the European Parliament are coded: 'Project of Integration – Level – Positive'. A defense of the current powers of the EP is coded: 'EU Polity – Level – Positive'. If it concerns *what the EU decides* upon, or policy fields and issues affected by European integration, we are talking of the scope of integration. An argument that the EU should not have a say in foreign policy or that agriculture should be renationalised is coded as: 'EU Polity – Scope – Negative'. If it concerns *who is affected by the European Union or who affects the EU*, whether talking of countries or societal groups, we are coding this as the inclusiveness of integration. An argument against Turkish membership of the EU is coded as: 'Project of Integration – Inclusiveness – Negative'. An argument that big business has too much influence in the EU, that the EU is elitist (i.e. excluding ordinary citizens) or that letting Romania and Bulgaria in was a mistake, is coded as: 'EU Polity – Inclusiveness – Negative'. An argument that one's own country interests are adequately represented in the EU, is coded as: 'EU Polity – Inclusiveness – Positive'. To put it very simply then: *Level is about power and a more or less federal Union; scope is about issues and policy domains; and inclusiveness is about the relationship between the EU and people, whether grouped on nationality, religion, class or anything else.*

There may – again – be difficult situations. For instance, arguments for a more social or greener Europe could be both positive about the scope, or the inclusiveness, of the Project (since it argues in favour of integration in a certain direction). If it is phrased in such general terms, where constituencies are not named or directly implicated, we code scope. If however, in the argument 'the EU should create a globalisation fund to finance re-education of people who lost their jobs due to integration or globalisation', the constituency is clearly mentioned. The plea could be rephrased as: 'the EU should actively affect the lives of more people in the future, who are now left out'. The last example would thus be coded as: 'Project – Inclusiveness – Positive'.

The third and final category 'Project of Integration' concerns plans for future integration, as opposed to integration already achieved and represented in the current EU polity. The Project may concern institutional change, enlargement, and pleas for a 'different' Europe or changes in the competencies of EU institutions. The same three distinctions applying to Polity – Level, Scope and Inclusiveness – also apply to Project.

Finally, whether an evaluation is 'positive' or 'negative' depends on the implications for European integration, as opposed to the tone of voice. Thus a comment such as 'those damn Eurosceptics are ruining everything' has a clear negative tone of voice, but is coded as: 'Principle of Integration – Positive'.

Principle of Integration [M_Principle]

1. Positive
2. Negative
3. N/A [no evaluation on Principle of Integration in this message]

EU Polity [M_Polity]

1. Level – Positive
2. Level – Negative
3. Scope – Positive
4. Scope – Negative
5. Inclusiveness – Positive
6. Inclusiveness – Negative
7. N/A [no evaluation on EU Polity in this message]

Project of Integration [M_Project]

1. Level – Positive
2. Level – Negative
3. Scope – Positive
4. Scope – Negative
5. Inclusiveness – Positive
6. Inclusiveness – Negative
7. N/A [no evaluation on Project of Integration in this message]

Keep in mind that a message may include one or more evaluations. Thus, it could transmit an opinion on all three categories of European integration, two or just one. Logically then, a message cannot have the value 'N/A' for all three of these variables. A message may, however, be highly complex and have multiple evaluations for each of the three dimensions of evaluation. In such a case, the coder will have to make a choice which of the evaluations is the primary one for each of the categories, since a single message cannot have more than one value per variable. *Unless one of the evaluations clearly is given more importance in the text than the others, prefer the first evaluation made.*

Also keep in mind that evaluations may be implied, but not made. Thus, when a message is positive about the Polity, it is implicitly also positive about the Principle. After all, most actors who support the EU as it currently exists are also in favour of the idea of cooperation between European countries to begin with. However, 'N/A' is coded in the Principle variable, unless the same actor actually makes an evaluation on the principle. Thus, as a coding rule, one cannot allocate values on dimensions of evaluation which the actor does not address in the text. In other words, only dimensions of evaluation discussed in the text are coded.

Finally, we code the justification of worth given in the message. This can be understood as an explicit reason given by the actor of the message for his evaluation – i.e. 'I want [...], because [...]', or it may be a vaguer context or motivation providing the background for the message. To find out whether there is a justification of worth, and if so, what it is, the coder should fill in the following sentence: 'European integration is positive/negative in light of our shared value of [...]'. If that sentence cannot be finished, try filling in the following sentence: 'The actor in the message implies that European integration should be evaluated with criteria of [...].' If the message and its context do not allow finishing either one of these test sentences, there is no justification of worth.

For example, the message 'the people know Britain is better off in the EU' holds a clear evaluation of 'EU Polity – Inclusiveness – Positive'. However, the word 'better' does not give us anything on the right criteria supporting this evaluation. Consequently, there is no possibility to finish either of the above two sentences and thus no justification of worth. On the other hand, the message:

'You are so in love with the idea of destroying Britain and creating the European superstate that you don't care about the practical results', does give a clear answer, namely 'practical results', which would fall under value 3: necessity. By the way, this message has two evaluations. It is both negative about 'the idea of destroying Britain' and about 'creating the European superstate'. This is coded as 'Principle – Negative' and 'Project – Level – Negative' within the same message.

Note that the justification of worth does not incorporate any positive attitude towards European integration. In other words, if the justification of worth of a particular message is democracy, the evaluations in that message may still either portray European integration as supporting democracy or as damaging democracy. As with other variables, in case of multiple justifications, prefer the first one given unless a later one is given clear priority. Consider the following example: 'The European Parliament should not be given more powers as it is an inefficient and unnatural institution. Even more important, it is not recognized by the citizens of the EU as legitimate.' Although the first justification given (inefficient) would point to value 3: Necessity, and the second (unnatural) to value 2: Culture, the last one, is given more importance and the right value should thus be 1: Democracy.

Justification of Worth [M_Worth]

1. Democracy [citizen influence, legitimacy, accountability]
2. Culture [tradition, identity, community values]
3. Necessity [governability, efficiency, effectiveness, obligations]
4. Economic Prosperity [economic growth, employment, wealth]
5. Safety [social security, stability of society, internal security, external security]
6. Other
7. N/A

These are all the variables and values involved in our study. It should be noted that our codebook necessarily forms an abstraction of reality. Thus, not every interesting aspect is captured in the coding. For instance, whether Euroscepticism targets the Euro, the European Commission or Turkey is not coded. Notes were made while coding on information that may be relevant, but is not captured by the coding scheme. This is used to illustrate and clarify the quantitative results in a qualitative manner in the country chapters.

Appendix III: Categorising EU polity contestation

In the introduction, we present a novel typology of EU polity contestation based on three distinct dimensions and the possibility to discursively present a positive or a negative evaluation of each of these dimensions. Building on previous attempts at classifying different forms or degrees of Euroscepticism (Kopecký and Mudde 2002; Szczerbiak & Taggart 2008c), we argue there is more to EU polity contestation than simply being 'in favour' or 'against'. Rather, we follow Morgan in distinguishing between three distinct dimensions of justification (Morgan 2005). These three dimensions are the principle of integration, the institutional set-up of the currently existing EU polity and the project of integration. Based on this, we developed a 2x2x2 table of possible forms of combinations of EU polity contestation. Of the eight theoretical possibilities, we ruled out two which we considered illogical arguments. The remaining six arguments are labelled Affirmative European, Status Quo, Alter-European, Eurocritical, Pragmatic and Anti-European. The typology is reproduced in Table A.1: Typology of EU Polity Contestation

Table A.1: Typology of EU polity contestation

Project of integration	Principle of integration			
	Positive		Negative	
	EU institutional set-up		EU institutional set-up	
	Positive	Negative	Positive	Negative
Positive	Affirmative European	Alter-European	–	–
Negative	Status-Quo	Eurocritical	Pragmatic	Anti-European

However, in practice, contributions to EU polity contestation in the public sphere rarely address all three dimensions of evaluation. Rather, the majority of evaluations in the form of messages we coded, address only one or two dimensions. Reality, therefore loads onto a 3x3x3 table where contributions to discourse can exclude one or two dimensions of contestation. Note that one combination – that of no evaluation on all three dimensions – is excluded, since this does not count as a contribution to EU polity contestation. We thus face 3x3x3-1=26 possible forms of EU polity contestation instances. The question then arises whether such real existing performances load onto our ideal-typical typology, and if so, how.

We now argue that all twenty-six forms of performances can be loaded onto our typology of EU polity contestation, with the exception of three combinations for which we need a seventh category. Whereas the original six represent lines of argumentation meeting the discursive standards for a 'sufficient' justification of EU legitimacy, the seventh category does not. That is, it consists of arguments which lack enough information to be placed in any of the six ideal-typical types of evaluation. Our categorisation rests first on the assumption that the three dimensions of polity contestation are generally not perceived to be independent from each other by those making the evaluations and the general audience. Secondly, we assume that evaluations are more likely to be negative than positive. That is, actors are generally more inclined to express disagreement than to express agreement in politics (Gamson 1968). This means that, once people make the effort to contribute a positive evaluation, this is more meaningful than when they contribute a negative evaluation as the threshold to do so is higher.

The main reason why most evaluations addressing one or two dimensions of contestation can be loaded onto our typology is that the three dimensions are not considered independent from each other (Vasilopoulou 2008). We assume that actors evaluating EU legitimacy, as well as the general audience of such evaluations, consider the three dimensions generally as ranked. That is, we assume that a positive evaluation of the third dimension of contestation – project of integration – builds on a positive evaluation of the first and second dimension unless explicitly stated otherwise. In other words, an argument in favour of further steps in integration in the future carries with it implicit acceptance of the principle of integration and the current institutional set-up. Similarly, we assume that a positive evaluation of the current institutional set-up of the EU carries implicit support for the principle of integration.

Secondly, we assume that people are generally more inclined to actively voice criticism than to voice support in politics. This is so, first, because 'voice' is often to be considered a form of action in response to an undesired situation (Hirschman 1970). It has consequently been specified that citizens with a combination of discontent about a political situation and the belief to be able to change this, are most likely to engage in politics (Gamson 1968: 48). This means that a negative evaluation of a particular dimension of contestation does not directly contribute to negative discourse on the other dimensions. After all, underlying opinion may be positive about the other dimension and just refrain from expressing it. In contrast, a claimant making a positive evaluation overcomes a greater hurdle to engaging in the public sphere, since it is easier or more natural to express criticism than it is to express support. Positive expressions of support in one dimension are thus understood to be supported by implicit positive evaluations of subordinate dimensions of legitimacy contestation, unless specifically evaluated as negative. In other words, if someone takes the effort to state his or her opinion on the EU or European integration online, and this opinion includes a positive evaluation on the project of integration or the institutional set-up of the EU, we assume evaluations on underlying dimensions are positive as well, and can thus be categorised as such unless explicitly argued otherwise.

Thirdly, we make a distinction in our three dimensions with regard to whether they address the EU as polity or European integration as political process (Morgan 2005). The second dimension is considered to address the EU as political entity or polity. The first and third dimension, in contrast, carry with it a historical dynamism of addressing the ongoing political project of European integration.

Table A.2: Possible EU polity contestation combinations, categories applied and frequencies

Principle	Institutional Set-Up	Project	Polity Evaluation	Frequency
Positive	Positive	Positive	Affirmative European	8
Positive	Positive	Negative	Status Quo	2
Positive	Positive	N/A	Affirmative European	23
Positive	Negative	Positive	Alter-European	16
Positive	Negative	Negative	Eurocritical	27
Positive	Negative	N/A	Eurocritical	35
Positive	N/A	Positive	Affirmative European	10
Positive	N/A	Negative	Status Quo	4
Positive	N/A	N/A	Affirmative European	22
Negative	Positive	Positive	-	0
Negative	Positive	Negative	Pragmatic	0
Negative	Positive	N/A	Pragmatic	1
Negative	Negative	Positive	-	0
Negative	Negative	Negative	Anti-European	16
Negative	Negative	N/A	Anti-European	26
Negative	N/A	Positive	-	0
Negative	N/A	Negative	Anti-European	5
Negative	N/A	N/A	Anti-European	29
N/A	Positive	Positive	Affirmative European	24
N/A	Positive	Negative	Status Quo	5
N/A	Positive	N/A	Status Quo	106
N/A	Negative	Positive	Alter-European	37
N/A	Negative	Negative	Eurosceptic	80
N/A	Negative	N/A	Eurosceptic	415
N/A	N/A	Positive	Affirmative European	87
N/A	N/A	Negative	Eurosceptic	149
N/A	N/A	N/A	-	1

Some of our categories (Affirmative European, Anti-European, Alter-European) rest, in particular, on their evaluation of the process of integration, whereas others (Status Quo, Pragmatic, Eurocritical) are shaped more by their opinion on the current institutional set-up of the EU, than by a particular vision on the process of integration. To mark this distinction, we pay particular attention to whether one or both types of dimensions are addressed in the evaluation. To give an example, a positive evaluation of the institutional set-up of the EU without evaluations on the other two dimensions, could, according to Table A.1 be an Affirmative European, a Pragmatic or a Status Quo evaluation. We categorise it here as Status Quo since 1) no dynamic dimension of legitimacy contestation is addressed (ruling out Affirmative European) and 2) a positive evaluation of the institutional set-up is understood to rest on a positive evaluation of the principle of integration, unless explicitly stated otherwise (ruling out Pragmatic).

Based on these three assumptions, we can provide a renewed short description of the basic characteristics of each of the six ideal types of polity contestation:

1. An Affirmative European argument consists primarily of a positive evaluation of the dynamics of the process of European integration. This means a positive evaluation (POS) of the principle of integration and/or a positive evaluation of the current status and/or future project of integration without any accompanying negative evaluations. Possible combinations can thus be:
    a. Principle *POS*, Current status *n/a*, Future project *n/a*;
    b. *POS, n/a, POS*;
    c. *n/a, n/a, POS*;
    d. *n/a, POS, POS*; or
    e. *POS, POS, POS.*
2. A Status Quo evaluation is characterised primarily by a positive evaluation of the EU institutional set-up. It differs from an Affirmative European argument in that there is no positive evaluation of either principle or project of integration, accept a combination of positive on principle and negative on project. It further differs from Pragmatic arguments in that there is no negative evaluation (NEG) of principle of integration. Status Quo combinations therefore are: *POS, POS, NEG; n/a, POS, NEG; n/a, POS, n/a.*
3. An Alter-European evaluation is primarily characterised by a negative evaluation of the institutional set-up, in combination with a positive evaluation of the project of integration. If the combination of this is present, the principle dimension does not affect the nature of the evaluation anymore. Combinations are therefore: *POS, NEG, POS; and n/a, NEG, POS.*
4. Eurocritical evaluations are characterised by positive evaluations of

the principle of integration in combination with negative evaluations of the institutional set-up, excluding a positive evaluation of the project as this would be considered an Alter-European argument. Possible combinations are therefore: *POS, NEG, NEG; POS, NEG, n/a.*

5. A Pragmatic evaluation is composed of a negative evaluation of the principle of integration in combination with a positive evaluation of the institutional set-up. Furthermore, we consider a combination of a negative evaluation on principle and a positive evaluation on project to be illogical and therefore exclude this from our typology. We also did not find this combination in practice. Possible combinations for pragmatic evaluations are therefore: *NEG, POS, NEG and NEG, POS, n/a.*

6. An Anti-European evaluation targets the dynamics of European integration rather than the currently existing EU polity and is, in that extent, close to the opposite of an Affirmative European evaluation. However, a negative evaluation of the project of integration without any other evaluations present does not tell us as much as a positive evaluation of the project. We can thus only count negative evaluations of the principle of integration without accompanying positive evaluations on other dimensions to load onto Anti-European evaluations. This includes the following combinations: *NEG, NEG, NEG; NEG, n/a, NEG; NEG, NEG, n/a and NEG, n/a, n/a.*

Of twenty-six possible combinations of evaluations, nineteen have thus been defined as fitting one of our six categories of polity contestation. Of the remaining seven combinations, three are ruled out as illogical as they combine a negative evaluation of the principle of integration with a positive evaluation of the project: *NEG, POS, POS; NEG, NEG, POS and NEG, n/a, POS.* One more combination (*POS, n/a, NEG*) does not directly fit the definition of a Status Quo evaluation, but comes close and will be understood as a form of Status Quo argument. Understanding our three dimensions as ranked (first assumption) it remains an open question whether such an evaluation carries an unspoken positive or negative evaluation of the institutional set-up. In other words, in terms of definition, it could fit either the Status Quo or Eurocritical categories of evaluation. However, since we assume people are inclined to make negative evaluations and not making them, thus, rather implies a positive attitude, we understand this combination as Status Quo, rather than as Eurocritical.

This leaves us with three so far unclassified possible combinations of polity contestation: *n/a, NEG, NEG; n/a, n/a, NEG and n/a, NEG, n/a.* They are clearly negative in tone, yet could all fit the definition of either Anti-European or Eurocritical evaluations. In addition, the second and third combination could fit the Status Quo and Alter-European categories respectively. Since we lack sufficient information to place these three types of polity contestation in our typology, we add a seventh category of 'underspecified negative evaluation' to our typology. This category will be labelled 'Diffuse Euroscepticism' to capture on the one hand the clear negativity enclosed, yet also indicate the relative under-specification. To be precise, the under-specification particularly concerns what would alleviate the discontent. In other words, the actor states a clear discontent with some aspects of the European Union and/or European integration without clarifying what could possibly be done to remedy this unease. This message is, in our opinion, neatly captured by the term 'Euroscepticism'.

Bibliography

Aarts, K. and Van der Kolk, H. (eds) (2005) *Nederlanders en Europa. Het Referendum over de Europese Grondwet*, Amsterdam: Bert Bakker.
— (2006) 'Understanding the Dutch "no": the euro, the east, and the elite', *PS: Political Science and Politics* 39(2): 243–246.
Abromeit, H. (2001) 'The constitutionalisation and democratisation of the European Union', in M. Haller (ed.) *The Making of the European Union*, Berlin: Springer Verlag.
Abst, K., Heerwegh, D. and Swyngedouw, M. (2009) 'Sources of Euroscepticism: utilitarian interest, social distrust, national identity and institutional distrust', *World Political Science Review*, 5(1). Online. Available DOI: <Available <http://dx.doi.org/10.2202/1935-6226.1057> (accessed 30 October 2012)
Adam, S. (2009) 'Euroscepticism and the mass media: an analysis of the form of contention in the German and French debates on a European constitution', in D. Fuchs, R. Magni-Berton and A. Roger (eds) *Euroscepticism: Images of Europe among mass publics and political elites*, Opladen: Barbara Budrich Publishers, pp. 193–211.
Adamski, W. (1998) 'Interes', in *Encyklopedii Socjologii*, Warszawa: Oficyna Naukowa.
Albrecht, S. (2006) 'Whose voice is heard in online deliberation?: A study of participation and representation in political debates on the internet', *Information, Communication & Society* 9(1): 62–82.
Alexa Internet, I. (2009) 'Alexa, the web information company', Online. Available <http://www.alexa.com/> (accessed 3 August 2009).
— 2010) 'Top sites in Poland', Online. Available <http://www.alexa.com/topsites/countries/PL> (accessed 30 October 2012).
AliceCsodaországban01 (2009) 'comment number 1213', Online posting. Available <http://forum.index.hu/Article/showArticle?na_start=300&na_step=30&t=9192316&na_order=> (accessed 7 June 2009).
Amouch, H. (2006) 'Moslim-jongeren op internet: een overzicht', Online. Available <http://www.denieuwereporter.nl/2006/04/moslim-jongeren-op-internet-een-overzicht/> (accessed 23 November 2009).
Anderson, C. J. (1998) 'When in doubt, use proxies: attitudes toward domestic politics and support for European integration', *Comparative Political Studies* 31(5): 569–601.
Anderson, P. J. (2004) 'A flag of convenience? Discourse and motivations of the London-based eurosceptic press', in R. Harmsen and M. Spiering (eds) *Euroscepticism: Party politics, national identity and European integration*, Amsterdam: Rodopi, pp. 151–170.

Antal, D. (2009) 'nagykolíció felé: az EP választások tétje', Online. Available <http://antaldaniel.blogspot.com/2009/06/nagykoalicio-fele-az-ep-valasztasok.html> (accessed 2 June 2009).

Árpád, T. (2009) 'Európai értelemben vett fasizmust!', Online. Available <http://w.blog.hu/2009/06/08/europai_ertelemben_vett_fasizmust> (accessed 8 June 2009).

Arthaud, N. (2009) 'Nathalie Arthaud (LO) : ''Les classes populaires n'attendent rien des élections européennes''', Online. Available <Available <http://europeennes.blog.lemonde.fr/2009/05/23/nathalie-arthaud-lo-les-classes-populaires-n%E2%80%99attendent-rien-des-elections-europeennes/> (accessed 23 May 2009).

Arwine, A. and Mayer, L. (2008) 'The changing bases of political conflict in Western Europe: the cases of Belgium and Austria', Nationalism and Ethnic Politics 14(3): 428–454.

Ash, T. G. (1993) *In Europe's Name: Germany and the divided continent*, New York: Random House.

Aspinwall, M. (2000) 'Structuring Europe: powersharing institutions and British preferences on European integration', *Political Studies* 48(3): 415–442.

Associated Newspapers Ltd (2009) *Mail Online*. Online. Available <http://www.dailymail.co.uk/> (accessed 6 August 2010.

Backhaus, M., Lambeck, M. and Walter, M. (2009) 'Warum sollte man heute zur Europawahl gehen?', Online. Available <http://www.bild.de/BILD/politik/2009/06/07/angela-merkel/interview-zur-europawahl-2009.html> (accessed 7 June 2009).

Baker, D., Gamble, A., Randall, N. and Seawright, D. (2008) 'Euroscepticism in the British party system: a case of fascination, perplexity and sometimes frustration', in A. Szczerbiak and P. A. Taggart (eds) Opposing Europe?: *The comparative party politics of Euroscepticism*, Oxford: Oxford University Press, pp. 93–116.

Baker, D., Gamble, A. and Seawright, D. (2002) 'Sovereign nations and global markets: modern British conservatism and hyperglobalism', *British Journal of Politics and International Relations* 4(3): 399–428.

Bakker, P. and Scholten, O. (2005) *Communicatiekaart van Nederland: Overzicht van Media en Communicatie*, 5th edn, Amsterdam: Kluwer.

Balme, R., and Chabanet, D. (2008) *European Governance and Democracy: Power and protest in the EU*, Lanham: Rowman & Littlefield.

Barlow, J.P. (1996) 'A cyberspace independence declaration', Online. Available <http://homes.eff.org/~barlow/Declaration-Final.html> (accessed 17 October 2012).

Bartolini, S. (2005) R*estructuring Europe: Centre formation, system building, and political structuring between the nation state and the European Union*, New York: Oxford University Press.

BBC (2009) 'Elections 2009', Online. Available <http://news.bbc.co.uk/2/hi/in_depth/europe/2009/election_09/default.stm> (accessed 9 July 2012)

Belle, G. M.-V. (1968) *Les socialistes belges et l'intégration européenne*, Bruxelles: Editions de l'Institut de Sociologie de l'Université libre de Bruxelles.

Belot, C. (2002) 'Les logiques sociologiques de soutien au processus d'intégration européenne: éléments d'interprétation', *Revue Internationale de Politique comparée* 9(1) : 11–29.

Belot, C. and Cautrès, B. (2004) *L'Europe invisible mais omniprésente*, Paris: Presses de Science Po.

Benhabib, S. (1996) *Democracy and Difference*, Princeton: Princeton University Press.

Bennett, l. W. and Entman, R. M. (eds.) (2001) *Mediated Politics. Communication in the Future of Democracy*, Cambridge: Cambridge University Press.

Bergounioux, A. and Grunberg, G. (2005) *L'ambition et le remords. Les socialistes français et le pouvoir* (1905–2005), Paris: Fayard.

Beste, R. and Kurbjuweit, D. (2009) 'Eine verkopfte Sache', Online. Available <http://www.spiegel.de/spiegel/print/d-65489957.html> (accessed 7 June 2009).

Bet El, I. (2009) 'Pity the eurosceptics', Online. Available <http://www.guardian.co.uk/commentisfree/2009/jun/05/europe-votes-eurosceptics> (accessed 14 November 2010).

Bild.de (2009a) 'Wahlkampf läuft auf Hochtouren', Online. Available <http://www.bild.de/BILD/politik/wahlen/06/02/entscheidung-europawahl/wahlkampf-laeuft-auf-hochtouren.html> (accessed 7 June 2009).

—— (2009b) 'Europawahl am Strassenrand', Online. Available <http://www.bild.de/BILD/politik/wahlen/05/27/europawahlen-wahlplakate-der-parteien/wer-hat-das-beste.html> (accesses 7 June 2009).

Binnema, H. and Crum, B. J. J. (2007) 'Resistance to Europe as a carrier of mass-elite incongruence: the case of the Netherlands', in J. Lacroix and R. Coman (eds) *Les Résistance à l'Europe: Cultures nationales, ideologies et stratégies d'acteurs*, Bruxelles: Université de Bruxelles, pp. 113–128.

Blome, N. (2009) '... aber warum gehen nur so wenige zur Wahl?', Online. Available <http://www.bild.de/BILD/politik/wahlen/06/07/wahlmuedigkeit-warum-europa/nicht-sexy-ist.html> (accessed 7 June 2009).

Blondel, J., Sinnott, R. and Svensson, P. (1998) *People and Parliament in the European Union: Participation, democracy and legitimacy*, Oxford: Clarendon Press.

Boer, B. (2005) 'Euroscepsis en Liberalisme in Nederland', in H. Vollaard and B. Boer (eds) *Euroscepsis in Nederland*, Utrecht: Lemma, pp. 129–150.

Bohman, J. (1996) Public Deliberation: Pluralism, complexity, and democracy, Massachusetts: Massachusetts Institute for Technology Press.

Bóka, J. (2009) 'Az EP-választás tétje', HVG-online. Online. Available <http://hirszerzo.hu/publicisztika/109966_az_epvalasztas_tetje> (accessed 28 May 2009)

Bolesch, C. and Gammelin, C. (2009) '"Weltmeister in riskanten Bankgeschäften"' Süddeutsche.de. Online. Available <http://www.sueddeutsche.

de/wirtschaft/eu-kommissar-verheugen-weltmeister-in-riskanten-bankgeschaeften-1.458276> (accessed 7 June 2009).

Boltanski, L. and Thévenot, L. (2006) *On Justification: Economies of worth*, Princeton, NJ: Princeton University Press.

Börzel, T. (2005) 'Mind the gap! European integration between level and scope', *Journal of European Public Policy* 12(2): 217–236.

Börzel, T. A. and Risse, T. (2000) 'When Europe hits home: Europeanization and domestic change', EUI Working Papers 2000/56, European University Institute. Online. Available <Available <http://cadmus.eui.eu/dspace/bitstream/1814/1696/1/00_56.pdf> (accessed 30 October 2012).

Brinegar, A. P. and Jolly, S. K. (2005) 'Location, location, location', *European Union Politics* 6(2): 155–180.

Bräuninger, T. and König, T. (1999) 'The checks and balances of party federalism: German federal government in a divided legislature', *European Journal of Political Research* 36(2): 207–234.

Bude, H. (1992) *Bilanz der Nachfolge. Die Bundesrepublik und der Nationalsozialismus*, Frankfurt a.M.: Suhrkamp.

Bulmer, S. (1992) 'Britain and European integration: of sovereignty, slow adaptation and semi-detachment', in S. George (ed.) *Britain and the European Community : The politics of semi-detachment*, Oxford: Clarendon Press, pp. 1–29.

Burawoy, M. (2009) 'Working in the tracks of state socialism', *Capital and Class* 33(2): 33–64.

Busch, K. and Knelangen, W. (2004) 'German Euroscepticism', in R. Harmsen and M. Spiering (eds) *Euroscepticism: Party politics, national identity and European integration*, Amsterdam: Rodopi, pp. 83–98.

Byrd, P. (2008) 'The Labour Party and the European Community 1971–1975', *Journal of Common Market Studies* 13(4): 469–483.

CafeBabel (2012) 'CafeBabel.com: the European magazine'. Online. Available <http://www.cafebabel.com> (accessed 31 October 2012).

Callot, E.-F. (1988) 'The French communist party and Europe: the idea and its implementation 1945–1985', *European Journal of Political Research* 16(3): 301–316.

Carey, S. and Burton, J. (2004) 'Research note: the influence of the press in shaping public opinion towards the European Union in Britain', *Political Studies* 52(3): 623–640.

Carlson, T. and Strandberg, K. (2005) 'The 2004 European parliament election on the web: Finnish actor strategies and voter responses', *Information Polity* 10(3–4): 189–204.

Cautrès, B. (2000) 'Les attitudes vis-à-vis de l'Europe en France', in B. Cautrès and D. Reynié (eds) *L'Opinion européenne 2000*, Paris: Presses de Science Po. pp. 97–120.

Cautrès, B. and Denni, B. (2000) 'Les attitudes des Français à l'égard de l'Union européenne: Les logiques du refus', in P. Bréchon, A. Laurent and P. Perrineau (eds) *Les Cultures politiques des Français*, Paris: Presses de Sciences Po. pp. 323–356.

CBOS (2003) 'Deklaracje udziału i głosowania w referendum akcesyjnym', CBOS Research Report, 2003/81, CBOS Public Opinion Research Center. Online. Available <http://www.cbos.pl/SPISKOM.POL/2003/K_081_03. PDF> (accessed 30 October 2012).
— (2008) 'Opinie o Traktacie Lizbońskim', CBOS Research Report, 2008/74, CBOS Public Opinion Research Center. Online. Available <http://www.cbos.pl/SPISKOM.POL/2008/K_074_08.PDF> (acessed 30 October 2012)
— (2009) 'Korzystanie z Internetu', CBOS Research Report, 2009/96, CBOS Public Opinion Research Center. Online. Available <http://www.cbos.pl/SPISKOM.POL/2009/K_096_09.PDF> (accessed 30 October 2012).
— (2010a) 'Społeczny odbiór kampanii wyborczej i udział polaków w e demokracji przed wyborami samorządowymi', CBOS Research Report, 2010/170, CBOS Public Opinion Research Center. Online. Available <http://www.cbos.pl/SPISKOM.POL/2010/K_170_10.PDF> (accessed 30 October 2012.
— (2010b) "Sześć lat obecności Polski w Unii Europejskiej', CBOS Research Report, 2010/56, CBOS Public Opinion Research Center. Online. Available <http://www.cbos.pl/SPISKOM.POL/2010/K_056_10. PDF> (accessed 30 October 2012).
Cebul, K. (2009) 'Wizje Unii Europejskiej w programach wyborczych partii politycznych i w wyborach w latach 2005 i 2007', in E. Skotnicka-Illasiewicz (ed.) 5 lat członkowstwa Polski w Unii Europejskiej w perspektywie społecznej, Warszawa: Wydawnictwo UKIE, pp. 162–187
Chryssochoou, D. (1994) 'Democracy and symbiosis in the European Union: towards a confederal consociation?' *West European Politics* 17(1): 1–14.
Conservatives (2009) 'Vote for change: European election manifesto', Online. Available <http://www.conservatives.com/Policy/Where_we_stand/Europe.aspx> (accessed 4 April 2010).
Contamin, J.-G. (2005) 'Les grèves de décembre 1995 : un moment fondateur?', in É. Agrikolansky, O. Fillieule and N. Mayer (eds) *L'altermondialisme en France. La longue histoire d'une nouvelle cause*, Paris: Flammarion.
Costa, O. and Magnette, P. (eds) (2007) *Une Europe des Élites? Réflexions sur la fracture démocratique de l'Union européenne*, Bruxelles: Editions de l'Université libre de Bruxelles.
Crespy, A. (2008) 'Dissent over the European constitutional treaty within the French Socialist Party: between response to anti-globalization protest and intra-party tactics', *French Politics* 6(1): 23–44.
— (2010a) 'When Bolkestein is trapped by the French anti-liberal discourse: a discursive institutionalist account of preference formation in the realm of EU multi-level politics', *Journal of European Public Policy* 17(8): 1253–1270.
— (2010b) Les résistances à l'Europe néolibérale. Interactions, institutions et idées dans le conflit sur la Directive Bolkestein. PhD Dissertation. Université libre de Bruxelles.

— (2011) 'Europe and Euroscepticism: "non-issues" in Belgian politics', in R. Harmsen and J. Schild (eds) *Debating Europe: The 2009 European Parliament elections and beyond*, Baden-Baden: Nomos, pp.17–32.

Crespy, A. and Verschueren, N. (2009) 'From Euroscepticism to resistance to European integration: an interdisciplinary perspective', *Perspectives on European Politics and Society* 10(3): 377–393.

Crum, B. and Fossum, J. E. (2009) 'The multilevel parliamentary field: a framework for theorising representative democracy in the EU', *European Political Science Review* 1(2): 249–271.

Csepeli, G. and Örkény, A. (eds) (2002) Gyűlölet és politika, Budapest: Minoritás.

Daddow, O. J. (2004) *Britain and Europe Since 1945: Historiographical perspectives on integration*, Manchester: Manchester University Press.

— (2006) 'Euroscepticism and history education in Britain', *Government and Opposition* 41(1): 64–85.

Dahlgren, P. (2005) 'The Internet, public spheres, and political communication: dispersion and deliberation', *Political Communication* 22(2): 147–162.

— (2009) *Media and Political Engagement*, Cambridge: Cambridge University Press.

Dale & Co (2011) 'About Iain Dale', Online. Available <http://www.iaindale.com/contributors/iain-dale> (accessed 9 July 2012).

Dandoy, R. and Pauwels, T. (2009) 'Belgique', Cahiers du Cevipol, 2009/3. Online. Available> Dandoy, R. and Pauwels, T. (2009) 'Belgique', in Nathalie Brack, Yann-Sven Rittelmeyer, and Cristina Stănculescu (eds), *Les élections européennes de 2009 : entre national et européen. Une analyse des campagnes électorales dans 22 Etats membres*, Cahiers du Cevipol 2009/3. Available < http://dev.ulb.ac.be/cevipol/dossiers_fichiers/cahiers-du-cevipol-2009-3.pdf > (accessed 11 June 2013), p. 21.

Dayan, D. and Katz, E. (1992) *Media Events: The live broadcasting of history*, Cambridge: Harvard University Press.

Della Porta, D. (2006) 'The anti-globalisation and the European Union: critics of Europe', *Notre Europe Policy Paper* 2006/22.

Delwit, P. (1995) *Les Partis Socialistes et L'intégration Européenne: France, Grande-Bretagne, Belgique*, Brussels: Editions de l'Université libre de Bruxelles.

Delwit, P., Kulahci, E., Hellings, B., Pilet, J.-B. and Van Haute, E. (2005) 'L'Européanisation de la représentation communautaire: le cas des partis francophones belges', *Politique européenne* 16: 83–102.

Deschouwer, K. and Van Assche, M. (2008) 'Hard but hardly relevant: party based Euroscepticism in Belgian politics', in A. Szczerbiak and P. Taggart (eds) *Opposing Europe? The comparative party politics of Euroscepticism*, Oxford: Oxford University Press, pp. 75–92.

De Telegraaf (2009a) 'Baskische partij mag toch meedoen aan verkiezingen', telegraaf.nl. Online. Available <http://www.telegraaf.nl/buitenland/3983495/__Baskische_partij_bij_verkiezingen__.html?cid=rss> (accessed 23 November 2009).

- (2009b) 'Ergernissen aan kosten Europa', telegraaf.nl. Online. Available <http://www.telegraaf.nl/binnenland/4057273/__Ergernissen_aan_kosten_Europa__.html?cid=rss> (accessed 23 November 2009).
- (2009c) 'PVV grootste in Rotterdam', telegraaf.nl. Online. Available <http://www.telegraaf.nl/binnenland/4086033/__PVV_grootste_in_Rotterdam__.html?cid=rss> (accessed 23 November 2009).
- (2009d) 'Wilders: uitslag pak slaag voor kabinet', telegraaf.nl. Online. Available <http://www.telegraaf.nl/verkiezingen/ep2009/4086159/__Wilders__uitslag_pak_slaag_voor_kabinet__2___.html?cid=rss> (accessed 23 November 2009).
- (2009e) 'Zweedse piratenpartij in Europees parlement', telegraaf.nl. Online. Available <http://www.telegraaf.nl/digitaal/4106708/__Zweedse_Piraten_Partij_in_Europees_Parlement__.html?cid=rss> (accessed 23 November 2009).

De Villiers, P. (2009) 'Quelle place pour les souverainistes en Europe?', lemonde.fr. Online. Available <http://www.lemonde.fr/elections-europeennes/chat/2009/05/19/quelle-place-pour-les-souverainistes-en-europe_1195523_1168667.html> (accessed 19 May 2009).

De Vreese, C. H. (2001) '"Europe" in the news: a cross-national comparative study of the news coverage of key EU events', *European Union Politics* 2(3): 283–309.
- (2003) *Framing Europe: Television news and European integration*, Amsterdam: Askant.
- (2007a) *The Dynamics of Referendum Campaigns: An international perspective*, London: Palgrave Macmillan.
- (2007b) 'A spiral of Euroscepticim: the media's fault?', *Acta Politica* 42(2–3): 271–286.
- (2007c) 'Visibility and framing of European integration in the media', in R. Holzhacker and E. Albæk (eds) *Democratic Governance and European Integration*, Cheltenham: Edward Elgar.
- (2009) 'Second-rate election campaigning? An analysis of campaign styles in European parliamentary elections', *Journal of Political Marketing* 8(1): 7–19.

De Wilde, P. (2007) 'Politicisation of European integration: bringing the process into focus', ARENA Working Paper Series, 2007/18, ARENA, University of Oslo. Online. Available <http://www.arena.uio.no/publications/working-papers2007/papers/wp07_18.xml> (accessed 30 October 2012).
- (2009a) 'Reasserting the nation state: the trajectory of Euroscepticism in the Netherlands 1992–2005', RECON Online Working Paper, 2009/01, ARENA, University of Oslo, Online. Available <http://www.reconproject.eu/main.php/RECON_wp_0901.pdf?fileitem=16662572 > (accessed 30 October 2012).
- (2009b) '"Welcome sceptics!" A pro-European argument in favour of eurosceptics in the European Parliament', *Hamburg Review of Social Sciences* 4(2): 59–73.

— (2010) *How Politicisation Affects European Integration: Contesting the EU budget in the media and parliaments of the Netherlands, Denmark and Ireland*, Oslo: Unipub.
— (2011) 'No polity for old politics? A framework for analyzing politicization of European integration', *Journal of European Integration* 33(5): 559–575.
De Wilde, P. and Trenz, H.-J. (2012) 'Denouncing European integration: Euroscepticism as polity contestation', European Journal of Social Theory. Published online before print March 14, 2012. Available DOI: <Available <http://dx.doi.org/10.1177/1368431011432968 > (accessed 30 October 2012).
De Wilde, P., Trenz, H.-J. and Michailidou, A. (2009) Euroscepticism in the 2009 European Parliament Election Campaign: Codebook for the analysis of evaluations of the EU's polity's worth in online debates, Reconstituting Democracy in Europe (RECON), ARENA, University of Oslo. Online. Available <http://www.reconproject.eu/main.php/Codebook.pdf?fileitem=4472861> (accessed 30 October 2012).
De Wilde, P. and Zürn, M. (2012) 'Can the politicization of European integration be reversed?', *Journal of Common Market Studies* 50(s1): 137–153.
De Winter, L. (2001) 'The impact of European Integration on ethnoregionalist parties', The Institut de Ciències Polítiques i Socials (ICPS) Working Papers, No. 195. Online. Available <http://ddd.uab.cat/pub/worpap/2001/hdl_2072_1270/ICPS195.txt> (accessed 30 October 2012).
Díez, T. (1999) 'Speaking "Europe": the politics of integration discourse', *Journal of European Public Policy* 6(4): 598–613.
Díez Medrano, J. (2003) *Framing Europe: Attitudes to European integration in Germany, Spain, and the United Kingdom*, Princeton: Princeton University Press.
Duchesne, S., Haegel, F., Frazer, E., Van Ingelgom, V., Garcia, G. and Frognier, A.-P. (2010) 'Between globalisation and integration: social differences and national frames in focus group discussions in France, French-speaking Belgium and Britain', *Politique européenne* 30: 67–106.
Duchesne, S. and Van Ingelgom, V. (2008) 'L'indifférence des Français et des Belges (francophones) pour leurs voisins Européens: une pièce de plus au dossier de l'absence de communauté politique européenne?', *Politique européenne* 26: 143–164.
Eder, K. and Kantner, C. (2000) 'Transnationale Resonanzstrukturen in Europa: eine Kritik der Rede vom Öffentlichkeitdefizit in Europa', in M. Bach (ed.) *Transnationale Integrationsprozesse in Europa*, Opladen: Westdeutscher Verlag, pp. 306–331.
Eder, K. and Trenz, H.-J. (2007) 'Prerequisites of democracy and mechanisms of democratisation', in B. Kohler-Koch (ed.) *Debating the Democratic Legitimacy of the European Union*, Boulder: Rowan & Littlefield, pp. 165–181.

Eichenberg, R. C. and Dalton, R. J. (1993) 'Europeans and the European Community: the dynamics of public support for European integration', *International Organization* 47(4): 507–534.
— (2007) 'Post-Maastricht Blues: the transformation of citizen support for European integration, 1973–2004', *Acta Politica* 42(2/3): 128–152.
Eilders, C., Neidhardt, F. and Pfetsch, B. (2004) Die Stimme der Medien. Pressekommentare und politische Öffentlichkeit in der Bundesrepublik, Wiesbaden: VS Verlag.
Electronic Frontier, F. (2009) Electronic Frontier Foundation- Homepage. Online. Available <http://www.eff.org/> (accessed 6 august 2009).
Entman, R.M. (1993) 'Framing: toward clarification of a fractured paradigm', *Journal of Communication* 43(4): 51–58.
Eriksen, E. O. (2005) 'An emerging European public sphere', *European Journal of Social Theory* 8(3): 341–363.
Esser, F. and de Vreese, C.H. (2007) 'Comparing young voters' political engagement in the United States and Europe', *American Behavioral Scientist* 50(9): 1195–1213.
Euractiv (2009) 'Lisbon Treaty shadow looms large over UK elections', euractiv. com. Online. Available> (accessed 16 October 2012).
Eurobarometer (2008a) 'Public Opinion in the European Union. Standard Eurobarometer 68: Autumn 2007'. Online. Available <http://ec.europa.eu/public_opinion/archives/eb/eb68/eb_68_en.pdf> (accessed 30 October 2012).
— (2008b) 'Public Opinion in the European Union. Standard Eurobarometer 69: Spring 2008'. Online. Available <http://ec.europa.eu/public_opinion/archives/eb/eb69/eb_69_first_en.pdf> (accessed 30 October 2012).
— (2008c) 'Public opinion in the European Union. Standard Eurobarometer 70: Autumn 2008'. Online. Available <http://ec.europa.eu/public_opinion/archives/eb/eb70/eb70_first_en.pdf> (accessed 30 October 2012).
— (2009a) 'Public Opinion in the European Union. Standard Eurobarometer 71: Spring 2009'. Online. Available <http://ec.europa.eu/public_opinion/archives/eb/eb71/eb71_std_part1.pdf> (accessed 30 October 2012).
— (2009b) 'Die öffentliche Meinung in der EU. Nationaler Bericht Österreich. 72: Autumn 2009'. Online. Available <http://ec.europa.eu/public_opinion/archives/eb/eb72/eb72_at_at_nat.pdf> (accessed 30 October 2012).
— (2009c) 'The Europeans in 2009', Special Eurobarometer 308. Online. Available <http://ec.europa.eu/public_opinion/archives/ebs/ebs_308_en.pdf> (accessed 30 October 2012).
— (2009d) 'Report Krakow. Eurobaraometer 72'. Online. Available <http://ec.europa.eu/public_opinion/archives/eb/eb72/eb72_pl_pl_nat.pdf> (accessed 5 May 2010).

— (2010a) 'Standard Eurobarometer 72: Factsheets UK'. Online. Available <http://ec.europa.eu/public_opinion/archives/eb/eb71/eb71_std_part1.pdf> (accessed 31 October 2012).
— (2010b) 'Public Opinion in the European Union. Standard Eurobarometer 73: Spring 2010'. Online. Available <http://ec.europa.eu/public_opinion/archives/eb/eb71/eb71_std_part1.pdf> (accessed 31 October 2012).
European Commission Representation in the United Kingdom (2009) 'Euromyths', Online. Available <http://ec.europa.eu/unitedkingdom/press/euromyths/index_en.htm> (accessed 7 June 2009).
European Parliament (2009) 'Results of the 2009 European elections', Online. Available <http://www.elections2009-results.eu/en/new_parliament_en_txt.html> (accessed 4 July 2009).
Evans, G. and Butt, S. (2007) 'Explaining change in British public opinion on the European Union: top down or bottom up?', *Acta Politica* 42(2): 173–190.
Facebook (2012) 'Facebook'. Online. Available <http://www.facebook.com/> (accessed 31 October 2012).
Fallend, F. (2008) 'Euroscepticism in Austrian political parties: ideologically rooted or strategically motivated?', in A. Szczerbiak and P. Taggart (eds) *Opposing Europe? The comparative party politics of Euroscepticism. I: Case studies and country surveys*, Oxford: Oxford University Press, pp. 201–220.
Fawn, R. (2003) 'Ideology and national identity in post-communist foreign policies', *Journal of Communist Studies and Transition Politics* 19(3): 1–41.
Financial Times (2009) 'Interview with Martin Schulz', 2 June 2009.
Fischer, S. (2009) 'Acht für Europa', spiegel.de. Online. Available <http://www.spiegel.de/politik/deutschland/0,1518,627188,00.html> (accessed 31 May 2009).
FitzGibbon, J. (2010) 'Civil society-based eurosceptic protest movements', paper presented at the UACES 41 Annual Conference, Exchanging Ideas on Europe: Europe at a Crossroads, Bruges, Belgium, 6–8 September 2010.
fn24 (2009a) 'Kitiltankák Orbánt Szlovákiából', fn.hu. Online. Available <http://www.fn.hu/kulfold/20090603/kitiltanak_orbant_szlovakiabol/> (accessed 3 June 2009).
— (2009b) 'Minden megy tovább június 8-án?', fn.hu. Online. Available <http://www.fn.hu/belfold/20090525/minden_megy_tovabb_junius_8/> (accessed 25 May 2009).
— (2009c) 'Németország aggódik Orbánért', fn.hu. Online. Available <http://www.fn.hu/belfold/20090602/nemetorszag_aggodik_orbanert/> (accessed 2 June 2009).
— (2009d) 'Szélsöbboldali elöretörést hozhat az EP-választás', fn.hu. Online. Available <http://www.fn.hu/kulfold/20090605/szelsojobboldali_eloretorest_hozhat_ep/> (accessed 5 June 2009).
— (2009e) 'Szélsöjobbal az EP-be?', fn.hu. Online. Available <http://www.fn.hu/belfold/20090519/szelsojobbal_ep_be/> (accessed 19 May 2009).

Foot, K. A., Xenos, M., Schneider, S.M., Kluver, R. and Jankowski, N.W. (2009) 'Electoral web production practices in cross-national perspective: the relative influence of national development, political culture, and web genre', in A. Chadwick and P. N. Howard (eds) *Routledge Handbook of Internet Politics*, London: Routledge, pp. 40–55.

Forster, A. (1998) 'Britain and the negotiation of the Maastricht Treaty: a critique of liberal intergovernmentalism', *Journal of Common Market Studies* 36(3): 347–368.

— (2002) *Euroscepticism in Contemporary British Politics: Opposition to Europe in the British Conservative and Labour parties since 1945*, London: Routledge.

Fossum, J. E. and Schlesinger, P. (2007) 'The European Union and the public sphere: a communicative space in the making?, in J. E. Fossum and P. Schlesinger (eds) *The European Union and the Public Sphere. A communicative space in the making?*, Abingdon: Routledge, pp. 1–19.

Fouetillou, G. (2007) 'Le web et le traité constitutionnel europeen: ecologie d'une localité thématique compétitive', *Réseaux* 144: 279–304.

Franklin, M. N. and Wlezien, C. (1997) 'The responsive public: issue salience, policy change, and preferences for European unification', *Journal of Theoretical Politics* 9(3): 347–363.

Fraser, N. (2007) 'Transnationalizing the public sphere: on the legitimacy and efficacy of public opinion in a post-Westphalian world', *Theory, Culture & Society* 24(4): 7–30.

Fuchs, C. (2006) 'eParticipation research: a case study on political online debate in Austria', Research Paper No. 1, ICT&S Center, University of Salzburg.

Fuchs, D. and Klingemann, H. D. (2011) *Cultural Diversity, European Identity and the Legitimacy of the EU*, Edward Elgar: Cheltenham.

Fuchs, D., Magni-Berton, R. and Roger, A. (2009) 'European cleavage, Euroscepticism and support of the EU: a conceptual discussion', in D. Fuchs, R. Magni-Berton and A. Roger (eds) *Euroscepticism: Images of Europe among mass publics and political elites*, Opladen: Barbara Budrich Publishers, pp. 9–32.

Føllesdal, A. and Hix, S. (2006) 'Why there is a democratic deficit in the EU: a response to Majone and Moravcsik', *Journal of Common Market Studies* 44(3): 533–562.

Gabel, M. J. (1998a) 'The endurance of supranational governance: a consociational interpretation of the European Union', *Comparative Politics* 30(4): 463–475.

— (1998b) 'Public support for European integration: an empirical test of five theories', *Journal of Politics* 60(2): 333–354.

Gabel, M. J. and Anderson, C. J. (2004) 'The structure of citizen attitudes and the European political space', in G. Marks and M. R. Steenbergen (eds) *European Integration and Political Conflict*, Cambridge: Cambridge University Press, pp. 13–31.

Gaffney, J, (ed.) (1996) *Political Parties and the European Union*, London: Routledge.
Gajda, A. (2009) 'Próba bilansu pięciu lat członkostwa Polski w Unii Europejskiej', in J. Barcz (ed.) *Pięć lat członkowstwa Polski w Unii Europejskiej: Zagadnienia polityczno ustrojowe*, Warszawa: Instytut Wydawniczy EuroPrawo, pp. 222–255.
Gamson, W. A. (1968) *Power and Discontent*, Homewood, Ill.: Dorsey Press.
— (2004) 'Bystanders, public opinion, and the media', in D. A. Snow, S.A. Soule and H. Kriesi (eds) *The Blackwell Companion to Social Movements*, Oxford: Blackwell Publishing, pp. 242–261.
Gavin, N. T. (2001) 'British journalists in the spotlight: Europe and media research', *Journalism* 2(3): 299–314.
Gazeta.pl (2009) 'Za wybory każdy Polak zapłaci 2 zł I 80 gr', Online. Available <http://wiadomosci.gazeta.pl/Wiadomosci/1,80708,6692461,Za_wybory_kazdy_Polak_zaplaci_2_zl_80_gr_.html> (accessed 17 December 2010).
GeenStijl (2009a) 'Rutger belaagd door EU-bejaarden in Almere', Online. Available <http://www.geenstijl.nl/mt/archieven/2009/06/rutger_belaagd_door_eubejaarde.html> (accessed 23 November 2009).
— (2009b) 'VERKIEZINGEN: Glunderende Geert & Blije Barry', Online. Available <http://www.geenstijl.nl/mt/archieven/2009/06/pvv_grote_winnaar_stijlloze_po.html> (accessed 23 November 2009).
— (2009c) 'Wees niet sneu. Stem voor/tegen EU', Online. Available <http://www.geenstijl.nl/mt/archieven/2009/06/wees_niet_sneu_stem_voortegen.html> (accessed 23 November 2009).
George, A. L. and Bennett, A. (2005) *Case Studies and Theory Development in the Social Sciences*, Cambridge: BCSIA, Harvard University.
George, S. (1990) *An Awkward Partner: Britain in the European Community*, Oxford: Clarendon Press.
Gerhards, J. and Schafer, M. S. (2010) 'Is the Internet a better public sphere? Comparing old and new media in the US and Germany', *New Media & Society* 12(1): 143–160.
Gifford, C. (2006) 'The rise of post-imperial populism: the case of right-wing Euroscepticism in Britain', *European Journal of Political Research* 45(5): 851–869.
— (2008) *The Making of Eurosceptic Britain: Identity and economy in a post-imperial state*, Aldershot: Ashgate.
Gitlin, T. (1998) 'Public sphere or public sphericules', in T. Liebes, J. Curran and E. Katz (ed.) *Media, Ritual and Identity*, London: Routledge, pp. 168–174.
Global and General Nominees Limited (2004) 'About Guido's Blog', Online. Available <http://order-order.com/2004/01/09/about-guidos-blog/> (accessed 10 April 2012).
— (2012) 'Guido Fawkes' blog... of plots, rumours and conspiracy', Online. Available <http://order-order.com/> (accessed 10 April 2012).

Gombár, C., Köröséyni, A., Lengyel, L., Stumpf, I. and Tölgyessy, P. (2006) *Túlterhelt demokrácia*, Budapest: Századvég.
Góra, M. and Mach, Z. (2010) 'Between old fears and new challenges: the Polish debate on Europe', in J. Lacroix and K. Nicolaïdis (eds) *European Stories: Intellectual debates on Europe in national contexts*, Oxford: Oxford University Press.
Gordon, P. and Meunier, S. (2002) *Le Nouveau Défi Français: La France face à la mondialisation*, Paris: Odile Jacob.
Google (2012) Google Reader. Available <http://www.google.com/reader> (accessed 4 September 2012).
Guardian, The (2009) 'European Elections', Online. Available <http://www.guardian.co.uk/politics/european-elections> (accessed 6 August 2009).
— (2011a) 'The Media 100 in 2011: 47. Paul Staines (Guido Fawkes' blog)', Online. Available <http://www.guardian.co.uk/media/2011/jul/24/paul-staines-mediaguardian-100–201> (accessed 9 July 2012).
— (2011b) 'The Media 100 in 2011: 93: Iain Dale' Online. Available <http://www.guardian.co.uk/media/2011/jul/24/iain-dale-mediaguardian-100–2011> (accessed 9 July 2012).
Guardian News and Media Ltd (2012) *The Guardian*, Online. Available <http://www.guardian.co.uk/> (accessed 9 July 2012).
Haas, E. B. (2004[1958]) *The Uniting of Europe: Political, social, and economic forces, 1950–1957*, Notre Dame: University of Notre Dame Press.
Habermas, J. (1989) *The Structural Transformation of the Public Sphere*, Cambridge: MIT Press.
— (2003) 'Why Europe Needs a Constitution: The chartering of Europe', in E. O. Eriksen, J. -E. Fossum, and A. J. Menéndez (eds) *Developing a Constitution for Europe*, Baden-Baden: Nomos Verlag, pp. 17–33.
Haesly, R. (2001) 'Euroskeptics, europhiles and Instrumental Europeans: European attachment in Scotland and Wales', *European Union Politics* 2(1): 81–102.
Hafez, K. and Skinner, A. (2007) *The Myth of Media Globalization*, Cambridge: Polity Press.
Haller, M. (2008a) *Die österreichische Gesellschaft: Sozialstruktur und sozialer Wandel*, New York: Campus.
— (2008b) *European Integration as an Elite Process: The failure of a dream?*, London and New York: Routledge.
Harmsen, R. (2004) 'Euroscepticism in the Netherlands: stirrings of dissent', in R. Harmsen, R. and M. Spiering (eds) *Euroscepticism: Party politics, national identity and European integration*, Amsterdam: Rodopi, pp. 99–126.
— (2008) 'The evolution of Dutch European discourse: defining the "limits of Europe"', *Perspectives on European Politics and Society* 9(3): 316–341.
Harmsen, R and Spiering, M. (2004) *Euroscepticism: Party politics, national identity and European integration*, Amsterdam: Rodopi.
Hartleb, F. (2008) 'Party-Based Euroscepticism in Germany', *The Romanian Journal of Political Science*, No.2, 13–30.

Hegedűs, I. (2004) 'Csatlakozás, népszavazás, alkotmányozás, európai választások', Médiakutató 2004(1): 103–114.
Heine, S. (2009) *Une Gauche Contre l'Europe? Les Critiques Radicales et Altermondialistes Contre l'UE en France*, Bruxelles: Editions de l'Université de Bruxelles.
Heller, M. (2010) 'Euroscepticism in the European Parliament elections of June 2009, country report: Hungary', Online. Available <http://www.reconproject.eu/main.php/RECON_WP5reportEuroscepticism_Hun.pdf?fileitem=19070977> (accessed 30 October 2012).
Heller, M. and Rényi, Á. (1996) 'Discourse strategies in the new Hungarian public sphere: from the populist-urban controversy to the Hungarian-Jewish confrontation', in Mänicke-Gyöngyösi, K. (ed.) *Öffentliche Konfliktdiskurse um Restitution von Gerechtigkeit, politsche Verantwortung und nationale Identität*, Frankfurt a.M.: Peter Lang, pp. 373–395.
Helmes, I. (2009) 'Wir treffen uns vor den Hünchen', suddeutsche.de. Online. Available <http://www.sueddeutsche.de/politik/750/469308/text/> (accessed 28 May 2009).
Hilal, N. (2007) *L'eurosyndicalisme par l'action. Cheminots et routiers en Europe*, Paris: L'Harmattan.
Hirschman, A. O. (1970) E*xit, Voice, and Loyalty: Responses to decline in firms, organizations, and states*, Cambridge, Mass: Harvard University Press.
Hírügynökség, F. (2009) 'Befejeződött a listavezetők csonka vitája', index.hu. Online. Available <http://index.hu/kulfold/eu/2009/valasztas/befejezodott_a_listavezetok_csonka_vitaja/> (accessed 5 June 2009).
Hivert, W.R. (2009) 'Anti-européens et euroconstructifs: Les communistes français et l'Europe (1945–1979)', Cahiers de l'Irice 4: 49–67.
Hix, S. (2005) *The Political System of the European Union*, 2nd edn, New York: Palgrave Macmillan.
— (2007) 'Euroscepticism as anti-centralization: a rational-choice institutional perspective', *European Union Politics* 8(1): 131–150.
Hix, S. and Marsh, D. (2007) 'Punishment or protest? Understanding European parliament elections', *The Journal of Politics* 69(2): 495–510.
Hix, S., Noury, A. and Roland, G. (2006) 'Dimensions of politics in the European Parliament', *American Journal of Political Science* 50(2): 494–511.
Hix, S., Noury, A. and Roland, G. (2007) *Democratic Politics in the European Parliament*, Cambridge: Cambridge University Press.
Hobolt, S. B. (2009) *Europe in Question: Referendums on European integration*, Oxford: Oxford University Press.
Hooghe, L. (2007) 'What drives euroskepticism? Party-public cueing, ideology and strategic opportunity', *European Union Politics* 8(1): 5–12.
Hooghe, L. and Marks, G. (2005) 'Calculation, community and cues: public opinion on European integration', *European Union Politics* 6(4): 419–443.
— (2007) 'Sources of Euroscepticism', Acta Politica 42(2/3): 119–127.
— (2009) 'A postfunctionalist theory of European integration: from permissive consensus to constraining dissensus', *British Journal of Political Science* 39(1): 1–23.

Hooghe, M. and Teepe, W. (2007) 'Party profiles on the web: an analysis of the logfiles of non-partisan interactive political internet sites in the 2003 and 2004 election campaigns in Belgium', *New Media Society* 9(6): 965–985.

Horváth, S. (2009) 'Az európai identitás diskurzuselméleti kérdései', *Politikatudományi Szemle XVIII*(4):105–125.

Hughes, J., Sasse, G. and Gordon, C. (2008) 'How deep is the wider Europe? Elites, Europeanization, and Euroscepticism in the CEECs', in A. Szczerbiak and P. Taggart (eds) *Opposing Europe? The comparative party politics of Euroscepticism. Vol. 2: Comparative and theoretical perspectives,* Oxford: Oxford University Press, pp. 181–207.

Hurrelmann, A., Krell-Laluhová, Z., Nullmeier, F., Schneider, S. and Wiesner, A. (2009) 'Why the democratic nation-state is still legitimate: a study of media discourses', *European Journal of Political Research* 48(4): 483–515.

Hyde-Price, A. G. V. (1990) 'Review: [untitled]; European Security beyond the Year 2000', *International Affairs* 66(2): 358.

Ilonszky, G. and Lengyel, G. (2009) 'Válaszúton: konszolidált vagy szinlelt demokrácia?', Politikatudományi Szemle, XVIII(1): 7–25.

Imig, D. and Tarrow, S. (eds) (2001) *Contentious Europeans: Protest and politics in an emerging polity*, Lanham: Rowman & Littlefield.

Index.hu (2009a) '267 hely a néppártnak, 159 a szocialistáknak'. Online. Available <http://index.hu/kulfold/eu/2009/valasztas/2009/06/08/267_hely_a_ neppartnak_159_a_szocialistaknak/> (accessed 8 June 2009).

— (2009b) 'Dávid ibolyát aggasztja a Jobbik'. Online. Available <http:// index.hu/kulfold/eu/2009/valasztas/david_ibolya_aggodik_a_jobbik_ miatt/> (accessed 7 June 2009).

Inthorn, S. (2006) 'What does it mean to be an EU citizen? How news media construct civic and cultural concepts of Europe', *Westminster Papers in Communication and Culture* 3(3): 71–90.

Ivaldi, G. (1999) 'La liste Pasqua – Villiers', *Revue française de Science Politique* 49(4) : 643–652.

— (2006) 'Beyond France's 2005 referendum on the European Constitutional Treaty: second-order model, anti-establishment attitudes and the end of the alternative European utopia', *West European Politics* 29(1): 47–69.

Jachtenfuchs, M. (2002) Die Konstruktion Europas: Verfassungsideen und institutionelle Entwicklung, Baden-Baden: Nomos.

Jamieson, K. H. (1992) *Dirty politics: Deception, distraction, and democracy*, Oxford: Oxford University Press.

Janicki, M. (2009) '"Czy ktoś przyzna, że się mylił?", Polska w Unii: pierwsze 5 lat', Polityka 17(2702): 3–6.

Jankowski, N. W. and Van Os, R. (2004) 'Internet-based political discourse: a case study of electronic democracy in Hoogeveen', in P. M. Shane (ed.) Democracy Online: The prospects for political renewal through the Internet, London: Routledge, pp. 181–194.

Jankowski, N. W. and Van Selm, M. (2008) 'Internet-based political communication

research: illustrations, challenges & innovations', *Javnost - the Public* 15(2): 5–16.
Jarosz, M. (2005) *Wygrani i Przegrani Polskiej Transformacji*, Warszawa: Instytut Nauk Politycznych PAN.
Jasiecki, K. (2004) 'Jak Polacy postrzegają członkostwo w Unii Europejskiej?', *Polska w Europie* 1(45): 89–110.
Jennar, R. (2009) 'Raoul Jennar (NPA) veut «dénoncer l'influence des groupes de pression» à Bruxelles', lemonde.fr. Online. Available <http://europeennes.blog.lemonde.fr/2009/05/25/raoul-jennar-npa-veut-denoncer-linfluence-des-groupes-de-pression-a-bruxelles/> (accessed 25 May 2009).
Jones, S.G. (1999) *Doing Internet Research: Critical issues and methods for examining the Net*, Thousand Oaks/London/New Delhi: Sage.
Jobbik (2009a) 'Jobbik 2009 EP agenda'. Online. Available <http://www.jobbik.hu/sites/jobbik.hu/down/Jobbik-program2009EP.pdf> (accessed 24 October 2012).
— (2009b) 'Jobbik 2009 EP agenda'. Online. Available <http://www.jobbik.hu/sites/jobbik.hu/down/Jobbik-program2009EP.pdf> (accessed 24 October 2012).
— (2012a) 'Válasz az SZDSZ kampányára' (Reply to the campaign of SZDSZ (liberal party)). Online. Available <http://www.youtube.com/watch?v=vj2U9lKotbU> (accessed 24 October 2012).
— (2012b) 'Az új erő EP-kampányfilmje' (The EP campaign spot of the new force). Online. Available <http://www.youtube.com/watch?v=aGX8IFGvsZo> (accessed 24 October 2012).
Juniper, T. (2009) 'The coming of the Greens', guardian.co.uk. Online. Available <http://www.guardian.co.uk/commentisfree/2009/jun/01/green-european-election> (accessed 16 October 2012).
Karlsen, R. (2010) 'Online and undecided: voters and the Internet in the contemporary Norwegian election campaign', *Scandinavian Political Studies* 33(1): 28–50.
Kevin, D. (2003) *Europe in the Media: Reporting, representations, and rhetoric*, Mahwah, N.J.: Lawrence Erlbaum Associates.
Klein, U. (2000) 'Tabloidized political coverage in the German Bild Zeitung', in C. Sparks and J. Tulloch (eds) *Tabloid Tales, Global Debates over Media Standards*, Lanham: Rowman and Littlefield, pp. 177–194.
Klingemann, H.-D., Volkens, A., Bara, J., Budge, I. and McDonald, M. (2006) *Mapping Policy Preferences II: Estimates for parties, electors, and governments in Eastern Europe, European Union and OECD 1990–2003*, Oxford: Oxford University Press.
Kohler-Koch, B. and Rittberger, B. (eds) (2007) *Debating the Democratic Legitimacy of the European Union: Governance in Europe*, Plymouth: Rowman & Littlefield.
Koole, R. and Raap, L. (2005) 'Euroscepsis en de Sociaal-Democratie in Nederland', in Vollaard, H. and Boer, B. (eds) *Euroscepsis in Nederland*, Utrecht: Lemma, pp. 109–128.

Koopmans, R. (2007) 'Who inhabits the European public sphere? Winners and losers, supporters and opponents in Europeanised political debates', *European Journal of Political Research* 46(2): 183–210.

Koopmans, R. and Statham, P. (eds) (2010) *The Making of a European Public Sphere,* Cambridge: Cambridge University Press.

Kopecký, P. and Mudde, C. (2002) 'The two sides of Euroscepticism: party positions on European integration in East Central Europe', *European Union Politics* 3(3): 297–326.

Korwin-Mikke, J. (2009a) 'Przy sobocie, przed robotą – czyli o wielkiej rurze', Online posting. Available <Korwin-Mikke.blog.onet.pl> (accessed 10 November 2009).

— (2009b) 'Popieram czerwonych', Online posting. Available <Korwin-mikke.blog.onet.pl> (accessed 10 November 2009).

— (2010) 'Blog', Online Posting. Available <http://korwin-mikke-blog.onet.pl/> (accessed 10 November 2009).

Koszta, D. (2009) 'Hogyan kampányolunk? Magyaros ízek az európai tányéron', Európai Parlamenti Szemle. Online. Available <http://www.corvinusembassy.com/ep/index.php?page=2&article=2&show=86> (accessed 4 May 2009).

Kriesi, H. (2007) 'The role of European integration in national election campaigns', *European Union Politics* 8(1): 83–108.

Kriesi, H., Grande, E., Lachat, R., Dolezal, M., Bornschier, S. and Frey, T. (2008) *West European Politics in the Age of Globalization*, Cambridge: Cambridge University Press.

Kritzinger, S. (2003) 'The Influence of the nation-state on individual support for the European Union', *European Union Politics* 4(2): 219–242.

Kursa, M. (2009) 'Eurokandydaci łowią w sieci', Gazeta Wyborcza. Online. Available <http://krakow.gazeta.pl/krakow/1,35824,6663703,Eurokandydaci_lowia_glosy_w_sieci.html> (accessed 31 October 2012).

Larsen, H. (1999) 'British and Danish European policies in the 1990s: a discourse approach', *European Journal of International Relations* 5(4): 451–483.

Lasica, J. D (2003) 'Blogs and journalism need each other', in M . Ludtke (ed.) *Journalist's Trade: Weblogs and journalism*, Nieman Report Fall 2003, Nieman Foundation for Journalism at Harvard. Online. Available <http://www.nieman.harvard.edu/reports/article/101042/Blogs-and-Journalism-Need-Each-Other.aspx (accessed 10 October 2012).

Leconte, C. (2010) *Understanding Euroscepticism*, Basingstoke: Palgrave Macmillan.

Lees, C. (2008) 'The Limits of Party-Based Euroscepticism in Germany', in A. Szczerbiak and P. Taggart (eds) *Opposing Europe? The comparative party politics of Euroscepticism*, Oxford: Oxford University Press, pp. 28–51.

Le Figaro (2009a) 'Baudis : l'atout de l'UMP, c'est la réussite de la présidence française de l'UE'. Online. Available <http://www.lefigaro.fr/

le-talk/2009/05/29/01021-20090529ARTFIG00527-baudis-l-atout-de-l-ump-c-est-la-reussite-de-la-presidence-francaise-de-l-ue-.php> (accessed 29 May 2009).
— (2009b) 'L'influence grandissante du Parlement européen'. Online. Available <http://www.lefigaro.fr/elections-europeennes-2009/2009/06/06/01024-20090606ARTFIG00117-l-influence-grandissante-du-parlement-europeen-.php> (accessed 5 June 2009).
— (2009c) 'UE: Barroso candidat à sa succession'. Online. Available <http://www.lefigaro.fr/international/2009/06/09/01003-20090609ARTFIG00406-ue-barroso-candidat-a-sa-succession-.php> (accessed 9 June 2009).
— (2009d) 'Alain Juppé - Michel Rocard : l'UE face à la Turquie'. Online. Available <http://www.lefigaro.fr/debats/2009/06/03/01005-20090603ARTFIG00385-alain-juppe-michel-rocard-l-ue-face-a-la-turquie-.php> (accessed 31 October 2012).
Leibfried, S. and Zürn, M. (eds) (2005) *Transformations of the State?*, Cambridge: Cambridge University Press.
Le Monde (2009a) 'Pour Mme Aubry, il y a un seul adversaire : l'UMP', lemonde.fr. Online. Available <http://www.lemonde.fr/cgi-bin/ACHATS/acheter.cgi?offre=ARCHIVES&type_item=ART_ARCH_30J&objet_id=1085966&clef=ARC-TRK-NC_01> (accessed 5 June 2009).
— (2009b) 'Indifférence?', lemonde.fr. Online. Available <http://www.lemonde.fr/idees/article/2009/06/08/indifference_1203896_3232.html> (accessed 8 June 2009).
— (2009c) 'J'ai bien l'intention de réparer l'affront de Lisbonne en allant voter', lemonde.fr. Online. Available <http://www.lemonde.fr/elections-europeennes/article/2009/05/29/j-ai-bien-l-intention-de-reparer-l-affront-de-lisbonne-en-allant-voter_1199924_1168667.html> (accessed 29 May 2009).
— (2009d) 'Nathalie Arthaud (LO) : ''Les classes populaires n'attendent rien des élections européennes''', lemonde.fr. Online. Available <http://europeennes.blog.lemonde.fr/2009/05/23/nathalie-arthaud-lo-les-classes-populaires-n%E2%80%99attendent-rien-des-elections-europeennes/> (accessed 23 May 2009).
Le Nouvel Observateur (2009a) 'L'Europe contre l'Europe', nouvelobs.com. Online. Available <www.tempsreel.nouvelobs.com> (accessed 27 May 2009).
— (2009b) 'LO : Nathalie Arthaud plaide pour une Europe "débarrassée des exploiteurs"', nouvelobs.com. Online. Available <http://tempsreel.nouvelobs.com/article/20090601.OBS8754/lo-nathalie-arthaud-plaide-pour-une-europe-debarrassee-des-exploiteurs.html> (accessed 01 June 2009).
Lepsius, R. M. (1989) 'Das Erbe des Nationalsozialismus und die politische Kultur der Nachfolgestaaten des "Großdeutschen Reiches"' in M. Haller, H.-J. Hoffmann-Nowottny and W. Zapf (eds) *Kultur und Gesellschaft*, Frankfurt a.M., New-York: Campus, pp. 247–264.

Le Soir (2009) 'Le salaire d'un eurodéputé : 7.665,31 euros bruts', lesoir.be. Online. Available <http://archives.lesoir.be/le-salaire-d-8217-un-eurodepute-7–665–31-euros-bruts_t-20090601–00NCDR.html> (accessed 1 June 2009).

Leszczyńska, K. (2009a) *Cztery wizje Europy*, Kraków: Nomos.

— (2009b) 'Wizje Unii Europejskiej na łamach wybranych tytułów prasy katolickiej w debacie nad Kartą Praw Podstawowych', in E. Skotnicka-Illasiewicz (ed.) 5 lat członkowstwa Polski w Unii Europejskiej w perspektywie społecznej, Warszawa: Wydawnictwo UKIE, pp. 214–234.

Lindberg, L. N. and Scheingold, S. A. (1970) *Europe's Would-Be Polity: Patterns of change in the European Community*, Englewood Cliffs, N.J.: Prentice-Hall Inc.

Linkfluence (2012) 'Wahlradar 09'. Online. Available <http://wahlradar.linkfluence.net/, last (accessed 26 October 2012).

Lord, C. (1992) 'Sovereign or confused? The "great debate" about British entry to the European Community 20 years on', *Journal of Common Market Studies* 30(4): 419–436.

— (1994) *British Entry to the European Community Under the Heath Government of 1970–4*, Aldershot: Dartmouth Pub.

Lubbers, M. and Scheepers, P. (2007) 'Euroscepticism and extreme voting patterns in Europe', in G. Loosveldt, M. Swyngedouw and B. Cambre (eds) *Measuring Meaningful Data in Social Research,* Leuven: Acco, pp. 71–92.

Ludlow, P. (2006) T*he European Community and the Crises of the 1960s: Negotiating the Gaullist challenge,* London: Routledge.

Ludtke, M. (ed.) *Journalist's Trade: Weblogs and journalism*, Nieman Report Fall 2003, Nieman Foundation for Journalism at Harvard. Online. Available <http://www.nieman.harvard.edu/reports/article/101042/Blogs-and-Journalism-Need-Each-Other.aspx (accessed 10 October 2012).

Lusoli, W. (2005a) 'The Internet and the European Parliament elections: theoretical perspectives, empirical investigations and proposals for research', *Information Polity* 10(3–4): 153–163.

— (2005b) 'A second-order medium? The Internet as a source of electoral information in 25 European countries', *Information Polity* 10(3–4): 247–265.

McCormick, J. (1999) *Carl Schmitt's Critique of Liberalism: Against politics of technology*, Cambridge: Cambridge University Press.

Mach, Z. (1993) *Symbols, Conflict and Identity: Essays in political anthropology*, Albany: State University of New York Press.

Mach, Z. and Niedźwiedzki, D. (eds) (2002) *Polska lokalna wobec integracji Europejskiej*, Kraków: Universitas.

McLaren, L. M. (2005) *Identity, Interests and Attitudes to European Integration*, Houndmills: Palgrave Macmillan.

— (2007) 'Explaining mass-level Euroscepticism: identity, interests, and institutional distrust', *Acta Politica* 42(2/3): 233–251.

McNair, B. (2009) *News and journalism* in the UK, London: Routledge.

Mair, P. (2000). 'The Limited Impact of Europe on National Party Systems', *West European Politics*, 23(4): 27–51.
— (2005) 'Popular democracy and the European Union polity', EUROGOV: European Governance Papers, No. C-05–03. Online. Available <www.ihs.ac.at/publications/lib/ep3.pdf> (accessed 31 October 2012)
— (2007) 'Political opposition and the European Union', *Government and Opposition*, 42(1): 1–17.
Mardell, M. (2009a) 'Declan's democracy', bbc.co.uk. Online. Available <http://www.bbc.co.uk/blogs/thereporters/markmardell/2009/06/s_25.html> (accessed 14 November 2010).
— (2009b) 'Invasion relived', bbc.co.uk. Online. Available <http://www.bbc.co.uk/blogs/thereporters/markmardell/2009/06/_malta_here_in_malta.html> (accessed 14 November 2010).
— (2009c) 'A walk on the Wilders side', bbc.co.uk. Online. Available <http://www.bbc.co.uk/blogs/thereporters/markmardell/2009/06/almere_near_amsterdam_three_bl.html> (accessed 14 November 2010).
Markowski, R. and Tucker, J. A. (2010) 'Euroscepticism and the emergence of political parties in Poland', *Party Politics* 16(4): 523–54.
Marks, G. and McAdam, D. (1999) 'On the relationship of political opportunities to the form of collective action: the case of the European Union, in D. Della Porta, H. Kriesi and D. Rucht (eds) *Social Movements in a Globalizing World*, Basingstoke, MacMillan, pp. 97–111.
Marks, G. and Steenbergen, M. R. (eds) (2004) *European Integration and Political Conflict: Themes in European governance*, Cambridge: Cambridge University Press.
Marks, G., Wilson, C. J. and Ray, L. (2002) 'National political parties and European integration', *American Journal of Political Science* 46(3): 586–594.
Martin, H.-P. (2012) 'Dr. Hans-Peter Martin, Der unabhängige EU-Abgeordnete und Autor'. Online. Available <http://www.hpmartin.net/> (accessed 29. October 2012).
Mau, S. and Mewes, J. (2012) 'Horizontal Europeanisation in contextual perspective: what drives cross-border activities within the European Union?, *European Societies* 14(1): 7–34.
Mazzoleni, G. (2003) 'The media and the growth of neo-populism in contemporary democracies', in G. Mazzoleni, S. Julianne and B. Horsfield (eds) *The Media and Neo Populism*, London: Praeger, pp. 1–20.
Media-analyse (2010) 'Media-analyse'. Online. Available <http://www.media-analyse.at> (accessed 22 October 2010).
Mei, W. (2008) 'Measuring political debate on the Chinese Internet forum', *Javnost-The Public* 15(2): 93–110.
Mellows-Facer, A., Cracknell, R. and Lightbown, S. (2009) 'European Parliament Elections 2009', *Research Paper* 09/53, London: House of Commons Library.
Meyer, C. (2009) 'Does *European Union politics* become mediatized? The case of the European Commission', *Journal of European Public Policy* 16(7): 1047–1064.

Michael Lerner Productions (2010) 'Netiquette'. Online. Available <http://www.learnthenet.com/learn-about/netiquette/> (accessed 13 July 2010).

Michailidou, A. (2008) *The European Union Online*, Berlin: VDM-Verlag Dr Müller.

Michailidou, A. and Trenz, H.-J. (2010) 'Mediati(zi)ng EU politics: online news coverage of the 2009 European Parliamentary elections', *Communications* 35(3): 327–346.

Mikułowski-Pomorski, J. and Gawlewicz, A. (2009) 'Rodzinna Europa: kształtowanie się wizerunku Unii Europejskiej w prasie polskiej w momencie akcesji Polski do UE (2004) oraz w piątym roku członkowstwa (2008)', in E. Skotnicka-Illasiewicz (ed.) 5 lat członkowstwa Polski w Unii Europejskiej w perspektywie społecznej, Warszawa: Wydawnictwo UKIE, pp. 188–213.

Milner, S. (2004) 'For an alternative Europe: Euroscepticism and the French left since the Maastricht treaty', *European Studies* (20): 59–81.

Milward, A. S. (2000) *The European Rescue of the Nation-State*, 2nd edn, London: Routledge.

Mokre, M. and Bruell, C. (2006) 'Chancen für EUropäische Öffentlichkeiten: Eine Analyse der medialen Diskursivierung der Wahlen zum Europäischen Parlament in Österreich', *EIF Working Paper Series*, No. 27/2006. Online. Available <http://www.eif.oeaw.ac.at/downloads/workingpapers/wp27.pdf> (accessed 31 October 2012).

Moravcsik, A. (1998) *The Choice for Europe: Social purpose and state power from Messina to Maastricht*, Ithaca, N.Y: Cornell University Press.

Morgan, G. (2005) *The Idea of a European Superstate: Public justification and European integration*, Princeton, N.J.: Princeton University Press.

Nádori, P. (2009) 'Takarodó után: az EP-választás tanulságai', komment.hu. Online. Available <http://www.komment.hu/tartalom/20090608-velemeny-erdekes-idok-jonnek-az-europai-parlamenti-valasztas-utan.html> (accessed 8 June 2009).

Nalewajko, E. (2003) 'Eurosceptyczne partie i ich liderzy w publicznej debacie o integracji prowadzonej w latach 2000–2003', in L. Kolarska-Bobińska (ed.) *Przed referendum europejskim: Absencja, sprzeciw, poparcie*, Warszawa: IPS, pp. 97–132.

Niedermayer, O. (1995) 'Trends and Contrasts', in O. Niedermayer and R. Sinnott (eds) *Public Opinion and Internationalized Governance*, New York: Oxford University Press, pp. 53–72.

Norris, P. (2000) *A Virtous Circle: Political communications in postindustrial societies*. Cambridge: Cambridge University Press.

— (2001) *Digital divide: Civic engagement, information poverty and the Internet worldwide*, Cambridge: Cambridge University Press.

NOS (2009a) 'Blij dat we er veel aan gedaan hebben', nos.nl. Online. Available <http://weblogs.nos.nl/europa/2009/06/09/blij-dat-we-er-veel-aan-hebben-gedaan/> (accessed 23 November 2009).

— (2009b) 'Maak meer afspraken op Europees niveau', nos.nl.

Online. Available <http://weblogs.nos.nl/europa/2009/05/28/maak-meer-afspraken-op-europees-niveau/> (accessed 23 November 2009).
— (2009c) 'Nederland, Europa en Geert', nos.nl. Online. Available <http://weblogs.nos.nl/europa/2009/06/05/nederland-europa-en-geert/> (accessed 23 November 2009).
Nu.nl (2009a) 'Berlusconi krijgt minder steun dan verwacht', nu.nl. Online. Available <http://www.nu.nl/verkiezingen-eu---nieuws/2003555/berlusconi-krijgt-minder-steun-dan-verwacht.html> (accessed 23 November 2009).
— (2009b) 'Dick Berlijn steunt VVD', nu.nl. Online. Available <http://www.nu.nl/verkiezingen-eu/1965274/dick-berlijn-steunt-vvd.html> (accessed 24 November 2009).
— (2009c) 'PvdA voorstander van Europese referenda', nu.nl. Online. Available <http://www.nu.nl/verkiezingen-eu/1968744/pvda-voorstander-van-europese-referenda.html> (accessed 23 November 2009).
— (2009d) 'Steun Nederlanders voor EU is breed maar broos', nu.nl. Online. Available <http://www.nu.nl/verkiezingen-eu/1966210/steun-nederlanders-voor-eu-is-breed-maar-broos.html> (accessed 23 November 2009).
— (2009e) ''Vetorecht lidstaten verlamt Europese Unie'', nu.nl. Online. Available <http://www.nu.nl/verkiezingen-eu---nieuws/1969940/vetorecht-lidstaten-verlamt-europese-unie.html> (accessed 23 November 2009).
— (2009f) 'Winst voor Eurosceptici en Eurofielen', nu.nl. Online. Available <http://www.nu.nl/verkiezingen-eu---nieuws/2002318/winst-voor-eurosceptici-en-eurofielen.html> (accessed 23 November 2009).
— (2009g) 'Winst Wilders vijzelt EU-interesse in Turkije op', nu.nl. Online. Available <http://www.nu.nl/verkiezingen-eu---nieuws/2003056/winst-wilders-vijzelt-eu-interesse-in-turkije-op.html> (accessed 24 November 2009).
Nugent, N. (1996) 'Sovereignty and Britain's membership of the European Union', *Public Policy and Administration* 11(2): 3–18.
Olsen, J. P. (2002) 'The Many Faces of Europeanization', *Journal of Common Market Studies* 40(5), 921–952.
Onet.pl (2009) 'onet.pl'. Online. Available <http://onet.pl> (accessed 19 September 2009.
— (2010) 'Blog ranking'. Online. Available <http://blog.onet.pl/0,37,ranking.html> (accessed 16 August 2010).
Origo (2009a) 'Forum'. Online posting. Available <http://forum.origo.hu/topik.jsp?id=271459&page=5> (accessed 7 June 2009).
— (2009b) 'A cseheket is nyugtalanítja Orbán kampánybeszéde', origo.hu. Online. Available <http://www.origo.hu/nagyvilag/20090602-a-csehek-is-nyugtalanok-orban-kijelentesei-miatt.html> (accessed 2 June 2009).
— (2009c) 'Fico tiltakozik Orbán kampánybeszéde miatt', origo.hu. Online.

Available <http://www.origo.hu/itthon/20090525-uszitasnak-tartja-ficoorban-kampanybeszedet.html> (accessed 25 May 2009).
— (2009d) 'Torz végeredmény miatt aggódik Göncz: az MSZP és az EP-választás', origo.hu. Online. Available <http://www.origo.hu/itthon/20090519-ep-valasztasok-mszp.html> (accessed 2 June 2009).
Osiatyński, W. (1996) 'Wzlot i upadek społeczeństwa obywatelskiego w Polsce', *Wiedza i Życie* 1996/10.
Palayret, J.-M. (2006) 'De Gaulle challenges the community: France, the empty chair crisis and the Luxembourg compromise', in J. -M. Palayret, H. Wallace and P. Winand (eds) *Visions, Votes, and Vetoes: The empty chair crisis and the Luxembourg compromise forty years on*, Brussels: Peter Lang, pp. 45–77.
Palikot, J. (2010a) 'Blog'. Online. Available <http://www.sejm.gov.pl/poslowie/posel6/279.htm> (accessed 10 November 2009).
— (2010b) 'Poletko Pana P.'. Online. Available <http://palikot.blog.onet.pl/> (accessed 20 November 2010).
Pankowski, R. and Kornak, M. (2005) 'Poland', in C. Mudde (ed.) *Racist Extremism in Central and Eastern Europe*, Basingstoke: Routledge, pp. 161–163.
Państwowa Komisja Wyborcza (2010) ' Państwowa Komisja Wyborcza'. Online. Available <http://www..gov.pl> (accessed 20 November 2010).
PAP (2009a) 'Eurowybory mogą przynieść sukces partiom skrajnym', wiadomości.wp.pl. Online. Available <http://wiadomosci.wp.pl/kat,1022301,title,Eurowybory-moga-przyniesc-sukces-partiom-skrajnym,wid,11178911,wiadomosc.html?ticaid=1b6fe> (accessed 17 December 2010).
— (2009b) 'J. Kaczyński: Dokonaliśmy kroku ku lepszej Europie', wiadomości.wp.pl. Online. Available <http://wiadomosci.wp.pl/kat,1022301,title,J-Kaczynski-dokonalismy-kroku-ku-lepszej-Europie,wid,11176940,wiadomosc.html> (accessed 17 December 2010).
— (2009c) 'Polacy to jeden z najbardziej biernych elektoratów', wiadomości.wp.pl. Online. Available <http://wiadomosci.wp.pl/kat,1022301,title,Polacy-to-jeden-z-najbardziej-biernych-elektoratow,wid,11162389,wiadomosc.html> (accessed 17 December 2010).
— (2009d) 'Europejska frekwencja najniższa w historii', tvn24.pl. Online. Available <http://www.tvn24.pl/12691,1604086,0,1,europejska-frekwencja-najnizsza-w-historii,wiadomosc.html> (accessed 17 December 2010).
— (2009e) 'Zamieszanie wokół odezwy to rąbanka partyjna', tvn24.pl. Online. Available <http://www.tvn24.pl/12690,1603138,0,1,zamieszanie-wokol-odezwy-to-rabanka-partyjna,wiadomosc.html> (accessed 17 December 2010).
— (2009f) 'PO wygrała w wyborach', tvn24.pl. Online. Available <http://www.tvn24.pl/12690,1602947,0,1,pierwsi-juz-dzis-przy-urnach-ale-na-pis-nie-zaglosuja,wiadomosc.html> (accessed 17 December 2010).

Papacharissi, Z. (2009) 'The virtual sphere 2.0: the Internet, the public sphere, and beyond', in A. Chadwick and P. N. Howard (eds) *Routledge Handbook of Internet Politics*, London: Routledge, pp. 230–245.

Pawlicki, J. (2009) 'Eurostrachy na lachy', wyborcza.pl. Online. Available <http://wyborcza.pl/1,75515,6697662,Eurostrachy_na_lachy.html> (accessed 17 December 2010).

PEBI (2009) 'Parlament Europejski Biuro Informacyjne w Polsce'. Online. Available <http://www.europarl.pl/> (accessed 5 May 2010).

Pelinka, A. (2002) 'Consociational democracy in Austria: political change, 1968 - 1998', *Acta Politica* 37(1–2): 139–156.

— (2004) 'Austrian Euroscepticism: the shift from the left to the right', *European Studies* 20(18): 207–225.

— (2006) 'Right-wing populism plus "x": the Austrian freedom party (FPOe)', in D. Caramani and Y. Mény (eds) *Challenges to Consensual Politics: Democracy, identity, and populist protest in the Alpine region*, Brussels: P.I.E. – Peter Lang, pp. 131–145.

Pellikaan, H. and Brandsma, G. J. (2005) 'Een Ruimtelijk Model voor Onderzoek naar Euroscepsis Toegepast of Nederlandse en Vlaamse Politieke Partijen', in H. Vollaard and B. Boer (eds) *Euroscepsis in Nederland*, Utrecht: Lemma, pp. 89–108.

Percheron, A. (1991) 'Les Français et l'Europe: Acquiescement de façade ou adhésion véritable?', *Revue Française de Science Politique* 41(3): 382–406.

Perrineau, P. (2005) 'Le référendum français du 29 mai 2005: L'irrésistible nationalisation d'un vote européen', in P. Perrineau (ed.) *Le Vote Européen 2004–2005: De l'élargissement au référendum français,* Paris: Presses de Science Po, pp. 229–244.

Petithomme, M. (2008) 'Is there a European identity? National attitudes and social identification toward the European Union', *Journal of Identity and Migration Studies* 2(1): 15–36.

Peter, J., Semetko, H. A., de Vreese, C. (2003) 'EU politics on television news', *European Union Politics* 4(3): 305–327.

Petter, I. and Griffiths, R. (2005) 'Gekke Henkie in Europa? Financiële *Euroscepsis in Nederland*', in H. Vollaard and B. Boer, B. (eds) *Euroscepsis in Nederland*, Utrecht: Lemma, pp. 45–70.

Pfetsch, B. (2007) 'National media in Europeanized public sphere: the openness and support of the press for European integration', in C. de Vreese and H. Schmitt (eds) *A European Public Sphere: How much of it do we have and how much do we need?*, Connex Report Series No. 2, Mannheim Centre for European Social Research (MZES), pp. 401–425.

Phibbs, H. (2009) 'Harry Phibbs: Cameron and his "new friends" in Europe won't be thwarted by Eurocrat smears', *Mail Online*, Available <http://www.dailymail.co.uk/debate/article-1190545/HARRY-PHIBBS-Camerons-new-friends-Europe-wont-thwarted-Eurocrat-smears.html> (accessed 16 October 2012).

Pilecka, M. (2009) 'Społeczna percepcja członkowstwa Polski w UE', 5 lat Polski w UE, Warszawa: *Urząd Komitetu Integracji Europejskiej.*

Pilet, J.-B. and Brack, N. (2009) 'The European and regional elections of 7 June 2009 in Belgium', *EPERN European Parliament Election Briefings* 33. Online. Available <http://www.sussex.ac.uk/sei/documents/epern-no-33-belgium-2009.pdf> (accessed 31 October 2012).

Pilet, J.-B. and Van Haute, E. (2007) 'Les réticences à l'Europe dans un pays europhile : le cas de la Belgique', in J. Lacroix and R. Coman (eds) *Les Résistances à l'Europe: Cultures nationales, idéologies et stratégies d'acteurs*, Bruxelles: Editions de l'ULB, pp. 211–225.

PiS, P. (2010) 'Program PiS – Unia Europejska'. Online. Available <http://mypis.pl/program-pis/kategorie/21-unia-europejska/artykuly> (accessed 7 January 2010).

Plasser, F. and Ulram, P. A. (2003) 'Striking a responsive chord: mass media and right-wing populism in Austria', in G. Mazzoleni, S. Julianne and B. Horsfield (eds) *The Media and Neo-Populism*, London: Praeger, pp. 21–43.

Pliszka, S. (2009) 'Odsetek osób dokonujących wpisów na forach (CBOS, 2005–2009)', internetstats.pl. Online. Available <http://www.internetstats.pl/index.php/2009/08/odsetek-osob-dokonujacych-wpisow-na-forach-cbos-2005-2009/> (accessed 29 October 2009).

Podgórzańska, R. (2007) 'Polityka zagraniczna w kampanii wyborczej Lecha Kaczyńskiego i Donalda Tuska – konfrontacja wizji', in B. Krauz-Mozer and K. Sobolewska-Myślik (eds) *Oblicza polskiego systemu politycznego*, Toruń: Wydawnictwo Uniwersytetu Wrocławskiego, pp. 134–151.

Politically-Incorrect (2009a) 'Europawahl: 21 Parteien buhlen um Wählergunst', www.pi-news.net. Online. Available <http://www.pi-news.net/2009/05/europawahl-31-parteien-buhlen-um-waehlergunst/> (accessed 26 May 2009).

— (2009b) 'AUF: Klare Position gegen Türkeibeitritt', pi-news.net. Online. Available <http://www.pi-news.net/2009/05/auf-klare-position-gegen-tuerkeibeitritt/> (accessed 30 May 2009).

Politikblogs.at (2012) 'Politikblogs.at' Online. Previously available at <http://www.politikblogs.at/> (no longer accessible).

Polska The Times (2009) 'Europejski pakt PiS z Libertasem', wiadomosci.wp.pl. Online. Available <http://wiadomosci.wp.pl/kat,1022301,title,Europejski-pakt-PiS-zLibertasem,wid,11164494,wiadomosc_prasa.html> (accessed 17 December 2010).

Pszczółkowska, D., Szacki, W. and Wroński, P. (2009) 'Europa skręca w prawo', wyborcza.pl. Online. Available <http://wyborcza.pl/1,76842,6697982,Europa_skreca_w_prawo.html> (accessed 17 December 2010).

Puhl, J. (2009) 'Schlechte Zeiten für Europa-Hasser', spiegel.de. Online. Available <http://www.spiegel.de/politik/ausland/0,1518,627590,00.html> (accessed 1 June 2009).

Ray, L. (1999) 'Measuring Party orientations towards European integration: results from an expert survey', *European Journal of Political Research* 36(2): 283–306.

Rayner, G. (2009) 'Guido Fawkes: the colourful life of the man who brought down Damian McBride', telegraph.co.uk. Available <http://www.telegraph.co.uk/news/politics/5173475/Guido-Fawkes-the-colourful-life-of-the-man-who-brought-down-Damian-McBride.html>(accessed 16. October 2012).

Reif, K. and Inglehart, R. (eds) (1991) Eurobarometer: *The dynamics of European public opinion*, London: MacMillan.

Reif, K. and Schmitt, H. (1980) 'Nine second-order elections: a conceptual framework for the analysis of European Election results', *European Journal of Political Research* 8(1): 3–44.

Reply! Inc. (2012) 'Bloglines Reader'. Online. Available <www.bloglines.com> (accessed 10 October 2012)

Reungoat, E. (2010) 'Des appropriations ordinaires de l'Europe. L'U.E. vue de l'ANPE', in A. Crespy and M. Petithomme (eds) *L'Europe Sous Tensions*, Paris: L'Harmattan, pp. 113–132.

Rigardi.org (2012) 'Rigardi.org: politik kommentiert'. Online. Available <http://www.rigardi.org/> (accessed 31 October 2012).

Risse, T. (2003) 'The Euro between national and European identity', *Journal of European Public Policy* 10(4): 487–505.

— (2010) *A Community of Europeans? Transnational identities and public spheres*, Ithaca: Cornell University Press.

Rittberger, B. (2003) 'The creation and empowerment of the European Parliament', *Journal of Common Market Studies* 41(2): 203–25.

Rittberger, B. and Schimmelfennig, F. (2006) 'Explaining the constitutionalization of the European Union', *Journal of European Public Policy* 13(8): 1148–1167.

Rohrschneider, R. (2002) 'The democracy deficit and mass support for an EU-wide government', *American Journal of Political Science* 46(2): 463–475.

Ronzheimer, P. (2009a) 'Jörn Thiessen als Nazi beschimpft', bild.de. Online. Available <http://www.bild.de/BILD/politik/2009/06/09/50-euro-strafe-fuer-nicht-waehler/joern-thiessen-als-nazi-beschimpft.html> (accessed 7 June 2009).

— (2009b) 'Wird die Wahl zur Geisterwahl?', bild.de. Online. Available <http://www.bild.de/BILD/politik/wahlen/06/06/europawahl-beteiligung/wird-die-wahl-zur-geisterwahl.html> (accessed 6 June 2009).

Ross, G. (2008) 'What do 'Europeans' think? Analyses of the European Union's current crisis by European elites', *Journal of Common Market Studies* 46(2): 389–412.

Rousselin, P. and Paoli, P.-F. (2009) 'Alain Juppé – Michel Rocard: l'UE face à la Turquie', lefigaro.be. Online. Available <http://www.lefigaro.fr/debats/2009/06/03/01005-20090603ARTFIG00385-alain-juppe-michel-rocard-l-ue-face-a-la-turquie-.php> (accessed 3 June 2009).

Rzeczpospolita (2009) 'Niewielkie zainteresowanie Polaków wyborami', rp.pl. Online. Available <http://www.rp.pl/artykul/17,251780_Niewielkie_ zainteresowanie_wyborami_do_europarlamentu.html> (accessed 5 may 2010).
Sanchez Salgado, R. (2009) 'How the EU creates its own protest', paper presented at the International conference bringing civil society in: *The European Union and the rise of representative democracy*, European University Institute, Florence, 13–14 March 2009.
Santamaria, Y. (1999) *Histoire du Parti Communiste Français,* Paris: Presses Universitaires de France.
Sauerwein, F., Brantner, C. and Dietrich, A. (2006) Europäisierung der österreichischen Öffentlichkeit: Mediale Aufmerksamkeit für EU-Politik und der veröffentlichte Diskurs über die EU-Erweiterung, *Forschungsbericht im Auftrag des Bundesministeriums für Bildung, Wissenschaft und Kultur,* Wien: Institut für Publizistik- und Kommunikationswissenschaft.
Sauger, N., Brouard, S. and Grossman, E. (2007) Les Français Contre l'Europe? Les sens du référendum du 29 mai 2005, Paris: Presses de Science Po.
Sauger, N. and Lauret, A. (2005) 'Le référendum de ratification du Traité Constitutionnel Européen: comprendre le 'non' français', *Les Cahiers du Cevipof*, 42.
Scheuer, A. (1999) 'A Political Community?', in H. Schmitt and J. Thomassen (eds) *Political Representation and Legitimacy in the European Union*, Oxford: Oxford University Press, pp. 25–46.
Schlesinger, P. and Kevin, D. (2000) 'Can the European Union become a sphere of publics?', in E. O. Eriksen and J. E. Fossum (eds) *Democracy in the European Union. Integration through deliberation?*, London: Routledge, pp. 206–229.
Schmitter, P.C. (2000) *How to Democratize the European Union ... And Why Bother?*, Lanham: Rowman & Littlefield.
Schneider, S. M. and Foot, K. A. (2004) 'The web as an object of study', *New Media & Society* 6(1): 114–122.
— (2005) 'Web sphere analysis: an approach to studying online action', in C. Hine (ed.) V*irtual Methods: Issues in social research on the Internet*, Oxford: Berg, pp. 157–170.
Schneiders, T. G. (ed.) (2009) *Islamfeindlichkeit: Wenn die Grenzen der Kritik verschwimmen*, Wiesbaden: VS Verlag.
Sherrington, P. (2006) 'Confronting Europe: UK political parties and the EU 2000–2005', *British Journal of Politics and International Relations* 8(1): 69–78.
Skotnicka-Illasiewicz, E. (2002) 'Opinia społeczna wobec integracji europejskiej', in E. Skotnicka-Illasiewicz (ed.) Społeczne aspekty integracji Polskie z Unią Europejską: Badania i ekspertyzy 2001–2002, Warszawa: Wydawnictwo UKIE, pp. 8–36.
— (2009a'Dynamika zmian świadomości społecznej w mijającym

pięcioleciu członkowstwa', in E. Skotnicka-Illasiewicz (ed.) *5 lat członkowstwa Polski w Unii Europejskiej w perspektywie społecznej*, Warszawa: Wydawnictwo UKIE, pp. 39–46.

— (2009b) 'Społeczne rekonstrukcje wizji Unii Europejskiej w latach 2004–2008', in Skotnicka-Illasiewicz, E. (ed.) *5 lat członkowstwa Polski w Unii Europejskiej w perspektywie społecznej*, Warszawa: Wydawnictwo UKIE.

Słodkowska, I. and Dołbakowska, M. (eds) (2006) *Wybory 2005: Partie i ich programy*, Warsaw: Institute of Political Studies, Polish Academy of Sciences.

Smith, A. (2009) 'The Internet's role in campaign 2008'. Online. Available <http://www.pewinternet.org/Reports/2009/6--The-Internets-Role-in-Campaign-2008.aspx> (accessed 31 October 2012).

Sokolewicz, Z. (2003) 'Polish debate on European Christian values: some thoughts on marginal issues of Poland's negotiations of membership of the European Union', in A. Z. Nowak and D. Milczarek (eds) *On the Road to the European Union: Applicant Countries' Perspective*, Warsaw: Warsaw University Centre for Europe, pp. 433–460.

Spiegel Online (2009a) 'Europawahl – gehen Sie hin?', forum.spiegel.de. Online posting. Available <http://forum.spiegel.de/showthread.php?t=6880&page=250> (accessed 7 June 2009).

— (2009b) 'Merkel dringt auf strenge Finanzregeln bis Juni'. Online. Available <http://www.spiegel.de/politik/ausland/0,1518,627875,00.html> (accessed 31 May 2009).

Spiering, M. (2004) 'British Euroscepticism', in R. Harmsen and M. Spiering (eds) *Euroscepticism: Party politics, national identity and European integration*, Amsterdam: Rodopi, pp. 127–150.

Stanyer, J. (2009) 'Web 2.0 and the transformation of news and journalism', in A. Chadwick and P. N. Howard (eds) *Routledge Handbook of Internet Politics*, London: Routledge, pp. 186–200.

Statham, P. (2008) 'Making Europe news: how journalists view their role and media performance', *Journalism* 9(4): 398–422.

Statham, P. and Gray, E. (2005) 'The public sphere and debates about Europe in Britain', *Innovation* 18(1): 61–81.

Statham, P. and Koopmans, R. (2009) 'Political party contestation over Europe in the mass media: who criticizes Europe, how, and why?', *European Political Science Review* 1(3): 435–463.

Stewart, W. (2010) 'Netiquette of sending', livinginternet.com. Online. Available <http://www.livinginternet.com/i/ia_nq_send.htm#flame> (accessed 13 July 2010).

Strandberg, K. (2008) 'Public deliberation goes on-line? An analysis of citizens' political discussions on the Internet prior to the Finnish parliamentary elections in 2007', *Javnost the Public* 15(1): 71–90.

Strasser, S. (2008) 'Europe's other', *European Societies* 10(2): 177–195.

Styczyńska, N. (2009) 'Euroscepticism in new member states: the case of Poland', *Contemporary European Studies Special Issue*: 138–143.

Sunstein, C. R. (2002) *Republic.com*, Princeton: Princeton University Press.
— (2007) *Republic.com* 2.0, Princeton: Princeton University Press.
Surel, Y. (2000) 'The role of cognitive and normative frames in policy-making', *Journal of European Public Policy* 7(4): 495–512.
Süddeutsche.de (2009) 'Keine Visionen, nür das Übliche'. Online. Available <http://www.sueddeutsche.de/politik/europawahl-die-wahl-im-schatten-1.448109-2> (accessed 7 June 2009).
Szacki, W. (2009) 'Pięć lat w Unii na piątkę', Gazeta wyborcza. Online. Available <http://wyborcza.pl/1,76842,6556556,Piec_lat_w_Unii_na_piatke.html#ixzz0nHUn6DCm> (accessed 29 October 2012).
Szalai, E. (2008) 'A kelet-európai átalakulás nagy kérdései és az értelmiség', Politikatudományi Szemle, 2008/03. Online. Available <http://poltudszemle.hu/index.php?option=com_content&task=view&id=265&Itemid=51> (accessed 31 October 2012).
Szczerbiak, A. and Taggart, P. (eds) (2008a) *Opposing Europe? The comparative party politics of Euroscepticism*. Volume 1: Case studies and country surveys, Oxford: Oxford University Press.
— (eds) (2008b) *Opposing Europe? The comparative party politics of Euroscepticism*. Volume 2: Comparative and theoretical perspectives, Oxford: Oxford University Press.
— (2008c) 'Theorizing party-based Euroscepticism: problems of definition, measurement, and causality', in A. Szczerbiak and P. Taggart (eds) *Opposing Europe? The comparative party politics of Euroscepticism*. Volume 2: Comparative and theoretical perspectives, Oxford: Oxford University Press, pp. 238–262.
Szewczyk, M. (2009) 'Eurowybory w Polsce cz. II Kampania Wyborcza', twojaeuropa.pl. Online. Available <http://www.twojacuropa.pl/174/eurowybory-w-polsce-cz-ii-kampania-wyborcza> (accessed 7 January 2011).
Taggart, P. and Szczerbiak, A. (2004) 'Contemporary Euroscepticism in the party systems of the European Union candidate states of Central and Eastern Europe', *European Journal of Political Research* 43(1): 1–27.
Taylor, P. (2008) *The End of European Integration*, London: Routledge.
Tazbir, J. (2004) Polska przedmurzem Europy, Warszawa: Wydawnictwo Twój Styl.
Technorati, I. (2009) 'Technorati'. Online. Available <http://technorati.com/> (accessed 6 august 2009).
Telegraph, The (2009) 'Expenses: How MP's expenses became a hot topic', telegraph.co.uk. Available <http://www.telegraph.co.uk/news/newstopics/mps-expenses/5294350/Expenses-How-MPs-expenses-became-a-hot-topic.html> (accessed 16. October 2012).
Terry, S. M. (2000) 'Poland's foreign policy since 1989: the challenges of independence', *Communist and Post-Communist Studies* 33(1): 7–47.
Teschner, J. (2000) 'No longer Europhlies? Euroscepticism in Germany in the 1990s', *Journal of European Integration* 22(1): 59–86.

Thomassen, J. and Schmitt, H. (1999) 'Introduction: political representation and legitimacy in the European Union', in H. Schmitt and J. Thomassen (eds) *Political Representation and Legitimacy in the European Union Oxford*: Oxford University Press, pp. 3–21.

Thomassen, J.J.A. (2005) 'Nederlanders en Europa. Een Bekoelde Liefde?', in K. Aarts and H. van der Kolk (eds) *Nederlanders en Europa. Het Referendum over de Europese Grondwet*, Amsterdam: Bert Bakker, pp. 64–86.

Tilly, C. and Tarrow, S. (2007) Contentious Politics London: Paradigm Publishers.

Total Politics (2011) 'Top 100 UK political blogs 2011'. Online. Available <http://www.totalpolitics.com/blog/259027/top-100-uk-political-blogs-2011.thtml> (accessed 9 July 2012).

— (2012) 'Total politics'. Online. Available <http://www.totalpolitics.com> (accessed 9 July 2012).

Trenz, H.-J. (2004) 'Media coverage on European governance: exploring the European public sphere in national quality newspapers', *European Journal of Communication* 19(3): 291–319.

— (2005) *Europa in den Medien: Die europäische Integration im Spiegel nationaler Öffentlichkeit*, Frankfurt a.M.: Campus.

— (2007) '"Quo Vadis Europe?" Quality newspapers struggling for European Unity', in J. E. Fossum and P. Schlesinger (eds) *The European Union and the Public Sphere: A communicative space in the making?*, Abingdon: Routledge, pp. 89–109.

— (2008) 'Understanding media impact on European integration: enhancing or restricting the scope of legitimacy of the EU?', *Journal of European Integration* 30(2): 291–309.

Trenz, H.-J., Conrad, M. and Rosén, G. (2009) 'Impartial mediator or critical watchdog? The role of political journalism in EU constitution-making', *Comparative European Politics* 7(3): 342–363.

Twitter (2009) 'What are hashtags?'. Online. Available <http://help.twitter.com/forums/10711/entries/49309> (accessed 6 August 2009).

Uhlig, D. (2009) 'Kto głosuje, a kto bojkotuje', wyborcza.pl. Online. Available <http://wyborcza.pl/1,76842,6703278,Kto_glosuje__a_kto_bojkotuje.html> (accessed 17 december 2010).

Usherwood, S. (2002) 'Opposition to the European Union in the UK: the dilemma of public opinion and party management', *Government and Opposition* 37(2): 211–230.

Van de Steeg, M. (2006) 'Does a public sphere exist in the European Union? An analysis of the content of the debate on the Haider case', *European Journal of Political Research* 45(4): 609–634.

Van der Brug, W. and Van der Eijk, C. (eds) (2007) *European Elections & Domestic Politics: Lessons from the past and scenarios for the future*, Notre Dame: University of Notre Dame Press.

Van der Eijk, C. and Franklin, M.N. (2004) 'Potential for Contestation on European Matters at National Elections in Europe', in G. Marks and M. R. Steenbergen (eds) *European Integration and Political Conflict*,

Cambridge: Cambridge University Press, pp. 32–50.

Van Stegeren, T. (2006) 'In gesprek met Dominique Weesie over de evolutie van Geen Stijl', denieuwereporter.nl. Online. Available <http://www.denieuwereporter.nl/2006/11/in-gesprek-met-dominique-weesie-over-de-evolutie-van-geenstijl/> (accessed 23 November 2009).

— (2007) 'Nieuws. Marokko.nl tegen professionele journalistiek: help ons stapje verder komen', denieuwereporter.nl. Online. Available <http://www.denieuwereporter.nl/2007/07/nieuwsmarokkonl-tegen-professionele-journalistiek-help-ons-stapje-verder-komen/> (accessed 23 November 2009).

— Vasilopoulou, S. (2009) 'Varieties of Euroscepticism: the case of the European extreme right', *Journal of Contemporary European Research* 5(1): 3–23.

Verbeke, G. (1981) Belgium and Europe: Proceedings of the International Francqui- Colloquium Brussels-Ghent, 12–14 November 1981, Koninklijke Academie Voor Nederlandse Taal-en-Letterkunde.

Vergeer, M. and Hermans, L. (2008) 'Analysing online political discussions: methodological considerations', *Javnost - the Public* 15(2): 37–56.

Verschueren, N. (2010) 'Réactions syndicales aux premières heures de l'intégration européenne', in A. Crespy and M. Petithomme (eds) *L'Europe sous Tensions: Appropriation et contestation de l'intégration européenne*, Paris: L'Harmattan, pp. 197–213.

Vobruba, G., Bach, M., Rhodes, M. and Szalai, J. (2003) 'Debate on the enlargement of the European Union, the enlargement crisis of the European Union: limits of the dialectics of integration and expansion', *Journal of European Social Policy* 13(1): 35–62.

Voerman, G. (2005) 'De Nederlandse Politieke Partijen en de Europese Integratie', in K. Aarts and H. van der Kolk (eds) *Nederlanders en Europa: Het Referendum over de Europese Grondwet*, Amsterdam: Bert Bakker, pp. 44–63.

Vollaard, H. (2005) 'Euroscepsis en Protestantisme in Nederland', in H. Vollaard and B. Boer (eds) *Euroscepsis in Nederland*, Utrecht: Lemma, pp. 151–176.

— (2006) 'Protestantism and Euroscepticism in the Netherlands', *Perspectives on European Politics and Society* 7(3): 276–297.

Vollaard, H. and Boer, B. (eds) (2005a) *Euroscepsis in Nederland*, Utrecht: Lemma.

— (2005b) 'Euroscepsis: ideologie of strategie?', in H. Vollaard and B. Boer (eds) *Euroscepsis in Nederland*, Utrecht: Lemma, pp. 9–14.

Wagner, P. (2008) *Modernity as Experience and Interpretation: A new sociology of modernity*, Cambridge: Cambridge University Press.

Walicki, A. (2000) Polskie zmagania z wolnością widziane z boku, Krakow: Universitas.

Wallace, H. (1995) 'Britain out on a limb?', *The Political Quarterly* 66(1): 46–58.

Wallace, W. (1986) 'What price independence? Sovereignty and interdependence in British Politics', *International Affairs* 62(3): 367–389.
Weber, T. (2007) 'Campaign effects and second-order cycles: a top-down approach to European Parliament elections', *European Union Politics* 8(4): 509–536.
Wessels, B. (1995) 'Evaluations of the EC: elite or mass-driven?', in R. Sinnott (eds) *Public Opinion and Internationalized Governance*, Oxford: Oxford University Press, pp. 137–162.
— (2007) 'Discontent and European identity: three types of Euroscepticism', Acta Politica 42(2–3): 287–306.
Wessels, W. (2004). 'Die institutionelle Architektur der EU nach der Europäischen Verfassung: Höhere Entscheidungsdynamik, neue Koalitionen?' *Integration* 2004(3)
Wessler, H., Peters, B., Brüggemann, M., Kleinen-von Köningslöw, K., Sifft, S. (2008) *Transnationalization of Public Spheres*, Palgrave Macmillan, Basingstoke.
Whitaker, R. (2009) 'What European election campaign?', reuters.com. Online. Available <http://blogs.reuters.com/great-debate-uk/2009/06/04/what-european-election-campaign/> (accessed 4 June 2009).
Więcław, E. (2010) 'Zmalało poparcie Polaków dla euro', parkiet.com. Online. Available <http://www.parkiet.com/artykul/10,924866_Zmalalo_poparcie_Polakow_dla_przyjecia_euro_.html> (accessed 07 May 2010).
Wikio (2009a) 'Wikio: Blogs your way'. Online. Available <http://labs.ebuzzing.co.uk/> (accessed 31 october 2012).
— (2009b), ' Top blogs: Politics (France)'. Online. Available <http://labs.ebuzzing.fr/top-blogs/politique> (accessed 31 October 2012).
— (2010) 'Top Blogs: Politics (UK)'. Online. Available <http://labs.ebuzzing.co.uk/top-blogs/politics > (accessed 31 October 2012).
Wikipedia (2010) 'Liste der Volksbegehren in Österreich'. Online. Available <http://de.wikipedia.org/wiki/Liste_der_Volksbegehren_in_%C3%96sterreich> (accessed 22 October 2010).
Wimmel, A. (2006) *Transnationale Diskurse in Europa: Der Streit um den Türkei-Beitritt in Deutschland, Grossbritannien und Frankreich*, Frankfurt a.M.: Campus.
Winter, M. (2009) 'Prügelknabe Brüssel', süddeutsche.de. Online. Available <http://www.sueddeutsche.de/politik/wahl-zum-europaeischen-parlament-pruegelknabe-bruessel-1.459395> (accessed 7 June 2009).
Wintrebert, R. (2007) Attac: la politique autrement?: *Enquête sur l'histoire et la crise d'une organisation militante*, Paris: La Découverte.
Wirtualna Polska (2009a) 'Wywiad z Arturem Zawiszą', wiadomości.wp.pl. Online. Available <http://wiadomosci.wp.pl/kat,1342,title,Artur-Zawisza-Libertas-towolnosc,wid,11074288,wiadomosc.html?ticaid=1a215&_ticrsn=3> (accessed 5 May 2010).
— (2009b) 'Znamy wyniki wyborów do Parlamentu Europejskiego', wiadomości.wp.pl. Online. Available <http://wiadomosci.wp.pl/

kat,1022301,page,2,title,Znamy-wyniki-wyborow-do-Parlamentu-Europ ejskiego,wid,11195709,wiadomosc.html> (accessed 17 December 2010).
— (2009c) 'To Parlament Europejski ustala co będziemy jeść', wiadomosci.wp.pl. Online. Available <http://wiadomosci.wp.pl/ kat,1022301,title,To-Parlament-Europejski-ustala-co-bedziemy-jesc,wid,11148270,wiadomosc_video.html> (accessed 17 December 2010).
— (2009d) 'Kampania wyborcza zniechęca Polaków do wyborów', wiadomości.wp.pl. Online. Available <http://wiadomosci.wp.pl/ kat,1022301,title,Kampania-wyborcza-zniecheca-Polakow-do-wyborow,wid,11154299,wiadomosc.html> (accessed 17 December 2010).
Wirtualnemedia.pl (2009). Online. Available <http://www.wirtualnemedia.pl/ artykul/najpopularniejsze-stacje-radiowe-w-grupie-wiekowej-30–60#> (accessed 29 October 2009).
Wiszniowski, R. (2008) *Europejska przestrzeń polityczna: Zachowania elektoratu w wyborach do Parlamentu Europejskiego*, Toruń: Wydawnictwo Uniwersytetu Wrocławskiego.
Witczak, B. (2009) 'UPR zapowiada ofensywę przeciw wprowadzeniu euro', upr.org.pl. Online. Available <http://www.upr.org.pl/main/artykul. php?strid=1&katid=17&aid=7757> (accessed 5 May 2010).
Witschge, T. (2008) 'Examining online public discourse in context: a mixed method approach', *Javnost-The Public* 15(2): 75–92.
Wodak, R. and Pelinka, A., (eds) (2002) *The Haider Phenomenon in Austria*, New Brunswick: Transaction Publisher.
Young, J.W. (2000) *Britain and European Unity, 1945–1999*, Basingstoke: Palgrave Macmillan.
Zappi, S. (2009a) '"L'Europe ouverte et solidaire" nouveau rêve de José Bové', lemonde.fr. Online. Available <http://www.lemonde.fr/elections-europeennes/article/2009/05/30/l-europe-ouverte-et-solidaire-nouveau-reve-de-jose-bove_1200225_1168667.html> (accessed 30 May 2009).
— (2009b) 'Le clivage oui-non perdure, quatre ans après le référendum européen', lemonde.fr. Online. Available <http://www.lemonde.fr/ cgi-bin/ACHATS/acheter.cgi?offre=ARCHIVES&type_item=ART_ ARCH_30J&objet_id=1084862&clef=ARC-TRK-NC_01> (accessed 29 May 2009).
Zimmermann, A., Koopmans, R. and Schlecht, T. (2004) 'Political Communication on the Internet, Part 2: Link structure among political actors in Europe', *The Transformation of Political Mobilisation and Communication in European Public Spheres Report* WP 4. Online. Available <http:// europub.wz-berlin.de> (accessed 31 October 2012).
Ziółkowski, M. and Jędrzejewska, S. (2009) 'Wejście Polski do Unii Europejskiej: przedstawienie procesu historycznego w dyskursie publicznym', in E. Skotnicka-Illasiewicz (ed.) *5 lat członkowstwa Polski w Unii Europejskiej w perspektywie społecznej*, Warszawa: Wydawnictwo UKIE, pp. 18–38.

Zuba, K. (2006) *Polski eurosceptycyzm i eurorealizm*, Opole: Wydawnictwo Uniwersytetu Opolskiego.

Zürn, M. (2006) 'Zur Politisierung der Europäischen Union', *Politische Vierteljahresschrift*, 47(2): 242–251.

Index

accountability 12, 145, 200, 219
   authorisation and 200
Anderson, C. 5, 179 n.3
Aubry, M. 86–7
Austria 18, 19, 61–78, 197–8
   Bündnis Zukunft Österreich (BZÖ) 19, 61, 63, 65, 69
   cultural identity and 66
   Czech Republic, relations with 63, 64
   EU membership and 62–3, 64
      1994 accession referendum 63
      Turkish accession debate 70, 72, 74–5
   Euroscepticism in 5, 7, 19, 61–2, 63–4, 65, 70, 116, 196, 197–8
      anti-Islamism and 70, 72
      EP 2009 elections and 69, 70–73
      far-right extremism and 61
      Haider debate and 64–5
      historical roots of 62–5
      parties and 19–20, 61, 69
      xenophobia and 70, 76
   Freiheitliche Partei Österreichs (FPÖ) 19, 61, 62, 63, 64, 65, 69, 71, 74, 106, 107 n.3
   Die Grünen – Die grüne Alternative 69, 70, 72
   immigration, attitudes to 64, 65, 66, 72
   Kronenzeitung 67, 68, 70, 197
   Liste Martin 19–20, 70, 106
   media populism in 66, 67, 68, 73, 74–7
      Euroscepticism and 5, 61, 66–7, 75, 76–7, 106, 196
      tabloid newspapers and 66–7, 69, 76, 77
      racism/xenophobia and 77, 197
   nationalism in 62, 65, 66, 75
   Nazism (Nazi) and 62, 63, 64, 65

   Österreichische Volkspartei (ÖVP) 64
      FPÖ coalition (2000) 64–5
   political system in 63
      consociational democracy and 66
   polity contestation EP 2009 analysis 30, 39, 42, 67–77, 114, 115, 151
      campaigning actors in 68–9, 197
      citizen-elite divide and 73
      election turnout 65, 67
      essence/substance of 70–1
      evaluations of integration principle 44, 50, 58, 70–7, 106, 196
      inclusiveness/exclusiveness dimension in 67, 72, 73
      integration, principle of and 71, 72
      justifications, evaluation of 67, 73–5
      legitimacy, discussion of and 71, 72–3, 197–8
      media coverage of elections 68–9, 76, 196
      online websites and 67, 73, 75, 76, 77, 197–8
      political blogs and 68, 69
      populist 'essentialist strategy' and 69–70, 71
      populist rhetoric and 69–70, 71, 72, 75, 76–7
   Die Presse 67
   right-wing populism and 61, 64, 65, 74–5
      logic of argumentation 75
      mass media, role in 66, 69–72, 74, 75, 76–7
      political blogs and 68, 69
      racism/extremism and 70, 72, 74, 77

Sozialdemokratische Partei Österreichs (SPÖ) 62, 64, 69
Der Standard 67, 74 n.9, 76, 77, 197
World War II and post-war culture 62–3, 64, 66
Benes Decrees and 64
authority 2, 4, 52, 69, 112, 158, 169
political 15, 47, 92, 196, 202, 203
High Authority and Common Assembly 138
inclusiveness and 69
legal 11
supranational 49, 196

BabelBlogs 39
CafeBabel 39
Barlow, J. P. 23 n.2
Barnier, M. 95
Belgium (French speaking) 18, 79–100, 198
Attac 82
Le Blog Politique 85, 86
Christen-Democratisch en Vlaams 82
Constitutional Treaty (2005) and 80, 82, 86
La Dernière Heure 85
as Europhile Member State 79, 82, 89
Euroscepticism in 7, 20, 79, 82, 84, 89, 99, 198
Flemish nationalists and 79, 82
radical left-wing parties 79, 82
trade unions and 82
Turkish membership and 84, 89, 95
ultra-liberal critique and 84
Fédération Générale du Travail de Belgique (FGTB) 82
Flanders (Flemish) 18 n.3, 79, 82, 84, 88
Forum Social de Belgique 82
Ligue communiste révolutionnaire 82
Lijst Dedecker (LDD) 84
Nieuw-Vlaamse Alliantie (N-VA) 82
Le Pan 85
Parti Communiste (PC) 82
Parti des travailleurs belges (PTB) 82
Parti Socialiste (PS) 82, 86
polity contestation EP 2009 analysis 20, 30, 42, 47, 80, 83, 84, 86, 88–9, 92, 93, 95, 96–7, 98, 99, 100, 137, 198
compulsory voting, effect of 88
data studied in 85–6
democracy, concern for 96
discourses of 80, 86, 99
elite/institutional distrust and 86, 89, 92–3, 99
EP campaign and 84, 86, 88, 89
French debate, influence of 89
integration project evaluation 39, 49, 59, 82–2, 86, 88–9, 92, 93, 95, 96–7, 98, 99–100, 115
media coverage of 83, 85–6, 88, 98, 196
necessity justification and 96–8
online news sites use of 85–6, 98
political blogs and 85, 86, 88
Radio Télévision Belge Francophone (RTBF) 85
Socialistische Partij Anders (SP.A.)
Le Soir 85, 86, 92, 93, 96
lesoir.be 85
Le Vif-L'Éxpress 85
Vlaams Belang 82, 84
Wallonia 18 n.3, 82
Benelux countries 138, 146
see also Belgium; the Netherlands
Berlusconi, S. 143
Besancenot, O. 84
Beyen, J. W. 138
Blair, T. 178
blogging, political 19, 21–2
citizen-elite divide and 54
micro-blogging and 22
as participatory journalism 21–2
Twitter and 22
see also internet; Facebook
Bohman, J. 40
Bokros, L. 133

Bolkestein Directive 79, 81
Boltanski, L. 35, 41
Bové, J. 84
Brown, G. 186

Cameron, D. 187
Chirac, J. 81
Christianity 74, 94, 114, 115 n.19, 156, 159, 167
civil society 2, 4, 59, 81–2, 82, 109, 139, 162–3
Cohn-Bendit, D. 84
collective will, formation of 3, 8, 22
    EP elections and 37, 195
    EU, evaluation of and 45
    media, role in 8
Common Agricultural Policy (CAP) 10
Council of Ministers 45, 138
Crespy, A. 2, 14, 79, 81, 82, 91
Csáky, P. 130
Czech Republic
    Austria and 63, 64
    Euroscepticism in 63
    Hungary, relations with 132
    EU polity contestation 39, 42, 44, 48, 50, *51*, 115, 196

Daddow, O. 173, 174, 175, 176, 178, 181
Dale, I. 183
Dávid, I. 132
de Gaulle, C. 79, 80
Delors, J. 11
democratic legitimacy, crisis of 202–3
de Villiers, P. 80, 83, 93
De Vreese, C. 4, 17, 23, 61, 180–1
Diez Medrano, J. 7, 35, 113, 174, 196
Dupont-Aignan, N. 83

Economic and Monetary Union (EMU) 177
EU polity contestation analysis
    convergence/divergence of 7–9, 19, 37, 39, 195
        existential/substantial debates and 8–9, 38, 39, 41, 42, 70–1, 200–1
    cross-country qualitative comparison of 18, 19–20, 36, 38–59, *69*, 195, 197–201
        cultural diversity and 36, 198
        EU institutional set-up evaluation *46, 47, 48*
        evaluations of integration principle/project 44–51, 197–8
        intensity of debate *42*
        number of EP election articles *29*
        trans-European online media, use of 19, 38, 195, *205*
        see also case studies under individual countries
    definition/concept of 2, 10, 79–80
        policy contestation, difference with 10
    EU legitimacy, relation to 10–11, 12, 79, 195
        citizen-elite divide in 53–4, 56, 58, 95
        legitimation/justification discourse and 13, 15, 52–3, 56–9
        polity dialectic, categories of 14–16, 52–3, *55*
    Euroscepticism and 6, 9–10, 11–12, 19
        'diffuse' Euroscepticism and 15, 40, 52, 54, 58, 59, 225
        discursive construction of 13–15, 16
        use of term in analysis 6, 11, 12, 15–16, 22, 225
    evaluations analysis 6, 9, 13–16, 21, 31, 34, 40–59, 195–6, 207–8, 220–5
        coding methodology 31–4, 41–2, 207–19
        diffuse evaluations, classification of 40–1, 54
        EU legitimacy categories 52–9
        inclusiveness of integration and 13–14, 43–8, 49–51
        justification of polity worth and

34–6, 39, 41, *55,* 56, *57,*
218–19
  level and scope of integration 13,
  14, *46,* 47–8, 49–51
  typology of 6, 9, 13–16, 21, 31,
  34, 40, 220–5
 public sphere perspective and 2–4,
 7–8, 22, 33, 58, 202
  online media and 23–4, 202
  web sphere, identification of 25, 26
 research design and methodology
 19, 21–36, 207–25
  Bloglines, use of 27, 31–2, 207
  clipping, use of 28, 29, 32, 207
  coding schemes 22, 25, 28, 30–1,
  32–3, 35, 38, 207–8
  data gathering and analysis 25–7,
  31–3, 38–9
  discourses and narratives used
  22, 34–6, 40, 52
  online news websites and 19, 21,
  22–4, 25–8, 52, 59
  political blogs, use of 19, 21–2,
  26, 38
  sampling challenges 25, 28
  salience and 1, 24, 37, 42, 56, 59,
  66, 68, 77, 86, 89, 98, 106,
  109, 121, 137, 180 n.4, 181
  n.5
  thread collection and 28–30,
  33–4, 207, 210–14
 website selection 26–8, 59
  Alexa.com 26 n.4, 124, 140, 164
  n.5, 182 n.6, 183
  BlogActiv 39
  Wikio blog rankings 183
  see also blogging, political;
  European Parliament 2009
  election study
EUObserver 39
Eurobarometer surveys 5, 43, 47, 81,
102–3, 122, 162, 165, 178, 179, 180
European Coal and Steel Community
(ECSC) Treaty (1951) 137
European Commission 7, 8, 16, 45

critique of 91, 92–3, 99, 112
European Defence Community 138
European Economic Community
(EEC) 138
European integration xvii, 1, 2, 10, 13,
200–1
 attitudinal studies and 4, 5
 Cold War and 62, 80
 Common Market and 40, 82, 84, 113
 communism and 62, 102, 158
 constitutionalisation and 1, 9, 12
 contestation of 3, 4, 9–10, 38, 56–9,
 100, 196–7, 200–1
  citizen-elite thesis and 53–4, 58,
  197
  Euroscepticism relation to 9,
  11–12, 38, 43, 54, 58
  existential debates, role of 200–1
  public opinion, construction of
  and 38, 53
 Europeanisation 3, 11, 37
 iron curtain, collapse of and 62, 155
 legitimation discourses and 13, 16,
 39, 40–1, 43
  justificatory discourses and 34–5,
  39, 41, 43, *57,* 197
  media debates role in 49, 50,
  53–4, 66, 104, 196, 197
 national government satisfaction,
 relation with 179 n.3
 national sovereignty, erosion of 96
 permissive consensus and 2, 4, 10,
 105, 111
 politicisation of 2, 4, 11, 37, 195
 polity contestation analysis 10, 12,
 37, 38–59, 195–201
  argumentation, lines of in 14,
  196
  evaluations of integration
  principle and 43–5, 48–51,
  111, 196–7
  mediated debates, effect on 39
  typology of evaluations 13–15,
  34–6, 43
 Treaty of Lisbon *see* Lisbon Treaty

Treaty of Maastricht 1, 80, 81, 103, 137, 181, 191
Treaty of Nice 103
see also Constitutional Treaty under individual countries; European Union (EU)
European Parliament (EP) 17, 45, 200
 critique of 92, 130
 elections in 8, 16–18, 37, 195, 201
  campaigning, and 17, 59, 195, 201
  media coverage of 9, 16–17, 18, 56, 59, 201
  polity contestation and 17–18, 59
  as 'second order' 8, 17, 33, 34, 37, 41, 102, 201
  status reform and 200
  turnout in 17
 national groups and MEPs 193 n.11
 powers of 14, 17, 96, 200
European Parliament 2009 election study xvii, 3, 16–18, 31–2, 38–59, 197–200
 comparative contestation survey 4, 16–18, 41–59, 197–200
  debates, types of 41–2
  intensity of polity debate 42, 43
  patterns of evaluation 56–8, 197
 cross-national qualitative sample 18, 18, 19–20, 36, 38–59
  data used in 38–9, 195
  integration principle, evaluation results 47–51, 196
  interactive news websites analysis 3, 5, 6–7, 27, 31–2, 38, 53–9, 195, 196
  article numbers per country 29
  trans-European online media and 19, 20, 195
  websites analysed 39, 59
 key findings of 195–201
 media impact on 20, 56, 59, 195–6, 201
  as EU critical 195–6
 voter participation in 86
 see also EU polity contestation analysis; European integration; under individual country case studies
European Union (EU)
 democratic deficit, critique of 14, 50, 56, 83, 112, 134, 198, 200
 democratic reform and 200
 foreign policy and 7, 145, 146, 216
 future of debate 196–202
 institutional set-up, evaluation of 43, 45–51, 200
  competencies, extent of 43, 47
  division of power and 43, 47
  inclusiveness of integration and 43, 45, 47–51
 Justice and Home Affairs and 16, 45, 148
 legitimacy and 7, 8, 35
  contestation of 1, 2, 6, 9, 10–11, 13, 14, 195, 197, 203
  democratic performance, questioning of 197, 200
  justificatory discourses and 34–5, 45, 113, 197
  online media, use of for 110, 195, 203
  referenda, use of and 9–10
 Stability and Growth Pact 151
 see also EU polity contestation analysis; European integration
Euroscepticism xvii, 1, 11, 43. 196
 as demand for accountability 12
 diffuse Euroscepticism 15, 40, 52, 54, 58, 59
 as EU polity contestation 6, 9–10, 11–12, 13–15, 16, 19, 22, 40, 52, 54, 58, 59, 225
 education level and 180
 'hard' and 'soft' distinction 6, 199
 identity politics and 1, 86, 95, 99, 103, 156, 159, 161, 163–4, 170, 173, 174, 175, 177, 178, 181, 182, 192, 199
 imperial (imperialism) and 159, 175, 181
 matrix of polity evaluation and 13,

15–16, 24, 43, *53, 55*
neoliberalism and 14, 79, 81, 82, 90, 99, 112, 198
renationalisation and 1, 72
online news media, role of in xvii-xviii, 19, 49, 54, 56
citizen-elite thesis and 54
public discourse of xvii, 1–2, 4, 10, 11, 43
research on 5, 6
focus on negative opinions in 6
shift towards 179, 194
as 'constraining dissensus' 194
see also under individual countries
Eurozone 34, 117, 186
crisis of 1, 15, 177, 196–7, 202–3

Facebook 26, 27, 28, 30, 39
Farage, N. 193 n.11
Fawkes, G. 183
Fimin, O. 198
The Financial Times 107 n.3
Finland 18
polity contestation 30, 39, 42, 44, 48, 50
Foot, K. 23, 25–6, 27–8, 31
Fortuyn, P. 139, 141
France 18, 19
Assemblée Nationale 79
Attac 81
Chasse, Pêche, Nature et Traditions (CPNT) 83, 87, 99
Debout la République 83
'empty chair crisis' (1965–6) 79, 80
Europe-Ecologie 84, 98
European Socialist Party and 83
European Union, attitudes to 79, 81, 93
Constitutional Treaty (2005) and 79, 81, 84, 86, 91, 98–9, 100, 121, 198, 203
integration and 79, 80, 81–2, 98
Turkish membership and 83, 86, 93–5, 96, 99
Euroscepticism in 80, 81, 89–90, 98, 99
leftist critical discourse and 81, 91
nationalist/sovereignist parties 83
Le Figaro 85, 92, 93, 95, 96
Front de Gauche (PG) 84
Front National 81, 83, 87, 99
Gaullism (Gaullists) and 80, 83
global justice movement and 81
immigration and 83
xenophobia/anti-Islamic attitudes and 99
Lutte Ouvrière (LO) 84, 87, 91, 94
Le Monde 85, 92, 94
Mouvement pour la France (MPF) 81, 83, 87
Nouveau Parti Anti-Capitaliste (NPA) 84, 87
Le Nouvel Observateur 85, *92*
Parti Communiste (PC) 80, 81, 85
Parti Socialiste (PS) 82, 83, 86–7
Plume de Presse 85
polity contestation EP 2009 analysis 20, 39, 42, 47, 79, 83–100, 198
anti-liberal discourse and 90, 91–2, 99, 198
citizen-elite divide and 95
data used in 85
ecological movements and 84
EP campaign and 83, 86–7
EU institutional distrust and critique 89–92, 93, 99–100, 198
integration project evaluation 48, 50, 79, 86–8, 89–92, 93, 98–9
justifications and 95–6, 99
left-wing, anti-capitalist rhetoric and 84, 91
media coverage and 85, 87, 88, 90, 91–2, 196
online news sites use of 79, 85, 198
political blogs and 85, 87, 88
populist arguments and 83
presidential election, focus on

and 86, 87, 98
presidential system in 86
Rassemblement du peuple français (RPR) 80
Sarkofrance 85, 87
l'Union pour un mouvement populaire (UMP) 83, 86, 87

Ganley, D. 83
Germany 18, 19, 101–17
Arbeit und soziale Gerechtigkeit–Die Wahlalternative (WASG) 101
BILD 108, 109
Bild.de 105, 106, *107*, 108, 109
Bild-Zeitung 104, 105, 106, 115, 141
Bildblog 105, *107*
Bundesbank 115 n.19
Bundesrat 101
Bundestag 101, 105, 108
Christlich Demokratische Union Deutschlands (CDU) 109
Christlich-Soziale Union in Bayern (CSU) 101, 104, 116
Constitutional Treaty and 103
Deutsche Volksunion (DVU) 103
European integration, attitudes to 101, 102, 103, 111–12, 114–15, 116
  decline in support for 102–3, 115, 116, 198
  enlargement and 111
  financial crisis, effect on 115
  national parliaments and 112, 114
  Turkish accession and 111, 115
European People Party 109
European Socialists 109
Euroscepticism and 7, 10, 101, 102, 103, 115–16
  EU legitimacy and 108
  externalisation of 107, 116
  'hard' of right-wing extremists 103–4
  media, role in 104, 105, 106, 116, 198
  regionalist autonomy and 101

unification, effect on 102
federalist system in 101
Freie Demokratische Partei 114
Die Grünen 20
Die Linke (Left Party) 101, 103, 104, 114, 116
mass media/internet 102, 103, 104, 110, 116–17
  citizen protest and 105
  online news media 105, 106, 116
  political blogs and 105, 106
  public-opinion making and 104, 105
  tabloid papers and 104, 105, 109, 116, 141
Nationaldemokratische Partei Deutschlands (NDP) 103
nationalism, right-wing 106
Partei des Demokratischen Sozialismus (PDS) 101
PI-news 105, 115
polity contestation EP 2009 analysis 20, 30, 42, 47, 105–17
  campaign, characteristics of 105, 106, 109, 114
  democracy, concerns expressed with 113, 114
  domestic elections, effect on 105–6, 108
  EP, power of 111–12
  EU institutional set-up and legitimacy 111–12, 113
  integration project evaluation 39, 49, 50, 101, 106, 111–17
  justifications used in 113–15
  media attention to 102, 106, *107*, 108–9, 196
  online websites/forums and 106, 110, 130–2
  partisan contestation and 101, 102, 103, 104, 105
  as 'second order' debate 105–6, 109
  substantial debate, lack of 109
  turnout/voter indifference and 108, 109, 112

values/culture, references to
114–15
populism and 104, 116
media, role in 104, 106, 116
pro-European attitudes in 10, 18,
20, 101, 113–14, 115, 198
'progressive Europeanism'
ideology of 101, 113, 116
Republikaner 103
(re)unification (1990) 102, 130, 198
financial burden of 102
*Sozialdemokratische Partei
Deutschlands* (SPD) 109
Der Spiegel 106
Spiegel Online 105, *107*, 112, 114
Süddeutsche.de 106, *107*, 108
Süddeutsche Zeitung 106, 108 n.4
Die Welt 105
Gifford, C. 176, 178, 181
globalisation xiv, 81, 91, 96, 100, 217
Göncz, K. 131
Greece, polity contestation in 30, 42,
49, 50

Habermas, J. 3, 22, 23 n.2
Hague, W. 186
Haider, J. 61, 63, 64–5
Heller, M. 120, 121, 122, 129, 198
Hungary 18, 19, 119–35
Austro-Hungarian Monarchy 120
Blog.hu 124
culture and identity in 119–20, 134,
135
public discourses and 120
developmental models and 119–20
EU integration, attitudes towards
120–1, 129, 131–2, 133–4, 135
economic gain and 120, 121, 133
German unification and 130
Euroscepticism in 19, 20, 63, 119,
120, 122, 127, 129, 131, 198
domestic politics and 121, 122,
134, 198
financial crisis, effect on 121, 121
media, role in 130, 196

Fidesz 124, 125, 127, 132, 199
Figyelő 124
Figyelőnet 123, 124, *126*
Gárda 122
Index 123–4, *126*, 131, 132, 133, 134
internet and media in 123–4
political blogs 123, 124–5
professional journalism websites
and 123
Jews (anti-Jewish) and 127
Jobbik 20, 122, 127, 128, 129, 131,
198
Magyar Demokrata Fórum (MDF)
132, 133
Magyar Igazság és Élet Pártja
(MIÉP) 122
Magyar Koalíció Pártja 130
Magyar Szocialista Párt (MSZP)
122–3, 131
Munkáspárt 129, 131, 132, 133
nationalism and 127, 132, 134, 199
far-right parties and 122, 127,
132, 134
Greater Hungary, resurrection of
120, 127, 132
trans-border activism and 127
1990 system change 120
[origo] 123, *126,* 131, 133, 134
political trust and 192
polity contestation EP 2009 analysis
30, 42, 120–35, 198–9
campaign characteristics of 123
democratic values and 133–4
domestic politics, focus on in 122–
3, 125, 127, 128, 129, 134
economic crisis, issue of 127
ethnic Hungarians, support of
125, 127
EU institutional set-up, critique
of 130–1, 132–4, 135
integration principle evaluation
of 49, 50, 122, 125, 128,
129–35, 196
justifications of 133–4
political far-right activism and

122, 127–8, 134, 135
  racist/xenophobic discourse and 127–8, 133
  online media and 123, 125, *126*, 127–8, 130, 132, 133–4, 135
  second-order campaigns and 125, 128
Reakció 123, 124, *126*
Roma population, racism and 122, 127, 128
Slovakia, relations with 125, 127, 130, 132
Soviet occupation of 119
Tatars 120
Trianon, Treaty of 120, 125, 132
W-For a Better Magyarland 123, 124, *126*

Iceland 131
in't Veld, S. 149, 150
International Monetary Fund (IMF) 127
internet
  citizen's voice/journalism and 23, 110
  deliberative discussion and 23–4
  liberal/open nature of 24
  netiquette and 23
  political communication and 23–4
    role in 23–4, 110
  RSS feeds and 27, 28
    Twitter and
      Hashtag 27 n.4, n.6, 28
      micro-blogging and 22
      polity contestation study, use in 26, 27, 28, 30, 39
      tweet 27 n.6, 30
  URL 26
  web sphere, concept of and 25, 26
    dynamism of 27–8
  web storms, definition of 25–6
  see also blogging, political; Facebook; mass media
Italy 65, 143, 193 n. 11

Jospin, L. 81
Juppé A. 93–4

Kaczyński, J. 157, 159, 164
Kaczyński, L. 157, 158, 159, 164
Koch-Mehrin, S. 114
Kohut, T. 198
Korwin-Mikke, J. 161, 164, 167, 168, 169
Krippendorff, K. 31
Kriza, B. 198

Laroes, H. 147
Latvia 178
Le Pen, M. 83
  Libertas 83, 161, 165
Lisbon Treaty 34, 58, 72, 91, 93, 95–6, 100, 103, 109, 111, 114, 121, 130, 134, 161, 166, 186–7, 191
  as negation of democracy 99, 165, 186
  2009 EP elections, effect on 140, 186

Maastricht Treaty (1992) 1, 80, 81, 103, 137, 181, 191
Madlener, B. 149
Mair, P. 1, 9, 10, 59, 200
Martin, H.-P. 63, 65 n.6, 69–70, 76, 106, 197
Martin, M. 186
mass media 3, 5
  content analysis xvi, 4, 6, 9, 19, 21, 22, 30, 31, 36, 38, 61, 155, 197
  EU coverage of 4, 16–17, 19, 52, 89, 180–1, 202
    EU contestation in xvii-xviii, 2, 3, 4–5, 6, 7, 20, 22–7, 37, 38, 39, 43, 52–8, 195–7, 201–2
    EU legitimacy and 17, 52–3, 196
    Euroscepticism, role in 89, 104, 180
    framing of issues and 180–1
  mediatization patterns of 5
  nation-state, reaffirmation of 180
  'traditional' media and 23, 54
  political intermediation in 22–3
  public debate, transformation of 3, 196

see also internet; under individual countries
media organisations 59
see also internet; under individual countries
media spheres 3, 7, 19, 39, 43, 195
mediatization 5
Mélenchon, J.-L. 84
MEPs (Members of the European Parliament) 20, 128, 129, 166–7, 187, 193, 201
Eurosceptic critique and 71, 90–1, 92–3, 96, 99, 130, 132, 133–4
Merkel, A. 108, 109, 115, 169
Mitterrand, F. 81
Moscovici, P. 95

Netherlands, The 18, 19, 137–53
Algemeen Dagblad 141
Anti-Revolutionaire Partij (ARP) 138
Christelijk Democratische Appèl (CDA) 138, 139
Christelijk-Historische Unie (CHU) 138
ChristenUnie 138, 139
Communistische Partij Nederland (CPN) 138
Constitutional Treaty 2005 referendum 6, 121, 137, 139–40
Democraten 66 (D66) 139, 140, 143, 149, 150, 199
European integration, attitudes to 137, 138, 145, 150, 199
citizen-elite gap and 139, 149, 152–3
Constitutional Treaty 2005 and 139–40, 149, 152, 199, 203
initial support for 138–9, 151
membership, consensus on 145
parties in opposition of 138, 151–2
Turkish membership and 139, 145, 148, 149, 152
Euroscepticism and 7, 10, 20, 137, 138, 139, 151–2
Constitutional Treaty (2005) change in 151–2
EP 2009 election analysis and 138, 198
party positions and 138–9
GeenStijl.nl 138, 140, 141
Gereformeerd Politiek Verbond (GPV) 138
GroenLinks 140
Ilse Media Group 141
Katholieke Volkspartij (KVP)
Marokko.nl 138, 140, 141–2, *143*
media and internet in 140–1
political blogs 140, 152
NOS.nl 138, 140, 141, *143*, 147
Nu.nl 138, 140–1, 143, 148–9, 150
Partij van de Arbeid (PvdA) 138–9, 143, 147
Partij voor de Vrijheid (PVV) 20, 106, 139, 149, 199
polity contestation EP 2009 analysis 39, 42, 137, 140–53, 199
data used in 140–1, 142
domestic issues and 140, 142, 143
EU inclusiveness and 146, 148
EU institutional set-up and 145, 146–7, 148, 152
evaluations of integration principle 44, 48, 50, 143, 145–50
existential debates and 143, 144, 145, 150, 151, 152
justifications and 144, 150–1
Lisbon Treaty and 140–2
media attention to 142–3, 152
online debates and 138, 142–4, 145, 146–8, 152
party politicians, evaluations of 149, 152–3
as 'second order' elections 140, 142, 144
2005 referendum, effect on 137, 140, 143, 149, 150, 151, 152–3, 199

populism in 139, 141, 151–2
Reformatorisch Politieke Federatie
    (RPF) 138
Socialistische Partij (SP) 139
Staatkundig-Gereformeerde Partij
    (SGP) 138, 139
De Telegraaf 141, 142, 143
Telegraaf.nl 138, 140
Volkspartij voor Vrijheid en
    Democratie (VVD) 139, 148
Nice Treaty 103

Orbán, V. 125, 130, 132, 199
Ostendorf, C. 146

Palikot, J. 164
Paris, Treaty of 138
Pasqua, C. 80
Poland 18, 20, 155–71
  Alliance of Democratic Left and
      Workers Union 165
  Catholic Church and 160, 162, 170
    Ours Daily 162
    Radio Maria 162, 165
  civic activity/political interest in
      157, 163, 170–1
  EU accession (2004) and 155–6,
      160, 163
    Catholic Church and 162
    farmers and 162
    as 'return to Europe' 155
    three-dimensional debate frame
        and 155–6, 170
  European integration, attitudes to
      155, 157, 159, 162–3, 168, 170–1
    Treaty of Lisbon, interest in 167,
        168
  Euroscepticism in 155, 156, 157, 170
    citizen-elite divide and 156, 170
    endangered economy and 156,
        157–8, 161, 163, 168, 170, 199
    endangered identity and 156,
        158–9, 163, 168, 170, 199
    EU democratic deficit critique
        159, 168

Eurosceptic/Eurorealist distinc-
    tion 157
  media and 162, 163, 165, 170
  online coverage 165, 166, 170
  party politics and 159–60, 199
European Parliament elections
  2004 elections 160, 161, 165
  2009 elections 20, 161, 165–71
  voter turnout and 163, 165, 169, 170
Gazeta.pl 167, 171
Gazeta Wyborcza 164
German relations 158, 159
The Highest Time 164
Independence and Democracy 160
Libertas 160, 161, 165
Liga Polskich Rodzin, (LPR) 158,
    159, 160, 161, 162
media and internet 162, 164, 166, 170
  Catholic Church and 162
  internet use, level of 166, 171
  political blogs in 164, 166, 171
  tabloid press 162, 171
  websites, professional journalism
      and 164
Narodowe Odrodzenie Polski
    (NOP) 161
Onet.pl 165
Platforma Obywatelska (PO) 163,
    164, 165, 169, 171
political trust and 192
polity contestation EP 2009 analysis
    42, 163–71, 199
  campaign issues and debates
      165–6
  EU democratic deficit critique
      168–9, 171
  evaluations of integration
      principle 39, 44, 48, 50, 115,
      166–71
  justifications of worth and
      168–9, 171
  nationalisation of politics and
      170, 171
  online media and 163–4, 165,
      166, 167, 168, 170, 171, 199

political trust and 170, 171
    as 'second order' elections 163
Polska The Times 162, 167, 171
Polskie Stronnictwo Ludowe (PSL) 158
Prawica RP 165
Prawo i Sprawiedliwość (PiS) 158, 159, 160, 161, 162, 164, 165, 166, 167, 171
Russia, relations with 158
Rzeczpospolita 162
Samoobrona 158, 161
Sojusz Lewicy Demokratycznej (SLD) 163
TVN24.pl 164
Unia Polityki Realnej (UPR) 159, 161, 164
Union for a Europe of the Nations 166
USA relations 159, 161
Wirtualna Polska 164
Pöttering, H.-G. 108, 109
public opinion, EU and 5, 6, 7, 179
    formation of xvii, 4, 6, 9, 37, 202, 203
        discursive dynamics of 7
        media's role in 3, 202, 203
        positive/negative interaction and 6
    European integration and xvii, 6, 37, 38, 53, 58
        citizen-elite divide and 53–4
        online news media, use of for 38, 58, 202
    political contestation, role in 37, 202
    rational choice institutionalist framework and 179
    see also EU polity contestation analysis
public sphere
    EU polity contestation, study of and 2–4, 7–8, 21, 22, 37, 58, 202
    cyber-optimist/cyber-pessimist divide and 23 n.1
    mass media, role in 3, 202
        fragmentation thesis and 202

online political sphere and 23, 24, 110, 202
    as translators 3
    perception formation in 2
    web sphere, definition of 25, 26
    see also EU polity contestation analysis, public sphere perspective

rational choice institutionalism 179
referendums, EU and 5, 9–10, 17–18
    see also under individual countries
RECON project xvii
representation (representative, representativeness), EU and 17, 37, 41, 61, 89, 114, 133–4, 179, 200–1, 202
    media populism and 75, 76
    MEPs and 71, 75, 130, 133
Rocard, M. 95, 96
Rohrschneider, R. 179
Rydzyk, T. 162

Sarkozy, N. 83, 84, 86
Sarrazin, T. 115 n.19
Schneider, S. M. 25–6, 27–8
Schulz, M. 107 n.3, 109
Schüssel, W. 64
Seguin, P. 80
Sherrington, P. 177–8
Slovakia 125, 127, 130, 132
social movements, EU and 4, 23
Spaak, P.-H. 82
Spain 143
Speroni, E. 193 n.11
Stadler, E. 74 n.9
Staines, P. 183
Statham, P. 177, 180, 181
Steinmeier, F.-W. 109, 130
Strache, H.-C. 63, 74
Styczyńska, N. 119 n.1, 121, 119
Sweden 143
    Euroscepticism in 5, 7
    Pirate Party 143
    polity contestation and 42, 48, 50, 196

Thatcher, M. 173, 176 n.1
Thévenot, L. 34, 41
Thürmer, G. 132, 133
Timmermans, F. 147
Tindemans, L. 82
Topolánek, M. 168
Tóta W., Á. 124
Trevor, J. 186 n.8
Turkey 7, 16, 70, 121, 132
Tusk, D. 158

United Kingdom 18, 19, 173–94
  British Broadcasting Corporation (BBC) 182, 184, 185, 187, 188, 191
  British National Party (BNP) 106, 177, 187, 194
  Conservative Party 176, 177, 181, 186–7, 192, 193
  The Daily Mail 182, 184
  EU accession (1973) 173, 176
  European Conservatives and Reformists (ECR) 193 n.11
  European integration, attitudes towards 18, 43, 112, 173–4, 176–7, 188–9, 200
    education level, effect on 180
    enlargement and 176–7
    EU institutional trust and 178–9
    existential discourse and 181, 182
    monetary union and 177
    utilitarianism and 179, 181
  European People's Party (EPP) 187, 193 n.11
  Euroscepticism in 5, 7, 10, 19, 116, 173, 176–80, 182, 187, 191, 192, 193, 194, 199
    Conservative elites and 175, 176, 177
    Constitutional Treaty and 178
    as 'constraining dissensus' 194
    distinct periods of 176
    exceptionalism, myth of and 173, 178, 199
    hard/soft Euroscepticism and 177
    historical background to 174, 175, 194
    left-wing critique and 175
    media reporting and populism 5, 106, 173, 180–1, 182
    national identity and 173, 174, 175, 178, 179, 181, 182, 191, 192
    party politics and 174, 175, 176–8, 181
    public opinion and 173, 174, 175, 179–80, 182, 192
    sovereignty, issue of and 173–4, 175, 177, 182, 191, 192
    use of term in analysis of 174–5
  Green Party 193
  The Guardian 182, 183, 184, 185, 187, 188, 191
  Guido Fawkes' blog 183
  House of Commons 186
  Iain Dale's Diary 183
  Labour Party 176, 178, 192, 193, 194
  Liberal Democrats 193
  Mail Online 183, 184, 185, 188, 191
  media and internet 173, 180–5, 187–8
    broadsheets and 181, 184
    citizen's journalism 183
    coverage of EU topics in 180, 181
    'Euromyths' website 181
    framing of EU issues in 181, 182
    party politics, link with 181
    political blogs and 182–3, 184, 185
    tabloid papers 141, 173, 181, 184
  political trust in 179, 192–3
  polity contestation, EP 2009 analysis 41, 42, 173, 182–94, 199–200
    data and sources used in 182–4
    domestic politics, link to 184, 192, 193 n.10
    EU institutional set-up, critique of 189, 191, 200
    Euroscepticism in 182, 187, 191, 192

    evaluations of integration
        principle 39, 44, 48, 50, 106,
        184, 188–9, 199
    justifications and 189
    Lisbon Treaty as issue 186–7, 191
    media coverage of 184–5, 187
    online media and 41–2, 43, 173,
        174, 182–5, 187–9, *190,*
        191–2
    parliamentarians expenses
        scandal, domination of 186,
        187, 189, 192–3
    as 'second order' elections 186,
        192
    voter turnout and 193
The Sun 181
The Telegraph 183, 186
Total Politics 183
2005 general election 178
UK Independence Party (UKIP) 19,
    106, 177, 193, 194
Wales 194
Westminster 178, 183

Van Baalen, H. 148
Van Stegeren, T. 141
Verdonk, R. 139
Verheugen, G. 109

Wilders, G. 20, 106, 116, 132, 139,
    142, 146, 149, 198, 199

Zawiska, A. 165
Ziobro, Z. 166

www.ingramcontent.com/pod-product-compliance
Lightning Source LLC
Chambersburg PA
CBHW071347290426
44108CB00014B/1466